HOYT S. VANDENBERG

0422-M-01

HOYT S. VANDENBERG
The Life of a General

PHILLIP S. MEILINGER

Originally published by

BLOOMINGTON & INDIANAPOLIS

New imprint by

AIR
FORCE
History
and
Museums
PROGRAM

Indiana
University
Press

MANUFACTURED IN THE UNITED STATES OF AMERICA

Library of Congress Cataloging-in-Publication Data
Meilinger, Phillip S., 1948–
Hoyt S. Vandenberg, the life of a general.
Bibliography: p.
Includes index.
1. Vandenberg, Hoyt Sanford, 1899–1954. 2. Generals
—United States—Biography. 3. United States. Air
Force—Biography. 4. United States—History, Military
—20th century. I. Title.
E840.5.V36M45 1989   355'.0092'4 [B] 88-45097
ISBN 0-253-32862-4
1 2 3 4 5 93 92 91 90 89

New imprint by the Air Force History and Museums Program, 2000

CONTENTS

FOREWORD to the new imprint

In this insightful consideration of Gen. Hoyt S. Vandenberg, Col. Phillip Meilinger has described the career of one of the major leaders of the United States Air Force. Born in 1899, General Vandenberg's career spanned the interwar years, World War II, the tumultuous postwar years, and the Korean War.

Vandenberg served in a variety of important operational as well as staff posts, providing him with an ideal background for positions of great responsibility. In World War II, as chief of staff of the Twelfth Air Force, and then the Northwest African Strategic Air Force, Vandenberg directed crucial air campaigns. In early 1944, Major General Vandenberg went to Europe as deputy air commander-in-chief of the Allied Expeditionary Forces and commanding general of the American air component. Subsequently, as commanding general of the Ninth Air Force, he was involved in planning the Normandy invasion. Late in the war, he returned to Army Air Forces headquarters as assistant chief of the Air Staff. In this capacity, he played a leading role in organizing the postwar Air Force.

After an interlude in 1946 as the first director of central intelligence for the Secretary of War, Vandenberg returned to Army Air Forces headquarters. In October 1947, he was appointed vice chief of staff of the newly independent United States Air Force and in April 1948, he succeeded Gen. Carl A. Spaatz as USAF chief of staff.

As chief of staff, Vandenberg headed the fledgling Air Force during a critical, tumultuous period. Shortly after becoming chief, he played a leading role in the Air Force presentation during the hearings on "the Revolt of the Admirals." Vandenberg's own testimony became a key ingredient in the persuasive case made by the Air Force for supporting the strategy of nuclear deterrence. Moreover, Vandenberg made the decision in late 1948 that the Air Force would emphasize a buildup of its nuclear deterrent forces. Concomitantly, Vandenberg was instrumental in bringing Gen. Curtis E. LeMay back from Europe to head the Strategic Air Command, thus initiating decades of SAC as the nation's premier nuclear deterrent force.

In addition to fighting roles and missions battles and inaugurating the Air Force's era of nuclear deterrence, Vandenberg led the Air Force during the Korean War, a period when the Air Force's budget increased greatly. General Vandenberg had to balance needs dictated by the Korean conflict against the requirement to sustain the Air Force's strategic deterrent in order to counter the Soviet threat.

As Colonel Meilinger emphasizes in this excellent study, General Hoyt S. Vandenberg was the Air Force's first Cold War leader and his leadership and vision set the standard for those who followed.

RICHARD P. HALLION
The Air Force Historian

PREFACE

General Hoyt S. Vandenberg, United States Air Force chief of staff from 1948 to 1953, played an important role in shaping military policy after 1945 and was a main participant in significant events of his time: unification of the armed forces and formation of an independent Air Force; the Berlin Airlift; the B-36/Supercarrier controversy; the formation of the Strategic Air Command, the development of the hydrogen bomb, and the Korean War.

After graduating from West Point in 1923, Vandenberg served as a fighter pilot for the next decade, becoming an outstanding flier and junior officer who was recognized as such throughout the Air Corps. In 1934, he began five years of educational assignments, which broadened his horizons and introduced him to the necessity of planning and sound staff work.

During World War II, Vandenberg served on the Air Staff in Washington, D.C., as an air planner for the North African and Normandy invasions, as a diplomat in Moscow, as chief of staff for a major command, as deputy of another, and as commander of the Ninth Air Force—the largest tactical air unit in history. In the harsh difficulties of war, Vandenberg consistently showed his ability to adapt and persevere. While others were competent in staff, planning, or command positions, he excelled at all three.

At the conclusion of the European war, Vandenberg returned to the Air Staff, where he was instrumental in the foundation of the Strategic Air Command. Army Chief of Staff General Dwight D. Eisenhower then selected him as War Department intelligence chief. Vandenberg totally reorganized that function in a scant three months. His efforts were so remarkable that President Harry S. Truman appointed him as director of the Central Intelligence Group—forerunner of the Central Intelligence Agency. After one year, Vandenberg returned to the Army Air Forces as deputy commander and was promoted to the rank of general—until then the second youngest American to achieve that rank. When the Air Force became independent in 1947, Vandenberg was its first vice chief, and upon the retirement of General Carl M. Spaatz the following year, Vandenberg became Air Force chief of staff.

Emphasis in this book is on Vandenberg's tenure as chief of staff. His life to 1948 reveals basic character traits, his impressive personal qualities, and the reasons for his rapid advancement. After rising to chief, his career merges with the great events of the Truman presidency. In 1948, the United States was confronted by the Berlin Blockade. Vandenberg's Air Force was to bear the brunt of that crisis by mounting the amazingly successful Berlin Airlift. Soon after, difficulties with the Navy culminated in the confrontation over the relative merits of strategic bombers and large aircraft carriers. The congressional hearings that resulted from this controversy were among the most divisive and bitter in recent American history.

As a result of continuing Soviet pressures in Europe, the North Atlantic Treaty Organization was formed in 1949, which brought increased military responsibilities to the United States. With the "fall of China" and the detonation of the Soviet's first atomic bomb, both in 1949, the United States embarked on a major program to develop a thermonuclear weapon. Vandenberg, a true "cold warrior" who distrusted the motives and goals of the Kremlin leadership, strongly supported this development. Soon after becoming chief of staff in 1948, he expressed strong feelings about the Communist menace.

> This philosophy opposed to ours is a suffocating thing, and it is spreading like a disease throughout a great portion of the world. We must stop this sickness—stop it cold—before it kills our friends. Our immediate job, therefore, must be to prevent the further spreading of germs by any international Typhoid Mary.[1]

But America's conventional military capabilities were deficient; and when North Korean forces exploded across the thirty-eighth parallel in June 1950, the country, as well as Vandenberg's Air Force, was unprepared. This shortcoming was soon rectified. At the time of his retirement in 1953, Vandenberg had transformed the Air Force from an understrength "shoestring air force" into the cornerstone of American military policy.

Vandenberg's concept of air power was crucial to his success because he struck a balance between the tactician and the strategist: advocating the primacy of strategic bombardment doctrine as a deterrent to war and a potentially decisive weapon, but never forgetting the necessity of tactical air support for the ground forces. The general's technical expertise as a pilot, combined with his managerial ability, dynamic personality, and aggressive leadership, made him a dominant and respected figure in the cold war era. Unfortunately, his early death in 1954, less than one year after retirement, along with his reticence to commit his innermost thoughts to paper, has caused his significance to be largely overlooked.

ACKNOWLEDGMENTS

I wish to thank Brigadier General Alfred F. Hurley, Colonel Carl W. Reddel, the United States Air Force Academy, and the Frank J. Seiler Research Laboratory for giving me the opportunity to continue my research. Dr. David MacIsaac at the Air Power Research Institute of the Air University was a major factor in my decision to study military history, while Brigadier General Jon A. Reynolds convinced me of the importance and need for telling the story of General Vandenberg. His own work detailing Vandenberg's early career was an essential and invaluable foundation for my book. I also greatly appreciate the advice and support of Professor John Shy at the University of Michigan.

Many details of General Vandenberg's life would have remained hidden had it not been for those individuals who graciously consented to personal interviews. Major General Hoyt S. Vandenberg, Jr., was absolutely essential to my work. His many hours of thoughtful reflection on his father's career were of the greatest importance. Also significant were interviews with Mrs. Gloria Miller, Generals Lauris Norstad, Earle E. Partridge, Leon Johnson, and Robert M. Lee; Lieutenant Generals Ira C. Eaker and Joseph Smith; Brigadier Generals Noel Parrish and Godfrey McHugh; Colonel Edward Hitchcock, and Walter Pforzheimer. In addition, I received dozens of letters from former associates of General Vandenberg that were also of great value in this work, but especially useful were the contacts with Colonels William Burt and Carroll F. Sullivan and Walter W. Rostow, who supplied me with documents and memories from their past.

Because most of the research was conducted in various archives, my task would have been impossible had it not been for the selfless efforts of several individuals. Of these, the most helpful and energetic was Duane Reed at the Air Force Academy's special collections branch—no job was too big or too small to warrant his prompt, thorough attention. The personnel at the Office of Air Force History in Washington, D.C., under the leadership of Dr. Richard Kohn, were also tremendously supportive: historians Herman Wolk, George Watson, Jr., and Walt Moody supplied essential historical criticism and expertise; and Lieutenant Colonel Elliott Converse, Bill Heimdahl, and Master Sergeant Roger Jernigan provided administrative and archival assistance. Spending three months at the Library of Congress made the friendly cooperation of Gary Kohn and Charles Kelly a great help to my research. CIA archivist Bill Henhoeffer; John Taylor at the National Archives Modern Military Branch; Lyman Hammond, Jr., curator of the MacArthur Memorial Foundation Archives; Dr. Richard Sommers at Carlisle Barracks; and Pressley Bickerstaff of the Simpson Historical Research Center also provided invaluable assistance. Crucial editorial advice and support were supplied by Major Steve Chiabotti, my colleague in the Air Force Academy Department of History.

HOYT S. VANDENBERG

Tradition means giving votes to the most
obscure of all classes—our ancestors. It is
the democracy of the dead. Tradition re-
fuses to submit to the small and arrogant
oligarchy of those who merely happen to
be walking around.

G. K. Chesterton

I | The Learning Years

Airplanes may kill you, but they ain't
likely to hurt you.

Satchel Paige

BEGINNINGS

Pieter VanDenBerg immigrated to America as the eighteenth century drew
to a close and the new Republic was born. Little is known of this Dutchman, except that he settled in lower New York state and that the courage and determination it took to move across the ocean to start a new life were transmitted to his
descendants. His grandson, Aaron VandenBerg, was a hard-working leather-
maker from Coxsackie, New York, a small town twenty miles south of Albany on
the Hudson River. As a young man he moved across state to Clyde and opened
his own harness-making business. In 1865, while the nation began to recover from
its grievous wounds, Aaron married Harriet Collins. Though a happy and successful match, tragedy cut it short. Their first child, William Collins, was born in 1869,
but Harriet died giving birth to Josephine five years later. The widower needed
a wife and his young children a mother, and so two years later Aaron married
Alpha Hendrick. The VandenBergs moved to Grand Rapids, Michigan, to start
anew; and there in 1884 a third child, Arthur, was born. Aaron opened a retail
sales shop that prospered and later expanded into a wholesale leather goods factory. But the times were not good, and the depression of 1893 drove him into
bankruptcy. The old man's business was broken and so was his heart; he never
really recovered from this setback.[1]

The two half brothers, William and Arthur, were separated by fifteen years
and thus were not close during their youth. When his father's business collapsed,

1

Collins, as William now preferred to be called, moved to Milwaukee and began his own career. The young man was enterprising and quickly became a local success, having several industrial and brokering interests, owning a bookbinding company, and serving as the assistant general manager of the Milwaukee Tractor and Electric Light Company. Photographs show him as fit and dignified, always nattily dressed, with dark, well-oiled hair and the handlebar mustache in style at the time. He cut a very dashing figure, and soon Pearl Kane, daughter of a wealthy hotel owner in town, caught his fancy. Although she was married, the feeling was mutual, and Pearl divorced her husband to wed VandenBerg.[2]

Pearl was a tall, strikingly handsome woman of imperial bearing with soft brown hair and piercing gray eyes. As she grew older her hair turned snow white, tending to heighten her beauty. This commanding presence, combined with a strong will, independent mind, and affluent background, made her a most formidable woman. She was also devoted to her family. When the first son, Hoyt Sanford, was born on January 24, 1899, Pearl named him in honor of relatives: Eli Hoyt was a favored uncle, and Sanford Kane was her father. Collins was enormously proud of his young "Buster" and wrote his parents soon after the happy event: "Our son is as husky as they make them, . . . and is as smart as a dozen whips. Doesn't talk as yet, but he is 'dead on' to everything that is going on in his vicinity."[3] A second son, Aaron Shedd, was born eighteen months later and named after Grandfather VandenBerg and Freeman B. Shedd, a close friend and business partner of Eli Hoyt. The VandenBergs lived in the Prospect Hill area of Milwaukee, and years later Hoyt reminisced about his childhood: playing ball in the local sandlots and swimming in the town water tank. It was an enjoyable youth.[4]

In 1910, after Pearl's mother became ill and returned home to Lowell, Massachusetts, Pearl urged Collins to move back East so that her mother could be looked after. Although Collins was reluctant to relocate, the dark-eyed Pearl was insistent. Collins sold his prospering business interests and moved to Lowell, a cotton mill town of nearly one hundred thousand located twenty miles north of Boston. There he bought a stately Victorian mansion at 386 Andover Street. The Hoyts, who had owned the house previously, operated a factory that produced tooth brush liquid, men's cologne, and other toiletry articles. The Hoyts, Shedds (who lived next door), and VandenBergs were among Lowell's elite. But forced by circumstances to abandon his chosen career in the prime of life, Collins never quite recovered; ambition waned and henceforth his time was spent selling insurance, traveling, and in leisure. Collins was a gentleman with family wealth that provided the VandenBergs with a comfortable life.[5]

Hoyt and his younger brother, Shedd, spent their teen years in Lowell. Hoyt was intelligent, poised, and athletic, participating in several sports while in high school: baseball, football, hockey, golf, and track. The outdoors held a special attraction for him, and throughout his life he was an avid hunter and fisherman, activities that helped keep him fit. Six feet tall and 140 pounds with a solid build—not an impressive upper body, but especially thick, muscular legs—he had cool, blue eyes, parted his hair down the center, smiled easily, and was unusually handsome. He was already quite popular with the ladies, and his bedroom walls were adorned with dozens of their photographs. Hoyt was also active in scouting and advanced to the rank of eagle—a feat of which he was always proud.[6]

The VandenBergs were a close-knit, affectionate family. Episcopalians, the boys attended Bible School on Sundays and were reared to be ethical and upright. Hoyt never became overtly religious, seldom attending church services as an adult, but the sense of personal integrity instilled by loving parents was to remain a prominent characteristic.[7] If there were any peccadilloes inherited during youth, it was a prejudice against the Irish. Pearl VandenBerg was known as a "Yankee through and through" who recognized a clear distinction between her class and the Irish immigrants who usually served as domestics and mill workers in Lowell. If this trait ever existed in Hoyt, however, it was quickly dispelled during his early military training by a leveling process that permitted little discrimination.[8]

During his high school years the First World War engulfed Europe, and Hoyt joined the cadet regiment at Lowell High, attaining the rank of captain. In 1916 the Mexican expedition fired youthful enthusiasm, and Hoyt wanted to volunteer for service. Collins dampened such talk, but did allow his son to attend the Plattsburgh Junior Camp at Plum Island, New York, in July 1916.

The Plattsburgh Camps, the novel brainchild of General Leonard Wood, were designed to instill patriotism and a sense of martial awareness in the citizenry. Those who attended the camps were often wealthy college students or businessmen. Indeed, Collins himself was a member of the Businessmen's Battalion. For young men between the ages of fifteen and eighteen, a special junior camp was established at Fort Terry on Plum Island, New York. For forty dollars, parents could send their sons to this sandy bit of land at the entrance to Long Island Sound to participate in the five-week program. A total of twelve hundred boys from twenty-four different states signed up and were taught the rudiments of military life. Every morning the troops would wake at 0545 and have a full day of drill, tactics, target practice, personal and camp hygiene, map making, and athletics. Instruction was provided by regular Army officers and West Point cadets. In the evenings there were movies and humorous skits put on by the boys themselves. At 2230 all retreated to their tents to rest for the arduous day to come. The experience was moving: "Merely to go to sleep with the notes of the bugle sounding taps, to wake in the morning under canvas at the sound of the first call, and to be up and ready for the day as reveille rings out, is something to be remembered all one's life."[9]

The movement was proud of the diverse backgrounds of its participants; there were sons of businessmen, bankers, farmers, and factory workers. Yet, when they put aside their mufti and donned the uniform, all became equal. An observer who attended "Camp Washington" on Plum Island articulated the purpose of the exercise:

It means being clean in body and mind. It means obedience and loyalty, because it is often only those in command who know which way is the straight way. It means bravery, for the straight way leads sometimes to danger. It means efficiency, for it avoids the wasteful ways around. It means democracy, for you cannot go the straight way if you play favorites.[10]

Though such sentiments sound hackneyed and banal today, Hoyt was moved by the experience, was promoted to cadet corporal, and told his father that he wished to become a professional soldier. Collins acquiesced, but suggested that if such was his desire, the proper avenue for the son of a gentleman was to attend the Military Academy at West Point and become an officer. This was no easy task because Hoyt had never excelled academically. On one occasion he had been withdrawn from school, spending several months in Biloxi, Mississippi, during his father's recuperation from a bout of typhoid. While there, Hoyt and Shedd had had a private tutor.[11] This disruption, the easy-going attitude of his parents, frequent vacation trips throughout New England during the school year, and Hoyt's own lack of interest in schooling, produced mediocre academic results. His performance was succinctly summed by an early teacher: "Hoyt has a quick bright mind—although not fond of concentrated application."[12]

For admission to the Military Academy one needed a political appointment and also to pass the daunting West Point entrance examination. In preparation for the test, Hoyt attended Columbian Preparatory School in Washington, D.C., to bolster his knowledge in mathematics and English. Years later, he remembered the anxiety of the lonely train ride and the three mile walk from Union Station to the boarding school. Though not an enjoyable year, it was a productive one. To better his son's chances for a political appointment, Collins then sent Hoyt to live with his brother, Arthur, who had remained in Grand Rapids and had, fortuitously, developed political connections. In 1906 the *Grand Rapids Herald* was a struggling newspaper sorely in need of dynamic management. Arthur Vandenberg was placed in command, given a handsome salary, and charged with making the enterprise a success. The daily's owner, United States Senator William Alden Smith, was well pleased with the results. In addition, Arthur was on the board of directors of the Grand Rapids Savings Bank, of which Smith was chairman.[13] It was intended that Hoyt live with his youngish uncle, establish Michigan residence by working as a clerk in the bank, and obtain a senatorial appointment from Arthur's mentor. In 1918, Hoyt passed the West Point entrance examination, and Senator Smith offered him the coveted appointment.

SCHOOL FOR SOLDIERS

Cadet Hoyt Sanford Vandenberg entered West Point on June 13, 1919, one day after the arrival of a new superintendent, Brigadier General Douglas MacArthur. At age thirty-nine, MacArthur was the youngest superintendent in a century. Army Chief of Staff Peyton March appointed the war hero, stating that West Point was forty years behind the times and in drastic need of revitalization.[14] This was no exaggeration. The school was in serious difficulties owing to outmoded academic procedures and the turmoil caused by the Great War. Five classes had been graduated in 1917–18 to provide more officers for the American Expeditionary Force. Congress favorably noted the financial savings involved and in May 1919 legislated that West Point would henceforth be a three-year school. Although the cadets welcomed such news, MacArthur did not. He was convinced that four years were necessary to produce a quality officer, and he lobbied immediately and continuously to reverse the Congressional decision. In the meantime, he labored to modernize the three pillars of the West Point edifice: athletics, academics, and military training. Time would show, however, that many of his efforts were of limited effect and duration.

Although MacArthur had not been a top athlete as a cadet, he appreciated the importance of conditioning, not only for physical stamina but for mental toughness as well. He therefore required that all cadets take physical education classes in the major sports and participate in intramural athletics two days each week.[15] His famous dictum, "Upon the fields of friendly strife are sown the seeds that upon other fields, on other days, will bear the fruits of victory," became a guiding principle. The general was also an avid fan of West Point's intercollegiate teams and spent many afternoons watching practice sessions. His enthusiasm seemed to be contagious, and the football team began to win games, especially against arch rival Navy. Such an accomplishment should not be dismissed too lightly. West Point cadets were almost totally isolated from the outside world, not even being permitted to leave post until after their first two years. In an age before the radio, news was gained through newspapers and magazines, but these were not readily available to cadets. Young women were permitted on the grounds for periodic "hops," but because only a few minutes were permitted to escort the ladies off-post after the last dance, romance occurred infrequently. Patrick Timberlake, one of Vandenberg's company mates, was put on report and forced to march "tours" for the egregious offense of dancing cheek-to-cheek.[16] Cadet life, though busy, was boring, and MacArthur, idolized by most of his young charges, brought a breath of fresh air into the gray walls on the Hudson with his emphasis on spirit, competition, and sportsmanship. Unfortunately, he was less successful in his efforts to improve the academic side of cadet life.

The Academy faculty was dominated by tenured professors who, although military officers, had long past forgotten the requirements of soldiering. For that matter, they had even forgotten the aims of higher education. One permanent professor expressed great pride at the fact that they taught no such frivolous subjects as sociology or psychology at the Point: "This is a professional college that makes no pretense to be a university . . . West Point is conservative. Perhaps it is not a bad thing to have a few strongholds of conservatism in an educational world where the roots of radicalism so soon and so widely take hold."[17] To MacArthur, this attitude was perverse. The Great War had demonstrated to him that new methods were needed. He tried to modernize the antiquated academic system, which consisted largely of rote memorization, daily quizzes, and working problems at the chalk board. The individual attention and academic discipline these methods engendered—because classes averaged a dozen or so students and each cadet knew he would be tested every day, he could hardly allow himself to fall behind—were commendable, but also dated. MacArthur advocated new courses in the social sciences, electricity, and aeronautics that challenged the cadets' intellect and forced instructors to teach, not merely listen to their students' recitations. Almost all of his instructors were West Point graduates who had no

education beyond their cadet training. This situation seemed intellectually inces-
tuous, but again, little was done to alter it.[18] One experiment was to have the
professors visit a civilian university for a month to observe and learn. But the
Academic Board—the real power at West Point—was dominated by the aged professors; the superintendent had but one vote. Almost always outvoted on key
decisions, MacArthur could only lament: "How long must we continue to prepare
for the war of 1812?"[19]

The third major area of cadet life to be attacked by the "young Mars" was
military training. Cadet life was a democratizing experience. Regardless of their
background, once freshmen ("plebes") entered the Academy gates they became
equals. All wore the same uniform, attended the same classes, and were subjected
to the same discipline. West Point was proud of the fact that in 1923 Emilio Agui-
naldo, Jr., entered as a plebe. Joining this son of the famous Filipino revolutionary
was Frederick Funston, Jr., son of the officer who had captured the elder Agui-
naldo. Now the sons were equals, at least in theory. Because it was prohibited
for cadets to obtain additional money from outside sources, even family wealth
was to little advantage. Unfortunately, such theory did not always prove true in
practice. Hazing and physical abuse had always been endemic at the Academy,
but conditions had become worse because of the war. A new class of plebes was
ordinarily given its basic training by first classmen (seniors). Although there were
excesses, first classmen at least had three years of experience and maturity; but
owing to the early graduations during the war, plebe indoctrination was being
conducted by men barely past basic training themselves. MacArthur, who had suffered severe hazing as a cadet, was afraid things would get out of control. In fact,
shortly before his arrival one plebe had committed suicide, allegedly because of
mistreatment by upper classmen.

It was MacArthur's intention that military training should be administered
by cadets acting as "proud gentlemen" and not as "common thugs."[20] The trenches
of France had impressed the general profoundly, and he felt that the previous
methods of discipline and training were no longer applicable in the age of the intelligent, patriotic citizen-soldier. The officers leading such men must be similarly
intelligent and trained along "broad, humane lines." After graduation it was too
late to begin teaching a new lieutenant how to take care of his men while in the
field. MacArthur had seen West Pointers assigned to occupation duties in Germany who were unable to cope with diverse problems involving social, economic,
and political factors, matters beyond their ken. MacArthur thought this shortcoming was largely an educational deficiency that could be remedied before commis-
sioning.[21]

MacArthur wanted cadets to be given more responsibility and to have an opportunity to lead and experiment, rather than merely follow the orders of the
Academy staff. That he arrived when only two classes were enrolled was seen as
a blessing because it offered a clean slate; the cadets had not (it was hoped) become too ingrained in the old, outmoded ways.[22] Tactical officers—the Army officers who supervised the cadets—were directed to monitor events closely. The
so-called beast barracks (summer basic training) was to be run by officers instead
of cadets, and a move was also made to strike at the root of the problem. Cadets

acted like children because they were treated like children, cooped up on the Academy grounds with no freedom and no social contacts. MacArthur granted cadets increased free time; they could venture off-post, even as far as New York City. In addition, Christmas and summer leaves were given, six-hour passes were allowed on the weekends, and cadets were authorized to visit the quarters of faculty and staff officers. They were even given five dollars per month to spend as they saw fit![23] During the summers the Corps had ordinarily encamped on Academy grounds at Fort Clinton, where they learned the rudiments of soldiering in the field. Now they were marched one hundred miles to Fort Dix, a *real* Army post, where they observed actual maneuvers and received instruction from qualified noncommissioned officers in the use of machine guns, artillery, chemical warfare (gas), and aviation.[24]

The purpose of these changes was to drag the Military Academy into the twentieth century, to treat men like men and to grant them some measure of responsibility. In this realm too MacArthur was foiled; the Point had endured over a century of tradition blithely unhampered by progress and there were many who were loath to change. Surprisingly, it was not just the alumni and "Old Guard" at the Academy who resisted such designs; many cadets did so as well.[25]

Although the tenure of a superintendent was ordinarily four years, MacArthur was transferred after only three. It was widely believed the early departure was owing to his attempts at change. His successor, Brigadier General Fred W. Sladen, moved quickly to reestablish the old ways by returning summer camp to Fort Clinton, taking away spending money and weekend passes, and restoring beast barracks to cadet supervision. Perhaps to signal his swing back to conservatism, Sladen declared soon after his arrival that the mission of West Point was to train platoon leaders, nothing more.[26]

Vandenberg, who experienced all this turmoil, had an undistinguished cadet career. He again demonstrated a knack for producing minimally acceptable academic work; his study habits were virtually nonexistent, and he was constantly in difficulty with the dean. Vandenberg was often late getting home for Christmas leave because he had to remain behind for special "turnout" exams. His grades were so low that only by passing these perennial "last chances" was he able to avoid disenrollment.[27] There was no question that he had the ability—later events would prove his mental sophistication and intelligence—but the motivation was simply not there. One classmate recalled that "Van," as he was now called by everyone but his family, often needed help with mathematics and engineering. He would wait until a major examination loomed and then belatedly seek assistance. One of the brighter men in A Company, Jerry Rusk, usually came to the rescue. Later, Vandenberg stated that he might not have made it through without Rusk's help.[28] However, another friend from those days concluded simply that Vandenberg could have done the work himself but was too lazy.[29]

Vandenberg's military performance was even worse than his academic work. Demerits for such infractions as sleeping in chapel, slouching at the dinner table, dirty rifle, late for class, and "improper expression during breakfast" (?) were a constant blot on his record.[30] During second class year (junior) he ranked a dismal

276 out of 293 in military efficiency and conduct, with a personal four-year high of 118 demerits (the "top" man in the class had 160 that year).[31] One of MacArthur's innovations was to have cadets rank each other on military ability and potential, a task previously performed by the tactical officers. Although Vandenberg was well liked by his classmates, they obviously were not in awe of his performance because it was they who repeatedly ranked him low.[32] As one classmate noted wryly: "Van was not a fileboner"—cadet slang for an ambitious classmate.[33] Like two cadet predecessors who would also become famous airmen, Henry H. Arnold and Carl M. Spaatz, Vandenberg was a "clean sleeve" and never attained cadet military rank. Later, he referred to the Academy as "the Dump" and told his son that "he slept through his four years." The cadet yearbook also notes his inclination for the "arms of Morpheus."[34]

The main reason for Vandenberg's poor performance was that he simply did not like the Academy. He had worked hard to secure an appointment—attending prep school for a year and then living with his uncle for an extra year—but West Point obviously did not live up to the expectations awakened on Plum Island. He wanted to resign as a plebe, but was dissuaded by an old friend from Lowell.[35] To Van the disciplinary system was demeaning, archaic, and counterproductive, despite MacArthur's exertions. Cadets were not taught leadership, and there was little opportunity for practicing it. The Corps was still run by the tyrannical tactical officers, and it was they who determined the rules and how they would be enforced.[36] Perhaps Vandenberg's permissive upbringing made him particularly unsuited for rigid regimentation. Possibly his maturity—he was already twenty years old as a plebe and one of the oldest men in his class—placed him above the oft-times childish hazing and harassment. Perhaps he was farsighted enough to look beyond the narrow traditionalism of the West Point system and see a future military organization based on more enlightened methods. Or perhaps he was angry.

Although MacArthur successfully reversed the decision to make West Point a three-year program, Congress thought it only fair to grant all cadets then serving the option to graduate after three years or remain for the full four. MacArthur did not welcome this breath of democracy into such a crucial decision and instructed his commandant, Colonel Robert M. Danford, to encourage those leaning toward the three-year option to reconsider. Danford and his staff hinted strongly that the future careers of those electing to graduate early would suffer. Two who remember the incident speak of "terrific pressure" applied on them to remain the extra year.[37] Another stated later that he had been deliberately lied to and told early graduation would not be permitted for him since he would not yet be twenty-one years old.[38] In the spring of 1920 the Corps was mustered, and each man stepped forward to state his decision. Those wishing to leave early were then taken aside and counseled once again by Colonel Danford. The final tally showed that the entire class of 1920 opted for four years; but seventeen from 1921 voted to leave early, as did twenty-seven from Vandenberg's class of 1922 (which then became the class of 1923).[39] Van elected to stay. One wonders why a cadet would choose to remain at West Point when he could instead be an officer with freedom, a commission, and a paycheck. Either the sense of comradeship and esprit was especially strong, which seems unlikely, or the pressure campaign of MacArthur and his staff was effective. Whatever Vandenberg's reasons for staying, love of West Point was clearly not one of them.

Fortunately, there were outlets for his frustrations. Vandenberg remained active in athletics and played left wing and defense on the Army hockey team for all four years, although he was not a starter and lettered only during his sophomore year. In addition, while a senior he was a starter on the polo squad that won five of its seven matches.[40] He also regularly attended the weekly hops and was known for his social graces. An activity record was kept on all cadets, awarding points for those who participated in various events, and this played a role in the graduation standing. Being a class officer, on the Honor Committee, in the choir, a Sunday school teacher, a cheer leader, or on the yearbook staff all earned points. Vandenberg garnered an impressive 722 such activity points; however, 710 of them were for escorting young ladies to hops.[41] Classmates from those days are virtually unanimous in describing him as slim, handsome (a real "Lothario"), outgoing, and friendly: "Van was a good dancer and very popular with the ladies. He had a mischievous twinkle in his eyes and was not at all shy. He was a very good looking cadet [who] made friends easily and was well liked."[42]

At one of these dances Van met Gladys Rose from nearby Sloatsburg, who was attending teacher's college. Glad was a remarkably beautiful and vivacious woman with amber eyes and long, auburn hair. Of Scottish descent, her father was a well-to-do realtor in Sloatsburg. Gladys, who owned her own car, attended many of the West Point dances, often staying on post with the family of Major Harold Loomis, a French instructor. In fact, her visits were so frequent that Loomis had a special brass visitor's pass made for her car so the post guards would quickly wave her through. Glad's loveliness and charm—almost coquettish—made her irresistible to the cadets. While attending a dance as the date of one cadet, she was introduced to Van, and after a single dance, Glad was "his girl."[43] After this initial encounter, Glad visited the Loomises even more frequently, where Van would call for her on the weekends, and they would walk the Academy grounds or go into New York City for the afternoon. Glad had been courted by many cadets, but it was Van who would win her hand.[44]

Significantly, there may have been another avenue through which the restless young man could channel his energy. There were others in Vandenberg's company who felt similarly exasperated and constrained by the juvenile and outmoded plebe system. These "radicals" hoped to correct this situation during their first-class year by introducing reforms into beast barracks: "Those who were in Summer Camp in '22 well remember that unquenchable spirit of reform that swept like wildfire through the Corps."[45] Attempts were made to humanize the disciplinary system and remove the excesses that were so demotivating. Whether or not Vandenberg played a role in such events is uncertain. Most underclassmen from A Company remember him as largely indifferent to plebes and their training. None could recall a single instance when he corrected a subordinate; one recalled him as an "invisible man who ignored most people, including plebes."[46] It is possible that he played a role behind the scenes, urging and nudging his classmates into a more mature approach to plebe training, but it seems more likely that his attitude was one of indifference.

Vandenberg had wanted to join the Cavalry upon graduation, but his lowly class standing of 240 out of 261 made entrance to this elite branch an impossibility. The last cavalry slot was taken by the man ranked 150.[47] Chance then intervened to play a significant role. The class of 1923 was the first to be offered the opportunity of entering the Air Service upon graduation. Brigadier General William ("Billy") Mitchell, the vibrant, dynamic air leader and hero of the First World War, had spoken to the Corps about the future of air power. In addition, a dashing young pilot had once landed on the Plain in a SE-5 pursuit aircraft, discussed his trade, and offered a flight to anyone interested; he had cut a most impressive figure.[48] Vandenberg was moved by such incidents and decided on an aviation career. That his only other choice, at number 240, was the Infantry, may have made flying seem all the more attractive.[49]

It might be said that Hoyt Vandenberg's cadet career was a failure; he had not excelled in any endeavor during his four years, and he left with a bitter taste. But the Academy cannot help but have an enormous impact on an individual, whether positive or negative. The feelings, experiences, and interpersonal relationships are too intense. Vandenberg left West Point with memories, as well as certain values and beliefs (if not necessarily those officially endorsed), that were shared by hundreds of other graduates. The vast majority of high-ranking generals with which he was associated during the rest of his life were among them; their destinies seemed always linked. Twenty-eight years after Vandenberg's graduation, an American president would ask him to travel half way around the world to assess a brother officer and Academy graduate whose performance had been deemed questionable. Upon completing his journey and after much reflection, Vandenberg agreed with Mr. Truman that General MacArthur—the man who was superintendent when he was a plebe—should be relieved of his command.

KICK THE TIRES AND LIGHT THE FIRES

Lieutenant Vandenberg attended pilot training at Brooks Field in San Antonio, Texas. Although experiencing difficulty at first, he applied himself far more seriously than he had at West Point and did well. His instructor pilot, Lieutenant Jimmy Taylor, had several years of teaching experience, and Van responded well to his direction. Van's fellow students remember him as a "good but not outstanding pilot."[50] Others were not so fortunate: nearly half of Vandenberg's fellow students "washed out," and six more were killed in air crashes, one of them Jerry Rusk, the close friend who had helped him with his studies at West Point. Rusk's death hit Van particularly hard. Death was to be the constant companion of airmen in the years ahead. Flying was a hazardous endeavor and Van was to see numerous friends and squadron mates killed in air crashes. Indeed, during World War II aircrews were engaged in the most parlous occupation encountered by American officers. This almost daily exposure to danger and death led many airmen to become jaded and fatalistic. Often, these feelings were manifested by cockiness and arrogance. Van was not immune to such tendencies. Of importance, several men who would play large roles in later years were at Brooks that year: Ben Chidlaw, Larry Craigie, Orval Cook, Benny Giles, "Opie" Weyland, and Ralph Royce.[51] It was also while in pilot training that Vandenberg began carrying a bag of "lucky coins" whenever he flew. He believed they kept him safe.[52]

During the Christmas break of 1923, things were sufficiently under control for Van and Gladys to wed. Although they had planned to wait until after the completion of his pilot training, the longing was too painful, and they decided to be married immediately. The nuptials took place at Saint Mark's Episcopal Church on December 26. Collins and Pearl VandenBerg took the train to Texas for the wedding and then remained with the newlyweds until the following April. This unusual decision set the pattern for the years ahead. Collins's early retirement left him a great deal of leisure time, and Pearl needed a warm climate, and so they usually spent the summer months with Shedd in Boston and the winter with Hoyt and his bride. Not surprisingly, Gladys grew to resent and dread the long, annual visits of her willful mother-in-law.[53]

After winning his wings in 1924, Vandenberg requested and received an assignment to the 3rd Attack Group, based at Kelly Field, across town from Brooks. This tour began a decade of association with pursuit-type aircraft that made Vandenberg an expert pilot and tactician. The mission of "attack" had developed during the First World War and consisted of aircraft being employed near the battlefield to bomb and strafe enemy troop concentrations, supply lines, communication centers, and other military targets. "Pursuit," on the other hand, was concerned with the concept of air superiority. Pursuit aircraft would sweep the skies of enemy planes to ensure that friendly reconnaissance, bombardment, and attack aircraft could operate unimpeded. Equally important, air superiority ensured that friendly ground troops were safe from enemy air attacks. In later years the distinction between "pursuit" and "attack" would blur somewhat as similar aircraft were used to perform overlapping missions. Significantly, although attack missions often bore resemblance to those of bombardment, attack pilots were averse to consider themselves bomber pilots—the butt of derogatory jokes around the bar. Although theoretically the most important mission was to become bombardment, in reality there was always more glamour attached to pursuit.[54] Vandenberg considered himself a "pursuiter."

As a measure of his flying ability, in 1926 the lieutenant was chosen for a role in the motion picture *Wings*, then being filmed in San Antonio. This epic, the last of the great silent movies and the first to win an Academy Award, was a tale of love and rivalry involving World War I pursuit pilots vying for the same woman. Starring Buddy Rogers, Richard Arlen, Clara Bow, and Gary Cooper, *Wings* cost two million dollars, a phenomenal sum in those days. Over two hundred aircraft were assembled for the filming, including several Spads and Fokkers brought from Europe. Three hundred pilots, most from the Air Service, were to do the actual flying. Van was selected to fly Rogers's aircraft, making the takeoff and performing the various acrobatics and dogfighting scenes. As the camera mounted on the front of his aircraft was activated, Van would duck down in his seat to reveal the grim visage of Rogers, who had been sitting behind him. When the camera was turned off, Van would reemerge from under the dashboard and regain control of the plane.[55]

To simulate being shot down in one of the dogfighting scenes, Van filled a large bag with flour and lamp black. His plan was to pitch up the aircraft at the appropriate moment, stall, and enter a spin. At that point he would open the bag and the cameras would record the downward spiraling Fokker trailing a thick plume of black smoke. It was a good plan. Unfortunately, when Van opened the bag its entire contents dumped back into the cockpit with him. Said the intrepid aviator later: "I was blinded, suffocated, bewildered and even unhappy." While Van gasped for breath and flailed his arms wildly to dissipate the smoke, the plane gyrated about the sky. Finally, Van was able to regain his vision and aircraft control moments before impact. Rolling to a stop he staggered from the cockpit and collapsed. The film crew ran over to him, ebullient. It was the most realistic near-crash scene they had ever witnessed. They asked if he would do it again.[56]

The Air Corps held annual gunnery competitions, and in the two in which he participated (1925 and 1926) Vandenberg did quite well. Earle E. ("Pat") Partridge was a main competitor in both these events. To his chagrin, Partridge claimed that he would begin practicing weeks in advance to hone his skills for the meet; Vandenberg never bothered to practice, yet still excelled.[57]

An incident that occurred en route to one of these gunnery meets paints an interesting picture of life in the Air Corps in 1926. Vandenberg and his crew chief, Sergeant Rudy J. Baros, took off from Bolling Field in Washington, D.C., and headed for West Virginia. About half way there it began to snow. As conditions worsened, Vandenberg descended and shouted to Baros to look for a suitable emergency landing field. A corn field was spied and Vandenberg landed. After talking to the local farmers, the two men hitched a ride into town, stayed in a hotel, and bought some gasoline for their craft. The next day Van had the farmer cut down a few trees in his take-off path and then departed. The weather was still poor and it was extremely cold in the open-cockpit biplane. Landing at a small town called Fairfield, the young pilot and his crew chief once again stayed in a hotel. When it was time to depart the next morning, however, Van confessed to Baros that he had no money to pay for his room or breakfast (a bowl of chili). The sergeant therefore cashed a check for five dollars, paid the bills, and the two hardy aviators continued on their journey. Hardly a glamorous life![58]

The young pilot served for three years in the 3rd Attack Group, eventually becoming the commander of the 90th Attack Squadron. Although such a position did not then have the authority usually associated with the term *commander*, it was nevertheless a distinction for a man so young.[59] Soon after Vandenberg's arrival, General Billy Mitchell visited the group to evaluate their performance. After being briefed on the tactics to be employed for the demonstration, Mitchell snorted that such methods would be useless in combat situations. He then briefed the pilots on the "proper" altitudes and tactics. Four pilots subsequently crashed their aircraft and died trying to negotiate Mitchell's spontaneously revised maneuvers, for which they had not been trained. The result was near mutiny.[60] This tragic incident illustrated a problem that would haunt air leaders throughout the interwar period. Air power at that time was "sensed" rather than demonstrated. American involvement in the First World War had not lasted long enough to formulate an effective strategic or tactical doctrine and allow it to be tested in combat. Mitchell and his followers would labor to write a formula for air power employment, but their efforts would take years, and until they could prove their contentions, many of their theories were just words.

In late 1927, the Vandenbergs moved to March Field, California, where Van became a flight instructor in the basic training aircraft, the PT-1, PT-3, and DH-4. It is often said that a pilot never reaches his full potential until he has been an instructor and allowed the opportunity to watch, guide, and correct other pilots and learn from their mistakes. This duty was among the most satisfying of his career, and years later Vandenberg would advise his son, who wanted desperately to become a fighter pilot: "Don't overlook a tour as an instructor pilot early in your career. You never really learn how to fly until you teach someone else."[61] The unique combination of flying and personal interaction appealed to Vandenberg. He soon acquired a reputation as an excellent instructor, and students having difficulty were often transferred to his care. One individual, though he was washed out, wrote Vandenberg afterwards that he was an outstanding instructor who seemed to know instinctively how to teach. The former student expressed his gratitude for Vandenberg's efforts and stated that had he been his instructor all along, he certainly would have won his wings.[62] He did, however, employ some unusual instructional techniques. Another of Van's students, future chief of staff John P. McConnell, provided an interesting insight into his instructor's "charm and personality." It seems McConnell had the bad habit of forgetting to fasten his seat belt before flight. To teach him a lesson, Vandenberg climbed his open-cockpit biplane to eight thousand feet and rolled the aircraft on its back: "Boy, I grabbed everything in that cockpit to stay in!"[63]

The Vandenbergs had two children: Gloria, born in 1925, and Hoyt, Jr., in 1928. "Gogo" and "Sandy," somewhat spoiled by frequent visits from doting grandparents, had a father who was dedicated and strict, but not demonstrably affectionate. On the other hand, Van seldom spanked his children. There were exceptions. Sandy remembered an incident when he and a friend had taken turns breaking out lights with a broom handle one evening. The lights smashed were the runway approach signals at Maxwell Field. The boys were soon caught, and the elder Vandenberg was severely chastened by his commander: "If you can't control your own son, how the hell can you control your men!" The seriousness of the youngsters' offense plus the stinging rebuke from a superior resulted in one of the worst hidings Sandy ever received from his father.[64] Van was not the type to play baseball with his son or push his daughter on a swing. Yet, the relationship between father and children was a close one, as evidenced by this Father's Day poem written by Gogo and Sandy:

F is for your face, so big and ugly
A is for your addle-pated brain
T is for your temper, hot and spicey
H is for your hair, ain't it a shame

E is for your ears, so big and flapping
R is for your rump so fat
Put them all together and they spell Father.
The sweetest guy in all the world.[65]

It takes a special closeness to write something that sarcastic.

Sundays were usually set aside for the family, and virtually every weekend all four would bundle into the car and drive to a nearby lake or forest preserve for an afternoon picnic. This was Van's time to relax with his family, but also to contemplate. At such picnics, while obviously enjoying the closeness of Glad and the kids, he would often sit quietly, thinking deeply, his mind many miles away. This was to be characteristic. Later in life, Van would often sit for long periods, staring out a window, ruminating. It was his way of arriving at difficult decisions. Free time during the rest of the week was reserved for Vandenberg's real passions: flying and golf.[66] He loved the air and flew constantly, not only in the local area but whenever a cross-country flight was available. Vandenberg was a hard worker who labored long hours to become a good officer; he was a dedicated, aggressive professional and an excellent pilot.

Van's love of the air was almost equaled by his love of golf. Glad was a "golf widow" who saw her husband off to the links nearly every free morning or afternoon he had. Even during his later years as chief of staff with an onerous work schedule, he found time to golf at least once a week. On the other hand, his flying and golfing skills were not matched by his usefulness around the house. He hated routine chores and was never accused of mowing a lawn or fixing a leaky faucet. Apart from flying machines, all things mechanical defeated him. Unlike many men who enjoy tinkering with cars in their spare time, he could not even find the hood-latch release. Nonetheless, this did not stop him from taking pleasure in a good automobile; as chief of staff he enjoyed driving a custom-made, powder blue Cadillac with a plush interior that included knobs and levers shaped like airplanes.[67] This disinclination toward understanding technology carried over into his career. His job was to fly airplanes; he left it to others to fix them. He did, however, ensure they were indeed fixed. In all aspects of his life it was one of his great strengths that he recognized his weaknesses and took steps to compensate for them. If he was personally uninformed on a particular subject, he admitted this shortcoming, but then found someone who was an expert and gave that person the responsibility and authority to ensure success.

Glad remained beautiful and shapely. She and Van were devoted to one another and protected their private times together. Having the children's grandparents visit so frequently allowed Van and Glad time to slip away by themselves, vacationing in Canada, Mexico, and Europe while the youngsters remained at home. Glad exercised an enormous influence on Van. She seemed to possess a sixth sense about people, their personality and trustworthiness. Van relied heavily on her advice and intuition throughout his career. Glad would meet Van's colleagues, watch, listen, size them up, and then pass on her intuitions. He did not always agree with her assessment or act upon such feelings, but he always listened. In addition, Van was basically shy. He was always well liked and friendly, but if given the choice, would have preferred to remain in the background. Glad would not allow this. She was too vivacious and gregarious to remain at home and too proud of her husband to let him hide his light under a basket. They were an incredible team.

After two years at March, the Vandenbergs were transferred to Wheeler Field, Hawaii, to join the 18th Pursuit Group. This was an enjoyable tour in which the lieutenant once again became a squadron commander, sharpening still further his leadership skills. His style of command was subtle; he led by example and seemed sincerely concerned about his subordinates' welfare. He did, however, make mistakes. In April 1930 his squadron received the new Boeing P-12s, and all were curious to test the performance of the aircraft. Without briefing them on his intentions, Vandenberg led his squadron up through the clouds to determine how high the new fighters would go. The P-12 was unpressurized, unheated, and lacked oxygen equipment. The aircraft were well over twenty thousand feet when the commander finally began his descent. Most of the pilots experienced hypoxia, and some even collapsed upon landing. Although he later apologized for such foolishness, the incident reflects Vandenberg's still-maturing personality.[68]

To Van, pursuit flying was an invigorating challenge. He enjoyed this new mission, and his family was so enchanted with Hawaii that he asked for an extension of his tour. He was dissuaded by his commander, who warned that staying in the Islands too long would sap ambition and distance him from the mainstream of the Air Corps. The rest of the family did not particularly agree with that line of reasoning, so leaving was difficult. As the Vandenbergs rounded Diamond Head on their long sea voyage back to the States, a flight of P-12s from the group flew overhead to say aloha. Sandy and Gogo burst into tears and refused to smile again for several days.[69]

The Vandenbergs returned to San Antonio, Texas, in September 1931 for an assignment at Randolph Field. Van was once again to be an instructor pilot, this time at the new "West Point of the Air." As before, he acquired a reputation as an outstanding pilot and officer who was sincerely concerned about his men. One of his students later said: "He was a man of charm and personality . . . a great guy."[70] Another described him in even more graphic terms:

> He was lighting a cigarette with cupped hands over which he trained on me the most piercing blue/gray eyes that I had ever seen—jaw to jaw. My hopes of getting the best instructor were instantly furnished substance as he looked the part in every respect—tall, lean, tanned by the weather, flight cap at the casual position, squint lines around the eyes, lips rather compressed and a rather stern expression that did not hide the gleam in those piercing eyes. And best of all, a hot pursuit pilot from foreign service—not like some of the other instructors without such a glamorous background.[71]

By the mid-1930s, Captain Hoyt Vandenberg was recognized by his contemporaries as one of the hottest pilots in the Air Corps. These early years as a junior officer—when he flew a bewildering variety of aircraft and amassed over three thousand hours of flying time—were crucial in establishing a foundation of technical competence and expertise.[72]

After three years at Randolph, in 1934 Vandenberg received orders to attend the Air Corps Tactical School at Maxwell Field, Alabama. Before he was to report, however, there was one final air challenge awaiting him. In February of that year, President Roosevelt had abruptly canceled all airmail contracts with the civilian air lines, alleging corruption in the awarding of those contracts. Not fully appreciating the gravity and complexity of the situation, the Air Corps commander, Major General Benjamin Foulois, volunteered his service to deliver the mail. This tragic interlude is usually referred to as the "Air Mail Fiasco," and with good reason. For four months the Air Corps flew the mail, initially in abominable winter conditions, with obsolescent aircraft. The Army flyers were not prepared to carry out these missions at night over unfamiliar terrain without proper instruments, any more than airline pilots could have flown in formation or accurately dropped bombs.[73] The demands of the two activities were totally different, and each required specialized training. Twelve pilots were killed in the sixty-six aircraft accidents that occurred while the Air Corps flew the mail. Although air leaders maintained that this performance was not appreciably worse than normal flying activities, in fact the accident and fatality rates were four times what they had been the year before.[74]

Vandenberg, like most Air Corps pilots, found himself pressed into service. One wintry night he took off in marginal weather and soon encountered severe icing conditions. Unable to maintain altitude, he began scanning anxiously for an emergency landing site. After circling for a few minutes he saw someone waving a light alongside a snow-covered field on the top of a low mountain. Van decided to take a chance and set down near the light and rolled to a stop without mishap. The man with the lantern came through the snow over to the plane, and when he held up the light to look at the pilot exclaimed: "Why, Captain Vandenberg, you don't remember me, but you were the check pilot who washed me out of pilot training a month ago! I just came up to this mountain to get away from it all and write a book. When I heard a plane circling overhead I knew it was in trouble and came out to have a look."[75] Vandenberg must have been carrying his lucky coins with him that stormy night.

IN QUEST OF A THEORY

In 1934, Vandenberg began a string of educational and staff assignments that were to fill out the other half of his professional character. The Tactical School was the intellectual center of the Air Corps. Aviators were never accused of being thinkers, but what theorizing was done concerning the proper roles and missions of air power took place at Maxwell. Attendance at the Tactical School was virtually mandatory for all officers aspiring to a command in the Air Corps, and the vast majority of high-ranking American air officers in World War II had either attended or instructed there.[76] The curriculum was designed to train students in the strategy, tactics, and logistics required for air power employment and was also instrumental in the formulation and codification of doctrine.

Vandenberg arrived at a highly significant time. Air power enthusiasts since Billy Mitchell had been pushing for an independent air force. The rationale used to support this demand was that air power was a unique force that had rendered traditional methods of warfare obsolete. The goal of war, it was often said, was to destroy the enemy army. Once accomplished, an invader could then march unhindered to the heartland and dictate peace terms. Mitchell argued that such thinking had mistaken means for ends. The true *goal* of war was the enemy's heartland, but defeating his army first was until then the necessary *means* to achieve it. Air power now obviated the bloody and protracted first step of engaging the enemy's ground forces. Airplanes could fly over slow-moving and static armies and strike directly at the enemy's vital center. Air power, as exemplified by strategic bombardment, was unique. Not only could it avoid the trench deadlock and its carnage, but it was also an effective and economical defense against sea invasion. Because of this uniqueness, it should not be tied to the ground army but should be independent. According to Mitchell, his bombing and sinking of the captured German battle cruiser *Ostfriedland* in the tests of 1921 heralded a new era in warfare.[77]

Such ideas, and especially Mitchell's impolitic way of expressing them, were not welcomed by the army hierarchy. When the Navy's dirigible *Shenandoah* crashed in a thunderstorm in September 1925 and its commander, an old friend of Mitchell's, was killed, the dam burst. Mitchell accused his superiors of "incompetency, criminal negligence, and almost treasonable administration." His unwarranted outburst earned him a court-martial.[78] Moreover, Mitchell's claims for the bomber aircraft of his day were clearly exaggerated. The lumbering, open-cockpit biplanes of the 1920s achieved a top speed of barely one hundred miles per hour, easy prey for enemy pursuit. Less than a decade after Mitchell's fall, however, new technology seemed to make his dreams attainable. The Martin B-10 bomber was an all-metal, twin-engine, cantilever monoplane with enclosed cockpits, retractable landing gear, and an internal bomb bay; it had a speed and altitude capability nearly equal to that of contemporary pursuit planes. The B-10 prototype had been flown in 1932, and the first production models were delivered to the Air Corps in June 1934—two months before Vandenberg arrived in Alabama. Coincidentally, he left Maxwell Field in 1935 just as the Boeing XB-17 made its maiden flight.

The effect of such aircraft on thinking at the Tactical School was profound. Major Donald Wilson and Captain Harold L. George, instructors there at the time, were vocal and zealous advocates of the strategic bombing theory. Their influence helped initiate a shift in Air Corps thinking toward bombardment. Wilson himself later admitted that the ideas expounded during that period were a radical departure from Army doctrine, and only the fact that Washington was unaware of what was being said at Maxwell allowed it to go unchallenged.[79] The importance of pursuit was clearly downplayed in the curriculum. In fact, Major Claire Chennault, the instructor and main champion of pursuit employment at the Tactical School, later claimed that there was a strong movement to drop the pursuit section altogether, and it was only the strong intervention of the Army ground forces instructors that convinced the commandant to retain the subject.[80] Such views must have been a jolt to the Captain Vandenberg who had had scarcely any contact with bombardment aircraft during the previous decade. The year at

Maxwell introduced him to a theory of air power employment that was fully to emerge fifteen years later when, as chief of staff, he would make the Strategic Air Command the cornerstone of American military policy.

Vandenberg's year at Maxwell was followed by more schooling: Command and General Staff School at Fort Leavenworth, Kansas. Unlike the Tactical School, Leavenworth was designed to instruct Army officers in all facets of their profession, but the focus was on the ground-based combat arms. Because the Air Corps was still part of the Army, air officers hoping for promotion were expected to attend Fort Leavenworth to become well-rounded. Unfortunately, the curriculum was boring and routine for airmen like Vandenberg. The course of study emphasized map reading and staff exercises. Students planned and led attacks, pursued a retreating enemy, conducted reconnaissance, and defended strong points. Supply, logistics, and transportation of large units in the field were also taught. Air power, however, was barely mentioned; only 5 of the 158 conference periods were dedicated to aviation, and these did not discuss its strategic employment. Apparently this omission was deliberate. The school's official history admits that the Army was so fearful of an independent air force that it refused seriously to discuss air power lest it "further inflame the matter." The air power concepts taught at Leavenworth in 1939 were the same as those taught in 1923.[81] Moreover, although there was an Air Corps representative on the faculty to introduce aviation to the ground officers, his influence was minimal because of the lack of modern aircraft available at the school to demonstrate air capabilities.[82] Aviators complained that too much time was spent on minutiae—how to emplace machine guns and the like. Pat Partridge later stated that Leavenworth was a "letdown after going to the Tactical School where they were really using their imagination and running exercises." He added that the Army still seemed to be "marching down the road at 2 1/2 miles an hour" instead of keeping pace with developments such as mechanization, then being introduced in Europe.[83] Vandenberg graduated in June 1936 near the middle of his class, respectable considering the caliber of the competition.

Major Ira C. Eaker, who attended Leavenworth the year after Vandenberg, wrote a light account of his tribulations as a student. The Command and General Staff School was referred to as "The Little House," to distinguish it from "The Big House" next door—the Federal Penitentiary. It was an old post, with large trees and reasonably good facilities. The students lived in an ancient and rambling converted barracks called the "bee hive" that was extremely hot and noisy. After shooting a few darts at the staid and unimaginative curriculum, Eaker saved his choicest barbs for the considerable emphasis placed on "equitation." Three afternoons each week were spent at the stables, thus underscoring the significance of the large sign at the main gate: "Horses Have Right of Way." Fortunately, the aged quadrupeds had been at Leavenworth for so long they were most tolerant of the inexperienced pilots assigned to ride them. Indeed, they could be very helpful: "Abbie Waller was wont to work his General Terrain Exercises sitting on the ground, holding his horse's reins, while the beast looked over his shoulder. Abbie would put down a solution on his map, then look up. If the horse shook his head, Major Waller promptly changed his set-up. It worked." Eaker concluded his article with advice to his fellow pilots: "don't ruin your eyes"—the course was not worth the effort.[84]

As usual with Vandenberg, it was the people, not the curriculum that he found stimulating; and although the course itself made little impact, he made or renewed friendships that would be of great importance in the years ahead: Charles Chauncey, John R. Deane, Leslie Groves, Lyman Lemnitzer, Ralph Stearley, Pat Timberlake, Vic Strahm, Louie Brereton, Tom Hanley, and George Stratemeyer.[85] Of far greater importance to Van, however, was making the acquaintance of fellow student Major Carl M. Spaatz, soon to be one of the great commanders of World War II. He too was unenthusiastic about attending school, and after his selection wrote: "I am going to Leavenworth not because I expect it will do me any good, but primarily because I am ordered there and secondarily to get away from here [Washington]."[86] Although eight years separated Spaatz and Vandenberg in age, their personalities complemented each other. "Tooey" had been a fighter pilot in the First World War and had shot down four German aircraft. He was a superior pilot and had participated in the famous "Question Mark" flight of 1929 that demonstrated the possibilities of midair refueling. Spaatz was a hard drinker "with a face like a rusty nail" who munched cigars and whose all-night poker games were legendary. He was a diamond in the rough, but he also had a knack for judging character and picking top subordinates; such an ability was never so evident as in his later support of Vandenberg.

In 1936, Captain Vandenberg returned to the Tactical School as an instructor in fighter tactics. It would seem that his background as one of the premier pursuit pilots in the Air Corps would have made him uniquely suited for this position. Surprisingly, this was not the case, and his two years at Maxwell proved remarkably unremarkable. The highly charged intellectual environment at the Tactical School still spawned endless debates over the proper role of air power, and these arguments occurred not just with ground-based Army officers, but between aviators as well. Although incendiaries like Wilson, George, Kenneth Walker, and Claire Chennault had by then departed, their replacements—Larry Kuter, Haywood "Possum" Hansell, and Muir "Santy" Fairchild—were just as vociferous. One would think that inserting a dedicated pursuiter like Vandenberg into this cauldron would have brought matters to the boiling point, but surprisingly, sparks did not fly; rather, tempers and rhetoric cooled. With the firebrand Chennault gone, pursuit doctrine decisively receded into the background, and strategic bombardment became the gospel of American air power.[87] Typically, Vandenberg played the role of arbitrator, referee, placator, and soother. He labored to effect cooperation and understanding, not inflame passions. His personality was one of his greatest strengths, and he used it to produce harmony.

Vandenberg was a good lecturer, but gave the impression that he would rather be doing something else, preferably flying.[88] His lectures were neither inflammatory nor controversial; he presented the "conventional" approach to pursuit doctrine, as demonstrated by the experiences of the World War and his own career. Before departing, Major Don Wilson had given Van directions on how to teach his course: "Pursuit is merely an element of antiaircraft defense." It was not to be used to escort bombers—that would be unnecessary—but rather to defend fixed bases and forces.[89] Vandenberg heeded these instructions, teaching that although the pursuit mission was a vital component of an air force, it had limitations. It was not an effective weapon against ground personnel; use as escort for bombardment was possible, though "uneconomical," and even as an interceptor pursuit was of dubious utility: "It is extremely unlikely that a general defense can be provided that is strong enough to successfully oppose an enemy penetration in force." Van admitted that "technology has favored bombers" to the extent that pursuit was relegated to a "point defense security force." He concluded one of his lectures gloomily by saying that pursuit's defensive capabilities were such that "it must lay new plans if it is to continue to wage a successful battle against the attacking airplane."[90] Another striking aspect of Vandenberg's Tactical School lectures was their incredible knowledge of the details involved in gun calibers, rates of fire, penetration capabilities of different ordnance, firing angles, and the like. It was obvious that he was exceptionally skilled in the technical aspects of his job. Significantly, in an essay published later, Vandenberg likened pursuit aircraft to a "mobile antiaircraft unit" that could be directed from the ground. Although he anticipated the need for an escort fighter to protect bomber formations, he painted the characteristics of such a mission in purely defensive terms: "the pursuit ship places itself between the possible enemy attack and the planes to be protected, thus greatly deflecting the attack itself. If the pursuit breaks off its protective duties for a fight, the friendly planes will be forced to go unescorted." This is bland stuff and sounds almost like an apology for pursuit.[91] Strange thoughts for a fighter pilot, but perhaps Vandenberg was already beginning to see beyond the narrow confines of his cockpit. It seems clear that Vandenberg was in the process of a profound philosophical transformation. Although never forgetting the importance of pursuit, he now began to realize the overriding primacy of bombardment. Fighter aircraft are not by themselves a war-winning weapon—bombers are.

Lieutenant Larry Kuter and his wife, Ethel, later recalled that Vandenberg never took the Tactical School very seriously, either as a student or as an instructor. They stated that although Van and Glad were an attractive and popular couple who attended the parties and enjoyed themselves, they were not socialites and did not feel a need to be always a part of the group. They were a complementary team—"sufficient unto themselves."[92] There was little social distinction between students and faculty; all mingled freely at the Officers Club and each others' homes. This was intentional; students and faculty alike were told: "this is a place where we want you to relax and take time off to try to think about what is going on. Get acquainted with your contemporaries." In fact, although students were graded on their work, they were deliberately not given their relative standing in the class, for fear it would lead to hostile competition and unnecessary study.[93] Vandenberg took this advice literally. He was outgoing and gregarious, but always preferred the company of men with whom he could unwind. Poker with the boys was his favorite card game; he shunned the "bridge set" and the cocktail circuit. He occasionally drank alcohol, but not to excess, and although he could swear, it was never in the presence of women. There was no hint of scandal in his private life; Van and Glad were devoted to each other and were best friends; they relied on each other's strengths and were a happy, supportive match.[94]

After two years in Alabama, Captain Vandenberg returned to school in 1938 when chosen to attend the Army War College at Fort Humphreys (presently Fort McNair) in Washington, D.C. This was a vitally important tour. As one observer noted, the list of War College alumni was a veritable "Who's Who" of the Army. Such an assignment for a man of his junior rank was unusual and indicated a promising future for Vandenberg. Although he had not achieved fame as a student or an educator, Vandenberg's reputation as an outstanding pilot, leader, and officer was reflected in annual efficiency reports and was largely responsible for this latest honor. To use the jargon of the selection board: "The most desirable candidates were the officers of great promise with curves of rising efficiency."[95] In addition, luck and timing were significant factors because new selection criteria specified for the first time that a certain number of Air Corps captains be chosen who had good records, had already attended Fort Leavenworth, and who were available for immediate reassignment. Not many officers fulfilled all these conditions; Vandenberg had "filled the squares" for such a tour while most others had not.[96]

The course of study at the War College was on a considerably higher plane than that of the Command and General Staff School. Instead of dealing with mundane map reading and tactical exercises, the War College addressed matters of national policy, the role of economic and social factors in war, and the formulation of foreign policy.[97]

The entire course followed a building-block approach and began with a month-long discussion of American military organization and doctrine. This was followed by a similar examination of the military forces of Great Britain, France, Germany, Italy, the Soviet Union, and Japan. The second phase examined mobilization plans, a subject that had been largely ignored in military circles up to that time. The student body was divided into several groups, and each was responsible for preparing various reports. Van's committee examined the mobilization of manpower for industrial purposes in the United States, trying to formulate the most efficient use of personnel in the event of a major war.[98]

The class then turned its attention to the foreign policy of the United States in Latin America. Army Chief of Staff George C. Marshall was particularly interested in this topic and directed the War College to look into it closely. Specifically, the students were to discover what threat Germany presented to Brazil and Argentina and to devise a course of action to oppose that threat.[99]

Having thus determined American military organization, policy, and capabilities, as well as those of potential foes, the students were then directed to use that knowledge to prepare war plans. The previous year the hypothetical enemy had been Germany, but new neutrality legislation that feared American involvement in European quarrels prohibited such a scenario for Vandenberg's class. Instead, pursuing the thread of hemisphere defense, the students were to draw up a plan for invading Mexico and installing a "friendly government." The preparation of these plans took seven weeks, and the results were impressive.[100]

The officers compiled an enormously large and detailed plan of attack involving joint operations acting on two axes—an overland strike toward Monterey, and an amphibious assault at Vera Cruz. Vandenberg was a member of the committee that prepared the Vera Cruz operations order. This scenario, consisting of two large binders, considered a host of factors including weather, terrain, climate, water supply, intelligence, logistics, occupation duties, and treatment of prisoners of war. Upon completion of their plan, the authors briefed it to the entire class, who then discussed its strengths and weaknesses.[101]

While studying the best method of subduing Mexico, the students were asked by the General Staff to consider another question: "What should be the military policy of the United States in the western Pacific with special emphasis on the Philippines?" In short: How should the United States defend the Islands against Japanese attack? The students concluded after a very lengthy examination that the Philippine archipelago was of crucial importance to this nation and must be staunchly defended.[102] As will be seen, this study was to have a significant impact on Vandenberg's strategic thinking.

Following this effort, there was a Command Post Exercise that postulated an invasion of America's northeast coast. The students had to organize, plan, and simulate fighting a defensive campaign to repel the invaders. Once again, the detail and thoroughness of these activities were impressive.[103] Because the Army was small and funds were short, large-scale maneuvers were impossible in the United States. These games were designed to take their place; therefore, every attempt was exerted to make them realistic. They seemed to succeed in that goal.

As at the Command and General Staff School, the personal encounters at the War College were at least as important as the academic curriculum. Again, there was little distinction between students and their teachers; all were professionals gathering to ponder and debate weighty matters. The actual technique used was for small groups to work together on a particular topic of study, and, after thrashing it out, to prepare a report and brief the entire class on their findings. "Lively discussion" would then follow.[104] The opportunity to meet and work with these top soldiers, sailors, and airmen, and to exchange views on crucial questions, was a rare gift. Vandenberg later maintained that this aspect made the War College one of his most important assignments.[105]

In retrospect, 1939 can be seen as a milestone in Vandenberg's life; he was slowly awakening to the importance of staff work. Heretofore, only flying had stirred his professional interest and elicited concentrated effort. As the commandant of the War College had stated in his welcoming remarks: "No one likes staff work, but what must be realized is that war *is* staff work—preparing for one is preparing for the other." After sixteen years, Vandenberg finally understood that fact. The timing was propitious, because only two months after his graduation war broke out in Europe, and Vandenberg's new duty was across town in the Plans Section of the Air Staff.

Campaigns and battles are nothing but a long series of difficulties to be overcome. The lack of equipment, the lack of food, the lack of this or that are only excuses; the real leader displays his quality in his triumph over adversity, however great it may be.

George C. Marshall

II | The War for Europe

Strategy is finding a sonofabitch whom you rank and telling him to take a place, and relieving him if he doesn't.

George S. Patton, Jr.

THE AIR STAFF

While Captain Vandenberg was attending the Army War College, the Air Corps had begun planning for a massive expansion. War threatened in Europe, and President Roosevelt declared in January 1939 that American defenses were "utterly inadequate." The Air Corps was especially deficient, consisting of only seventeen hundred aircraft and sixteen hundred officers; therefore, projections were hurriedly made to determine the size and composition of the necessary force. As each plan was drawn, however, it was almost immediately eclipsed by events. Within a year estimates had leaped from twenty-four combat-ready groups, to forty-one, then fifty-four, and finally to eighty-four. The main problem with these plans was that they simply did not contemplate fighting a war on the massive scale then being conducted in Europe. To complicate matters further, in May 1940 as German armies swept through western Europe, the president unexpectedly called for fifty thousand airplanes, an astounding figure. To underline his new-found attraction for air power, Roosevelt also appointed Robert A. Lovett as assistant secretary of War for Air, a post that he had declined to fill for the first eight years of his administration.[1]

Unfortunately, events were unfolding in Europe and the Pacific so rapidly that air planners could not keep up. One difficulty was that the Air Corps and General Staff did not agree on the basic mission of air power. An independent air force required heavy bombers for strikes in the enemy's rear; but a ground support arm had greater need of attack, observation, and medium bombers for close support near the battlefield. Moreover, the vocal debate over doctrine within the Air Corps itself on this same issue had not disappeared. The result of this constant tug between factions produced near chaos.[2] Although much studying, reporting, and projecting took place, few aircraft were actually built. One airplane builder commented in exasperation that the Air Corps plans for mobilization were nothing but "hogwash."[3]

The new chief of the Air Corps Plans Section, Lieutenant Colonel Carl Spaatz, needed able officers to bring order to this confusion and in April 1939 requested that Captain Hoyt Vandenberg, his classmate at Fort Leavenworth four years previously, be assigned to his staff. The request was approved. Managing the expansion program was the major responsibility of the Plans Section, and for the next two years Vandenberg was occupied in this effort, attempting to resolve the thorny issues of what to buy and in what quantity, as well as ensuring that there were bases to house the new aircraft and personnel to maintain them.[4]

The Air Corps had been pushing expansion for years and was eager to carry out the president's designs, but a major obstacle soon appeared that was to cause anxious moments for air leaders. Not only did Roosevelt want to build an American air force, he also wanted to supply the British, French, Chinese, and others. Although increased production orders were a welcome incentive to an American aircraft industry just emerging from a debilitating depression, there were simply not enough aircraft yet being produced to satisfy all needs. When General Hap Arnold, chief of the Air Corps, balked at these plans, he received a pointed warning from President Roosevelt that his negative attitude would soon get him reassigned to Guam unless he "played ball."[5] Since speed was essential, quantity temporarily outweighed quality as America rearmed. On several occasions Vandenberg directed that proposed aircraft modifications be halted in the interest of hurrying specific models into production.[6] During this period he had the delicate task of balancing national defense and training needs against the desire to send planes to the "future allies" who were taking the war to the enemy. Vandenberg matured quickly during this period, but the pressures of war preparation led to mistakes. In March 1941, Van advised Spaatz not to develop drop tanks or other range extension devices for pursuit that would allow the escorting of heavy bombers. He believed that the escort function was "incompatible with the mission of pursuit." This atypical display of rigid dogmatism would prove extremely costly over the skies of Europe. Fortunately, Vandenberg made such errors of judgment infrequently.[7]

Another area under Spaatz's purview was war plans. There were no "air war plans" as yet, only air appendixes to War Department plans. Arnold pushed for a separate unit, but was consistently rebuffed and told it was "fundamental" that only one agency be responsible for Army planning.[8] Air Corps leaders nevertheless had their own ideas on the proper way to win a war. Building on the study he had participated in at the Army War College a few months previously, in September 1939 Vandenberg wrote a lengthy memorandum for Spaatz addressing strategic air operations in the Far East. Assuming war with Japan, the memorandum offered three possible roads to victory: an invasion force, a naval blockade, and a sustained air offensive. An invasion force of sufficient strength was not deemed feasible because there were no suitable supply bases within two thousand miles of Japan to maintain such an army. A naval blockade was also unfeasible because the blockading ships would need air cover, and no airfields were available. On the other hand (using classic Tactical School logic), because Japan's industry and population were densely concentrated in certain areas, they were particularly susceptible to air attack: "It is probable that sustained air attack alone would be sufficient to force Japanese acquiescence in our national policies."[9]

To mount this air attack, secure bases and a strategic air force were necessary. Hawaii was too distant—thirty-nine hundred miles from Japan. The solution was either to extend the range of bombardment aircraft to four thousand miles—an unlikely option—or to locate bases closer to Japan. Excluding territory then occupied by the Soviet Union and Japan, the only possibilities left were China, Guam, and the island of Luzon in the Philippines—all within two thousand miles of Tokyo. (Not coincidentally, the B-17 had a range of two thousand miles.) After eliminating China and Guam for political and strategic reasons, Luzon remained. Dismissing the concern that such a base would present a major target for a Japanese preemptive strike, Vandenberg opined confidently:

> If an air base were prepared and available in Luzon, a suitable striking force could fly from peace-time stations to the Philippines immediately upon the outbreak of hostilities. Such a striking force could establish an air defense zone about the Island of Luzon and prevent its seizure by Japan by interdiction of its overseas expedition.[10]

Preventing an attack would be possible by employing three groups of medium bombers (200 aircraft) and three reconnaissance squadrons (75 planes). But this would suffice only to stop a Japanese invasion; to prevent an air assault would require additional forces: two groups of heavy bombers (64 planes), three more reconnaissance squadrons, and three groups of interceptor fighters (150 planes). This force (total: 565 aircraft) would ensure the defense of Luzon. In order to conduct the strategic air offensive, six more heavy bomber groups (200 planes) and six reconnaissance squadrons (150 planes) would be necessary. Vandenberg recommended to General Arnold through Spaatz that airfields and facilities be built on Luzon and that forces be specifically earmarked for transfer, although they would not actually be sent until "the threat or outbreak of hostilities."[11]

There are several interesting aspects to this memorandum. The strategic war plans of the United States at that time called for abandonment of the Philippines because they were believed indefensible. This postulate, as detailed in RAINBOW 5, would be reaffirmed in early 1941 at the so-called ABC talks with Great Britain.[12] This decision would begin to change only in July 1941 after Germany invaded the Soviet Union. It was then feared that Russian preoccupation with Germany would leave a power vacuum in Asia that Japan would be tempted to fill. To help prepare for this eventuality, General Douglas MacArthur, retired and living in Manila, was recalled to active duty and made commander in the Philippines. His "contagious optimism," coupled with the "startling success" of B-17 raids by Britain in the European war, induced the War Department to believe that the Philippines could become a self-sustaining fortress. Talk of abandoning the Islands was scrapped; and plans for defense and reinforcement were substituted, with air power playing a special role.[13] General Marshall's change of mind was evidenced when he wrote Arnold in July that he was "unalterably opposed" to any more aircraft shipments to the Soviet Union until the Philippine defenses were improved.[14]

Although only thirty-five B-17s and 178 fighters were located in the Philippines by the time of Pearl Harbor, 270 more bombers and 130 fighters were slated to arrive by March 1942.[15] When it is noted that this would have left a total of only seventeen B-17s in the United States, it is apparent how radical a change had occurred in American thinking over the previous months. In November, Marshall held a press conference in which he reiterated the high priority being given to Philippine defense. He feared, however, that the movement of aircraft to the Islands had been completed with such secrecy that the Japanese might not be aware of it; hence, the buildup's deterrent value was wasted. Prophetically, Marshall stated that the "danger period" was the first ten days of December: "If we get by that we're OK until February. By then MacArthur will have plenty in the Philippines."[16] The token air force available in Luzon on December 8, 1941, hopelessly inadequate, was soon destroyed by Japanese attackers. Nevertheless, it is interesting to speculate on what effect the scheduled 600-plane deterrent force would have had on events. It is more interesting to imagine the 900-plane strike force envisioned by Vandenberg in 1939.

It is a positive commentary on Vandenberg's intelligence and foresight that he pushed for a defensive force on Luzon nearly as large as the entire combat strength of the Air Corps at that time. It is also illuminating that he, a fighter pilot, would have the breadth of vision necessary for such a broad strategic plan based primarily on bombers; moreover, that he looked to the Pacific at a time when the eyes of most others were riveted on Europe. Relatively defenseless on December 7, the Philippines fell in four months, and it would be three years before they could be retaken. A strong and defensible position on Luzon could have had a powerful impact on the course of the Pacific war. To be sure, there was simplistic and illogical thinking in this study: no mention is made of aircraft carriers; a blockading force of submarines scarcely needs air cover; and advanced bases for an air offensive could just as easily be used to protect the invasion or sea blockade that had quickly been shrugged off as "inadequate." Nevertheless, these criticisms are glaring only in hindsight; the strategic vision and boldness displayed are commendable.

Vandenberg's concern with the defense of the Philippines was not ended. As the Battle of Britain unfolded in late 1940, the vulnerability of bombers to effective fighter aircraft that were combined with radar and a central control network became apparent. Air Chief Marshal Hugh Dowding, head of the Royal Air Force Fighter Command, visited the United States in early 1941 and assured Major Vandenberg, who had been promoted in March 1940, that a defense of Luzon was viable.[17] Whether Vandenberg's efforts were a factor in the mid-1941 decision to defend and reinforce the Philippines, such moves were destined to be too little and too late. Seven radar sites were scheduled for the Philippines, but only two were operating by December 7, and the entire defense communications network was inadequate.[18]

As war with Japan approached, promotion and responsibility came quickly. In November 1941, Vandenberg was promoted to lieutenant colonel and assigned to the Operations and Training Section of the Plans Division. General Arnold was concerned with Japanese activities in the Pacific islands, but had no accurate intelligence.[19] He therefore directed Vandenberg to send two aircraft on a long-range photographic reconnaissance mission to overfly the Japanese-held islands of Jaluit, Truk, and Ponape (in the Caroline and Marshall Island groups) to monitor a possible military buildup. Army Chief of Staff General George C. Marshall sympathized with Arnold's concern and authorized the highly classified mission. This was a grave decision, and the pilots of the two planes, fully armed B-24s, were instructed to defend themselves in the event of attack by Japanese forces. The requisite orders were dispatched, but the Army's adjutant general, Major General E. S. Adams, who normally sent such messages, had not been notified. Upon seeing a copy of the order sent without his approval, Adams hurried to the Plans Division to court-martial whoever authorized "such an act of war." Vandenberg replied blandly that he had sent the order but had done so on the oral directive of General Marshall. Preparations continued, and the aircraft winged westward on their secret sortie. The first B-24 arrived in Hawaii on the morning of December 5; it was still there two days later when it was destroyed along with most of the Pacific Fleet.[20]

On December 7, Van and Glad were talking in the kitchen of their Westchester apartment on Cathedral Avenue while Gloria was reading a book and Sandy was listening to a Redskins football game on the radio. The broadcast was interrupted to announce the Pearl Harbor attack. Van grabbed the car keys and headed for his office in the Munitions Building. He returned home for supper, had Glad pack a small suitcase, and then returned to the office for the next two days. He was especially busy because the chief of his section, Colonel Earl Naiden, had been caught, quite literally, with his pants down. Apparently, Naiden had taken off that weekend on a tryst with General Arnold's secretary. He could not be reached.[21]

In late January 1942, Vandenberg received the silver eagles of a colonel and took over as chief of the Policy Section of the Plans Division. Besides being in a position of significance, he stayed in daily contact with General Arnold and accompanied the chief to Britain in May 1942 to discuss aircraft allocations.[22] During the next few months, Vandenberg was deeply involved in aircraft shipments to both American and Allied units: B-17s to Australia, T-6Bs to South America, B-24s to China, night fighters to Britain, and P-40s to the "Flying Tigers." In truth, Vandenberg was responsible for allocating virtually all aircraft produced in Britain and the United States to all the Allies, based on their needs and attrition. He held an extremely important position and handled it admirably.[23] Part of his success was directly attributable to his personality; he got along with virtually everyone. At that time, most coordination could still be accomplished on a face to face basis, much of it over a round of golf or on another social occasion. Van was most effective in such environments, and this ensured smooth relations with other staff members.[24]

Vandenberg had performed exceptionally well while on the Air Staff; in August 1941, a comparison of efficiency ratings shows that he was rated the top major on Arnold's staff with twenty-four others below him.[25] As a consequence, rapid promotion followed, and in June 1942 Vandenberg was nominated for promotion to brigadier general. He was rejected, but the reason is unclear. An associate in Plans maintained that it was common knowledge within the office that the president himself had disapproved the promotion because of Vandenberg's earlier push for Philippine defense and also the political connection with his uncle, the Republican senator.[26] This explanation seems inadequate—others of greater rank had also advocated such ideas and not suffered—besides, it had become the accepted national policy over a year previously. As for his relationship with Uncle Arthur, such an explanation would assign to President Roosevelt a pettiness and vindictiveness that would be out of character. It also attributes a political importance to the airman that appears questionable. Another contemporary thought the pass-over was simply owing to Vandenberg's upcoming transfer to a combat assignment overseas, which he had requested to liberate him from a desk. Had Vandenberg remained on the Air Staff, a star would probably have been his, but the desire for action was too great and seemed a small price to pay for glory.[27] It does appear, however, that Vandenberg himself and several others on the Air Staff were expecting his promotion. As he was getting ready to board a transport plane for London at the end of June, Spaatz smiled at him and then silently slipped a set of stars into his pocket. When the brigadier's list was published the following week, however, Vandenberg's name was not on it.[28] Vandenberg's labors on the Air Staff were finally rewarded in September 1942, when he received the Distinguished Service Medal for his "ability, energy, judgment and brilliant professional knowledge" in planning the vast expansion of the Army Air Forces (AAF) to meet global commitments, while at the same time assisting the buildup of Allied air strength.[29]

NORTH AFRICA

In mid-July 1942 Colonel Vandenberg accompanied Generals Marshall and Arnold and the president's close advisor, Harry Hopkins, to London for discussions regarding American aircraft shipments to Britain. The result of these meetings was the "Arnold-Towers-Portal Agreement" that scheduled nearly three thousand combat aircraft to England during the coming year. It also decreed that American combat units stationed in Britain would remain "homogenous" and not be used to fill out British units.[30] These issues settled, the war leaders turned to the question of the Second Front. The United States wanted to attack Germany quickly, but determining the optimum location for such a strike was difficult. General Marshall believed that a limited invasion of France (codenamed SLEDGEHAMMER) should be attempted in 1942 to establish a bridgehead for a major invasion that would take place in 1943.[31] This proposal was supported by American air leaders because it allowed a continued buildup in England for a bombing offensive against Germany. If an invasion were launched in a different theater, it was feared the bomber offensive would be downgraded in importance and its air units drained to support the new attack site.[32] The British, however, were absolutely opposed to a cross-channel invasion in 1942, believing the chances of success were too small. The prime minister and his military advisors proposed something less ambitious: an invasion of French-held North Africa. Though Marshall objected, seeing this as a distraction from the major theater of war, the British were insistent. President Roosevelt deferred to his allies and project TORCH was launched.[33]

Vandenberg remained in London for a week and met daily with General Spaatz, who was now the senior air officer for the European Theater of Operations, United States Army (ETOUSA). Although at first these talks centered on SLEDGEHAMMER, the decision of the president signaled a speedy shifting of gears.[34] As usual, Spaatz was impressed with his young protégé and wrote Arnold urgently requesting that Vandenberg be assigned to his staff. The chief concurred and Vandenberg became the air planner for TORCH.[35]

Even though the venue for attack had been decided, debate did not end, and disagreements over the details continued. Arnold pointedly wrote Marshall on August 29 that it was "generally accepted that the North African operation has *less than a 50% chance of success*," and in order not to diminish those odds still further, all available aircraft should be diverted to the operation. The Far East and Europe would have to wait.[36] Marshall agreed, but General Spaatz did not; he favored a strategic air offensive against Germany, and from his position at ETOUSA was instrumental in directing the Eighth Air Force to that goal. It was apparent that the aircraft Arnold thought necessary to ensure TORCH's success, especially the bomber component, could come from only one source. The Eighth Air Force had the only American heavy bombers and trained crews in the European theater, and it was to be denuded to supply the new Twelfth Air Force. Spaatz wired Arnold on at least four occasions, protesting that stripping the Eighth would jeopardize the war effort and delay ultimate victory over Germany. He pleaded for the Eighth Air Force to be left alone, but to no avail.[37] Admitting defeat, on October 31 Spaatz wired Arnold that although he objected to his aircraft being diverted to Africa, at least they were not being sent to the Pacific![38] Characteristically, when TORCH was launched the following month, he backed it totally.

General Arnold chose Brigadier General James H. Doolittle, recently returned from Tokyo, to be commander of the new Twelfth Air Force; he was a controversial choice. First, he did not get on well with the TORCH commander, General Dwight Eisenhower, who had requested either Spaatz or Ira Eaker for the position. The first meeting between Eisenhower and Doolittle was not auspicious: the airman's prewar reputation as a racing pilot, unconventional soldier, and affluent executive for Shell Oil Company had preceded him. A replacement was sought. Marshall and Arnold agreed that if Doolittle was really not wanted, perhaps someone else could be found, but they were confident the Medal of Honor winner would perform capably. Eisenhower acquiesced. Arnold's decision also raised eyebrows among airmen because Doolittle had not been in uniform throughout the interwar years. It was felt that he had not paid his dues, and the Twelfth Air Force plum should go to someone who had, but Arnold recognized Doolittle's outstanding leadership qualities and stuck to his decision.[39] Later events would prove that the selection was a sound one.

Arnold did, however, include a safeguard by personally choosing Doolittle's staff for him. Although ordinarily a commander's prerogative, Arnold wanted to ensure that top-notch officers were on hand. Vandenberg was appointed chief of staff and Colonel Lauris Norstad the deputy for Operations. This was the first close contact between "Van and Larry," and soon the two became close personal and professional friends whose careers were intertwined thereafter. In fact, the entire Twelfth Air Force staff soon became like one big family during this first great adventure.[40] The importance of this assignment on Vandenberg's career cannot be exaggerated. Except for the Eighth Air Force, which was just beginning operations against Germany, the Twelfth was soon to be the only substantial combat unit in action against the enemy. To be chosen as chief of staff of this crucial force was indicative of the tremendous confidence that Arnold had in Vandenberg. It was now essential that his performance match those expectations.

The TORCH planning staff was headquartered on the fifth floor of Norfolk House in London. Van lived in a nearby flat and ate in local restaurants. The invasion was slated for November, only three months distant, so conferences lasted sixteen to eighteen hours per day, seven days a week, with Vandenberg meeting daily with Eisenhower, General Mark Clark, and Doolittle. Originally, it was decided to land at two sites on the Mediterranean shore of North Africa, Oran, and Algiers. The air support would consist of Doolittle's Twelfth Air Force supporting the western landing—largely an American affair—and Air Marshal William Welsh's Eastern Air Command supporting the British in the east. Although Doolittle's force was three times the size of Welsh's, the two men were equals and reported directly to Eisenhower. When a third landing was added at Casablanca on the Atlantic coast of Africa, Doolittle's force split its resources to cover the new beachhead.[41]

Vandenberg was concerned about the growing scope of the invasion, telling Clark in late August that he had only one-fourth the air power necessary to ensure the operation's success. Although later he would be noted for his ability to work well with his British colleagues, at this early stage Vandenberg was skeptical. He told Clark that the British were not committing enough air strength to TORCH and that they were attempting to bleed off some of the Twelfth's forces to support their own sector. What was worse, they were acting like wise older brothers and constantly trying to take control of both planning and operations.[42] Fortunately, he was able to get over these initial irritations and work smoothly with the British for the remainder of the war.

The final plan for TORCH anticipated that land-based air power would play only a minor role in the actual landings because there were no airfields available nearby. Instead, aircraft would be held in readiness in England and at Gibraltar while the beaches were covered by carrier-based fighters. A top priority of the ground forces upon landing was to secure airfields so that the air armada could deploy to North Africa. There were also several squadrons of P-40 fighter planes loaded on the decks of aircraft carriers that would be launched as soon as bases were secured, and land at the newly acquired fields to begin operations. The aircraft from the North would soon follow.[43] As the invasion date approached, Doolittle wrote Arnold exuberantly: "I have the best staff, the best commanders and the smoothest running organization in the Air Force . . . our key people are really tops. . . . We have a job—a hard job—to do. We are looking forward with pleasant anticipation to the altogether successful accomplishment of it."[44]

On November 5, Doolittle and Vandenberg left London for Gibraltar in B-17s. En route, Doolittle's aircraft was attacked by German fighters, the copilot was badly wounded, and the general jumped into his seat. The damaged Fortress escaped by finding a friendly cloud in which to hide. Not an auspicious beginning.[45] Doolittle and Vandenberg remained with Eisenhower in the tunnels of Gibraltar, monitoring events electronically, when, on November 8, 1942, the combined American and British amphibious forces landed in the face of desultory resistance. An intelligence report before the invasion had stated that the French Air Force in Morocco had poor training and efficiency, but high morale. The report noted dryly that the French "retain a confidence in themselves and their aircraft which is not entirely justified."[46] French Dewoitine fighter planes did duel British Seafires and American Navy aircraft over the beaches, but by the afternoon of the first day the airfield at Tafaraoui, near Oran, was in American hands, and Doolittle ordered the 31st Fighter Squadron to depart Gibraltar south. The following afternoon he and Vandenberg left the rocky labyrinth in a heavily escorted B-17 for their new home. Headquarters was soon established in the Standard Oil Building in downtown Algiers.[47]

Numerous problems immediately arose in the austere conditions of North Africa. Aircraft replacements were constantly delayed, and trained aircrews were scarce. Doolittle reported in late December 1942 that nearly 75 percent of his crews were either untrained or only partially trained. There was also a severe bomb shortage, and many missions were flown with short loads for the first two months after the invasion. Added to these shortages was the abominable condition of the African airfields. Never very good, before the French had surrendered at Tafaraoui they had blown up the sewer system, flooding the airfield and turning it into a quagmire. As a consequence, it could not support the heavy and medium bombers employed by the Twelfth. To illustrate the problem, when Doolittle's B-17 landed at Tafaraoui and taxied clear of the runway, it promptly sank into the mud, and four tanks were required to pull it out.[48] Owing to the lack of motor and rail transportation from the ports, it was impossible to acquire the materials necessary to transform the sod and dirt airfields into hard surface. Eventually, the heavies moved to the desert airstrip at Biskra, where mud was no longer a problem; even so, environmental difficulties continued throughout the campaign. Once it stopped raining, the dust became a major concern, generating some ingenious solutions: "To protect the pitot static tube from dust, we slip on an old GI sock. At night we cover up the canopies with old mattress covers. . . . The shell extractor chutes have small openings which would permit sand to enter to jam the guns if we didn't cover them. So we paste paper over the openings. With a razor we cut little slits."[49]

The living conditions were extremely difficult and were exacerbated by an Arab culture alien to most Americans. The heat was oppressive, the bugs omnipresent, and the odor unbearable. In addition, the water was unfit to drink and the local food was inedible. As a consequence, the troops lived on K-rations,

Spam, and cheap wine. Cigarettes were severely rationed, even for full colonels like Van, and hard liquor was simply unattainable. Typically, however, Van did receive two bottles of Scotch from a staff member because on one of his trips back to London he had located the man's lost footlocker among the thousands left in a warehouse. Writing to Sandy, Van's main complaint was with the Arabs who stole constantly and who were prone to commit acts of sabotage.[50] North Africa held little charm for Vandenberg in 1942.

As the French resistance in Algeria and Morocco collapsed, Eisenhower's forces prepared to move into Tunisia. A reorganization became necessary to extract Doolittle's forces from the west and employ them in the forthcoming campaign. Air Chief Marshal Arthur Tedder, air officer commanding Middle East, had been pushing for a reorganization for some time. In his view, the two air leaders under Eisenhower violated the unity-of-command principle. He believed that the existing situation was inefficient and failed to provide adequate close air support for the ground forces. Instead, he proposed an overall air commander under Eisenhower who would determine how to parcel out air power based on operational requirements.[51] Tedder himself was the likely candidate for this position. Although Eisenhower saw merit in the suggestion, he preferred Spaatz for the job and in early December designated him the deputy commander for Air, Allied Force. Significantly, although Spaatz moved down from London to fill this new position, he did not relinquish control of the Eighth Air Force through his ETOUSA role. Wearing two hats effectively allowed him to maintain control over all American air power in Europe.[52]

Eisenhower's decision was not well received by some. Tedder was amazed that Spaatz, who "lacked operational experience and knowledge," was placed in such a position.[53] As a result, the issue was brought up at the Casablanca Conference the following month, and the TORCH forces were reshuffled once again. Under pressure from Churchill and his chief air advisor, Air Marshal Charles Portal, the infant Allied Air Force under Spaatz was interred, and the Middle Eastern Theater was separated from the European Theater for the first time. This maneuver forced Spaatz to sever his connections with ETOUSA. The Mediterranean Air Command under Tedder was then formed and controlled all allied air units in Africa. It consisted of three main organizations, the most important of which was the Northwest African Air Forces (NAAF), commanded by Spaatz.[54] The NAAF was then organized along functional lines. The Northwest African Strategic Air Force (NASAF) was given to Doolittle, with Vandenberg remaining as his chief of staff.

The NASAF contained most of the allied heavy and medium bombers (about six hundred aircraft: B-17s, B-25s and B-26s; P-38s and P-40s for escort; and four wings of British Wellingtons), and was responsible for striking targets behind enemy lines such as transportation centers, port facilities, and Axis shipping in the Mediterranean. Largely as a result of the bombing, enemy shipping tonnage soon dropped by two-thirds, and a total of 185 merchant ships were sunk with another 110 probable.[55] As the campaign in North Africa moved toward a successful conclusion, NASAF increasingly hit targets in Sicily, Sardinia, and Italy, far removed from the desert ground action. In fact, the target priorities assigned to

NASAF in January were as follows: the eviction of Axis forces from Africa; strikes on Axis air and naval forces in the Mediterranean; direct support of the Sicilian landings; and destruction of oil refineries at Ploesti, Rumania. By April 1943 most of the missions flown by NASAF were against Sicilian or Italian targets.[56]

In December 1942 Vandenberg received the star of a brigadier that had been denied him six months previously. He had been supported in this quest by the Air Force hierarchy that thought the promotion was overdue. Shortly after Vandenberg's arrival in London, Major General George Stratemeyer had written Spaatz:

> Vandenberg was recommended for his promotion and that I am sure that it would have gone through had he not volunteered for his present assignment in England. General Arnold thought that he would have been one of the best minds available to you and for the work that he is doing. I feel confident that Vandenberg felt that such an assignment would probably bring about his promotion, but it just worked out to the contrary. Had he stayed there at A-3, he would be a brigadier general today. Because of his present assignment, I feel rather sure that his name was taken off the list so if you can see your way clear to do so, it is recommended that you recommend Vandenberg for promotion. There is not a more deserving officer on the Air Staff than he is to become a brigadier general.[57]

Once TORCH was underway, Doolittle approached Eisenhower, explained that Vandenberg was performing excellently, and recommended him for promotion. Eisenhower agreed and on November 22 forwarded the proposal to General Marshall. Approval soon followed.[58]

Doolittle and Vandenberg were kindred spirits in many respects and worked well together. Both loved the air and flew numerous unauthorized combat missions in British and American aircraft. Vandenberg logged twenty-six combat missions, mostly in the B-25 and B-26, and considered it effective leadership to let the men "see the brass go flying." He flew as a copilot, gunner, and observer on these sorties, and for his "gallant and courageous leadership" was awarded the Silver Star, Distinguished Flying Cross, and five Air Medals. He led by example.[59] On one occasion during a premission briefing, a B-26 tail gunner stood up and shouted hysterically that he would not fly; he could not take it any longer. There was a stunned silence in the room until Vandenberg said softly from the rear: "Why, that's all right, Sergeant; I'll take your place."[60] Vandenberg was not supposed to fly combat because he was privy to Top Secret Ultra information—the highly classified intelligence consisting of broken German codes. Those who had access to this material were told not to fly combat for fear they would be captured and under duress divulge the existence of the broken codes. In North Africa this rule was widely circumvented, largely because Doolittle himself so loved to fly and refused to stand down. On one occasion he and Vandenberg flew together on a B-26 mission that lost three of six aircraft.[61] Finally, Eisenhower called Doolittle into his office and told him bluntly that he could either be a major general and command NASAF, or he could be a lieutenant and fly airplanes. Which did he prefer? Doolittle understood; he and Vandenberg refrained from combat thereafter.[62] As the campaign moved toward a conclusion, Doolittle was proud and pleased as he congratulated his command: "An amateur Air Force has gone out against one of the best professional Air Forces in the world and on equal footing with it has kicked hell out of it."[63] It was indeed an impressive initiation.

The North African experience was of immense importance to Vandenberg, as indeed it was to American air power in general. Many of the men with whom Vandenberg would work in the years ahead were main actors in the TORCH drama: Eisenhower, Bradley, Patton, Clark, Spaatz, Doolittle, Norstad, Larry Kuter, Joe Cannon, Pete Quesada, and Pat Partridge. As in the past, Vandenberg's superiors were impressed by his performance, and they lauded him for his achievement in organizing NASAF in the face of "almost insuperable difficulties due to lack of time, experienced personnel, and equipment."[64] It is also important to note that Vandenberg was not only introduced to combat and all its complexities, but within the realm of strategic air power. For the first time in his career, Vandenberg was directly involved with strategic bombing operations concerned with more than just the immediate tactical situation on the battlefield. The purview of the fighter pilot was continuing to broaden. Although he would return to tactical aviation in mid-1944, this experience with heavy bombers and strategic doctrine was of use later in his career.

Vandenberg was only indirectly concerned with close air support operations in North Africa, but the lessons learned there would shape tactical air doctrine for the remainder of the war. At the outset of the campaign there was a constant struggle between the ground and air commanders to decide who would control air power. Most ground leaders desired to have a clearly defined air unit assigned to them at all times to strike targets they deemed appropriate. Air leaders, on the other hand, resisted attempts to divide their resources, believing that air power should remain concentrated to strike quickly and decisively. They maintained that this inherent flexibility and ability to intervene en masse gave air power its decisiveness.[65] Close air support was unsatisfactory in the early months of TORCH as soldiers and airmen labored to convert prewar theory into combat practice. Official doctrine followed Army thinking, but it was not effective in either the American or the British experience. Based on his desert campaign, General Bernard Montgomery firmly concluded in September 1943:

> Nothing could be more fatal to successful results than to dissipate the air resources into small packets placed under command of army formation commanders, with each packet working on its own plan. The soldier must not expect, or wish, to exercise direct command over air striking forces.[66]

As the war progressed, air power grew increasingly independent of Army control, and airmen gradually took charge—North Africa was the crucial first step in this process. Spaatz, in his typically outspoken manner, asserted that it was time to realize that the war would be prolonged indefinitely unless it was fought "by the modern method of Air assisted by Armies and Navies."[67] In July 1943, the Army published a new doctrine manual dealing with air power employment that was based on the previous year's wartime experience; the entire first three paragraphs were printed in capital letters and stated boldly:

Land power and air power are co-equal and interdependent forces; neither is an auxiliary of the other. . . . The inherent flexibility of air power is its greatest asset . . . control of available air power must be centralized and command must be exercised through the air force commander if this inherent flexibility and ability to deliver a decisive blow are to be fully exploited.[68]

Somewhere, Billy Mitchell must have been smiling.

Upon returning to Washington after the African campaign, Vandenberg resumed duties on General Arnold's staff. While there, he accompanied Arnold to the Quadrant Conference in Quebec. During his tenure in Washington, Vandenberg was closely watched by a young captain who was working as one of Arnold's speech writers. James Gould Cozzens was a sensitive and observant man who studied people and events at AAF Headquarters, making copious mental notes for future use. In 1948 Cozzens won a Pulitzer Prize for *Guard of Honor*, a somewhat steamy novel of war, sex, and racism. The time is 1943 and the setting is an airfield in Florida. A racial incident has occurred on the base, and Washington is concerned. The Old Man, General Arnold, sends his "Deputy Chief of Staff for Assassination," Brigadier General "Jo-Jo" Nichols, to investigate. The young general is a friend of Spaatz and confidant of Arnold. He is a West Point graduate, described as handsome, debonair, wise, a good flyer, equable, and clinical. Nichols is deadly serious about the war; he has fought in North Africa with distinction and upon returning to Washington accompanied Arnold to the Quebec Conference, where he briefed Roosevelt and Churchill. Nichols is known as a "good man" who is fair and honest. He is especially adept at getting people to speak their mind and reveal their inner thoughts. He tells humorous anecdotes with a deadpan seriousness for which he is famous. These stories always have a moral, always seem appropriate, and always contain a slight admonitory edge. He supports the Old Man totally and is determined that his orders are followed completely and unreservedly. It is obvious that Nichols has a bright future in the separate Air Force that will undoubtedly follow the peace.

Cozzens patterned Nichols on Vandenberg. His portrait is remarkable.[69]

MISSION TO MOSCOW

When Germany invaded the Soviet Union in June 1941, Premier Stalin frantically sought help from Britain, asking Churchill to send twenty-five or thirty divisions to fight in the Caucasus. Although the request was bizarre—there were only ten divisions in the entire British Army at the time—it is significant because Stalin was seeking allied troops on his territory.[70] As the immediate peril passed such requests became infrequent.

Although the United States was not yet a belligerent, it was President Roosevelt's policy to aid "anti-Axis forces." When Averell Harriman visited Moscow in September 1940 to discuss lend-lease, Stalin presented a long list of needed items that included heavy bombers (B-17s and B-24s). General Arnold had anticipated such a request and quickly refused. The Air Corps was still weak, but the chief was especially concerned about the paucity of strategic bombers. There were but a handful available, and he resisted sending them to the Soviet Union where they would not be used effectively by the untrained, tactically minded Soviets.[71]

By the following May, the United States was also at war, and plans to hit Germany directly began brewing in the mind of General Arnold. He envisioned bomber bases at several points on the periphery of the German empire: England, North Africa, the Middle East, China, and the Soviet Union. He discussed his ideas with the president, who agreed to advance them to Stalin. At the Moscow Conference of August 1942, it was proposed that a combined British-American air force consisting of several hundred aircraft be based in the Ukraine. Stalin seemed receptive to the idea, saying that he would "gratefully accept."[72] As soon as air planners tried to work out the details, however, the Soviets began to backtrack. Taking the position of the previous year, they said planes were needed, not people. Instead of an Allied air force, Stalin countered with a request for heavy bombers to be flown by Soviet aircrews. Once again Arnold was adamant, but the president seemed to be softening on the question.[73] In an effort to head off such a possibility, Arnold wrote a boldly worded memorandum to General Marshall spelling out his rationale for opposing the request: it was a wasteful diversion of scarce resources; the Soviets did not know how to use such equipment; there were too few heavy bombers for American use without squandering them on the Soviet Union. In a disarmingly frank manner Arnold asserted: "Our policy of aid to Russia, in which I concur heartily, is based upon the necessity for hurting Germany, and not upon any desire to help Russia."[74] Arnold wanted sustained, mass bombing by American planes flown by American crews. Roosevelt concurred; there would be no B-17s for the Soviet Union.

Arnold then took a different tack to obtain Soviet bases. A foreign ministers' conference was scheduled in Moscow for October 1943 at the same time a new American ambassador, Averell Harriman, and a new chief of the military mission to Moscow, Major General John R. Deane, were to arrive. General Arnold proposed that rather than giving bombers to the Soviets or stationing an Allied air force on Soviet soil, "shuttle bases" be provided instead. The aircraft operating from England and Italy did not have sufficient range to strike targets in eastern Germany and return home. Bombers could, however, make such attacks if they then continued east and landed in the Soviet Union—a comparatively short distance. After rearming and refueling, the fleet would depart for home, bombing Germany again on the way. This procedure would open up previously invulnerable targets in northeastern Germany, promote Allied good will, and confound the German defenses that would be forced to redeploy to meet the new threat from the east. This last rationale was considered particularly useful in light of the upcoming Normandy invasion. Every German plane distracted to the Eastern Front was one less to worry about over the French beaches. There was also another motive for the American desire to plant shuttle bases on Soviet soil.[75]

The war against Japan was predominantly an Army and Navy affair. The Japanese Empire was so large that it was not yet possible to strike at its heart—the Doolittle raid notwithstanding. The largely amphibious forces of MacArthur and

Nimitz were slowly inching their way toward the Home Islands, while air power was either based on aircraft carriers or conducting strikes in support of the ground forces. General Arnold itched to hit Japan directly with strategic bombing as was then being done to Germany, but not even the new B-29s had the range to strike Tokyo from Hawaii or New Guinea. The simple map exercise described by Captain Vandenberg in 1939 was still applicable: with Guam, Luzon, and much of China in enemy hands, the only locale left to base an air force from which to strike Japan was the Soviet Union. Arnold believed as early as December 1941 that he would be able to obtain bases near Vladivostok from which to bomb Japan.[76] But Stalin and the emperor were not at war, and so the bases were not forthcoming. The idea did not die; Arnold thought that war between Moscow and Tokyo would break out eventually, and when it did, he would have his precious bases. Until then, airfields in the Ukraine would provide operational and administrative experience and serve as a precedent for future cooperation. This hope, never to be realized, kept air leaders pursuing the chimera of entente long after it had proven futile.

After Brigadier General Vandenberg returned to Washington from North Africa in June 1943 again to serve on Arnold's staff, he was chosen to accompany Harriman and Deane to Moscow with instructions to negotiate an agreement for American bases. Besides his professional expertise, it is likely that Vandenberg's affability and aplomb were factors in Arnold's decision to send him to Moscow. The young airman's patience would soon be severely tested. It was assumed the mission would take six weeks; Vandenberg remained in Moscow for three months.

Harriman, Deane, and Vandenberg left Washington on October 16, 1943. Stopping in London, Vandenberg attempted to persuade the British to collaborate on the shuttle bombing concept, but the night tactics employed by Bomber Command were not conducive to such a scheme, and Air Marshal Arthur Harris politely declined.[77] Taking a circuitous route through Jerusalem, Baghdad, and Persia, the diplomats arrived in Moscow on October 18, the day before the conference was to start, and were greeted by a guard of honor playing "The Star Spangled Banner." Deane, Vandenberg, and Major General Sidney P. Spalding, who handled lend-lease matters, shared an apartment in the American embassy overlooking Red Square. From the window, Van could see many soldiers walking the broad avenues, but few civilians. The Americans were not restricted in their movements, and there was some opportunity to meet the people and fraternize over a drink of vodka. For example, Vandenberg attended an afternoon picnic with several Soviet air officers, which he reported as quite productive. In addition, he visited aircraft factories in the Moscow area and spoke with engineers and workers. He was greatly impressed by their determination and energy, later remarking that he could hardly imagine American workers operating so feverishly and in such austere conditions.[78] Over the next few months Vandenberg would spend his free time walking about the city, taking Russian language lessons, and shooting pool at Spaso House. He often complained about the intense cold, against which he drank vodka, and the periodic power failures.[79] A member of the attaché's office who had been in Moscow for over a year recalled that he and the other "old timers" looked with "amused tolerance at the enthusiasm of the 'quick fix' artists who dropped in to straighten things out overnight . . . who in general found themselves in a sort of revolving door and back on the street wondering what the hell, if anything, they had accomplished."[80] General Vandenberg was in store for an education in diplomacy.

At the first meeting with Foreign Minister V. M. Molotov and his staff, Vandenberg attempted to impress the Soviets with a short lecture on the efficacy of strategic bombing, complete with slides of a recent mission that had destroyed a Focke-Wulf aircraft factory at Marienburg. His effort was well received, although one Soviet airman was heard to comment that "all altitudes above fifteen feet over the tree tops are wasted." Deane, carried away by the seeming good will in the air, stepped forward to talk specifics. He asked for the Soviet Union to make ten air bases available for the Americans, to improve the exchange of weather information between the two countries, and to institute more effective air transport facilities. Molotov appeared shocked at such requests and replied flatly that these issues would "need study."[81]

Two days later Molotov informed Deane and Vandenberg that their proposals had been agreed to "in principle." The soldiers were elated; after only a few days they had scored an impressive diplomatic triumph. Such feelings quickly evaporated. A hint of what was to come occurred at the conference's termination when Molotov refused to include Deane's proposals in the official communique.[82] A few days later Deane visited the office of General A. Y. Vyshinsky to discuss details of the arrangement to which Molotov had agreed, but was thunderstruck when the general received him with an icy stare and a prolonged, insulting harangue that criticized the United States for stalling on the opening of the Second Front and for not fighting courageously in Italy. Vyshinsky then said discussions dealing with the shuttle bases would be held "in due time"; Deane was dismissed.[83] This type of treatment would occur on several more occasions.

The following week, Vandenberg met with Colonel General A. V. Nikitin to discuss tactics and aircraft employment. Things went smoothly, and the two airmen seemed to get on well together until the matter of bases was mentioned. Nikitin then stated crisply that he was not yet empowered to discuss the matter, but that "data was being assembled and discussions should start in a few days." Vandenberg then asked for permission to visit the front and witness Soviet close air support operations, especially to see how the American P-39 Aircobras were being employed. He was told that his trip would be arranged.[84]

Weeks passed, however, and the Military Mission was studiously ignored. Advice and assistance were sought from Washington to help break the impasse. With the Tehran and Cairo conferences looming, it was hoped that guns of a greater caliber could be brought to bear on the stolid Soviets. General Arnold spoke to the president about the stalled negotiations and stressed their importance to the defeat of Germany. He also mentioned the Siberian bases and how useful they would be in the war against Japan. Roosevelt agreed to mention the matter to Stalin. Vandenberg also went to Cairo and Tehran, perhaps briefing the president personally, and the matter was broached to the premier. Stalin promptly agreed "in principle" and directed Molotov to work out the details. Deane and Vandenberg were once again elated. Deane noted dryly in his memoirs that he hurried back to Moscow to increase his staff in order to handle all the American-Soviet cooperation that would be coming his way.[85]

Once again such hopes proved ill-founded; little happened, and the telephones at the Military Mission remained silent. Vandenberg met with Soviet officers on several more occasions, but because nothing of substance was accomplished, he began to grow restive. His original orders were due to expire, and he was expected at a new assignment—the planning staff in London working on OVERLORD. His tenure was extended until a breakthrough was accomplished.[86]

Ambassador Harriman took up the issue with Molotov and was once again told of "agreement in principle." Still nothing happened. In early January, Harriman cabled Washington that he was getting a "complete runaround" on the bases issue. He concluded that if progress was not made soon, he would take the matter up with Stalin personally.[87] One month later he did so. Surprisingly, Stalin was receptive to Harriman's overtures and discussed the entire operation in great detail. The ambassador was impressed by the generalissimo's technical knowledge and his appreciation for the many problems involved in such an operation. Stalin did not agree to everything Vandenberg had requested—instead of ten air bases there would only be three, and instead of two thousand American ground personnel, only twelve hundred would be allowed. There were also restrictions regarding such things as equipment for the men and aircraft, targeting, and reconnaissance flights. More significantly, all efforts to address the Siberian bases were avoided; Stalin merely said the proposal would be studied. Nevertheless, this discussion signaled real progress.[88] Within the next few days more was accomplished than in the previous three months. Deane was impressed by the cooperation between Vandenberg and the Red Air Force representatives. "Airmen world over are a people apart," he noted, "they seem to be much more cooperative, casual and energetic" than their ground based counterparts.[89]

Unfortunately, the result of Vandenberg's labors proved ephemeral. The three air bases near Kiev were soon built, and the first mission of Operation FRANTIC was scheduled for June 2, 1944. Led by Lieutenant General Ira Eaker, it landed at Poltava, the main base, amid much fanfare. Medals were presented, speeches delivered, and cameras whirred. Deane tabbed the event "the high tide of our military relations with the Soviet Union."[90] From then on things went downhill quickly. Conflicts over targeting, supply, fraternization with the local populace, and air traffic control procedures grew continuously. On the night of June 21, German aircraft attacked Poltava and destroyed over fifty American aircraft that had landed there earlier in the day. This raid, the second most costly of the war for the Army Air Forces, left bitter feelings. There was little Soviet antiaircraft protection at the bases, none of the German raiders were shot down, and Soviet airfield controllers would not allow American fighter aircraft to take off to duel with the attackers.[91]

Two months later the Warsaw Poles rose against their German masters in anticipation of imminent liberation by the advancing Red Army. Unfortunately, the Soviets stalled on the far side of the Vistula River, and the Polish resisters were crushed before they could be rescued. When Roosevelt and Churchill proposed that the shuttle bases be used in an operation to air drop supplies to the belea-guered Poles, Stalin flatly refused. The bases were for bombing Germans, not feeding Poles. The acrimony that arose from this tragedy was the death knell of FRANTIC. No more missions were flown, and the bases were closed.[92]

Although Vandenberg's venture into diplomacy was as successful as could be expected, the shuttle bombing concept itself was a failure. None of the reasons originally advanced for the operation were fulfilled: all of the targets hit were within range of bombers based in England and Italy. (The Soviets chose the targets and inexplicably would not allow those in northeast Germany to be struck.) The German defenses were not baffled; there is no evidence that any Luftwaffe units were pulled from France in order to bolster the Eastern Front. Ultra intercepts indicated that the Luftwaffe was aware of the shuttle bases, but their response was to improve their route-tracking information in the East, not to send interceptors.[93] Siberian bases for the B-29 armada were never granted; after the capture of the Marianas Islands in late 1944, Arnold finally stopped pushing the issue. As for the intention of fostering good relations between allies, the official Army history concludes that FRANTIC was a success because valuable experience was gained in negotiating and dealing with the Soviets.[94] Perhaps, but if such contact was valuable, it was also largely negative. Most negotiators left Moscow with feelings of frustration and disillusionment over the constant delays, rigid and bureaucratic Soviet decision-making apparatus, distrust bordering on paranoia, and bluntness akin to rudeness. Admiral Kemp Tolley, a member of the military mission, later remarked: "The Soviets did what they wanted, usually in a brutal manner without any finesse at all."[95] It is likely that Vandenberg left with similar feelings. As a junior member of the negotiating team he was given scant deference: "The Soviets respected only power, influence, and rank. They dealt with Deane directly because they knew he was a protégé of Marshall's and held the authority of the Joint Chiefs of Staff. Vandenberg was just another messenger boy [who] got thrown an occasional bone."[96] If such was indeed the treatment received, it must have had a powerful impact on the young general who four years later would be Air Force Chief of Staff and facing those same Soviet officials and generals during the Berlin Blockade crisis. The words of General Spaatz on the significance of this mission to Vandenberg's future outlook are of weight.

> General Vandenberg's visit to Russia was one of the most enlightening experiences of his career. He was impressed by the restless energy of Red technicians and the importance attached to the building of Red air power. He gained an understanding of Soviet progress which caused him to call attention repeatedly, both in high councils and in public statements, to the generally unrecognized threat of growing Russian power in the air.[97]

LIBERATING FRANCE

When Vandenberg arrived in London in February 1944, he joined the combined staff drawing up plans for OVERLORD. This work had already been going on for several months, but was in a state of confusion. In the first place, the planners were needlessly and foolishly scattered all over the London area while working on various aspects of the problem. In addition, most of the planners were Army officers who knew little about air power.[98] Consequently, upon Vandenberg's arrival in this imbroglio there were several burning issues in need of resolution, most regarding the role air power was to play before and during the invasion.

Heeding the lessons of previous campaigns, it was decided early in the planning process that under the Supreme Commander Allied Expeditionary Force, General Dwight Eisenhower, would be three coequal commanders for air, land, and water. The Allied Expeditionary Air Force (AEAF) was slated to include the Tactical Air Force (TAF) under Air Marshal Arthur ("Mary") Coningham, and the Ninth Air Force of Lieutenant General Lewis Brereton. Because the AEAF commander would also be responsible for the air defense of Great Britain, it was expected that he would be British. Air Chief Marshal Trafford Leigh-Mallory was chosen for the post.

Leigh-Mallory, the son of a stern clergyman, had enlisted in the infantry during the Great War and had been wounded at Second Ypres. He received a commission, transferred to the Royal Flying Corps, and advanced in rank during the interwar years. In the Battle of Britain he had commanded the illustrious 11th Fighter Group and had become a well-known figure in Britain.[99] Leigh-Mallory was a fighter pilot throughout his career, and was described by contemporaries as hot-blooded, brusque, "wanting everything his own way," aggressive, "too much high-hat and Oxford accent business," tactless, and dogmatic. He was usually at odds with his superior, Air Marshal Arthur Tedder, whom Eisenhower had chosen as his deputy, as well as his chief subordinates, Coningham and Brereton. The impact of personalities is always important, but especially so in coalition warfare when national pride and interests are at play. The Allied leaders had difficulty getting along; this was particularly the case with Leigh-Mallory. Because Tedder questioned Leigh-Mallory's ability to command such a large force, he had appointed Coningham to head the TAF—without notifying "LM," whom Coningham detested. Unfortunately, throughout the campaign Coningham's command was primarily responsible for supporting Montgomery's 21st Army Group. Monty did not like Mary and usually went over his head to LM, or worse, under his head to Coningham's deputy, Air Vice Marshal Harry Broadhurst—who, by the way, had been appointed by LM without Coningham's consent! Added to this, Brereton could hardly stand to be in the same room with LM.[100] It was all very confusing.

When it initially appeared that air support for the invasion would be primarily concerned with close air support on the beaches and their immediate vicinity, Leigh-Mallory's selection seemed reasonable and elicited slight comment. It had early on been decided that the AEAF commander would have "administrative control" over all Allied air power. This did not particularly upset the American air leaders because they defined this term, as the British official history relates with a straight face, as embracing "the award of decorations and decisions about promotion and pay."[101] Soon, however, it became obvious that the massive air support demanded by Eisenhower called for far more than merely the fighter planes and attack bombers earmarked for the AEAF. Eisenhower insisted on the use of American and British strategic bombers. This was an entirely different matter, and as Eisenhower noted, not even the British (including Churchill) trusted the air marshal for such a task, although they had specially selected him for the position.[102] Air Marshal Arthur Harris of Bomber Command was an extremely capable and forceful personality who held the confidence of the Prime Minister, often dining alone with him at Downing Street. General Spaatz, leader of the United States Strategic Air Forces (comprised of the Eighth and Fifteenth Air Forces), was similarly influential. Apart from personalities, it was also a fact that it was the bombers of these two men that had thus far been primarily responsible for carrying the war to Germany. Noted victories in far-off Africa and Sicily were gratifying, but after the London blitz it was a powerful morale factor that each day and night there were hundreds of aircraft lifting off from Britain to bomb the enemy heartland. Indeed, Bomber Command had already lost forty thousand crewmen in the war, more than the entire British army to that point.[103] Both of these bomber forces had become powerful and influential entities that enjoyed a wide degree of operational independence.

Since January of the previous year, when the Casablanca Conference had sanctioned the start of the Combined Bomber Offensive, codenamed POINT-BLANK, airmen had labored to destroy the war-making potential of Germany and render invasion unnecessary. In late January 1944, Harris wrote that if left alone his airplanes could bring Germany to its knees by April. Spaatz believed likewise, maintaining as late as July that if he had just thirty consecutive days of good weather his bombers would finish the war by year's end.[104] It was bad enough having to admit that such hopes were overly sanguine, but it was even worse to see the offensive against German heavy industry, which finally seemed to be taking effect, diverted to the destruction of railroads and bridges in France. The final straw was talk of appointing a "tactical flyer" like Leigh-Mallory as temporary custodian of the "heavies."[105]

Because of such turmoil, Leigh-Mallory soon found himself in the untenable position of having responsibility for the air campaign to ensure the success of OVERLORD, but without the authority to control the air forces necessary to guarantee that success. To add further insult—for Eisenhower realized Leigh-Mallory's unpopularity—Eisenhower had appointed his old friend Air Marshal Arthur Tedder as his deputy with the result that any orders issued by the AEAF chief that were unwelcome to his subordinates were inevitably made known to Tedder for his support against them; and not infrequently, Tedder overrode Leigh-Mallory. Close observers also noted that both Harris and Spaatz were at best uncooperative, and at worst downright hostile. Spaatz was the worst, studiously doing his best to ignore LM. What was demanded in this situation was a supreme commander for air; someone who could "send orders and not ambassadors to the strategic air forces." Although Tedder played this role to some extent, he was never able to gain full control of the maverick airmen.[106]

The issue of air support for OVERLORD evoked one of the most vociferous and lengthy debates of the European campaign. As early as December 1943, Eisenhower had begun questioning whether he would have authority over the heavy bombers. In January, he wrote Arnold that he did not wish to use terms or language that would "startle anyone," but he intended to have his way. Arnold soon agreed, but the British continued to drag their feet regarding Bomber Command. Finally, during an unsatisfactory discussion with Prime Minister Churchill on the matter, Eisenhower threatened to "go home" unless he was given control over Harris. Churchill surrendered.[107] Thus, the question of *which* airplanes would be used now turned to *how* they would be used. Professor Solly Zuckerman, a noted biologist before the war, had been an operations analyst for Tedder in North Africa and Sicily and was now charged to draw up an air plan that would most effectively seal off the invasion area from German reinforcement. His solution, usually referred to as the transportation or rail plan, called for a systematic and sustained attack on the French railroad network. Leigh-Mallory supported this plan unreservedly, which to Spaatz and Vandenberg clearly demonstrated the man's limited strategic vision. Also not surprisingly, all the ground commanders involved strongly approved of Zuckerman's scheme as well. General Omar Bradley commented:

> For untold years we infantrymen had been subjected to the glib, enticing arguments of strategic air power advocates, who unfailingly promised a quick-easy-cheap victory through air power. But I had seen the reality . . . Air Power had not lived up to the glamorous advance billing. . . . I argued fervently for the destruction of the French transportation system.[108]

For his part, Spaatz saw Zuckerman's proposals as a wasteful dispersion of air power. He maintained that rail systems were notoriously difficult to destroy—a line cut one day was repaired the next—such targets were more suitable for the medium bombers of the AEAF. To use B-17s to plow up wheat fields and railroad tracks was an egregious misuse of air. He pushed instead for a far-reaching campaign against the German oil industry. Although admitting that the effect of such attacks would not be as immediate as the transportation plan, the end result would be far more devastating: the *entire* German war machine would gradually grind to a halt.[109] Spaatz's position was implacable, and Leigh-Mallory asked Vandenberg to intercede with his countryman to try to soften his stance. It was to no avail. Spaatz was adamant.[110] Somewhat surprisingly, Tedder rejected Spaatz's view and instead favored the rail plan. Although realizing the importance of oil, he felt the effect of striking it could only be felt in the long term. OVERLORD was only weeks away, and destroying the transport network would more effectively hinder German movement in the short term.[111]

Air Marshal Harris also protested the rail plan, but gave different reasons. He maintained that such a campaign would endanger French lives. His night bombers were far less accurate than their American daylight counterparts, and he confessed that they were not capable of the pinpoint accuracy the transportation plan required. He pointed out that because the numerous near misses would be falling on French and Belgian soil, this was an important consideration. Harris estimated there would be between 80,000 and 160,000 civilian casualties.[112] Vandenberg also felt strongly about the idea of destroying French morale with what could be misconstrued as indiscriminate bombing. Such arguments swayed

Churchill, who was acutely attuned to the political implications of devastating France from the air. Long after military leaders had fallen in step behind the rail plan, Churchill still refrained from giving it his support. It was not until Roosevelt convinced him that military considerations should predominate in this case that he gave his approval.[113]

Another important factor to Spaatz was the belief that it was absolutely essential to destroy the German Air Force and gain air superiority. In order to accomplish that task, the Luftwaffe must be lured into battle. The transportation plan would not be sufficiently threatening to the German forces to guarantee that the Luftwaffe would rise to contest it, but the black life blood produced by the eastern refineries would undoubtedly be defended at all costs. For the past year Spaatz's beloved "Forts" had suffered grievous losses, but now long-range escort fighters were arriving in ever-increasing numbers, and he ached for revenge. It was a cardinal tenet of American theorists since Billy Mitchell that command of the air was a necessary prerequisite for victory, and Spaatz would not relinquish such beliefs. Tedder agreed with the basic concept of gaining air superiority, but thought the time was too late to stake everything on hitting the Luftwaffe.[114] Tedder's views were to prove decisive.

In an emotionally charged meeting of the top Allied military leaders for OVER-LORD held on March 25, 1944, the rival transportation and oil plans were presented for discussion. After acrimonious debate lasting several hours, Eisenhower opted for the railroads over the refineries.[115] Events would soon show, however, that this decision was not as definite as it first appeared.

Leigh-Mallory's deputy at AEAF was Major General William Butler, a somewhat pedestrian airman who had managed to alienate almost everyone at AEAF headquarters, as well as Generals Spaatz and Brereton. It was not all Butler's fault. Anyone placed in such a position would have had a difficult time reconciling the desires of his various masters. Butler was simply not up to the task. In early March, Eisenhower asked him to step down.[116] Vandenberg was selected as his replacement because his personality made him better suited than most to get along with the choleric LM, as well as the American air leaders, but also because he was tough enough to stand up for AAF interests. He assumed his duties on March 25, the day of the climactic meeting at Saint Paul's School that decided upon the rail plan. At the same time, he was given a second star.

Vandenberg's relations with Leigh-Mallory got off to a rocky start when he reported to AEAF headquarters at Bentley Priory in Stanmore and realized that the entire "combined" staff, save himself and his assistant, were British. The Air Marshal explained that he felt more comfortable with British methods of operation, and so he had relieved the American officers. Vandenberg was outraged by this slight, but Spaatz advised him to stay his anger so as not to upset relations.[117] Some time later when two American air generals attended the daily staff meeting, referred to as "morning prayers," Leigh-Mallory summarily dismissed them from the room, saying their attendance was unnecessary.[118]

General Vandenberg was in a difficult position. Though recognized as a tactical expert with sound combat experience, he had long since broadened his horizons beyond the narrow focus of a fighter pilot. He was and would remain a staunch advocate of strategic bombardment as a war-winning weapon. His tactical experience and strategic theory were a unique blend that gave him a foot in both camps without ever becoming too closely associated with either. Nevertheless, his tendency to think in terms of "strategic" air power was often in conflict with his AEAF commander. To make matters worse, his old friend "Tooey" Spaatz gave him clear guidance regarding where his true loyalties should lie:

> Conference with General Spaatz, at which time I pointed out my dual role of coordinating interests for air, loyalty to C-in-C, AEAF [Leigh-Mallory] and the task of guarding the operational use and fulfilling the administrative requirements of the American Component. General Spaatz directed that the number one priority was to be the safeguarding of the interests of the American Component and suggested that I make this clear to General Eisenhower and ask for his concurrence. . . . Later General Spaatz and I met General Eisenhower, at which time these matters were discussed and General Eisenhower concurred. Then met ACM Tedder and discussed the position of AEAF with SHAEF and the Allied Tactical Air Force, the Ninth Air Force, the Eighth Air Air Force, etc.[119]

This is a striking admission; it would seem that Leigh-Mallory's deputy, superiors, and colleagues had all agreed in advance to conspire against him. Caught between Spaatz and Leigh-Mallory, Vandenberg was placed in an untenable position. How could he balance loyalty to his superior, his friendship with Spaatz (who was also a superior), dedication to his nation and service, his personal desire for advancement, and, most important, the necessity of defeating Germany? Typically, he played the role of referee, a thankless but essential task. That he was successful in this melancholy part is evidenced not only by his continued support from Spaatz, but also by the respect won from the British. Solly Zuckerman, an important British civilian on the AEAF staff, recognized Vandenberg's predicament, but was convinced that he was absolutely loyal to Leigh-Mallory. Air Commodore E. J. Kingston-McCloughry, chief of staff for the AEAF, was similarly sensitive to Vandenberg's plight and his efforts at maintaining a balance: "it was General Vandenberg himself . . . who said that after he really got to know the man he realized Sir Trafford was one of the whitest and best British leaders with whom he had worked."[120] The next few months would be most challenging for the new major general.

The March 25 directive stated that "depleting the German Air Force to ensure command of the air" was a primary mission of the strategic air forces, and Spaatz seized upon this statement to continue his POINTBLANK strategy.[121] Vandenberg was a willing assistant, arguing with Leigh-Mallory that proposed bombing missions were inefficient and that more suitable targets should be sought. If his reasoning failed to move Leigh-Mallory, he contacted Spaatz or his former commander, General Doolittle, who was now running the Eighth Air Force, and advised them of the proposed target selections. They would then prepare suitable arguments about why such a mission could not be conducted. If all else failed, they would appeal to Tedder.[122] The conflicting loyalties and responsibilities inherent in such actions must have been difficult for Vandenberg.

At every opportunity, attempts were made to bomb targets thought more appropriate than those specified in the daily mission orders. At first rebuked for such tactics, Spaatz told Eisenhower he would resign unless allowed to strike the refineries whenever his bombers could be spared from the rail targets.[123] On April 5, the Ploesti marshaling yards were slated for destruction; as the official history blandly states: "Most of the 588 tons of bombs, with more than coincidental inaccuracy, struck and badly damaged the Astra group of refineries near by." Ploesti's oil was attacked again on the fifteenth and twenty-fourth of April. In truth, *both* strategies were employed to support OVERLORD, rail and oil.[124] The Normandy area was effectively sealed off, to the obvious pleasure of the ground commanders; the Luftwaffe fighter force was lethally wounded and failed to make a serious appearance over the beaches on D-Day; and the refineries began to suffer the damage that would eventually lead in large measure to the collapse of the Reich's military forces. Ultra intercepts confirmed that the German leaders were concerned about the fuel attacks that were having serious effects on the war effort. In the period from March to June 1944, the Luftwaffe's fuel supply had plummeted from 927,000 tons to 50,000 tons. After the war, German Armaments Minister Albert Speer declared that it was the oil raids of May 1944 that decided the war.[125] As a result, proponents of air power have often asked: what if Spaatz and Harris had been allowed to continue their air offensive undisturbed?

When the Allied troops went ashore at Normandy on the morning of June 6, 1944, Major General Vandenberg jumped into a P-38 and headed for the beaches. Although the visibility was poor, the view was spectacular. He wrote his parents that it was immensely gratifying to work so hard on planning an operation and then finally see it executed. Returning to Stanmore, he entered the war room and noted to his chagrin that there was very little information displayed on the battle maps concerning the American landings, whereas the British sites were clearly and copiously marked. He was shocked. After asking why there was not a single mark on "Omaha" or "Utah," he was told there had been no requests for reconnaissance. Hardly a suitable answer; reconnaissance was essential and such flights should have been launched as a matter of course. Vandenberg stormed into the office of Air Vice Marshal Stephen C. Strafford and insisted that something be done; it was, but "ten hours too late" as far as he was concerned. He blamed this incident on the fact that all the Americans had been removed from the war room except those one or two who were being used as "messenger boys."[126] On a lighter note, Vandenberg's air transport chief, Colonel Ralph Bagby, disappeared the night before the invasion and did not surface until a week later. He had talked his way onto a glider plane loaded with members of the 101st Airborne Division and landed with them behind German lines, where he took part in the initial fighting on the morning of D-Day. Upon returning to Stanmore, Vandenberg first chewed Bagby thoroughly and then recommended him for a medal.[127] The man who had flown over two dozen unauthorized combat missions himself could hardly be too punitive.

The following weeks were spent planning air strikes to support the Allied troops bottled up near the beaches and laboring to destroy the launching sites of the dreaded new "flying bombs" (V-1). Vandenberg landed at Cherbourg soon after it fell, noted the bodies of German soldiers lying everywhere, and was shot at by snipers. He was particularly fascinated by the V-1s: "It's an amazing gadget—If the Huns could only apply such ingenuity toward their *military* effort I believe they would reap a greater reward—It is uncanny however to hear and see them and realize no one is directing them."[128]

Disagreements with Leigh-Mallory over staffing and target selection continued, and as the invasion forces failed to break free from the beachhead, the comments of the Allied leaders became increasingly anxious and acerbic. Most such barbs were directed at Montgomery, whose prelanding predictions increasingly rang hollow. On June 14, Coningham warned that things were not as rosy as Montgomery was painting them and that there were elements of a crisis developing. Tedder agreed. Monty retorted that they were being alarmist; things were going according to plan. Leigh-Mallory suggested that heavy bombers be used to soften up the German positions in front of Montgomery at Caen. The other airmen rejected the idea. On June 16, Coningham began badgering Montgomery to admit that his original plans had failed and that it was now necessary to devise a new solution. The latest effort, Operation EPSOM, was sarcastically referred to as a "Break-in" at Caen. Leigh-Mallory confided glumly to his diary that he feared another Anzio. He suggested once again that heavy bombers be used to "carpet bomb" the German defenders. This time, his colleagues began to listen.[129]

Another offensive, GOODWOOD, was launched by Montgomery on July 19. Following Leigh-Mallory's advice, nearly two thousand bombers of Bomber Command as well as the Eighth and Ninth Air Forces pounded the enemy positions near Caen in an attempt to "unstick" Montgomery. To no avail. The following day Leigh-Mallory admitted he was "bitterly disappointed" in the meager results of the attack. The performance of the Army was "monstrous." Even so, Generals Eisenhower and Omar N. Bradley were much impressed by the bombing's effectiveness and determined to try it again further west, at Saint-Lô.[130]

General Bradley suggested that for his plan, Operation COBRA, the Eighth and Ninth Air Forces be directed to carpet bomb the area near Saint-Lô, after which his forces would pour through the resultant gap into the open French countryside. Realizing that something had to be done to break out from the beach area, the air commanders agreed to mount another maximum effort to support the ground forces. The tactical employment of the American heavy bombers caused disagreement.

Leigh-Mallory and Bradley wanted the heavy bombers to track parallel to the front lines, thus theoretically never flying over friendly troops. They thought this plan would lessen the chance of "short bombs," or those released too soon and thus threatening friendly forces. Spaatz and Doolittle, however, insisted on a perpendicular bomb pass. Because the target area was five miles in width, but only one mile deep, they argued that to employ a parallel track would expose the bombers to enemy antiaircraft fire for a much longer period of time. Moreover, Bradley specified that the bombardment last only one hour; a narrow, parallel eam would take over twice as long. Finally, the target area was just beyond a clearly defined road. If the bombers held release until after passing it, they were assured of not dropping short. A parallel pass would risk the danger of lateral drift, and all the bomb group commanders agreed with this line of reasoning. Vandenberg was still concerned about the perpendicular tactics, but deferred to the bomber commanders. Even so, some misses were inevitable in an operation of this size and General Bradley was told by Leigh-Mallory to expect some accidents. He accepted the risk providing the bombardment was successful in blowing open a hole for his troops.[131]

COBRA was scheduled for July 24, but because of miserable weather was postponed until the following day. Tired of sitting behind his desk, Vandenberg grabbed his aide, and the two jumped into a light aircraft and headed for the battlefield. The sight was spectacular, but strong winds and heavy smoke obscured the road below, which was not as large and prominent as it appeared on the map, and the high-flying B-17s began straying off target. Several dozen of the fifteen hundred airplanes—flying perpendicular to the front—released their loads too soon, and the result was over one hundred American soldiers killed, including Lieutenant General Lesley McNair. General Bradley was livid. He later claimed the perpendicular bombing attack was unauthorized: "I have seldom been so angry. It was duplicity—a shocking breach of good faith." When confronted, Spaatz replied he had never agreed to a parallel pass, a response Bradley termed an outright lie. Doolittle said simply and somewhat callously: "Well, the bomber shouldn't be in this sort of close support business, it isn't the thing they are trained to do."[132]

The official investigation that followed the incident (conducted by the AAF), exonerated the airmen in theory, although blaming the short bombs on individual personnel error. Spaatz concluded crisply that unforeseen crosswinds were a major culprit and that "all our bombing experience shows that lateral error [parallel] is greater than range [perpendicular] error."[133] Even so, the air strikes caused incomparably more harm to the German defenders. Although enemy casualties were light, the destruction of equipment and materiel, plus the effect on enemy morale, was massive. General-Leutnant Fritz Bayerlein, commander of the Panzer-Lehr Division, had no doubts about the bombing's effectiveness and related this story after his capture:

> The waves of planes kept coming, like a conveyer belt, seemingly without end. From 0930–1230 all his communications were totally knocked out and he was using runners. The front line was a moonscape and at least 70% [of his troops] were out of commission, either dead, wounded, crazed or dazed. All 30-40 of his tanks were knocked out. He was forced to withdraw.[134]

Field Marshal Karl R. Gerd von Rundstedt, German commander on the Western Front, echoed this statement, declaring categorically that the carpet bombing at Saint-Lô was the most effective, as well as the most impressive, tactical use of air power in his experience. Eisenhower and Bradley agreed, saying that the breakout would have been impossible without the strikes.[135] Overall, air leaders were gratified by the successes, dismayed by the short bombs that killed McNair and the others, but still inclined to believe that heavy bombers were best used in a strategic role.

Vandenberg's diary is disappointingly terse on the events taking place in France during the month of July. He apparently was distracted by events more personal.

In mid-1944 it was proposed that an Allied Airborne Army be formed consisting of two paratroop divisions and the IX Troop Carrier Command, transferred from the Ninth Air Force. Eisenhower first considered Vandenberg for the job because he was "imaginative and energetic." It is also likely that Eisenhower was aware of Vandenberg's difficult position at AEAF. Cooperation with allies was one of Eisenhower's litmus tests for high command. Vandenberg met that challenge. General Marshall was amenable to Eisenhower's suggestion, but then the supreme commander reconsidered; although acknowledging Vandenberg's excellent qualifications, he feared the young major general had neither the rank nor the prestige for the position—Generals Matthew Ridgway and Frederick Browning (British army) would outrank their commander.[136] Eisenhower suggested that Vandenberg be promoted if it could be done "without too great embarrassment." He was convinced that Vandenberg could perform the job superbly, but he had to have three stars.[137] Marshall was unwilling to take this step so instead proposed that Lieutenant General Lewis Brereton, then commander of the Ninth Air Force, be given the new army; Vandenberg would then replace him. Brereton, who had been one of Vandenberg's instructors at the Command and General Staff School and thought he was "one of the most promising young officers in the Air Force," also recommended Van as his replacement.[138] It is also likely that Arnold and Spaatz were simply disenchanted with Brereton's performance and wished him removed; from this point on his career entered an eclipse from which it never reemerged. One Army commander described Brereton as "taciturn almost to the point of rudeness and inclined to be too stubbornly an airman in matters pertaining to the air and ground."[139] Bradley, who had to work closely with the tactical air commanders in order to attain his objectives, did not think Brereton was sincere, energetic, or cooperative. Bradley asked Eisenhower to find a replacement for the pompous Brereton.[140]

General Spaatz confidentially notified Vandenberg on July 16 of his impending transfer. He was elated; after walking on egg shells at the AEAF for five months he was eager for a change.[141] Two more potential hurdles presented themselves. Major General Ralph Royce, who was slated to take over as Leigh-Mallory's deputy, was not highly regarded by Vandenberg, thinking his tactical ideas "ridiculous." For his part, Royce feared he did not possess the requisite prestige for the position of deputy, and proposed to Spaatz that he be given command of the Ninth for four to six weeks to enhance his reputation as a commander. Vandenberg was shocked and no doubt liked Royce even less.[142] Spaatz eventually shelved the idea, but a more serious obstacle presented itself when Brereton suggested that the *entire* Ninth Air Force be combined with the two airborne divisions to form one massive unit; he would agree to command it. General Bradley supported the idea. He appreciated the support given by the Ninth to his 12th Army Group in the six weeks since the invasion began, and the vision of such an impressive fighting machine under his control must have been enticing. This suggestion also faded.[143]

On August 4, 1944, Vandenberg received his long-awaited orders to take command of the mighty Ninth Air Force. The young general had good credentials for such a position. His performance had already won him two Distinguished Service Medals, a Silver Star, Distinguished Flying Cross, Legion of Merit, and five Air Medals. Even in wartime when decorations are relatively easy to obtain, such a collection is impressive. More importantly, his superiors and British allies recognized his ability and had progressively nudged him into positions of increasing responsibility and prominence. Vandenberg had done well in Washington, Africa, Moscow, London, and France; now would come his first opportunity for independent command.

THE NINTH AIR FORCE

When Vandenberg assumed command of the Ninth Air Force on August 8, it contained nearly 180,000 personnel, 4,000 aircraft, and was the largest tactical air unit in history. The organizations that comprised the Ninth were the IX and XIX Tactical Air commands (a third, the XXIX, was added in mid-September), the IX Bomber Command, an Engineers Command that was responsible for building and repairing the 285 airfields used by the Ninth Air Force in the course of the European campaign, the IX Air Defense Command (an antiaircraft unit), and a large supply organization.[144]

The men who commanded these units were outstanding, and two deserve special notice. The IX TAC was led by Major General Elwood R. Quesada. "Pete" was a forceful, dynamic, handsome, and independent bachelor who had earned his wings in 1925 and then served as aide to Major General James Fechet, chief of the Air Corps. In 1929 he had been a crew member, along with Spaatz and Eaker, on the "Question Mark" endurance flight that had demonstrated the potential of midair refueling. During the 1930s he was the private pilot for Assistant Secretary of War F. Trubee Davison and then aide to Secretary of War George Dern. His political connections were formidable. Quesada had been commander of the 12th Fighter Command in North Africa before taking over the IX TAC in October 1943. He was held in high regard by most, and the ground commanders with whom he worked considered him an ideal airman. In December 1944, Bradley rated him the fourth best American general in the theater behind Spaatz, Walter Bedell Smith, and Courtney H. Hodges.[145] On one occasion he offered to take General Eisenhower along in his P-51 on a fighter sweep. With more enthusiasm than sense the supreme commander agreed. After taking off and heading over enemy territory, however, Quesada realized the foolishness of his action and quickly took his passenger back to headquarters.[146] Because of his operational experience and tactical expertise, it is probable that Quesada expected to command the Ninth Air Force when Brereton left (Vandenberg outranked him by less than a month). Although the two worked together amicably, there seemed always to be a tension between them. Later, Quesada would say that he and Vandenberg were neither friends nor enemies, but they had exchanged some "unpleasantries."[147] One member of the Ninth Air Force staff thought that Vandenberg was afraid of Quesada. That is doubtful, but it is possible that Quesada's ability and seniority allowed him more latitude and independence than Vandenberg granted his other subordinates. The IX TAC was responsible for providing support to the First Army under Lieutenant General Courtney Hodges.

The XIX TAC was led by Brigadier General Otto P. Weyland. "Opie" was a brash and fun-loving Texan who had been in Vandenberg's pilot training class at Brooks Field. A fighter pilot throughout his career, he had arrived in the theater in November 1943 to command a fighter group. Tendered the XIX TAC in March 1944, he was directed to provide air support for the newly formed Third Army under George Patton. The two men became fast friends and a legendary team. Said Patton: "It was love at first sight between the XIX Tactical Air Command and the Third Army."[148] Van also liked Opie.

The mission of the Ninth Air Force was to provide air support for Omar Bradley's 12th Army Group, and Vandenberg resisted all attempts to distract him from that task.[149] During the preceding months the air-ground team had hammered out a system of cooperation that was eventually to run like a fine watch. Constant liaison was maintained between the air and ground leaders at the top echelons: Vandenberg's headquarters was situated near Bradley; Weyland's near Patton, and so forth. There was to be no leading from the rear. The airmen attended the daily staff meetings of their Army counterparts in order to be intimately familiar with their dispositions and intentions. This allowed the airmen to plan and prioritize their own operations so as to maximize the effectiveness of the air support given. It is important to note that there were airmen assigned to the army staff and ground officers to the TAC staffs; this helped ensure smooth coordination. In fact, Vandenberg's initial chief of staff was an infantry officer.[150]

Vandenberg's responsibility was to coordinate the activities of the TACs to ensure that their resources were being used most effectively and that they were not taking off on a nonessential tangent. If one sector had unusually high activity, he would often shift a fighter group or two from one TAC to another. It must also be remembered that there were far more than just fighter pilots in his command. Indeed, the vast majority of the 180,000 troops were support personnel belonging to the supply and engineer units. There were thousands of tons of supplies and gasoline moved daily, and Vandenberg held the ultimate responsibility for the smooth operation of this massive enterprise. At the higher echelons, Van worked closely not only with Bradley but also with Spaatz, Doolittle, Brereton, and Coningham. Most combat operations in the European Theater required detailed coordination between the various units these men commanded, and Van was adept in such situations.[151]

After one such high-level conference, Van and Colonel Palmer Dixon, a member of his staff, were flying back to Ninth headquarters while engaged in a loud and animated discussion. Suddenly, Dixon, who was piloting the aircraft, looked around and failed to see anything familiar. Landing in a friendly looking field, the men asked a French farmer where they were. Thirty miles behind German lines. Vandenberg and Dixon quietly climbed back into their craft and hurried home.[152]

At the lower levels, the cooperation was also close. When the American armies were on the move, there was a pilot attached to each tank squadron—termed an "air-ground cooperation officer" (ACO)—who was equipped with a VHF (very high frequency) radio to allow him to converse with the four-ship fighter-bomber formations constantly overhead. Aircraft would range up to thirty-five miles from the columns seeking enemy troops and fortifications and report this intelligence to the tankers below. The tank commanders or ACOs would similarly relay information to the pilots above. If targets were located, the "jabos" (short for *jagdbomber*) would attack; if additional firepower was needed, a radio call to TAC headquarters would generate the scrambling of "armed recon" aircraft to the scene. The ACOs were also supplied with portable radar sets that allowed them to vector the "jabos" toward the target area, bring them down through an overcast to hit the objective, and then vector them back out and up through the cloud deck—a sophisticated and effective operation. These air-ground teams soon became adept at spotting well-hidden German gun positions and cooperating to eliminate them. On many occasions when antiaircraft fire was too intense for the fighters to operate comfortably, they would request counter-battery fire from their ground partners to eliminate the menace. Eventually, this procedure was even used at night as radar-equipped P-61 Black Widows began arriving in the theater.[153]

This system was never more effectively employed than in the fall of 1944 when Patton's Third Army began its dash from Brittany to the Loire. At the time Vandenberg assumed command, Patton requested that the XIX TAC be used to guard his southern flank. Weyland assured him that if the weather was good, his planes would keep all German forces at least thirty miles from his columns. In addition, Ultra intercepts confirmed that no major German attacks were expected against that flank. Not being distracted with this chore, Patton streaked eastward in a huge enveloping movement.[154] The results achieved were remarkable. On August 14 while strafing an enemy column, Thunderbolt pilots noted that the German soldiers below were waving white flags at them. Realizing that they wanted to surrender, the fighters radioed the nearest American ground forces with their location and requested a detachment to pick up the three to four hundred prisoners. The planes then orbited the area at low altitude, keeping watch, until American forces arrived.[155]

More impressively, the following month Major General Eric Elster sought to surrender his command of twenty thousand men and two women at Beaugency Bridge on the south bank of the Loire River. The constant and devastating air raids he had been suffering were simply too intense. Because air power had been instrumental in his decision to surrender, Elster requested that the American air commander be present at the ceremony. Weyland attended and received a number of Lugers from the German officers—one of which was sent to Vandenberg. Patton was so impressed he offered Opie command of a corps.[156] On August 17, Patton wrote Marshall: "The cooperation between the Third Army and the XIX Tactical Air Command . . . has been the finest example of the ground and air working together that I have ever seen."[157]

Those were heady days. In an illuminating letter to Vandenberg in late August, Quesada invented a mock war conference taking place in Bradley's headquarters. "Monty," Bradley, Lt Gen Miles Dempsey, and Hodges are discussing whether they should advance. All are against the idea; Monty's troops lack tooth-brushes, and he will not move until his men are fully equipped; Hodges had not yet found a suitable chateau on a lake to use as his headquarters; Bradley does not feel Patton has cleared the way sufficiently to ensure a safe general advance; Dempsey (commander of the Second Army) concurs with all of the above. Vanden-berg and Quesada are also present at the fictitious meeting, shouting progressively louder: "Christ, why don't we move?" and "Goddammit, let's go!"[158] Patton was a favorite of the airmen, and the feeling was mutual. After liberating a supply of enemy whiskey, the Third Army commander sent a consignment to the Ninth with his best wishes: "My dear Vandenberg, if it were not for the Ninth Air Force and its affiliated units, we would not be able to capture the liquor which it gives us great pleasure to present to our comrades of the air."[159] When Vandenberg pinned on the stars of a lieutenant general in April 1945, Patton held a parade in his honor.

Vandenberg enjoyed this period immensely. He flew often and frequently visited his units to award medals, listen to the complaints of the men, and play volleyball or ping-pong. On one such trip he dropped his P-47 into a fighter group commanded by an old friend, Colonel "Dyke" Meyer. Van knew that the unit had recently transitioned into the P-51 and asked how it was working out. Meyer was heavy with praise and suggested they grab two Mustangs and go for a ride down to the Riviera for dinner. Van thought it an excellent idea, but confessed that he had not yet been checked out in a P-51. No problem. Meyer would start the air-craft for him, point out the various switches and buttons, then jump out so Van could get in. Meyer then looked at the big Thunderbolt and mentioned that he had never flown a P-47. That was no problem either. Van would likewise fire up his ship and give a quick brief to Meyer before exiting. By means of running back and forth between the cockpits, each pilot got his plane started and the other briefed. Then the two lifted off and headed south, smack into a thunderstorm. Pitched about in the lightning and darkness, the two aviators in their unfamiliar aircraft struggled to keep each other in sight. Arriving at Cannes, both men headed for a bar. They agreed that perhaps it would be best to fly their own planes home.[160]

Vandenberg tried to build a rugged, gung-ho image by wearing outlandish, distinctive clothes such as the GI woolen helmet liner that made him look like a cross between a "lumber jack and a Russian peasant." One witness remembered: "Van was wearing his limp flier's cap and his famous disreputable trenchcoat, a battered old garment held together by a knotted belt from which the buckle long since had been lost, and on which he wears no insignia of rank."[161] To an extent, this was an affectation. While at his headquarters, photographs and descriptions always portray him as impeccably dressed in an immaculate uniform. But it is al-most a truism that air leaders consciously and ostentatiously dispensed with the finer points of military discipline when among their troops—the sloppy uniforms, "50-mission crush" hats, and lack of saluting are common depictions. Perhaps this was because flying was considered a young man's game, and if an air commander wished to participate, he must look and act youthful. Or perhaps because in the air (especially in the fighter units), combat was usually performed by officers; and leading fellow officers is quite different from leading enlisted men. For whatever reason, Vandenberg, like Patton, cultivated an image that was designed to inspire his men. It seemed to work.

With his staff, Van was considerate, but also aggressive and efficient. Upon arriving at headquarters he quickly replaced many of Brereton's people who were thought to be too parochial in dealing with the other commands, especially the British. He then reorganized the headquarters, instituting a "deputy system" in which colonels were appointed to act in his name. This system, which he later employed as chief of staff, presumed the delegation of authority. Vandenberg was never a "details" man, refusing to become bogged down in the daily minutiae of his command. He hated paperwork, complaining that too much reading would ruin his eyes. Instead, he dwelt on a broader plane and left the routine to his subordinates. He managed by exception, leaving his deputies alone unless it became evident that something was going wrong, then he would intervene. When action became necessary he invariably moved quickly and politely. He was seldom if ever seen angry and never raised his voice, pounded his fist on the desk, or stood people at attention while upbraiding them. Former staff members speak continually of his compassion, deference, and politeness. Most considered him an ideal commander.[162] It is interesting that the Germans also held him in high regard. An intelligence document captured by the British during the war evaluated several Allied air leaders. It described Vandenberg as follows: "One of the most capable General Staff Officers in the American Army Air Corps. Pupil of West Point Military Academy. Known as the organizer of strategic warfare against Reich territory. Was destined to be commander-in-chief of the strategic air forces in the Far East." The report then concludes tenuously: "Not particularly well liked among the units. Also has difficulties with those American Air Corps commanders who have risen from the ranks [Quesada?]."[163]

Though not all air strikes had such impressive results as the Elster surrender, the good weather of August and early September provided a fertile hunting ground for the Ninth. As the American armies headed toward Argentan, a giant noose began tightening about the German forces. Realizing their danger, they fled eastward to escape through the increasingly narrow funnel of the Falaise Gap. As one enthusiastic pilot put it, "The whole goddam German army is moving through the Gap!"[164] Rich pickings. Although many escaped from the trap so slow to spring, it appeared the frenetic war of movement was only beginning. In fact, it was about to end temporarily.

Main activities of the Ninth were bridge-busting and railway interdiction, and the medium bombers of the IX Bomber Command were especially adept at the latter. Initially, the intent of the interdiction campaign was to prevent German reinforcement and supply. General Patton also wanted the bridges hit, but to stop the Germans from escaping his grasp—a crucial distinction.[165] Soon, he asked that the bridges be left intact for American use; it was taking too long for his engineers to rebuild them. As a way of acknowledging that the Ninth's mission had shifted from air superiority to ground support—the Luftwaffe was largely destroyed by late 1944—Van sought out those pilots who had proven most effective at destroying bridges, trains, and supply depots. These "busters" were singled out for special praise and recognition. This was an interesting tactic by Vandenberg and illustrates his keen eye for public relations. Air Force exploits needed continually to be brought to the public's awareness. The prodigious feats of Patton's Third Army could not be allowed to dominate the headlines.[166] In September, General Montgomery convinced Eisenhower to break temporarily from the broad front strategy and allow him to attempt a narrow, concentrated thrust against the German lines. Bradley's army group was, therefore, slowed and supplies diverted to Montgomery so that he could launch his rapier thrust to the Rhine. More to the point, the entire logistic system of the Allies began to snap under the strain of the rapid advance from Normandy. There was little food or ammunition and, more importantly, there was no fuel. Patton moaned: "My men can eat their belts, but my tanks have got to have gas." The Ninth resumed its efforts to interdict German reinforcement while the American armies impatiently waited through their forced inactivity.[167] The Allies continued to move forward, but on a much tighter rein than during the halcyon days of August.

In addition, as the weather deteriorated with winter's approach, the Ninth was increasingly grounded, flying only one-third as many sorties in October as it had in August. This had a noticeable impact on the ground campaign. "There's lots of times," noted a platoon leader, "when we can't move an inch and then the P-47s come over and we just walk in almost without a shot."[168] The preponderance of American air power had achieved almost total air superiority. The Army's official history states succinctly: "Few of Patton's troops ever saw more than a single German plane at a time. . . . Either the Luftwaffe lacked the planes and gasoline to make a major effort or the American fighters cut down the enemy short of the goal."[169] In mid-November, a new attempt, QUEEN, was made to blast through the German lines east of Aachen employing a preparatory bombardment of over forty-five hundred aircraft—far more than were used at Saint-Lô. To ensure there would be no accidents, air and ground commanders met at Vandenberg's headquarters to iron out the details. The assault forces were pulled back nearly four thousand yards from the target area, and the bombers were to open and lock their bomb bay doors over the English Channel to preclude an inadvertent drop on American troops.

The assault began on the morning of November 16, with over ten thousand tons of bombs rained on German defenses. There were few mishaps, and only one American soldier was killed in the bomb avalanche. The effect on the German soldiers was slight, however, because the American troops were so far back from the front. By the time they reached the impact area, the dazed defenders were beginning to come to their senses. A German prisoner said later: "I never saw anything like it. These kids . . . were still numb 45 minutes after the bombardment."[170] Unfortunately, the First Army could not move quickly enough to exploit the temporary paralysis of the German defenders, and on the first day QUEEN advanced a mere two miles.[171] Even so, General Bradley warmed to the idea of air support. In December 1944, he told newsmen: "The confidence . . . in air support has been firmly established, and now you cannot find a ground commander who will think of an operation without thinking in terms of air as well. . . . [the] German Army and Air Force in their heyday never had the degree of cooperation that we have."[172]

Hodges had failed; now it was once again Patton's turn. In early December he sat down with Vandenberg, Spaatz, and Doolittle to discuss his plan for a breakout that would get the war rolling again as it had in August. Air preparation was essential. The airmen proposed a massive two or three-day bombardment that left Patton jubilant; he was certain this assault would break him loose to the Rhine. The plan was approved by Eisenhower and set to begin on December 19.[173]

The three airmen left Patton's headquarters to fly home. Spaatz and Doolittle, flying in one aircraft, noted tracer bullets whizzing past their canopy. Assuming they had been jumped by a German fighter, the generals dove for the trees to escape. Vandenberg, alone in the aircraft behind, followed. The bullets continued and grew in intensity. Suddenly, Spaatz realized the rounds were coming from the ground; some of Patton's troops had mistaken them for Germans and opened fire. Both aircraft escaped, but upon landing, Spaatz phoned Patton to vent his ire. Upon hearing the situation, Patton bellowed with laughter. Spaatz hung up, sighed, and then smiled thinly: "You just can't stay mad at George."[174]

On December 16, Vandenberg, along with Brigadier General Frederick L. Anderson representing the Eight Air Force, Colonel Robert M. Lee, Solly Zuckerman, and other staff members, visited Quesada at Spa, Belgium. After spending the night in Quesada's chateau, Vandenberg and Anderson planned to brief Generals Hodges and William H. Simpson on the bombing operation scheduled for the nineteenth. Because Hodges was busy upon their arrival, the airmen began briefing Simpson. Hodges then interrupted the meeting to announce that the assault was off, the supposedly quiescent Germans were beginning to stir. The conference adjourned, and the airmen returned to Quesada's villa to spend the night, but upon waking in the morning learned that the Germans had launched a major offensive; indeed, there were reports that enemy paratroopers had landed nearby. What was more disconcerting, Hodges's headquarters had packed up and moved to Liège during the night without informing Quesada! Vandenberg strapped on a revolver and suggested that everyone fly back to his headquarters at Luxembourg City, but the fog precluded that possibility. Feeling helpless, the airmen wandered about the headquarters of the IX TAC, whose airplanes were also grounded. Finally, Vandenberg decided to drive back to his command post. Because the Germans had penetrated close by to the south, he detoured to the West and stopped at Paris, visiting with Spaatz at his headquarters to discuss a plan for containing the German offensive.[175] Vandenberg requested that additional air units be placed under his control, and Spaatz agreed. The Ninth Air Force would be shifted and shuffled like a "fire brigade" to whichever sector it was needed the most.[176] The Battle of the Bulge had begun.

There was little that air power could do to stem the German breakthrough. Hitler had planned his weather well; one hundred-foot ceilings and dense fog made air strikes nearly impossible. Quesada asked for two volunteers to fly a reconnaissance mission, hoping at least to pinpoint the location of the enemy columns. The volunteer pilots flew their F-5s (P-38s armed with cameras instead of cannons) at tree-top level most of the flight and did locate an enemy armored unit. The Germans were advancing on Stavelot, a scant twenty-two miles from Liège, a major supply depot whose loss would be disastrous. Thunderbolts were launched below the clouds to hit the armored columns, and the results were impressive: 126 tanks, armored vehicles, and trucks destroyed and an additional 34 damaged. Reconnaissance the following day revealed that the Germans had abandoned their attempts on Stavelot; this was a classic instance—seldom seen—of air power halting an attack singlehanded. Still, such episodes were isolated because the weather precluded extensive air operations.[177]

Whether or not it was owing to General Patton's prayer for good weather to smite the enemy, on December 23 the skies finally cleared, and the Ninth was able to act. Vandenberg planned a two-pronged attack; first, he borrowed a bomb division from the Eighth Air Force and sent it, along with his own IX Bomber Command, to destroy the bridges, railroads, and road intersections behind the German lines to dry up their reinforcement. Colonel-General Alfred Jodl (head of the operations staff of the Armed Forces High Command) testified later: "We still had lots of material and sent it to the front in hundreds of trains, but the trains got there only after weeks or not at all."[178] German commanders were unanimous in acknowledging the impact of the tactical air strikes. After Reich Marshal Hermann Goering's capture, Vandenberg asked him which tactical operations had caused him the most damage. Said Goering:

> The attacks on the Marshalling Yards were most effective, next came the low-level attacks on troops, and then the attacks on bridges. The low flying airplanes had a terror effect and caused great damage to our communications. Also demoralizing were the umbrella fighters, which after escorting the bombers would swoop down and hit everything, including the jet planes in process of landing.[179]

Second, Vandenberg borrowed two fighter groups from the Eighth Air Force and, along with his own commands, directed them against the German armored columns. From December 23 to 27, the Ninth flew 5,291 sorties, with the enemy forces around Bastogne singled out for a hammering. There were mistakes— nearly 150 civilians and American soldiers were killed at Malmedy by friendly aircraft—but overall the air strikes were devastating. Once the skies were clear, the winter weather worked to American advantage as the "jabos" followed telltale tank tracks into the forest to find targets. The Luftwaffe was conspicuous by its absence, and the ubiquitous fighter-bombers of the Ninth soon made daylight operations virtually impossible for the German Army. Sepp Dietrich, the butcher-turned SS general, complained after his capture that the American fighter planes showed no respect for general officers.[180] As the German offensive stalled and then retreated, Brigadier General Anthony McAuliffe, commander of the beleaguered Bastogne garrison, thanked Vandenberg for the "tremendous support" that was a "vital contribution" to his division's successful defense. Von Rundstedt later said ruefully that if not for Allied air power he could have taken Paris.[181] Basking in success, Vandenberg stated: "We have bottlenecked the enemy's supplies and throttled his offensive power. The results underscore the fact that tactical air power has come of age."[182]

On January 15, 1945, Vandenberg's portrait appeared on the cover of *Time* magazine. Inside, there was a highly complimentary article that described him in glowing terms.

> He combines the energy of an athlete with mature judgment. He is dead serious and fluent about anything having to do with aviation, . . . He rates as one of the top U.S. Air Force's thinkers as well as doers, with a talent for staff work and planning, and an added gift of good looks and attractive, easy manner.[183]

The article then documented his woeful West Point record, the fact that he was the nephew of a prominent senator, and that he was highly regarded by both British and American military leaders. This was followed by a lengthy paragraph that apparently caused Vandenberg some anxiety:

> If other top airmen [read Arnold and Spaatz] had any criticism of the Ninth, it might be that its bosses had got to working too closely with ground-force commanders. . . . Somewhere in the process of whole-hearted cooperation, the air commander may find himself being seduced into giving extra ground support at the expense of sound tactical doctrine.[184]

It is understandable why such a charge would cause Vandenberg consternation. What did it mean? Was the story prompted by someone above who was trying to give him a message? A member of his staff, Colonel Richard Hughes, paints an unflattering picture of Vandenberg and his response to the *Time* article. It seems necessary to quote extensively from his unpublished memoir because it is virtually alone in its vivid negative criticism of Vandenberg, whom Hughes perceived in a light like few others—at least of those who would put their thoughts on paper:

> General Vandenberg was extremely handsome, looked many years younger than his real age, and was completely unsure of himself professionally and socially. . . . He was definitely a sub-normal type, intellectually. However, he had an almost animal-like instinct for self-preservation, and his ready acceptance of me as his Chief of Intelligence reflected only his strong desire to have someone on his staff who was in General Spaatz's close confidence, and who, if need arose, could easily explain and, if necessary, excuse, his actions, or the lack of them, to the General. . . . In my own particular field, intelligence and planning, General Vandenberg knew less than the average American Air Force General.[185]

Hughes then states that the *Time* article made his commander "almost frantic" and scared "the insecure Vandenberg almost to death." In response, Hughes was ordered to "dream up some semi-strategic operation immediately" to restore the general's credibility. The result was a heavy interdiction campaign in the Ruhr, about to fall to the Allies in any event, which concentrated on bridges and rail centers. The plan was presented to Vandenberg, who "pounced on it like a starving lion." The air strikes were carried out, the Ruhr was overrun, and "in General Vandenberg's mind his professional reputation was saved."[186]

Such animosity is difficult to handle. The representation of a handsome and affable but shallow and political general is an enticing one. Vandenberg *was* handsome and affable, and his meteoric rise to high rank needs an explanation. That his career progression can be explained by political connections, both in and out of the Army, is one such theory. But Hughes's argument lacks grace. It is not logical that Vandenberg, a major general who had known Spaatz for over a decade, would need a colonel to intercede on his behalf; or that he could be considered ill-informed on planning and intelligence matters when he had spent much of the previous six years in that area. In fact, the Ninth's intelligence officer, Colonel Palmer Dixon, had become ill and was sent back to the States. Vandenberg had then asked Doolittle for the loan of his intelligence chief. Doolittle said no, so Van turned to Spaatz, who assigned Hughes to the position. He was not, therefore, someone that Vandenberg had requested or even known very well.[187] As for the Ruhr isolation campaign, on February 8 Vandenberg did approach Supreme Headquarters, Allied Expeditionary Force (SHAEF) with plans for the operation, and both Bradley and Tedder supported it enthusiastically. Germany desperately needed the coal and steel supplies of the Ruhr, and its isolation would "soon have a catastrophic effect on Germany's capacity to carry on the War." Indeed, Vandenberg confided to his diary that he had to force the Ruhr program "practically down [Hughes's] throat."[188] Had the colonel been less obviously hostile to Vandenberg, his interpretation would be more believable.

It seems more likely that Vandenberg quickly advanced in rank because of his success in every task and position he was given. Whether as a staff officer in Washington, a planner in London, a diplomat in Moscow, a combat pilot and chief of staff in North Africa, or in his ticklish position as deputy of the AEAF, Vandenberg had performed well and elicited unstinting praise from superiors. Nevertheless, this would have meant nothing if he had failed as the commander of a combat unit. He did not. There were others in the Air Corps hierarchy who had begun the war with great promise. Vandenberg was not the only youthful flyer on December 7, but eventually the Monk Hunters, Larry Kuters, Possum Hansells, Don Wilsons, and Ken Wolfes fell by the way because they did not have the ability, or luck, to succeed. They were outstanding officers and leaders to be sure, but a crucial element seemed lacking. Though it sounds somewhat flippant to include chance as a factor in such vital matters, it is nonetheless at play. Bradley later remarked on the role of luck in his own career:

> I would say luck plays an awfully large part in your success. You have to be able to perform when the opportunity occurs; however, the opportunity doesn't occur for everyone. I was very lucky, being at the right place at the right time to get a good job, and having a lot of good people to help me do it.[189]

For Vandenberg, the command of the Ninth Air Force during the last eight months of the European war was the galvanizing test that assured his professional future.

It must be admitted, however, that Van's timing for a command was most propitious. The Luftwaffe, although not yet dead, was wobbling severely, and although there were a great many planes still available—including jets—the best German pilots were gone. The invasion had succeeded, and the Allies were firmly established in France. Indeed, when Vandenberg assumed command of the Ninth Air Force in August, the beginning of the end was in sight; the Allies continued to grow in strength, while the Axis powers continued to weaken. It is quite possible that Vandenberg would have been equally successful had he been given a major command a year earlier. Fortunately, he did a superb job when he was given the chance.

Generals Arnold and Spaatz were two of the most pragmatic, calculating, and ruthless of military leaders; they demanded results, and friendship was not nearly enough to win their favor—they had already relieved many old friends. It is not possible to imagine these men being swayed by a winning smile and firm handshake. For years both Arnold and Spaatz had observed Vandenberg's performance. They knew his capabilities. Hoyt Vandenberg did not become the protégé of Arnold and Spaatz because he was good company, but because he was good.

The question of strategic versus tactical air power also needs to be addressed. Vandenberg never forgot the tactical experiences of his early career and was unable fully to accept the claims of those who advocated strategic air power. He recognized the primacy and potential of heavy bombers, but he never overlooked the necessity of tactical air for supporting the ground forces. Whereas Spaatz and Doolittle often seemed to oppose *in principle* the use of heavy bombers in a tactical role, Vandenberg recognized that there were occasions when such bombing was a valuable weapon, if only in the minds of the ground commanders benefiting from the support. Because the Army Air Forces were not yet independent, it was essential to gain the confidence of Army leaders to secure separate air power. It has been said that the impressive performance of the Eighth Air Force in destroying the German economy assured independent status for the airmen. Perhaps not, perhaps it was the Ninth Air Force, because the close cooperation established by Vandenberg with Generals Bradley, Patton, Hodges, Simpson, J. Lawton Collins, and the rest allayed their fears of being left without air cover in a future conflict. Army leaders were unwilling to release their precious air support without assurances. Bradley's bitter comment at the time of the debate over the transportation plan that he was tired of the "glib, enticing arguments" of strategic bombing advocates brings the matter into sharp focus. Bradley never trusted Brereton, but he did trust Vandenberg and thought he carried out his duties with "extraordinary competence." Bradley told Eisenhower in January 1945 that he would not settle for any other airman as his strong right arm.[190] When the war ended and the Air Force pushed for its freedom, Eisenhower was Army chief of staff; he was succeeded by Bradley, and he in turn by Collins. Old friends. It is not unreasonable to speculate that Arnold and Spaatz were aware of Vandenberg's gifts for accommodation, and they supported his career for that reason. Air Force independence was vital; it might be more attainable if Army leaders saw Vandenberg as heir apparent.

In sum, Vandenberg had performed exceptionally well in every position held during the war. Whereas others lacked the adaptability or perseverance to cope with unexpected and complex problems, he consistently succeeded. He was one of the top air leaders of the war who had proven himself in conference, combat, and command. On May 1, 1945, Spaatz penned an efficiency report on Vandenberg that described him as "alert, keen and brilliant" with a "most pleasing" personality that generated confidence. The report concluded that Vandenberg was "one of the most brilliant of our young officers."[191] As he arrived back in Washington in May to serve again on the Air Staff, General Arnold welcomed him warmly: "I want you to know that I have personally been proud of your achievements and that I count on your ability and judgment in the final prosecution of this war."[192] The future was bright.

Whenever science makes a discovery, the
devil grabs it while the angels are debating the best way to use it.

Alan Valentine

III | *Preparations for Command*

Science is in the saddle. Science is the dic-
tator, whether we like it or not. Science
runs ahead of both politics and military affairs. Science evolves new conditions to
which institutions must be adapted . . . let
us keep our science dry.

Carl M. Spaatz

THE ATOMIC STRIKE FORCE

Lieutenant General Vandenberg left Europe in May 1945. Because of War
Department policy, returning heroes arrived home at different times and at different places so that the entire nation could join in the welcome ceremonies. Vandenberg flew into San Antonio, Texas, en route to his new assignment on the Air Staff
in Washington. During the first few weeks there were numerous calls for speeches
and appearances around the country. Vandenberg responded to many of these requests, on one occasion sharing the podium with Clark Gable—former B-17 tail
gunner—and was introduced by a certain young reservist, Captain Ronald Rea-
gan. At most of these engagements Vandenberg hailed the performance of his illustrious Ninth and called for the formation of a separate Air Force.[1]

Returning to familiar surroundings on the Air Staff, Vandenberg headed the
Operations, Commitments, and Requirements Division and immediately became
involved in postwar planning.[2] The abrupt and dramatic conclusion of the Pacific
conflict in August forced military men to rethink basic premises of war and peace
in the atomic age. Airmen pointed triumphantly to the new weapon that had devastated two cities and announced that protective oceans were no longer a guarantee of American security. The atom bomb could destroy a nation and win a war
and, significantly, because of the weapon's enormous size and weight, as yet only
aircraft could deliver it. The implications of Hiroshima needed serious thought,
so in October 1945 General Arnold directed three of his top men, Generals

Spaatz, Vandenberg, and Norstad, to study the issue. The results of their efforts, referred to as the Spaatz Report, were in many respects an updated version of what air theorists had been advocating for decades.

The Spaatz board went about its task in two stages. The first report, produced at the end of October, said nothing startling. After a lengthy recapitulation of strategic bombing doctrine and its practice in the war, the generals drew predictable conclusions. In future wars, it would "undoubtedly" be the Air Force that first engaged the enemy. The atomic bomb's awesome destructiveness meant that an enemy surprise attack could decide a war because there would be no time for mobilization. The United States must, therefore, maintain a strategic bombing force in being capable of either "smashing an enemy air offensive, or launching a formidable striking force." In short, the Air Force "on the alert" was to be America's new first line of defense—and offense—in the future.[3]

The report continued that in order to carry out its mission, the Air Force needed seventy combat groups (about ten thousand aircraft), and four hundred thousand personnel, which included strategic, tactical, and air transport units. More importantly, the air component must have "full parity and coequal status with the Ground and Naval forces" in the framework of a unified Department of National Defense. This first Spaatz Report concluded that the defense of America was best assured by an "irresistible offensive capability" armed with atomic bombs.[4] This was one of the few occasions when the new weapon was mentioned. Its omission was deliberate because the following month the three generals took another look at military strategy, focusing specifically on atomic weapons.

The second Spaatz Report began by noting that current atomic weapons could utterly devastate a four-square-mile area, but that future weapons could be developed that would obliterate an area of up to ten square miles. The generals then made several assumptions: other nations would eventually develop atomic weapons and the means to deliver them; strategic air bases around the world would be available for American use; the B-29 and its descendants would remain the prime carrier for atomic weapons; a bomb stockpile would be established; and the United States would never again have time to arm after war had begun.[5]

This was an interesting start. Although most of these postulates are logical and give little pause, three catch the eye. First, the idea of needing overseas bases from which to launch a strike is a sharp break from the past policy of isolation. Already the air leaders had realized the new world role that America was to play. It is quite possible that this new understanding occurred to Vandenberg first. In October 1942, he had told Spaatz that the AAF should start planning for self-contained airfields around the world for use after the war. When it is considered that this statement was made by a mere colonel prior even to the North African invasion, it is remarkable. The quest for overseas bases would indeed become a crucial issue during the decade following the war.[6]

The second assumption of interest was the claim that the airplane would remain the prime carrier for atomic weapons. This was a highly contentious assertion that both the Army and Navy would vigorously challenge in the years ahead.

Finally, the generals reiterated the warning of the first report: that future wars would no longer provide the luxury of leisurely mobilization. This belief was to figure prominently in all subsequent Air Force thinking as the airmen strove to build a large, peacetime force.

The report then discussed potential targets and frankly acknowledged that not all were suitable for the atomic bomb. In many cases conventional bombs would be more efficient and effective. Besides, the new weapon was expected to exist only in very limited numbers, and it would be unwise to spend them on frivolous targets.

The report then stressed three more essential elements for a postwar Air Force: an effective air defense, a vastly expanded intelligence network, and an urgent upgrading of research and development.[7]

The first requirement, an effective air defense, was seen as necessary to American security, but events would soon make such a system expendable. Severe budget cuts imposed on the military necessitated the elimination of certain missions and weapons. Vandenberg was to decide that the best defense was a good offense; an active air defense system was made a low priority.

The call for a greatly expanded intelligence organization is important. This too probably indicates Vandenberg's influence. The report decried the lack of an effective intelligence system before the war. Because there would be no time to mobilize in the event of a future war, the nation would have to be well prepared in advance. One aspect of this preparation was a large strike force in being, but the other side of that coin was the knowledge of a potential enemy's intentions and capabilities. As will be seen, Vandenberg felt strongly about this issue and would soon have the opportunity to act upon his beliefs.

The final recommendation of the Spaatz board was a strong call for continued research and development, especially in the atomic field. There was, however, a complication to be overcome. Although the Air Force possessed the only delivery capability for the atomic bomb, airmen had been largely frozen out of the weapon's development program. The Manhattan Engineering District, jealously guarded by Major General Leslie R. Groves, was an Army and Navy project; few outsiders had access to its secrets. Spaatz and his colleagues recommended that a new post be created on the Air Staff—deputy chief of staff for research and development—and that someone of the caliber of Major General Curtis E. LeMay be appointed as its head. In his memoirs, LeMay disingenuously remarked that the appointment surprised him because he had little experience and knowledge of such technical matters. It appears, however, that the cigar-chewing combat leader was selected for other reasons. He was just the type of forceful, blunt, and goal-oriented individual who could break down the protective façade erected by Groves. LeMay's task was not so much to monitor the design of new aircraft engines as to strong-arm Groves into allowing the Air Force a voice in atomic development.[8]

Soon after assuming his new duties, LeMay proposed to Groves that the AAF assume responsibility for the procurement, storage, assembly, and transportation of the bombs. The Manhattan District would retain the responsibility for research and development, fabrication, and delivery to the AAF. Groves flatly declined, and the airmen were irritated. Every aspect of the new weapon was so highly classified that even critical members of the operational units tasked to deliver it were not given sufficient information to perform that duty. This was a major obstacle because the bombs required special handling, assembly, and transportation arrangements that took laborious training. Knowledge was power, and the AAF had little knowledge. General LeMay worked to change these circumstances, but it would take time.[9]

The story for the next two years was one of continuous conflict over these crucial issues. The AAF, not yet independent, was becoming paranoid because the one weapon so necessary for its institutional future was denied it. The Army and Navy, perhaps fearing their own inferiority in an atomic age, repeatedly used their seniority to elbow the upstart Air Force out of a dominant role. There were many bitter debates over who would exercise primary responsibility for the special weapons, but for the most part LeMay was frustrated in his attempts to gain entrance to the atomic sanctum. Indeed, when the Atomic Energy Commission was formed in January 1947 to replace the Manhattan District, it was even more secretive than its predecessor.[10] As the official historians of the AEC phrased it, "It seemed that the Commission had the exaggerated idea that its control of atomic energy information was a sort of sacred trust which took precedence over even military requirements."[11] It would be two more years before Vandenberg, as Air Force chief of staff, was able to pick the atomic lock and gain authority to act as the executive agent for the Joint Chiefs of Staff in atomic matters.

Lieutenant General Ira Eaker, now deputy commander of the AAF, was also concerned about the atomic bomb and its impact on his organization. How many groups should be trained for the atomic mission? There was only one unit so designated at the time, and Eaker feared that Congress and the War Department might conclude that that was all the strategic air force needed. Perhaps several groups should receive atomic training.[12] Along the same lines, a member of Eaker's staff suggested that the unit not even be called the "atomic bombing force," or any similar term, since it would immediately call attention to the fact that it was the only such group in existence. Specially train it, yes, but do not single it out.[13] In order to help clear the air, Eaker asked Vandenberg to study the matter.[14]

In January 1946, Vandenberg wrote a lengthy, detailed directive that established guidelines for the proposed "atomic strike force." He called for an organization manned with the most competent personnel, the best equipment, and the most advanced aircraft in the Air Force. This unit should be based near the atomic storage area at Albuquerque, New Mexico, so as to maintain an "extremely close and continuous coordination and liaison with the Manhattan District Project with particular regard to the development, manufacture, handling, and general technical aspects of the bomb itself." (Once again, the fear of being kept at arm's length from the new weapon is evident.) The force must be ready to deploy worldwide at short notice, although the actual decision to do so would come from the president. It was expected that the aircraft would deploy to forward bases first, with the bombs themselves remaining in New Mexico until needed for delivery. Specific units were designated to form the strike force: the 509th Composite Group—the original B-29 unit that had staged the combat strikes from Saipan—was designated as the nucleus to train two more bomb groups. Eventually, all medium and heavy bomb groups would be so capable.[15] Vandenberg noted various tactics that could be used by the atomic strike force: the group could penetrate enemy airspace in a mass as had been common in the European war; a single aircraft could attack at night or in bad weather; or individual aircraft could be launched simultaneously in a widely dispersed strike. The unit should be prepared for all such methods, but it was imperative that the actual bomb drop be carried out under radar conditions—visual drops were inadequate.[16]

This memorandum demonstrates clearly that Vandenberg had completed a long philosophical journey. His background and education were now complete; he was a total airman and air-power advocate. Although a fighter pilot at heart, he now believed in the primacy of bombardment. Vandenberg's varied experience and training better prepared him for the future than any of his contemporaries, and that truth would soon become apparent.

Two months after Vandenberg's memorandum, General Spaatz reorganized the AAF into three major combat air commands: Air Defense Command (ADC), Tactical Air Command (TAC), and the Strategic Air Command (SAC). The mission of ADC was defense of the continental United States, while that of TAC was close air support for the Army and Navy. SAC, of which the 58th Bomb Wing (atomic capable) was the prime component, was charged with conducting intense and sustained long-range offensive operations in any part of the world using the latest and most advanced weapons.[17] To a great extent SAC was patterned after the blueprint drawn by Vandenberg in January. The first SAC commander was General George C. Kenney, "MacArthur's airman," who had led the highly successful Far East Allied Air Forces during the Pacific war. In the years ahead, he and Vandenberg would have their differences.

SPY MASTER

When General Dwight D. Eisenhower returned from the Crusade to become Army chief of staff in November 1945, he reorganized the War Department General Staff. He was particularly concerned about his Intelligence Division (G-2), and a special committee was appointed under Assistant Secretary of War for Air Robert A. Lovett to study the matter. The three-man committee, of which Vandenberg was a member, was highly critical of Army intelligence and recommended its complete revision. The report began by charging that Army intelligence was dangerously inadequate for the tasks that lay ahead. During the war there had been an "incredible" lack of cooperation between intelligence users and producers, and the G-2 function had been held in such low regard that it seldom attracted quality personnel. The report specifically recommended that the head of the G-2 Division should have high rank and possess the unquestioned confidence of the Army as a whole; that intelligence should be placed on a par with operations, supply, and war planning in practice and not just name; an intelligence school should be established to train career intelligence specialists; and that these individuals receive equal consideration on promotion boards. The men concluded that the defects within G-2 were fundamental to the degree that a total reshaping was necessary if it was successfully to perform its new peacetime mission in the atomic age.[18]

Eisenhower doubted that the situation was quite as bleak as painted, but agreed there was a need for reorganization. Consequently, on December 20, 1945, he told General Spaatz, Arnold's successor as commander of the Army Air Forces, that he wanted the man who diagnosed the disease now to effect a cure. He wanted Vandenberg as his new G-2. Spaatz concurred, and Vandenberg assumed the position on January 26. He was not enamored with this new job, telling his parents that "Ike wanted him to straighten out a real mess that has been going on since before the war." He declared glumly that it was a place where he could "get his throat cut with no difficulty." What was worse, there would be little time for golf.[19]

Vandenberg had been in close contact with intelligence operations throughout the war. In fact, he was interested in all aspects of the mysterious new form of information called "communications intelligence," which consisted of intercepting and exploiting enemy radio messages. If these were encrypted in the high-grade cipher that employed the complex "enigma" machine, the product was termed "Top Secret Ultra," or simply Ultra. If plaintext (unencrypted) or low-grade ciphers were used, the information was dubbed "Y." Because of its importance, Ultra was more rigidly segregated and protected than other forms of intelligence.

The Ninth Air Force had a group of signals intelligence specialists who plucked German messages out of the airwaves both day and night. Ultra signals could not be deciphered at the unit level, and were thus relayed to Hut 6 at Bletchley Park, near London. Once decoded, those Ultra intercepts thought relevant were transmitted to the field commands concerned. At Ninth Air Force Headquarters two dozen or so individuals were aware of Ultra's existence, and only two, Van and Bob Lee, were given daily briefings on the subject. The information obtained from Ultra was often of great importance, but one had to be careful how it was used. As General Quesada colorfully commented: "I assure you that Ultra didn't permit us to do something tomorrow. You were not allowed to respond to Ultra tomorrow. If you did you would get your ass kicked out of the theater so fast it would make your head swim."[20] Notwithstanding Quesada's caution, if cleverly handled, Ultra could be put to use quickly. In one instance an intercept indicated that a large number of enemy trucks were bivouacked in a certain forest. Vandenberg launched reconnaissance aircraft to examine several areas, one of which was the suspected forest. Sure enough, the trucks were spotted visually, air strikes were ordered, and within hours over four hundred vehicles were destroyed.[21]

Y traffic was also of great importance. At times it consisted merely of German pilots talking to their ground controllers. Their language was not in code except for coordinates and the like. These codes were quickly broken, providing near real-time intelligence information to the Ninth Air Force: enemy aircraft would report their position to their base, these messages were intercepted and decoded, and fighters would be launched to engage.[22] It was a very efficient system.

What bothered Vandenberg about both Ultra and Y was that, except for a handful of Americans, the entire interception and decoding network was in the hands of the British. Vandenberg wanted access to the raw data and more intelligence personnel in his command to handle such duties. In February 1945, he wrote Washington that the "lack of an Air Force organization for the control of 'Y' would seriously prejudice our operations in war and our development and research in peace." The utter dependence on the Royal Air Force for such material was "a bad situation." He advocated the development of an Air Force intelligence system on a par with the British; with peace looming, friendly relations and equal access to British sources would no longer be guaranteed.[23]

In addition, on February 12, 1945, Vandenberg had been placed in charge of the training of all Office of Strategic Services (OSS) agents worldwide.[24] What precisely this position entailed is unknown; Vandenberg's papers contain no more than a cryptic diary entry. But it is apparent that he was well aware of the capabilities and activities of the secret organization—information that he would use later. Similarly, there is no evidence that Vandenberg had contact with Major General William ("Wild Bill") Donovan, the famed war hero and leader of the OSS, but many of Donovan's ideas regarding clandestine activities would later be adopted by Vandenberg.

Donovan had written to President Roosevelt in November 1944 advocating an entirely new intelligence setup after the war. He proposed a "central authority" reporting directly to the president that was to collect intelligence and be responsible for the final evaluation of all intelligence within the government. This authority required an independent budget, but it should not have any police or law enforcement functions. It would perform "subversive operations" abroad.[25] Although Roosevelt seemed favorable to the proposal, a copy of Donovan's memorandum was soon leaked to an unfriendly newsman. The resulting furor over what was depicted as a proposed *Gestapo* unit caused the president to back off. He told Donovan to wait patiently for a few months until things quieted down. By the time things were quiet, however, Roosevelt was dead, and the new president, Harry S. Truman, had little use for "Wild Bill."[26]

This was the background with which General Vandenberg approached his new duties on the General Staff. His predecessor, Major General Clayton Bissell, was not effective. One staff member recalled his lamentable attention to detail at the expense of the broad view. Producing multicolored viewgraphs for the morning briefing became a top priority in G-2. On one occasion he was displeased with the physical arrangement of the offices within his division. Bissell ordered everyone to move, and while this was taking place, all the phones were disconnected. The day was June 6, 1944.[27] Into this morass stepped Vandenberg. First, he instituted an intelligence school at Fort Leavenworth to train people for the new and complicated duties of collecting, filtering, and analyzing raw data. Before the war there had been virtually no such thing in the Army as a "career intelligence officer." Most of those chosen for such service during the war were in the fields of advertising, newspapers, or publicity. Vandenberg realized that professionals were needed for the tasks ahead—people trained in economics, statistics, and engineering, who also had a firm foundation in military intelligence procedures and requirements. He also pushed for more funds in a secret budget. Asking for a "blank check in trust," Vandenberg insisted that a large, well-organized and worldwide intelligence apparatus was necessary for the United States: "In my opinion, the vital importance of effective military intelligence is not generally understood. Our first line of defense is neither the Navy nor the Air Force, but Intelligence."[28]

Another imperative was to clean up the shambles left by rapid demobilization. Donovan's OSS had been disbanded by President Truman in September 1945, and the remnants of the people, equipment, codes, and networks were then split, with some being given to the State Department, while most (90 percent) went to G-2. Vandenberg thus inherited a sizable contingent of trained agents ready to carry on their work of "espionage and related special operations" around the world. This tended, however, to confuse the situation further as the influx of new personnel flooded the unprepared War Department. Reorganization was imperative. Vandenberg first grouped all administrative, coordinating, and planning responsibilities under a single executive director. The remaining activities were formed into functional offices: intelligence, security, combat intelligence and training, the Army Security Agency, and collection. The result was a far more streamlined and coherent intelligence organization.[29] What had been even more disconcerting during the war was the lack of cooperation between G-2, the Office of Navy Intelligence (ONI), the State Department, and the Federal Bureau of Investigation (FBI). These different organizations seemed continually to be in competition with one another and working at cross purposes.[30] In order to avoid wasteful duplication of effort and confusion, some type of national centralizing body was necessary.

This type of problem had been forcefully brought home to Vandenberg on January 1, 1945. On that day, the Luftwaffe launched major strikes against Ninth Air Force airfields. The damage was heavy, but it could have been far worse. The day before, Y intelligence had learned that "Operation Goldrigen" was scheduled for New Year's Day. Unfortunately, the signals experts did not know what that meant. The previous week, a prisoner of war interrogation had revealed that an operation called "Goldrigen" was planned that would be an all-out attack on Allied airfields, but he did not know when it would take place. Fortunately, Vandenberg had directed his intelligence chief to review information from all sources and compose a composite picture of enemy capabilities. On New Year's Eve, the various puzzle pieces were fitted together and the attack planned for the following morning was revealed. Vandenberg ordered his fighters alerted for dawn takeoffs and to wait in ambush for the Luftwaffe. Although the mass attacks were still punishing, the Ninth suffered losses only one-third as great as Coningham's TAF that had not reacted as quickly to the intelligence clues.[31] Vandenberg had learned a valuable lesson.

It was this problem of centralization that prompted President Truman to move for a Central Intelligence Group in January 1946. He told his chief legal counselor, Clark M. Clifford, that the confusing and contradictory reports he was receiving from the various intelligence entities were cluttering his desk and helping him not at all. He said that he had gone through all the evidence relative to the Pearl Harbor disaster and concluded that the lack of cooperation between the Army and Navy's intelligence teams had been responsible for the surprise. It was therefore necessary to have some central agency to put all the pieces together and to ensure such things did not recur.[32] As a result, on January 22, 1946, Truman issued a directive establishing the National Intelligence Authority (NIA) that consisted of the secretaries of War, Navy, and State. It was their duty to make sure that all foreign intelligence activities were planned, developed, and coordinated to guarantee the most effective accomplishment of the intelligence mission. To assist the NIA a Central Intelligence Group (CIG) was formed, headed by a Director of Central Intelligence (DCI).[33]

It was soon apparent that there were serious structural flaws in the president's plan. First, the CIG was not a governmental *agency*, but merely an interdepartmental *group* whose personnel were borrowed from the Army, Navy, and State departments for a temporary period. The group could not hire anyone; it asked for leftovers. Similarly, it had no budget; all funds had to be garnered from surplus in the other departments. In addition, the CIG was not authorized to "collect" intelligence, only to correlate, evaluate, and disseminate. This meant that it had no spies; it merely gathered the reports from the other agencies and combined them for presentation to the NIA. In practice, this quickly amounted to a hasty stapling together of various cables and memoranda with little attempt at interpretation. The DCI himself, though responsible to the NIA, was not a voting member of that body; hence, he held essentially the same status as the heads of the other intelligence services.[34]

There were even those who resented the CIG's existence. The Navy had fought it, seeing it as a precedent for "unification of the armed forces," the sinister *bête noire* of all admirals who clung tenaciously to their separate service. Eisenhower apparently believed that Admiral Chester W. Nimitz, chief of Naval Operations, was dragging his feet on the issue of centralized intelligence, and so he directed Vandenberg to effect the cooperation that others seemed reluctant to impose.[35] Besides the Navy, the FBI of J. Edgar Hoover was also recalcitrant. Hoover's organization had expanded enormously during the war because of the threat of foreign agents and subversion. Hoover probably expected to head the new CIG, which would then be combined with his beloved FBI. President Truman, however, had no intention of giving one man that much power, and upon realizing this, Hoover fought the CIG tenaciously; if it were not controlled by him then it would be emasculated.[36] Finally, the State Department looked upon the CIG as encroaching on its traditional territory. State had long gathered information on foreign powers through its embassy personnel around the world. It too resented the new organization that seemed to be dictating how foreign events should be interpreted and acted upon.[37]

In short, Truman's creation was an anemic organ with no arms or legs, a small voice, and no visible means of support—but with numerous predators. To make matters worse, the first DCI had no intention of expanding his position, protecting his turf, or flexing his muscles. Rear Admiral Sidney Souers had wanted to retire from his position as Navy intelligence chief, but was prevailed upon by President Truman to remain in uniform and head the new CIG. After reluctantly assuming his new desk, the admiral was asked what he wanted to do. "I want to go home" was the reply. Although from Missouri like the president, Souers was not one of Truman's cronies. In fact, one observer thought Truman liked Souers because he was not ambitious or "wanting something." Nevertheless, Souers was not a forceful personality and had not the stomach for the tough fight that a truly effective CIG would have provoked.[38] During the four months of Souers's tenure, the CIG was an inconspicuous entity.

When considering a successor, Souers decided upon General Vandenberg for several reasons. First, he thought it important that the director be military, but the position should be rotated between the services, and it was the Army's turn. Second, the CIG had no statutory authority because it had been established by an executive order. Acquiring legal legitimacy might require friends in Congress, and the nephew of the powerful senator from Michigan would no doubt have such friends.[39] Another consideration was Vandenberg's known skill, evidenced during the war, at developing teamwork among diverse individuals. If anyone could break the personality logjam in the intelligence community, he seemed to be the one. His brief tenure at G-2 had been truly remarkable; one columnist wrote that Vandenberg had achieved more in two months than all the other intelligence chiefs had in twenty years. Vandenberg had also headed the State-Army-Navy Communications Intelligence Board, charged with coordinating all signals intelligence within the United States and also effecting cooperation with the British. The British-US Agreement, or BRUSA (later renamed UKUSA) was negotiated in March 1946 under Vandenberg's tenure. This enormously important agreement established the official basis for continuation of the wartime relationship in the field of communications intelligence. Vandenberg knew only too well how vital this cooperation had been to winning the war.[40] In addition, Vandenberg's three-star rank also seemed to ensure the group would have some degree of protection from pressures by the other services and departments. Vandenberg outranked the other intelligence chiefs (in fact, he had outranked Souers), and this provided some leverage in achieving cooperation. Most importantly, he was known for his ability.[41]

When offered the job, however, Vandenberg expressed reluctance, which Souers thought was owing to his ambition to command the AAF. Souers pointed out to him that the DCI position was an excellent stepping stone to such aspirations because he would gain "visibility" working closely with the Secretaries of War and Navy and, more importantly, the president. Besides, Souers asked Vandenberg "if he thought that they would make him Chief of Staff just because he was pretty."[42] The general finally relented, and Souers recommended him to Admiral William D. Leahy, chief of staff to the president. Leahy concurred with Souers and wrote General Eisenhower, asking him to release Vandenberg for the vacant post. The chief hesitated, saying he did not want to part with his new G-2 but would think it over. Outflanking Eisenhower, Leahy then informed President Truman on May 9, 1946, that the new DCI should be an officer of proven ability in the intelligence field, possess superior executive skill, and have "established prestige." He told the president that Vandenberg, head of G-2 for the previous four months, was the only Army officer who filled those specifications.[43] President Truman then told Secretary of War Robert Patterson that he had thought about the matter and decided Vandenberg was the proper man for the job because he knew the intelligence business "from A to Z," was a diplomat, and would be able to get along with State and Navy. Under such pressure, the Army chief relented and after meeting with Vandenberg, Truman appointed the general as DCI effective June 10, 1946.[44] That Vandenberg would have his hands full was apparent. When the appointment was made public, one reporter commented: "It will take all of Vandenberg's boldness, enthusiasm and charm, and his airman's broad view of the world, to make anything of his as yet rootless organization."[45]

Vandenberg plunged into his new office with customary vigor; in the CIG he had the nickname "Sparkplug." He had brought with him several colonels from G-2, and this cabal closeted themselves away for a week to rethink the mission of the CIG. After their seclusion, Vandenberg and his staff announced their plans for the future. First, the group had to be expanded; second, it had to be reorganized; and third, it needed enabling legislation. Vandenberg had big plans for the "Company" and made it clear that he would do things differently from his predecessor. As one observer put it, Vandenberg was ambitious and "inclined to rock any boats" on the way to his goal.[46]

Under Admiral Souers, the CIG had contained seventy-one people; Vandenberg requested three thousand. More money was also sought, an extra ten million dollars, which nearly doubled the current CIG budget. He pushed to have all federal espionage and counterespionage activities outside the limits of the United States under his control, and also insisted that monitoring of foreign press and radio broadcasts be done by the CIG. In short, Vandenberg wanted *all* raw data gathered by *all* intelligence sources to pass through his agency so it could be screened and filtered, believing that was the only way an accurate picture of the world situation could be presented. He pushed hard to gain a separate budget for the CIG, thus ensuring a degree of freedom and independence from the other departments. It would not be necessary to reveal the size of the budget; in fact, it would be undesirable from a security standpoint to do so. The amount could be hidden within the appropriations of the other departments, as long as it was clear the money belonged to the CIG.[47] The ability to hire and fire was also imperative. Because the other departments supplied the people, the CIG was at their mercy. If, for example, the State Department disagreed with a certain policy or decision, it could effectively throttle the group by withholding the necessary personnel needed to implement it.

Soon after, Vandenberg moved to expand his authority still further. He absorbed the rump of the OSS clandestine organization that had been given to the Army G-2, and renamed it the Special Operations Office. He then took over the task of collecting and examining data concerning foreign atomic energy programs, a task previously performed by Major General Leslie R. Groves in the Manhattan Engineering District.[48] It is interesting that at the same time Vandenberg was moving on Groves, General LeMay was also hitting him on the flank concerning control of atomic weapons development. Was this a planned, two-front attack by the AAF to undermine Groves's position?

When engaged in the effort to assume responsibility for atomic intelligence, Vandenberg briefed the Atomic Energy Commission on his duties. The chairman, David Lilienthal, remembered the occasion:

A discussion of "foreign intelligence" by a slim young fellow—Gary Cooperish—turned out to be General Hoyt Vandenberg, head of "clandestine" intelligence—his word. The talk cannot be committed to paper—not now—but it sounded like a Hitchcock movie and the quite tall young man like a character just off the set.[49]

Although Groves and Lilienthal resisted the encroachments of the CIG, the real friction came from J. Edgar Hoover over the issue of Latin American operations, a province of the FBI. Fear of Nazi infiltration had precipitated a great increase in counterintelligence activity in Latin America during the war, and Hoover was adverse to relinquishing control. After a struggle, Vandenberg won his point, but Hoover was not a good loser. The FBI immediately began to pull its agents from the south before CIG personnel were available to take their places. When Vandenberg requested that they be left temporarily and replaced at a systematic rate, Hoover replied it was "impractical." The assistant secretary of state for American republics affairs, Spruill Braden, lent his support and also requested Hoover to relent, but to no avail. Finally, Admiral Leahy prevailed upon the FBI chief to stay his anger. Leahy then told Vandenberg to ease off on Hoover, deal with him directly and not through underlings, and avoid hiring any former FBI agents for the CIG. Even so, although Hoover slowed the recall of his agents, it was rumored that "the CIA agents [sic] arrived in the morning to find the FBI files burned and the FBI agents booked for departure that afternoon."[50]

One of the main functions of the CIG as Vandenberg saw it was to gather intelligence from the other agencies, combine it with information gathered from his own organization, and fit these pieces into a comprehensive, logical, and accurate picture for presentation to the president. The other agencies were suspect because of their own particular biases and areas of concern, but the CIG could and should be above such parochialism. In order to perform this task adequately, Vandenberg felt it necessary to become a collection agency—an activity not specifically authorized in the Group's original charter. The general did it anyway, later admitting that he interpreted his directive rather broadly.[51]

Once he had decided to collect intelligence, the next step was fairly simple: the agents to perform this task—the OSS people—had already been transferred from the Army. Even so, the main focus of such operations, the Soviet Union, was largely an enigma. Even after four years of wartime alliance, the Kremlin leadership was still mysterious and unknown; there were few, if any, American agents operating in Moscow in 1946, although the Soviets had been operating in Washington, New York, London, and Paris for thirty years. Much of the information on the Soviet Union was obtained from former German intelligence agents, especially General Reinhard Gehlen's network.[52] This was a serious shortcoming for the United States because it helped foster and perpetuate mistrust, speculation, and misjudgment: "It was our almost total ignorance of what was going on in the 'denied area' behind the Iron Curtain that helped create the false image of a superpowerful Soviet Union."[53] A few well-placed sources could have helped penetrate this shield and see a truer picture. Vandenberg understood this fact and labored to establish such an intelligence network. In late June, he hired George F. Kennan, recently returned ambassador to Moscow, as a consultant for one month. Kennan had authored the now-famous "long telegram," followed by the "Mr X" article in *Foreign Affairs* that preached a policy of containment. At that time, Kennan was considered the foremost American expert on the Soviet Union. Vandenberg thought his expertise would "contribute immeasurably to the accuracy and adequacy" of CIG reports.[54] Although the first American agents to enter the Soviet Union did not do so until after Vandenberg had left the CIG, ironically, they parachuted in from an aircraft flown by the Ninth Air Force.[55]

A more mundane but no less important source for piercing the dark shroud of the Iron Curtain was American citizens abroad in business and scientific communities, and various educational and religious organizations. Vandenberg's agents contacted these individuals upon their return to the United States from sensitive areas and listened to their views on what they had just seen.[56] In addition, he moved to use the offices of American journalists. In December 1946, Vandenberg wrote Arthur Sulzberger of the *New York Times* explaining the importance of the CIG and asking if he and his newspaper could "render assistance in accomplishing our assigned task."[57] Sulzberger pledged his fullest support. Vandenberg was seeking access to the "For Your Information Files," confidential reports sent by reporters to the home office that discussed rumors, tips, hunches, and unsubstantiated information not yet suitable for publication. Such information could be a gold mine, and the DCI knew it. The requests were granted and proved to be a valuable intelligence source. It is likely that Vandenberg made similar "special arrangements" with the other major media organizations.[58]

As an increasing volume of information began to flow into the CIG, Vandenberg tackled the next obstacle: presenting the total picture. When he was G-2, Vandenberg had begun an intelligence newsletter for major commanders around the globe. This paper, which was prepared two or three times weekly, contained information that might be useful to those in occupation duties or American defense. One or two pages in length, these reports warned commanders of events such as the Soviet occupation of northern Persia or the latest developments in Soviet military technology.[59] Admiral Souers had attempted a similar report for the president's use, but because the other intelligence agencies refused to allow the CIG to include any analysis, it became little different from the estimates it was designed to replace. Vandenberg wanted to rectify this shortcoming, arguing with the Navy and State Departments that if he had to obtain the approval of everyone in each case, the NIA would become a "debating society" and nothing would be accomplished.[60] Vandenberg insisted that he, as DCI, be the arbiter in deciding what should be included in the daily reports to President Truman, and that it should include analysis, not merely raw intelligence. The State Department continued to resist, but Vandenberg proceeded by his own lights; occasionally, however, his reports included a "dissenting opinion" from Foggy Bottom.[61] The DCI also suggested a weekly summary that would deal more with long-range estimates, something not suitable for the daily reports. Once again there was opposition, but Vandenberg continued to push the idea and when President Truman in

July 1946 asked for a CIG estimate of Soviet intentions, the opportunity was seized. For two days, Vandenberg and his staff labored over the report that was presented on July 26. Significantly, the study was not coordinated with the other intelligence chiefs beforehand, causing immediate protest from State and Navy. Vandenberg apologized and said he would try to do better in the future.[62]

The weekly reports were fairly short, usually two or three pages, the length a busy chief executive could be expected to handle. It is significant that these papers were surprisingly mild in tone. Although the cold war was in its formative stages, Vandenberg avoided the hardness that was to be prevalent in government statements a few years hence. In August 1946, for example, he wrote that the threats of Premier Stalin concerning Turkey and Yugoslavia were merely propaganda for internal consumption and a "war of nerves"; there was little danger of overt aggression. In September and October 1946 and again in January 1947, Vandenberg expressed similar sentiments, discounting Soviet military action as being caused by economic, social, and subject nationality problems. The United States should be watchful and prepared, but there was no reason to act precipitously.[63]

Clandestine intelligence collection and prophetic reports were important, but another of Vandenberg's major goals was to attain statutory status for the CIG. One of the key issues of the immediate postwar era concerned "unification," the combination of the Army, Navy, and an independent Air Force into a single Department of Defense. The legislative proposals for this scheme usually included provisions for a Central Intelligence Agency that would solve Vandenberg's concerns. He was reluctant, however, to tie his hopes for the CIG to this vehicle because unification was a very controversial issue being fiercely resisted by the Navy. He visualized this fight dragging on for years and thought it would be faster and easier to obtain separate legislation for the group.[64]

Soon after arriving at CIG, Vandenberg was given a briefing by Lawrence R. Houston, the group's general counsel. Houston had been working on proposed legislation for several weeks and showed Vandenberg his efforts. They were a detailed charter that addressed all the concerns about the CIG's structural flaws that Souers, Vandenberg, and others had already noted. Vandenberg liked the proposal, it went even further than he had originally contemplated, and directed Houston to continue. The result was a lengthy document calling for new legislation to include a separate budget, independent status, and the DCI reporting directly to the president and sitting on the proposed National Security Council. In fact, after studying the question firsthand, Vandenberg arrived at conclusions similar to those advanced by General Donovan more than two years earlier. Houston took the draft to Clark Clifford, who was the White House representative coordinating the proposals of the various agencies involved in the new legislation. Clifford was surprised at Houston's submission: "I thought you were to be a small coordinating group!" Houston said, "No, we are to be an operating agency."[65] Clifford promised to study the CIG proposal carefully.

On January 23, Clifford unveiled a draft of the proposed unification legislation that included a section on intelligence. It was a shock. The suggestions of Vandenberg and Houston had been ignored, and Clifford's proposals would leave the CIG as weak as before. With a strong personality like Vandenberg in charge, the group could hold its own, barely, but anyone less dynamic needed a stronger statutory position. That same day Vandenberg visited the White House and complained that the proposals did not address the difficulties of funding, staffing, and responsibilities.[66] Once again, Vandenberg considered separate enabling legislation, but after much thought elected to stick with the proposed National Security Act and keep the CIG section of that act as general as possible. The unification issue would provide enough fireworks; there was no need for him to add gasoline.

It appears Vandenberg may have discussed this problem on several occasions with his Uncle Arthur, seeking advice on the strategy that would best secure the desired statute. Whether "Unk" could offer more than political advice to his favored nephew is unknown. The CIG legislative counsel, Walter Pforzheimer, recalls that the general would often state that he had to see the senator; the two would drive to his office, where the senator and the general would speak privately. Pforzheimer was never told what was discussed; he wondered why Vandenberg even asked him to go along.[67]

Pforzheimer remembers Vandenberg as a tremendously forceful, dedicated, and hard-working individual. The DCI was very informal at the office, usually wore civilian clothes, and would often come into his staff members' offices just to chat: "Van would walk in smiling, sit down and put his feet up on *your* desk and ask what was going on." Vandenberg had an open mind on most matters and was approachable. If he thought an individual had doubts regarding a certain course, he would sit back in his chair and ask: "You aren't really satisfied with the decision, are you?" He wanted dialogue, not yes-men. What most impressed Pforzheimer was Vandenberg's intellect. He never gave the impression of being a scholar, but he was very intelligent. The first time the young lawyer had to brief his chief he found him sitting behind his desk reading a newspaper. Van told him to start talking. Pforzheimer did, but noticed that Van continued to read the paper, paying little attention. When Pforzheimer finished, Van said "thanks" and the meeting was over. Pforzheimer was irritated and left thinking, "what a lightweight." A few days later, however, Vandenberg stopped Pforzheimer in the hall to ask some questions regarding the previous briefing, which he quoted verbatim. After this happened on several other occasions, Pforzheimer realized that there was far more to the DCI than met the eye. He did not underestimate him again.[68] It was not unusual for Vandenberg to employ such tactics to catch people off balance. He would frequently feign indolence to strangers. Invariably, they would let down their guard, confide in him, speak too freely, and attempt to take advantage. All the while Vandenberg would sit behind his mask, watching and evaluating.

When the unification hearings began in Congress, Pforzheimer attended a few of the sessions and was surprised at the rough handling being given the witnesses: "Congress was loaded for bear." He then went to Vandenberg and suggested that the DCI attend one of these sessions to get a sample of what would be in store for him when it was his turn. Vandenberg thought it an excellent idea. The two men went over to Congress the next two days; Vandenberg also noted the treatment meted out to high-ranking generals and admirals. He returned to his office and warned his staff to prepare his testimony very carefully. Vandenberg then visited the office of Senator Chan Gurney, chairman of the committee he would testify before, asking for guidance. This was a wise move that broke the ice.[69]

When he appeared before the Armed Services Committee, Vandenberg began by assuring the senators that the pending bill would give the United States the best intelligence system in the world, which was essential to the national security. Vandenberg reasoned that the earth had shrunk dramatically since the advent of the atomic age—another Pearl Harbor could prove disastrous. The ad hoc apparatus formed during the war eventually provided a massive amount of raw data, but nowhere was there an agency charged with coordinating this information. The result was monumental waste. The war system had been only a stopgap measure; indeed, most of the significant intelligence had been supplied by the British. In the words usually quoted in the newspaper accounts of the hearings, Vandenberg stated:

> The United States should not . . . find itself confronted with the necessity of developing its plans and policies on the basis of intelligence collected, compiled, and intercepted by some foreign government . . . the United States should never again have to go hat in hand, begging any foreign government for the eyes—the foreign intelligence—with which to see. We should be self-sufficient.[70]

In executive session a few months later, Vandenberg returned to clear up the concerns of some lawmakers, stressing that the CIA should possess no police, subpoena, or law enforcement powers; he did not intend to contest domestic jurisdiction with the FBI. As for covert activities, the general stated that such matters were overdramatized and exaggerated, but they were essential and he recommended that they be sanctioned.[71]

Vandenberg's eleven-month tenure at CIG was moderately successful. The goals he set, though sound, were not totally attainable in such a short time. It would be more accurate to conclude that a detailed blueprint had been drawn which other men at other times could build upon. As one reporter commented, the intelligence system of the United States was "infantile" compared to other nations, but Vandenberg had gone a long way toward rectifying that shortcoming. Unfortunately, the helm was surrendered to a "lackluster leader" who failed to exploit the advantages prepared by Vandenberg.[72] Of importance, the path staked out in 1946 was a true one; there is no evidence of wrongdoing or extralegal activity. The scandals revealed in the seventies—the drug experiments on unsuspecting individuals, domestic spying on student radicals and dissidents, and mail interceptions—did not begin until years after Vandenberg's departure.[73] When asking for a "blank check in trust," he did so as one who would honor that charge.

On April 30, 1947, President Truman wrote Vandenberg that General Eisenhower requested his return to the Army Air Forces for important duties. He added that he regretted losing Vandenberg because his task had been "exceptionally well performed."[74]

Lieutenant General Ira C. Eaker, deputy commanding general of the Army Air Forces, decided to retire in early 1947. Eaker felt that the nation was heading into serious trouble with the Soviets, and he could be more valuable leading a fight against their encroachments out of uniform. He also felt it necessary for the "older men" to step aside now that the war was over and give "new blood" a chance to move upward. Finally, his thirty years were enough; he was tired and wanted to go fishing.[75] The emphasis on youth was strong within the AAF. In April 1943 Arnold had written Spaatz that it was time to get rid of the older officers who had outlived their usefulness: "It is vitally necessary that we ease out such men and make room at the top for those more junior officers who have not been left on the roadside by the parade." Spaatz was told to look for young men who could "carry on after we pass out of the picture."[76] Spaatz had listened closely. Vandenberg's prestigious and somewhat unexpected honor was a giant step upward. Admiral Leahy wrote in his diary that Vandenberg was being groomed as Spaatz's successor. *Newsweek* echoed that observation, and the prophecy gained credibility when Vandenberg received his fourth star on October 1, 1947. Such a promotion for a man of his youth was surprising. When the war ended there were twelve airmen who outranked him; although many of these retired, there were still three lieutenant generals who were senior. At forty-eight he was the second youngest American ever to reach the rank of full general; only U. S. Grant had advanced more rapidly.[77] Of far greater significance, Vandenberg returned to uniform just before unification of the armed forces.

UNIFICATION

Unification of the armed forces was a bitter and laborious process. The separate cabinet departments of Navy and War had existed since the first years of the Republic. Though attempts to achieve cooperation between the services had often been explored, they had scant success. In 1903, the Joint Board was formed, which, although a precedent, produced few results; even in the First World War, joint action was largely nonexistent. During the Great Depression, Congress looked at unification as a potential economizing move, but General Douglas MacArthur, then Army chief of staff, stated in 1932 that any such attempt would be fraught with potential disaster, and only enemies of the United States would welcome such an amalgamation.[78] Before 1939 all the service secretaries and service chiefs opposed any form of unification.

Nevertheless, the outbreak of World War II made it apparent that the "mutual cooperation" exercised by the Joint Board in the past was inadequate. Global war against powerful enemies necessitated unity. Moreover, on a more pragmatic note, American military leaders found themselves at a disadvantage when conferring with their British counterparts because they could not match the efficiency of the Imperial General Staff. As a consequence, the Joint Chiefs of Staff were formed in 1941, which allowed them to conduct business with their allies on a more equal footing. After March 1942, the Joint Chiefs were composed of Admiral William D. Leahy, chief of staff to the president and ranking member (although presiding officer, he had no command authority), General George C. Marshall, Army chief of staff, Admiral Ernest J. King, chief of naval operations, and General Henry H. Arnold, commanding general of the Army Air Forces. Although the AAF was still a part of the Army, Arnold was given a seat on the JCS so that he could treat with the Royal Air Force—which was an independent arm—on an equal basis. Even so, it was recognized that Arnold was subordinate to Marshall, and he never publicly disagreed with his chief throughout the war.[79]

One of the first problems addressed by the JCS concerned unified theater commands. The stakes were too high to allow admirals and generals to operate autonomously, as had been the case in the past. Unified commands were established that gave one man command of all land, sea, and air forces located in his theater of operations. Although the Pacific command structure tended to bend this rule somewhat, the Army looked upon unified commands as an important precedent.[80]

In early 1943, General Marshall directed General Brehon Somervell, commander of the Army Service Forces, to explore the requirements for demobilization. Somervell's planners quickly realized that any attempt to judge the size of a postwar army required knowledge of what character such an organization was to take. They recommended that a single department with a joint staff from all the services be established at the highest echelons in Washington, as well as in the theater commands overseas. Unification was deemed necessary because the former Joint Board system had not only been proven inadequate in wartime but, because of the growing complexity of modern war, was also inadequate in peace. War Department spokesmen claimed that the Navy's bureau system of organization was archaic; it perpetuated inefficiency and dissension. The tightly organized staff system of the Army was hailed as far more conducive to the needs of modern war. (Upon hearing this rationale, Navy Undersecretary James V. Forrestal commented sarcastically that until he could see the Army control the Corps of Engineers and General MacArthur, he would remain unimpressed.)[81] Somervell's planners also believed that unification would be more economical. Although precise figures were seldom given, it was often stated thereafter that substantial savings of money and materiel would be saved by unification. General Spaatz said in June 1946 that the defense budget could be cut by as much as one-third.[82]

In addition, the Joint Chiefs had worked well together during the conflict, but there was no legislative basis for their existence. General Arnold was particularly worried about this point because the War Powers Act and Executive Order 9082 stated that the JCS would automatically dissolve six months after the end of hostilities. The AAF might then lose the foot that had taken such time and labor to put in the independence door. It should also be pointed out that, although air leaders were firm advocates of unification, it was with the clear understanding that unification must include an independent Air Force.[83]

In November 1943, General Marshall approved Somervell's study and its recommendation for a unified defense establishment. This was the first time that he publicly backed unification. Admirals King and Leahy, however, disputed the Army's findings. Indeed, when Marshall suggested that the Joint Chiefs of Staff consider the matter of unification (Somervell's study was merely an internal Army project), the Navy refused even to agree to the proposal in principle. They feared that to charge planners with the task of studying postwar military requirements based on the premise of a unified defense establishment was stacking the deck. They were not convinced unification was desirable or necessary, even in theory, and they refused to agree. The Army, on the other hand, felt such guidance was necessary, or else the planners' task would be too vague. Deadlock resulted, and the JCS could only agree that the matter needed further study.[84]

The following year, partly under pressure from Congress, which was also exploring the issue of unification, the JCS formed a joint committee, headed by Admiral James O. Richardson, to examine the matter of a postwar defense department. The Richardson Committee, composed of two Army and two Navy members, submitted its report on April 11, 1945. The committee had interviewed fifty-six high-ranking combat officers, including MacArthur, Eisenhower, Nimitz, and Admiral William F. Halsey, all of whom supported the committee's majority conclusions favoring a single department of the armed forces.[85] Nevertheless, Admirals Leahy and King repudiated these findings and refused to endorse the recommendations. On October 17, 1945, the report and the separate Navy view on its conclusions were submitted to President Truman.

To lessen the impact of this study, Navy Secretary Forrestal asked an old friend and business associate, Ferdinand Eberstadt, to look into the subject. Eberstadt, whose staff was composed of young naval officers, not unpredictably reached conclusions that were quite different from those of the Richardson Committee. He opposed unification under one head and instead called for the JCS to continue as they had during the war. He proposed separate cabinet-level departments for sea, land, and air, a national security council, a central intelligence agency, and a national resources board. Specifically rejected were a single defense department, defense secretary, or military chief of staff. The Navy used these proposals as the basis for its unification position during the next two years. In the event, its vision of the future was more accurate than that of the War Department.[86]

While the JCS was wrestling with the unification question, Congress was also studying it. In late 1945 both the House and Senate held extensive hearings and called numerous witnesses from military and civilian life to testify. Almost without exception all Army witnesses favored unification, with the Army Air Forces becoming independent. It appeared that an independent Air Force was an idea whose acceptance was finally acknowledged by Army leaders. Air power had played a major role in the war, and Arnold had worn five stars while sitting on the Combined Chiefs of Staff. In addition, airmen like Joseph T. McNarney, Frank Andrews, and Lewis Brereton had commanded ground forces, and their loyalty and team spirit were appreciated. It is also possible that General Marshall, realizing the inevitability of a separate Air Force, supported the idea in the hope of maintaining a close working relationship with air leaders. Given the intractability of naval opposition, an ally was always welcome.[87]

On the other hand, Navy witnesses at the hearings opposed both unification and a separate air force. Those admirals who had earlier told the Richardson Committee that they favored such proposals now reversed themselves. Their reasons were disarmingly open: they feared losing influence in a unification scheme; they feared losing access to the president via a Navy secretary; they feared losing naval aviation to the Air Force; and they feared losing the Marine Corps to the Army. Admiral John Towers put the matter frankly in 1946: "I fear . . . that the Army Air Force advocates of a separate air force have well established in mind the plan, upon realization of a separate service, to absorb naval aviation. Approximately 40 percent of our post-war Navy is aviation. Its loss would be completely disastrous to the Navy."[88] Another admiral said simply that naval matters were "too damned complicated for any outsider to understand."[89]

The fact that the Navy was concentrating so heavily on air power is a fascinating study in pragmatism and flexibility. For decades the Navy had been dominated by the doctrine of Alfred Thayer Mahan and the battleship admirals who worshipped him. Most of the sea leaders of World War II were of this old guard.[90] Secretary Forrestal realized, however, that the days of battleship warfare were over, and that the Navy must concentrate on aircraft carriers that could be deployed worldwide. Naval planners called for a postwar budget that allotted 53 percent of the funds to naval air.[91]

It has been claimed that Forrestal's affection for aviation stemmed not from doctrinal motives regarding the superiority of carriers over battleships, but from practical economic considerations. The Navy had always based its budget projections, and therefore the size and composition of the fleet needed, on the strength of its most likely enemy. In 1945 it was clear that the only potential enemy was the Soviet Union, which had virtually no navy, so another system for determining force size must be found. Forrestal saw that naval aviation could perform far more missions than "control of the sea lanes." Diversification of the water role could be translated into more ships—aircraft carriers—more personnel, and more funds. The fundamental principle of traditional Mahanian doctrine—that ships fight ships—was being transformed. Navy leadership was not slow to appreciate the importance of atomic weapons, although they often claimed publicly to the contrary, and realized that future growth was largely dependent on acquiring a piece of the atomic pie. In 1947, the Navy began to design carriers that could launch aircraft large enough to haul the new weapon.[92]

In truth, the Navy had some justification for fearing that a nascent Air Force would have designs on its aircraft. During the House hearings of 1944, Assistant Secretary of War for Air Robert A. Lovett had testified that he envisioned a separate Air Force that would take over all of the Navy's land-based aviation, including that used for long-range reconnaissance, antisubmarine warfare, and the protection of shipping.[93] One of the more outspoken air power advocates, Lieutenant General Jimmy Doolittle, told Congress in 1945 that the battleship was obsolete and the aircraft carrier was becoming so: "The carrier has two attributes. One attribute is that it can move about; the other is that it can be sunk."[94] General Spaatz was equally indiscreet: "Why should we have a Navy at all? . . . There are no enemies for it to fight except apparently the Army Air Force. . . . The only reason for us to have a Navy is just because someone else has a Navy and we certainly do not need to waste money on that."[95] Perhaps the most tactless outburst was made by Brigadier General Frank Armstrong.

> You gentlemen had better understand that the Army Air Force is tired of being a subordinate outfit. It was a predominant force during the war, and it is going to be a predominant force during the peace, and you might as well make up your minds whether you like it or not, and we do not care whether you like it or not. The Army Air Force

is going to run the show. You, the Navy, are not going to have anything but a couple of carriers which are ineffective anyway, and they will probably be sunk in the first battle.[96]

The Marine Corps was as fearful about the designs of the Army and Air Force as were the naval aviators. Many, including Eisenhower, made no secret of their opinion that the Marines had grown too large and had become a "second army," complete with their own tanks, artillery, and air support. When it was noted that the Corps had the special mission of amphibious operations, soldiers retorted that Normandy was the greatest such exercise in history and no Marines had taken part. Once again Spaatz was blunt; there need only be enough Marines to guard ships, wave visitors through the gates of Navy shore installations, and protect American embassies in foreign countries.[97] General Arnold had accentuated these fears when he called for the "ruthless elimination of all arms, branches, services, weapons, equipment or ideas whose retention might be indicated only by tradition, sentiment or sheer inertia."[98] It is not difficult to recognize at whom his attack was directed.

The aim of Navy and Marine Corps leadership was to maintain their primacy as the first line of defense, using new weapons, but without the constraints of a unification scheme. With such luminaries as Admirals Leahy, King, Nimitz, and Halsey, as well as Navy Secretary Forrestal, testifying strongly in Congress against all unification proposals, matters were delayed for two years.[99] President Truman's patience wore thin; in early 1947 he directed the services to reach agreement, or he would reach it for them. Although President Roosevelt had never taken a public stance on unification, Truman had long held the belief that military reorganization was necessary: "One of the strongest convictions which I brought to the Presidency was that the antiquated defense setup had to be reorganized quickly as a step towards insuring our future safety and preserving world peace."[100] One observer wryly noted: "When Mr. Roosevelt, an ardent collector of ship models and Assistant Secretary of the Navy from 1913 to 1920, died and his place taken by Mr. Truman, the commander in 1918 of Battery D, the time had obviously come."[101]

In an effort to comply with the president's wishes and resolve differences, the Army appointed Major General Lauris Norstad to work with Vice Admiral Forrest Sherman to seek compromise. After many months of difficult work, an acceptable middle ground was discovered. On January 16, 1947, the two men wrote the president that they had "reached agreement on all aspects of the unification problem."[102] The breakthrough occurred when the Army agreed to Navy demands that there not be a single military department, but instead three equal cabinet level divisions for the Army, Navy, and Air Force. The Navy feared that a single service secretary would deny them ready access to the president and Congress, but the compromise solution removed this fear. In addition, the Army dropped demands for a chairman of the Joint Chiefs who would be the ranking military man and advisor to the president. To many, this proposal smacked of a "man on horseback."[103] (When passed, the National Security Act provided for a chief of staff to the president—the position held by Admiral Leahy—but he possessed little real power and was far removed from what the Army had desired.)

Congressional climate regarding the proposed legislation was favorable to the Navy. The chairman of the newly formed House Armed Services Committee was Carl Vinson, former chairman of the defunct Naval Affairs Committee. Vinson was a long-standing friend of the Navy and could be expected to protect its interests.[104] Perhaps realizing this, the Army—and especially members of the Army Air Forces—attempted to sway congressional opinion to their point of view. Extensive lobbying was done by the War Department, even to the extent of sending each congressman a copy of William Bradford Huie's book, *The Case Against the Admirals*, a blatant anti-Navy diatribe.[105]

Even aside from such machinations, the legislation might not have passed had it not been for Forrestal. Sensing that opposition to unification was no longer conducive to Navy interests, he threw his support behind the proposed bill. His action took the last ounce of steam out of the senior admirals still opposed to reorganization.[106]

Vandenberg's feelings about unification echoed those of his fellow airmen; to him it was a logical evolution. In December 1945, he stated that a unified command like that in Europe, coupled with a separate air arm, was essential to avoid the "bickering, compromise, delay and waste that comes from disunity at the top." He believed that unification was a "practical and economical way of safe-guarding the taxpayers' money." He did not think that either the Army or the Navy would "lose its identification." He stated on numerous occasions that the Air Force had no intention of absorbing naval aviation.[107] Realizing the necessity of making a strong alliance with the Army, Vandenberg wrote Norstad that the time was "peculiarly appropriate" to brief the new chief of staff (Eisenhower) on the goals of air leaders so that he would be on "our side."[108] Such precautions were probably unnecessary. Eisenhower was a staunch supporter of unification and air power, lending his considerable prestige to the issue early on.

Vandenberg played a more direct role after returning to uniform in May 1947 following his year at the CIG. As Spaatz's deputy, he worked closely with his Army counterpart, Lieutenant General J. Lawton Collins, to facilitate a smooth transfer to independence. The main issues to be settled concerned the service and supply personnel. The Air Force needed a large number of these people in order to function effectively, and the generals had to decide how many would be transferred to the Air Force. Vandenberg and Collins attempted to resolve all such difficulties rather than submit them to the Eisenhower/Spaatz level for decision. In this they were largely successful. Their relations were so effective and amiable that complete agreement was reached on over two hundred basic items in a matter of weeks. President Truman was greatly impressed and termed the relationship a "record of cooperation." It was one of the few times he could pay such a compliment.[109]

On July 26, 1947, the National Security Act became law. The act was a compromise and none of the services was completely happy; it provided for a federation, not a unification. There were to be three separate executive "departments"—Army, Navy, and Air Force—administered by a National Military "Establishment." The Secretary of Defense had an "office," but no staff to assist him. Moreover, the service secretaries were granted the express right to go over his head to the president if they so wished. General Eisenhower remarked that under such a setup the Defense secretary was "nothing more than a damned switchboard operator." The secretary did not "administer" the establishment, he "coordinated" it.[110] This distinction, administration versus coordination, was seen by the first Air Force secretary, Stuart Symington, as one of the National Security Act's greatest weaknesses. Symington was an old colleague of Forrestal, and the two argued a great deal over the new establishment and the defense secretary's role. Symington foresaw that a weak administrator was worse than none at all; Forrestal disagreed. After his years of experience with the Navy, Forrestal was conditioned to fear the specter of a powerful secretary. He would soon change his mind.[111]

President Truman offered the mantle of defense secretary to Robert Patterson of the War Department, but when he turned it down for personal reasons, the job was accepted by Forrestal.[112] The last safeguard to Navy interests thus seemed to click into place. Although strenuous efforts had prevented the complete merger preferred by the War Department, there was no cause for rejoicing among the admirals. Unification, however limited, had indeed taken place against naval opposition. Moreover, the vociferous and proselytizing Air Force had gained separate status, anathema to the seamen. Finally, and most important of all, the crucial issue of specific roles and missions assigned to each service was not spelled out in the National Security Act. The president intended to address that thorny problem in an executive order, reasoning that the commander in chief should make such decisions, not Congress: in that the legislative branch did not command military forces, it should not attempt to write specific functions into law. But an executive order can easily be changed by another executive order, and it was the question of roles and missions that would serve as the fuel for interservice rivalry in the following years.[113]

We do not want war any more than the
West does, but we are less interested in
peace than the West, and therein lies the
strength of our position.
                              Joseph Stalin

IV | First Challenges

If you aren't fired with enthusiasm, you'll
be fired with enthusiasm.
                              Vince Lombardi

THE MAN

One of the remarkable aspects of Hoyt Vandenberg in 1948 was the image
he presented to his contemporaries and the news media; almost without exception
they remarked on his youth, vigor, and good looks. One aide from the CIG recalled
that when Vandenberg walked past, the secretaries would "swoon." He once saw
Van at a Washington Senators baseball game with Lauris Norstad and Air Force
Secretary Stuart Symington: "You never saw such pulchritude! The women were
falling all over themselves trying to get a look at them."[1] Another aide recalled
that the Chief was so handsome and "debonair" that when he walked the halls
of the Pentagon, the secretaries would hurry out of their offices just to watch him
pass. Another said simply that he was the best-looking man in American public
life. Marilyn Monroe named him as one of the three men with whom she would
most like to be stranded on a desert island; the others were Joe Dimaggio and—
Albert Einstein.[2]

When the Air Force became independent, Vandenberg personally took a
major role in designing a uniform for the new service. He decided upon a blue
suit with silver buttons. Upon receiving the first models, Vandenberg and Norstad
visited the White House to sell the president. Truman was favorably impressed
and told the generals now to convince Congress. Vandenberg had an idea. Remembering an officer who had been in the Ninth Air Force and whose size and
build were similar to his own, Vandenberg called Colonel Richard Sims to his office. The confused and anxious Sims arrived to find the chief of staff looking at

the new uniforms. Vandenberg told him to put on the one with the eagle insignia. Vandenberg himself donned the garb of a sergeant. He then handed the befuddled colonel a copy of a speech he had written that was to be read to Congress. Sergeant Vandenberg then opened the door for the colonel and announced it was time to go. Walking one step behind and to the left and opening doors for his superior as he went, the sergeant escorted the colonel to the Senate Armed Services Committee. Sims read his prepared address that talked of the new uniform and took pains to point out that the new officer dress was nearly identical to that of the enlisted men. He then turned and announced that he wished to introduce the enlisted garb, presently being worn by Air Force Chief Hoyt S. Vandenberg. There was a stunned silence in the room and then pandemonium broke loose. The senators rose to their feet and began cheering. The new uniforms were approved and Vandenberg solidified his relations with Congress.[3]

When the uniform was issued to everyone, Vandenberg demanded that it be worn properly. One of his techniques was to stop an Air Force officer who was wearing his hat with the stiffening grommet removed (thus affecting a "50-mission crush" reminiscent of World War II), ask to see the hat, and then throw it in the trash. He reasoned that the news media tended to look down on the Air Force as consisting of immature "wild-blue-yonder boys." If the airmen wished to be treated like professionals, then they would have to look the part.[4] Vandenberg well understood the benefits of a supportive news media.

Vandenberg at forty-eight was six feet tall, weighed 165 pounds, and had a thirty-inch waist. He still played golf regularly and shot in the low eighties. Whenever an old friend was in town Van tried to break away for a round at "Burning Tree." He was good enough, and popular enough, to play in the National Celebrities Golf Tournament with Bob Hope, Bing Crosby, Ben Hogan, and Sam Sneed. When he drank liquor it was Scotch (Haig and Haig), martinis, or Mexican beer, though still not to excess. At home he preferred tea. He enjoyed fine clothes and was an excellent, though conservative dresser. On the links, however, he displayed a certain panache, wearing shorts and outlandish shirts—it was rumored that he bought them from the same tailor that served President Truman. He smoked continuously—Chesterfields, Cuban cigars, and a pipe—although he resolved to quit every January, and usually did for thirty days or so. As noted earlier, he also liked fancy cars, and drove a posh, custom-made Cadillac.

The general was a Bing Crosby fan and loved to dance, as did Glad. He loved to sing, but could not carry a tune in a bucket. He was still shy, especially with strangers, even though his ready smile made him seem approachable and friendly. As one friend remarked: "It is easy to get acquainted with Van, but hard to know him well. Most people never really figure him out." Vandenberg had many acquaintances but few close friends. He preferred to keep people at arms' length. Perhaps all the friends he had lost in peace and war, beginning with Jerry Rusk in 1923, had hardened him. He confided in no one but Glad. He was consistently described as shy, polite, and proper: "Can he help it if he is tall and handsome, polite as a small boy at his first party and looks like Joe College?"[5] In fact, his politeness could be a problem. Sandy remembered that while he was washing the car one day his father arrived home in a black mood and stormed into the house. Sandy looked to his dad's driver for an explanation. The story was told with a barely concealed grin. A young captain in the chief's office had asked for several autographed photos for friends and family. Van obliged. Later it was discovered that the young man was a homosexual and had indeed sent many photos to his friends. As FBI agents tracked down his illicit contacts they began discovering numerous photographs of the chief signed, "with my sincere best wishes."[6]

Van still considered himself a good pilot and insisted on flying; his personal aircraft was a converted B-17 that he flew himself, commenting: "Most of the strategic mistakes of the German Air Force were made by generals who no longer knew the air." During the war he was selected by a women's magazine as "Mr. America"; in 1948 Vandenberg crowned the Shenandoah Apple Blossom Festival Queen; he presented the Walter Camp Memorial Trophy for the Touchdown Club to Notre Dame All-American quarterback Johnny Lujack; and in December 1949 he appeared on the cover of *Life* magazine modeling sports clothes. Though such distinctions would seem incongruous for a general officer today, he was the perfect choice at that time: "At 49, he looked like a college senior playing the last act in 'Cavalcade.' His handsome face was unlined, his grey-blue eyes were sharp and piercing, and his hair was touched with proper streaks of distinguished grey at the temples."[7] Even General Omar Bradley, soon to be chairman of the Joint Chiefs of Staff, was impressed: "Van was as handsome as a movie star and cool as a cucumber."[8] Contemporary photographs bear out such descriptions.

When Vandenberg returned home from the war, Glad and the children were still living in the apartment on Cathedral Avenue. Van looked around and said they had been living there since he was a captain; now he was a lieutenant general and it was time to move on base at Bolling Field. Sandy objected. He did not want to spend his senior year at Anacostia High School. Dad said no problem, he would take care of that; he would have someone pick Sandy up every morning and take him to school, then bring him home every afternoon. Sandy liked that idea, although he later would trade the staff car for a jeep. His friends at school were much impressed. When chosen as vice chief, the family moved again, to quarters at Fort Myer.[9]

The Vandenbergs seldom went to the theater on post because it had a special row reserved for them. This was so embarrassing to the general he refused to go. Instead, the latest movies were borrowed and shown at home. He liked stories where strong-willed men overcame strong-willed women. He did not like sad movies, and whenever a film started to become melancholy, he would leave the room and pick up a book. His favorites were westerns, which he read by the bagful, but also science fiction and Dick Tracy. He also enjoyed crossword puzzles—he and Glad would race to see who finished first. After the war he temporarily became a photography buff. Poker and gin rummy were still his favorite card games.

It was somewhat difficult for Glad and Van to readjust to each other in 1945. While he had been in Europe becoming a hero, she had been plodding along, keeping her family together, raising two teenagers and running the household.

Glad had become used to being independent and there was some tension when Van returned home in glory. Theirs was certainly not an uncommon problem; tens of thousands of other couples experienced similar troubles. Van and Glad worked through them the way they had their previous problems—long talks and love. Nonetheless, Glad was not quite the same thereafter. She too had matured greatly during the war and had become her own woman. Like her husband, she did not suffer fools gladly and once even asked one of Van's aides to deliver an order to the officers' wives concerning a project she had in mind. The aide was taken aback, saying that he could not. "Van has charge of the men, why don't I have charge of the women? He issues orders to the men; why can't I issue orders to the women?"[10] She was a formidable woman, but Van remained devoted to her, deferring to her judgment, heeding her advice, and showering her with affection. When Glad fell and broke her arm in 1950, Van bought her a mink coat, prompting the remark: "I can't wait till I break a leg!"[11]

Vandenberg still remained surprisingly free of vices. The pressures and temptations that so often inflict men of his position and power were absent. A flaw in this image was his opinion of blacks. During the war he had been negatively impressed by the performance of the all-black 322nd Fighter Group. In a memorandum to General Arnold in October 1945, Vandenberg maintained that it had been more difficult to train Negroes owing to their "lower than average intelligence." Moreover, after being activated for combat, the group had scored only one-third as many aerial victories as the remaining three fighter groups (all-white) in the parent wing. He concluded heavily:

> Due to lower average intelligence, the demonstrated lack of leadership, general poor health, and extremely high elimination rate in training, it is far more expensive to train Negro officer personnel than white. Also statistics indicate that the end product obtained in Negro training is much less efficient than that obtained in white. . . . [therefore] further training of Negro personnel cannot be economically justified.[12]

A colleague from the war years also relates the rather astounding story that Vandenberg so believed in the inherent inferiority of blacks as combat pilots that he went for an afternoon drive in Washington, D.C., to prove his point. Vandenberg drove about until he spotted a black behind the wheel of an automobile; he would then head straight at him. Inevitably the black would give way first—no aggressiveness or determination—QED.[13] This tale, though perhaps apocryphal, is not totally at variance with Vandenberg's written remarks to Arnold. It was not that he was overtly or viciously racist, but rather that he sincerely believed the black was deficient as a combat officer. It is important to note that this prejudice was shared by most high-ranking officers in the services at that time.[14] It is therefore characteristic and to his credit that when President Truman in 1948 directed the services to integrate, Vandenberg complied unreservedly. Once again realizing that there were areas in which he was inexpert or uninformed, he chose a man, Lieutenant General Idwal D. Edwards, who wholeheartedly and enthusiastically supported the president's policy. Though there was resistance to change by some, Vandenberg made it clear to all his commanders that anything less than full cooperation and compliance were unacceptable. This directive was so unequivocal that the Air Force achieved total integration in 1949—the first service to do so.[15]

At home, Vandenberg had changed little. He still had an aversion for household chores, though his rank now gave him an excuse to avoid such things more honorably. Van had a sweet tooth, and would often bake a cherry pie in the evenings, which he was occasionally known to share with his family. He enjoyed arguing with his children at the dinner table and would often deliberately provoke them to express their thoughts and feelings, training them to think logically and systematically. Father had other peculiar ways of making people think.

Sandy had a problem late one night that he simply had to discuss with his dad. Waking him up, Sandy said he needed to talk. Dad asked: "Now?" Yes, it was important. Both men trundled down the hall in their pajamas to Sandy's room and sat cross-legged on the bed facing each other. Sandy had fallen into something less than love with a neighbor girl who came from an extremely wealthy family. She was beginning to talk of marriage. Although he did not feel a similar emotion, the monetary aspects appeared promising. He asked: "Dad, can a guy marry just for money?" Father stared at him thoughtfully and said, "Sure." Sandy, taken aback, queried: "He can?!" Father unblinkingly responded again: "Sure. Any other questions, son?" Crushed, Sandy muttered he thought not. "OK. Good night, son." Having expected a long-winded philosophical discourse on love and marriage and receiving a shock instead, Sandy sat there for the rest of the night thinking things out for himself. He decided against matrimony.[16]

Van hated cats but loved dogs. During the war he had been given a handsome, buff-colored bulldog puppy by Prime Minister Churchill, appropriately named "Winston of Alderhouse." Nicknamed "Alfie," the pup would often fly with Van or ride with him in the front seat of his jeep. He had free run of Ninth headquarters and was often seen chewing on furniture legs. Unfortunately, the mutt had been so spoiled overseas that he returned to America with no manners whatsoever. Glad threw him out.[17]

As a father Van seemed closer to Gloria than to his son. When Sandy graduated from high school, his parents had already made plans for the evening and did not attend the ceremony; Gloria went instead. The young man was deeply hurt by this rejection, but it appears that his father realized his error and tried to make amends thereafter.

Even though Van had not been happy at West Point, it was still his strong desire that Sandy go there as well. During the war he wrote his son, chiding him for his poor performance in school, noting that he too had been a lazy student, but it was a fault that had to be overcome. He would correct Sandy's letters for punctuation and spelling, which Van thought were "stinko," and warned that Sandy would have to shape up if he wanted an appointment to the Academy. Sandy did improve and did enter West Point in 1947, but he was unhappy. One day he called his father and told him he wanted to resign. Van told him to hang on, he would fly up there shortly. Wearing civilian clothes and notifying only the Academy superintendent that he was on post, Van met Sandy at the cadet library to talk. Everything was wrong—the plebe system, the Mickey Mouse discipline, the academics—everything. He just wanted to quit and come home. Dad listened quietly and said: "O.K., go pack your suitcase and fly back with me." Sandy was startled: "Well, dad, I'll have to out-process. It will probably take a couple of weeks."

"No problem, I'll take care of all that, just go grab your toothbrush."

"Well, now, wait a second, dad. I have to see some of my buddies, and—well, get ready."

"Oh, well, Sandy, let me know when you're ready, in a few weeks or so, and I'll come back and get you."[18]

Sandy, of course, did not resign, even enjoyed the Academy, and did well—far better than his father had many years before. On one occasion, however, the cadet was having difficulty with calculus and feared he would have to forego Christmas vacation so he could study. Upon hearing this the chief offered to fly up to West Point, move in with his son, and help him with his calculus. Based on the elder Vandenberg's cadet academic record, one wonders what possible help he could have provided. But it was a nice thought. Over Christmas leave another year, Sandy and a classmate, Myron Slatter, were visiting in Washington, and when it was time to leave, Sandy announced he would have to get going: it was a long train ride back to the Point. "No problem, son, I'll fly you both back. We'll land at Stewart Field, only take us an hour." The two cadets settled back and relaxed. A few hours later the three men headed out to Andrews where the chief's B-17 and its crew were waiting for them. En route the weather became extremely rough; Myron became violently airsick. Struggling forward to the cockpit, Sandy saw his father behind the yoke, arms outstretched, body taut, his brow heavy with perspiration; the aircraft pitched about as lightning flashed and hail beat against the windscreen. "No problem, son, just a little weather; we'll be through it soon." After what seemed an interminable period the aircraft landed, and there was a staff car waiting for the still-shaking cadets. Father said: "Good-bye, good luck, this car will take you back to West Point." Back to West Point?! Unfortunately, Stewart Field was socked in; they were forced to land at Mitchel Field at the southern tip of Long Island. It was about a three-hour drive up to West Point. Sandy and Myron were of course late, were written up, and had to serve punishments. Van wrote his parents breezily that poor Sandy had gotten into trouble again. Can't budget his time. Was late getting back to school after Christmas leave. Gonna have to learn. When appearing before the Battalion Disciplinary Board to receive his "award," Sandy was subjected to a long harangue by an infantry major who admonished him sternly: "Based on my experience in World War II, one should never rely on Air Force aircraft; they are *never* on time!"[19]

In the summer of 1949 when the chief decided to visit Europe to relive memories and renew acquaintances from his war years, he asked his son to go along. While staying in London's Columbia Hotel, Sandy amused himself by making water bombs, which he dropped on unsuspecting passersby from his seventh-floor window. His father saw him and asked sternly what he was up to. Upon hearing, a slow smile broke across the chief's face, and he asked if he might have a go.

It was great fun. Later, the travelers arrived in Paris and one evening the old comrades were having a particularly good time in the bar, so Sandy went to bed. Well after midnight, he was roused by the chief, looking for more francs; it was his round and he was broke. It was noted that the old man's voice was a bit huskier and his moves somewhat more deliberate than normal.[20]

In 1951, Sandy graduated from West Point and reminded his father that a new car had been promised in reward for the momentous event. The two men flew to Detroit, bought a new Oldsmobile, and then drove it back to Washington. For fifteen hours father and son were alone together to talk. It was an experience to be cherished. Only a year later Lieutenant Vandenberg's new auto was struck head-on by a drunk driver, and Sandy spent eleven months in bed. The chief had his son moved to Walter Reed Hospital in Washington, where he visited him three times a week. They would talk and play checkers; a flask was usually smuggled in, and the two would get "jolly."[21] It is an old proverb: when your son grows up, treat him like your brother.

THE CHIEF

After forty years, the Air Force was independent; General Carl Spaatz was the first chief of staff and Vandenberg his vice chief. But Spaatz was tired, and with the great battles of the war and unification now behind, the mundane rebuilding of the Air Force was too much effort. During his last months in uniform, matters seemed to drift. It was time to go, but who would be the successor? Joseph McNarney, George Marshall's deputy during the war and then Eisenhower's successor as commander of the ETO, was still the ranking general. His prestigious position and reputation within the Army was, however, a two-edged sword—he had been away from his service for too long. There were rumors that Arnold did not like McNarney, thinking him insufficiently air-minded. After the war, Arnold did not want McNarney on his staff, and so McNarney served as the occupation commander in Germany and then a United Nations advisor.[22] George Kenney also had seniority, but he too was suspect. In fact, both McNarney and Kenney outranked Spaatz and far outranked Van, but Vandenberg was to be chosen. Why?

Lauris Norstad maintained that it was owing to his close relationship with Spaatz that went back a dozen years; Van was known and trusted. Laurence Kuter thought there was no clear front-runner, but Van seemed the reasonable and natural choice. Robert Lee believed that younger men were needed. The Air Force was new; it needed new ideas and new leaders. Laurence Craigie said it was simply a question of ability; his old friend had excelled in every job given to him.[23] There is no question Vandenberg wanted the position. One associate commented that he had been "running for chief since the war ended."[24] It will be remembered that his predecessor at the CIG also noted that desire. Vandenberg himself told an associate that as a student at the Army War College he had heard several high-ranking generals speak and realized he was as competent as they; he too could become a general, and was spurred to achieve that ambition.[25]

There were, however, rumors concerning Vandenberg's selection, and the most prevalent dealt with the role of his Uncle Arthur, who had become a powerful force in American politics. Neither the senator nor the general trumpeted their relationship publicly because they realized that too close an association was inadvisable. In a letter to columnist Walter Lippmann, Arthur explained:

> I could very easily embarrass my distinguished nephew in *his* work—just as he could easily embarrass me in mine—if we did not both scrupulously avoid a "family pipeline." As result, we have also rather amazingly avoided *any* public criticisms about "too many Vandenbergs" in high place. Such criticism—warped by unfriendly motives—could easily impair the efficiency of both of us.[26]

Even so, the two men were very close. Hoyt and his family often visited "Unk" at the Wardman Park Hotel in Washington, using the underground entrance to avoid notice. Usually Glad and the children would remain in the front room while the men went to the kitchen "to discuss politics." The subject of these conversations can only be guessed, but foreign policy was certainly an issue. Senator Vandenberg later said that it was the arguments of his nephew that finally coaxed him from his isolationist shell into supporting the United Nations and North Atlantic Treaty Organization.[27] It also seems apparent that Arthur was very fond of his nephew and treated him like a surrogate son, perhaps because of his disappointment over his own son. He wanted Hoyt to succeed and was justifiably proud when he did.[28]

The question of the senator's influence on the general's career is a difficult one, and much must be inferred. Certainly, Arthur's political connections had obtained Hoyt an appointment to West Point in 1919, giving an advantageous start to his military career, but for the following decade there was little contact between the two men. Arthur entered the Senate in 1928, but bearing in mind that he was a conservative Republican and an isolationist, it can hardly be claimed that he helped his nephew during the 1930s. In fact, the reverse may have been the case, and Arthur hoped that he was not a hindrance to Hoyt's military career. (As mentioned previously, there were some who thought that Hoyt had been passed over for promotion to brigadier general in 1942 because of his name.) During the war it is clear that the younger Vandenberg rose on his own merit—Generals Marshall, Eisenhower, Arnold, and Spaatz pushed for his advancement, not politicians. The crucial period thus becomes the three years following the war.

Arthur Vandenberg was one of the main architects of the bipartisan foreign policy, which ensured President Truman of Republican support in his diplomatic efforts. From his position on the Senate Foreign Relations Committee, Vandenberg was frequently touted as presidential timber for 1948. Consequently, skeptics opined that a deal of some sort had been struck between the White House and the Vandenbergs: Arthur traded his support in foreign policy for his nephew's career. Air Force Secretary Stuart Symington rejects this as slander; President Truman and the Vandenbergs were not made of such stuff, and vigorously maintains that Hoyt Vandenberg was selected for chief of staff because he was the best man available. Symington relates that Spaatz came to his office and announced that he was planning to retire and it was time to choose a replacement; he had two men in mind, McNarney and Vandenberg. Symington, replying that such operational matters were out of his line, suggested they talk to General Eisenhower, Army chief of staff. When asked his opinion, Eisenhower responded that the "combat man" (Vandenberg) should get the job.[29] Spaatz said later that he chose Vandenberg because he trusted him and because his broad experience gave him the best overall understanding of the Air Force and its mission.[30] This is cogent logic. Vandenberg had served in numerous positions on the Air Staff before, during, and after the war; he had held various responsibilities in several combat commands; and he had been War Department G-2 and then DCI. These experiences, plus his political acumen and diplomatic skills, gave Vandenberg a breadth of knowledge unsurpassed by any other airman. To believe a conscious plan existed to maneuver Hoyt Vandenberg into the position of chief with the connivance of his uncle suggests that he did not deserve the post and that someone better qualified was deliberately bypassed. This in turn would lead to the conclusion that Spaatz, Eisenhower, Leahy, Symington, Forrestal, and Truman—the men responsible for deciding the matter—were all more concerned with politics than with the nation's best interests. That idea is not credible.

Although there was unquestionably a certain amount of prestige involved in being the nephew of a senator—one photograph shows Lieutenant Vandenberg in Hawaii with his uncle and a two-star admiral; when the senator visited he had to be entertained, and his nephew as well—it is perhaps fair to conclude that the senator had a neutral, or perhaps even negative impact, on his nephew's career until 1945. By then, Hoyt's reputation was so well established he needed no assistance, but the political connection with Arthur may then have had an unconscious or subliminal influence on the Army and AAF hierarchy, which recognized that such an affiliation could be an asset to the Air Force. Even so, such arguments would have more weight either if Arthur had been a Democrat. Indeed, Arthur had alienated the Thomas Dewey supporters within the GOP by making it apparent that he favored an Eisenhower candidacy.[31] But Dewey was the Republican nominee in 1948, and if Dewey had a favorite airman, it was General George Kenney.

There were some in uniform who expressed concern over Vandenberg's appointment. First, his youth troubled some of the older men. Lieutenant General Ennis Whitehead, commander of the Far East Air Forces, wrote his old friend George Kenney relating the discontent over how senior officers were being treated: "The Air Corps and the spirit thereof which we knew and worked for for years is no longer in existence. . . . I mean the fact that the effect of the present handling of Senior officers and constant maneuvering to get them out of the way has resulted in a spirit that penetrates down through all ranks of officers."[32] Realizing this, Vandenberg consciously tried to treat the Old Guard with deference. For example, to fill the position of vice chief of staff he chose Muir "Santy" Fairchild, commander of the Air University, who was five years his senior and a member of the Old Guard. Fairchild was jumped from two stars to four and brought to Washington. As usual, Vandenberg's conciliatory personality had positive results. General Kenney, disappointed that he had been rejected for the position of chief, wrote Vandenberg that he had expected the job himself, but knew the Air Force was in good hands: "After all, that is what both of us are really concerned over." Kenney then assured him of "personal loyalty and utmost cooperation for the hard work that seems to be facing us."[33]

Second, Vandenberg was viewed by some as too mild and agreeable; it was feared the Navy and Army would be able to manipulate the new Air Force. General LeMay, for example, thought the new chief "lacked personal force" and would fall easy prey to the admirals.[34] Events would prove, however, that although pleasant and friendly most of the time, Vandenberg was also an "icy sonovabitch to whom friendship meant nothing when the chips are down." It was noted that when discussing serious matters he had a smile of steel; when you saw it, you knew the hatchet was about to fall. Nevertheless, on several occasions in the years ahead he would be required to relieve commanders—old friends—who were not measuring up, and that was difficult. General Norstad recalled that one man in particular who had to go was too close; Van simply could not tell him personally, so he asked Norstad to break the news in his stead. Although a weakness for a man in his position, it also demonstrates Vandenberg's compassion, but more importantly, reveals a strength. The man was relieved; the alternative, too often taken by lesser leaders, would have been to work around the individual, provide an alternative power source, cover for him. Because Vandenberg knew such actions were counterproductive, he took steps to ensure the right thing was done, even on those few occasions when he was unable to do it himself.[35]

Other critics claimed the new chief was a "lightweight" and pointed to his behavior at press conferences and congressional hearings, when he would often sit "dreamlike, chewing absently on a cigar, until someone asks him a question." One colonel recalled being summoned to brief the joint chiefs on a certain issue. He noted that Bradley, Collins, and Admiral Denfeld were sitting at the table erect, attentive, and bemedaled, while Vandenberg was leaning back, coat off, legs stretched out straight in front of him, staring at the ceiling. The colonel thought his behavior rude and complacent. Apparently, the other chiefs were used to it.[36] Major General Donald Wilson believed that Vandenberg was not a "top-notch efficient officer." He was likeable and had a pleasing personality, but "he didn't begin to measure up to the bright boys."[37] This "intellectual lightweight" charge has been refuted by those who worked most closely with him. General Norstad and others have said that, although not a "philosophizer," he was an extremely intelligent man who would concentrate intensely on problems until he devised a solution. He had a great deal of very uncommon common sense. He was consistent, logical, had an unusual ability to go to the heart of a problem, and was extremely persuasive in discussion.[38]

His Army and Navy colleagues found him a formidable adversary, but they also thought him professional and dignified. He did not become vindictive or petty; Vandenberg remained above the name calling and mudslinging rife among the services. Spaatz later said that this was one of his greatest strengths; he refused to become emotionally involved in key issues, and he did not make enemies. Members of the news media noticed this trait quickly, commenting that whereas Arnold and Spaatz had approached the fourth estate with an air of belligerency, Vandenberg was always smooth and friendly. Walter Cronkite later commented that, "of all the generals, Hoyt Vandenberg certainly was among the warmest in his relations with the press. He would brief one or a dozen of us, and I always felt we got the straight scoop from him."[39]

Vandenberg had remarkable self-control and seldom lost his temper. When angry, he did not raise his voice, but merely grew more quiet, and his jaws tightened. When contemporaries were asked if they had ever seen Vandenberg angry or lose his temper, all save one said no. General Robert Lee was the dissenter. He remembered accompanying the chief to a series of meetings in the Pentagon. Unfortunately, there was a scheduling conflict; Van was expected in a JCS meeting at the same time he was to meet with Defense Secretary Lovett. Van told Lee to attend the JCS meeting in his stead. Lee said he could not; he had another briefing that required his presence. Vandenberg stopped dead in his tracks, wheeled on Lee and said in a voice barely above a whisper: "Bob, why can't you get yourself organized!" then stalked off.[40]

Finally, there were those who worried about his possible preference for tactical air power. In fact, Vandenberg's five-year tenure as chief saw bombardment, in the form of SAC, become the dominant military force in the nation. Some would even claim that he favored bombers too much, that close air support dangerously atrophied during his tour. This was to become a controversial issue in 1949, and the Korean War would show whether or not such a charge was accurate.[41]

When it was announced that Vandenberg was to be the new chief of staff, there were dozens of congratulatory letters that flowed into his office, but none was more warm and welcome than that from General Hap Arnold.

> We have seen you handle responsibility, and know your ability "to get the job done." . . . From my experience I believe you will come to know that the challenge of your position is too big to permit you to have "goals," as such: You will find you are able to have new vistas, only—from different viewpoints; new horizons, from different directions; for the inherent challenge of Air Power is as limitless as man's imagination itself. So don't let the few snags you may run into from time to time discourage you, nor lessen your enthusiasm.[42]

Two months later the new chief encountered his first "snag."

BERLIN

America found itself in a major cold war crisis in 1948 over Berlin, where tensions with the Soviets had been increasing for some time. The American military governor in Germany was General Lucius D. Clay, a stately and distinguished southern gentleman who was the son of a Georgia senator and direct descendant of the famous orator. On March 5, 1948, he sent a startling cable to Washington stating that he had felt previously that war with the Soviets was unlikely for "at least ten years," but had changed his mind because of various intangible impressions and now believed that war could come with "dramatic suddenness."[43] At the same time, Admiral Leahy noted in his diary that unconfirmed reports indicated that the Soviet Union was making preparations for a move into

Europe within three months.[44] The Czechoslovakian coup had occurred the previous month, and the tension was palpable. Although the CIA reported that war was "unlikely in the next sixty days," the Air Force refused to concur in the estimate, murmuring that the situation was not stable. The CIA did, however, predict the Soviets might blockade Berlin in an attempt to isolate the Allied forces there.[45]

These fears gained credence when the Soviets began tightening the screws on West Berlin. There had never been a written guarantee of surface access to Berlin from the Allied occupation zone in West Germany, and on March 30 the Soviets used this oversight to impose severe restrictions on all rail and road traffic into the city. General Clay reacted aggressively, informing Washington that he would not allow interference with Allied rail lines, and had instructed his guards to "open fire if Soviet soldiers attempt to enter our trains."[46] General Bradley later remarked dryly that if he had had any hair on his head that cable would have made it stand on end.[47] Secretary of the Army Kenneth Royall quickly wired Clay *not* to fire unless fired upon. Clay did send a train into the Eastern zone to test the response, but the Soviets merely pulled a switch and shunted the train onto a siding, where it remained for several days until Clay had it "ignominiously withdrawn."[48]

The Soviets were concerned about Allied plans to constitute a West German government, and also the Allied refusal to evacuate the divided city—perhaps they believed that pressure would hasten a withdrawal. On June 19, the Soviets cut off all passenger trains and road traffic to Berlin and limited freight trains to one per day. Two days later all rail and barge traffic was stopped. The American response was confused and tentative. President Truman failed to convene the National Security Council, the apparatus recently created for just such a crisis. The Joint Chiefs were similarly not consulted or adequately informed about the situation, a circumstance Bradley and Admiral Leahy much resented. Instead, the president told his close advisors, Secretaries Forrestal, Lovett, and Royall, that the United States would not evacuate Berlin, period. It was not until July 22 that the National Security Council was convened, but by then tentative decisions had already been made.[49]

In order to demonstrate American resolve, General Clay requested on June 27 that a group of B-29s be sent to Europe. Vandenberg supported such a move because he had been trying to shift additional SAC units into Europe for some time, and the blockade offered him the opportunity.[50] Vandenberg turned to his war comrade Lord Tedder, then chief of the RAF, and asked him if it would be possible to deploy B-29s to England. Tedder was agreeable, but stressed that he would have to consult his government. Approval was obtained from Prime Minister Clement Attlee and his Cabinet, and the B-29s were sent. Apparently there was little officially committed to paper on this arrangement. The foreign secretary, Ernest Bevin, wanted it that way, stating that there would be no formal agreements; rather, that "long-standing arrangements for visits of goodwill and training purposes" would be the rubric under which the bombers would be accepted.[51] Writing in *Newsweek*, recently retired General Spaatz emphasized the significance of this event and described the potency of the ninety heavy bombers sent to England as "comparable to a fleet of 79,200 fully loaded B-17s carrying TNT . . . and these demonstrations have not been lost on the rest of the world, including Soviet Russia."[52] Most observers accepted this judgment at face value, but it now appears that the B-29s may have been less of a threat than originally thought.

The 58th Bomb Wing at Roswell Field still had only one atomic-capable group at that time, the 509th. Because of the unusual size, shape, and arming procedures of the atomic weapons, only specially modified aircraft (SADDLETREE) could carry them. These modifications were extensive and expensive, but also essential because unmodified aircraft could not drop an atomic device. The only SADDLETREE planes were the dozen or so in in the 509th, and it did not deploy to England. General Curtis LeMay, commander of United States Air Forces Europe (USAFE), stated bluntly that the B-29s sent to England "weren't too much good"; not only did they not have an atomic capability, "they didn't have the capability of much of anything."[53] The B-29 crewmen were told they were on "normal training missions," although the rumor was widespread that they were going to be used for hauling coal.[54] It is apparent now that the initial groups of B-29s sent to Britain were not atomic capable. It was not until the following July that the first squadron from the 509th was deployed. Therefore, if the B-29 move of July 1948 was sabrerattling, it was also a bluff.[55]

Although the planes capable of delivering atomic weapons were not deployed, were the devices? Bomb assembly facilities had already been built in England, but the atomic cores were not under military control. As a result of the Berlin crisis, Vandenberg and the Joint Chiefs pushed for a transfer of custody from the AEC to the military. They argued that the delay involved in a transfer of weapons during an emergency would be prohibitively long and would endanger national security. All the service secretaries supported this opinion, as did Forrestal. On July 21, the secretary of defense and David Lilienthal, chairman of the AEC, met with President Truman. Lilienthal argued passionately against the transfer proposal, maintaining it would jeopardize civilian control over the military. After listening to the opposing arguments, Truman said he would think the matter over. Later, he informed Forrestal that the bombs would not be transferred; he did not want some "dashing lieutenant colonel" starting World War III.[56] The Atomic Energy Commission retained custody. It was not until the Korean War that Vandenberg persuaded President Truman to transfer custody to the Air Force. Nevertheless, two highly placed officials who should know the facts of the incident told me confidentially, but in emphatic terms, that the devices were indeed shipped to England: "We were not of a mind to bluff." Whatever the truth, most laymen thought the atomic strike force had been positioned for action; more informed observers, including the Soviets, were probably uncertain. In any event, if the B-29 deployment was an attempt to force the Soviets into blinking first, it failed; the blockade was not lifted.[57]

As a temporary expedient, General Clay had requested an airlift to supply needed items, and LeMay concurred. General Curtis E. LeMay was perhaps the top combat air commander of the Second World War. Gruff, cigar-smoking, and blunt, he spoke his mind and worried little about his popularity: "I don't mind being called tough because I find that in this business it's the tough guys who lead the survivors."[58] When asked by Clay if he could deliver coal to Berlin,

LeMay answered that he could deliver anything. Brigadier General Joseph Smith was placed in charge of the airlift and told to assume that it would last two or three weeks—negotiations would surely break the impasse quickly.[59]

LeMay was opposed to an extended airlift and so advised Washington. The transport aircraft under his command were intended for war mobilization and evacuation in the event of an emergency, not for hauling food and coal.[60] Vandenberg agreed, and on June 30 impressed upon his JCS colleagues the drawbacks of such an operation. The number of aircraft necessary (primarily four-engine C-54s) for an effective airlift would cut Air Force capability by over one-half. It would be impossible to carry out the emergency war plan and conduct an airlift simultaneously. Moreover, the airfields housing the air fleet would be highly vulnerable to Soviet attack, and in a few minutes over 80 percent of the Air Force heavy transport capability could be lost. The Joint Chiefs concurred: "Continued air supply for Berlin as a long-term operation is not feasible. Hence, unless ground routes are established, our position in Berlin will eventually become untenable." The JCS did not, however, advocate an armed convoy—although they directed General Clay to draw up plans for one. They realized that such a step was "fraught with the gravest military implications including the risk of war." Their proposed solution was ambivalent—negotiate a settlement. Vandenberg and the Joint Chiefs wanted neither an airlift nor an armed convoy.[61]

By the end of July, negotiations had clearly failed and President Truman called a meeting of the National Security Council to discuss options; General Clay was summoned from Germany. At the crucial meeting of July 22, 1948, the alternatives of an airlift versus an armed convoy were argued. Clay, who had originally pushed strongly for a show of force, now changed his mind; the realities of the situation were compelling: the Soviets outnumbered the Allies by a margin of twenty-four divisions to two. Moreover, although lauding the staunchness of the British, he totally distrusted the resolve of the French. Vandenberg no doubt shared such sentiments, knowing that the French Air Force had been heavily infiltrated by Communists.[62] Clay did not wish to bluff. Vandenberg, still opposed to a major airlift, reiterated his concern regarding the impact such a massive operation would have on the rest of his commitments and the possibility of losing his fleet in a Soviet attack. The Joint Chiefs agreed. President Truman asked Vandenberg if he preferred to risk an armed convoy. No, but his command's capability would be severely crippled by an airlift. The president pointed out that a war would also severely cripple his command's capability. Seeing that he was losing ground, Vandenberg then countered that the single airfield in Berlin was not adequate to handle the scale of activity envisioned. General Clay interjected that a new runway, Tegel, was already under construction. Vandenberg admitted defeat. The airlift was on.[63]

Once the decision was made, Vandenberg gave it his full support. Within a week, he despatched Major General William H. Tunner to take charge of Operation "Vittles." "Willie the Whip" had been commander of the Hump operation over the Himalayas during World War II and was by common assent the world's expert on mass airlift. The decision to send Tunner to Germany was a wise one;

however, precisely whose idea it was to put him in charge is murky. Major General Laurence Kuter was the commander of the newly formed Military Air Transport Service (MATS) and later recalled approaching Vandenberg to suggest that MATS run the airlift and that his deputy, Tunner, be put in charge. Tunner, on the other hand, maintained that he suggested it to Kuter; but his commander was noncommittal; so he went to Vandenberg. The chief was reticent until General Albert C. Wedemeyer, a member of the General Staff who had just returned from Berlin, finally convinced him that the airlift would be extremely complicated and that Tunner should be put in charge. Wedemeyer, who had been Tunner's superior during the Hump airlift, related that "Ton-Mile" had performed "unbelievable feats" during the war and was ideal for the task. Vandenberg was cool to these suggestions, believing that Smith was a good man and perfectly capable of running the operation. He soon changed his mind, decided on Tunner, and the results were outstanding. Although he had enormous respect for Smith, who had been his roommate at West Point, the chief realized that an airlift of this magnitude required special expertise. General Smith was hurt and disappointed, feeling certain the task was within his capability, but he did not question his old friend.[64] Tunner flew to Wiesbaden, and noted the chilly atmosphere on arrival:

> We went to Germany and reported in to LeMay. He wasn't very pleasant, he was very cold. He said, "Well, you'd better get started." So I said, "Tell Smith I'm here and taking over." He said, "Goodbye." I said, "Goodbye," and that's about all the conversation we ever had.[65]

Tunner was impressed by the spirit and desire of the "Vittles" aircrews, but what he saw also seemed inefficient and dangerous. He moved quickly to introduce procedures that would eventually become standard in all airlift operations and were already employed by most airlines. Flight plans, weather briefings, aircraft servicing, and unloading were all prepared in advance by ground crews. Each pilot was no longer required to check in at several different offices while on the ground in Berlin, the offices came to the aircraft; even coffee and doughnuts greeted the arriving crews. More radio marker beacons were installed to help pilots keep track of their exact position, radio transmissions were simplified, and air traffic control was systematized with aircraft landing around the clock at three-minute intervals. If for any reason an inbound airplane went "missed approach" and was unable to land, it was sent back to its takeoff base. In the past, overworked controllers had placed such airplanes in holding patterns over Berlin, thus further congesting the airways. In marginal weather—the rule rather than the exception—such practices invited calamities.[66]

Under Tunner's guidance the airlift soon became a marvel of efficiency and reliability as tonnage and sortie rates climbed markedly. Eventually a fleet of three hundred American and British cargo planes were delivering over 5,600 tons of supplies daily—far more than Clay had requested or even thought possible.[67] When Vandenberg visited Berlin in August, he was visibly impressed. Characteristically, he worried about his crews and realized that their morale was the real key to a successful airlift. Upon hearing the men had not been receiving their mail, he "raised hell" and said it would be corrected. The men had to know some-one cared about their efforts. They also had to be assured that their families back home were secure—many had left for Germany with virtually no advanced notice. Vandenberg instructed his commanders throughout the Air Force to pay particular attention to the needs and welfare of the airlifters' dependents—some still stranded in foreign countries. He initiated Project Sleighbells to deliver Christmas presents and letters back and forth.[68] Such attentions were perhaps just as important to increased productivity as the efficiency measures invoked by Tunner. As morale and tonnage figures continued to soar, the crews became increasingly enthusiastic. Many aircraft would rig small, handmade parachutes to which were attached bundles of candy. On takeoff from Berlin the "Bon-Bon Bombers" would jettison their cargoes to waiting crowds of children.[69]

One aspect worrying Vandenberg was the pressure the Airlift was placing on Air Force capabilities. As he foresaw, Berlin swallowed up a growing number of transports. By February 1949, "Vittles" was employing 287 cargo planes, and there were few left for other commitments. When the British asked for the loan of twenty-four Air Force C-54s, Vandenberg's staff examined their resources. There were a handful of airframes at training bases, some were being used for VIP transportation, forty were loaned to commercial airlines, and two dozen were in the Far East. MacArthur's staff "non-concurred strenuously with the mere idea" of giving up their transports.[70] Vandenberg instructed his commanders to dig deeply and do more with less. In one instance he apologized to the Army's Pacific commander in Hawaii—overzealous subordinates had confiscated his personal plane. The Air Force was stretched to the breaking point. Kuter implored Vandenberg to leave him alone since his command had only twenty-six planes left![71] Planners even contemplated converting new B-36 bombers into massive cargo planes that could haul sixty thousand pounds, but the cost and time needed were prohibitive.[72]

Meanwhile, the political situation continued inconclusively. The central question of how important Berlin was to the United States was often asked by the JCS, but never answered. As Tunner requested more and more airlift, Vandenberg grew increasingly restive. Soviet fighters had begun harassing his planes in the Berlin air corridors, barrage balloons had been suspended at different points to interfere with air traffic, and occasional ground firing had been reported. It was recommended that fighter escort be provided.[73] It appeared to some that the Soviets were trying to goad the United States into a fight. Colonel R. B. Landry, military aide to the president, wrote a memorandum to Admiral Leahy in which he spelled out his fears: "It seems to me that within the next three months, unless the Western states should yield, and they can never do this, the situation will come to a head and there will be war."[74] Defense Secretary James Forrestal was also pessimistic, and in early September he and the Joint Chiefs visited the White House to voice their apprehensions. That night President Truman wrote in his diary: "Have a terrific day. Forrestal, Bradley, Vandenberg (the Gen., not the Senator!), brief me on bases, bombs, Moscow, Leningrad, etc. I have a terrible feeling afterward that we are very close to war. I hope not. . . . Berlin is a mess."[75]

General Vandenberg directed USAFE to prepare for evacuation to Britain, destroying its facilities and equipment as it departed. Once established in England, it was to "interdict Soviet communications at specifically designated points." General John K. Cannon, who had replaced LeMay, responded that he was woefully unprepared for offensive operations. He could evacuate, but he could not fight.[76]

In early October, Van reported to the JCS that he fully supported American foreign policy but pointed out that the Air Force could not continue "Vittles" indefinitely without seriously jeopardizing American security.[77] On October 13, General Bradley reiterated to the NSC that the Airlift was putting enormous strain on military capabilities; moreover, the issue of increasing Soviet belligerence was becoming worrisome. Bradley stated that the Air Force could send in fighter escort, but only if the NSC had decided that "war in the near future and for the Berlin cause is acceptable." The NSC was stunned; such bluntness was unexpected and unwelcome. The JCS was accused of "getting the jitters" and "trying to pass the buck." The question of whether or not Berlin was worth fighting for was never answered; fortunately, it never had to be.[78] The Soviets did not want war any more than did the Allies.

When the Soviets relented and reopened the land lines in May 1949 the West had achieved an enormous psychological victory. Allied popularity increased dramatically throughout Germany, while that of the Soviets declined. Winston Churchill observed: "The spectacle of the British and Americans trying to feed the two million Germans in Berlin, while the Soviet government was trying to starve them, has been an object lesson to the German people, far beyond anything words can convey."[79] The Berlin Airlift was perhaps the West's greatest victory of the cold war.

The Berlin crisis showed deficiencies in the national decision-making apparatus. During the initial stages of the confrontation, the JCS had been largely ignored and had had no say in the decision on whether to resist blockade or launch an airlift. Civilian leaders and General Clay largely determined the course of action and then communicated directly with either the service chief involved or the commander on the scene. JCS involvement was not significant until October, and then it was resented (Bradley's "war scare"). One reason for this confusion was the National Security Act that had set up the NSC and the JCS. There was no statutory requirement that the Joint Chiefs be consulted. This deficiency was not corrected until 1949, when the act was amended and the Joint Chiefs became standing members of the National Security Council. As for Berlin, General Bradley said later: "We were very, very lucky."[80]

For Vandenberg's Air Force it was an excellent opportunity to demonstrate its ability and professionalism. After initial hesitation, the chief had acted dramatically and effectively. He chose the right man for the task, and his troops did not let him down. Besides giving valuable experience in a major airlift operation—experience that would be tested the following year in Korea—it also illustrated the necessity for a large, strategic cargo plane. Overall, the Airlift moved nearly 2.5 million tons of cargo (mostly coal) in over 275,000 flights. Sixty airmen were killed in air crashes.[81] It was a most impressive display of air power as an instrument of peaceful diplomacy, and Vandenberg summed it up well:

Above all the Berlin Airlift has provided the United States Air Force an opportunity to demonstrate to the American people, whose instrument it is, and to the world at large, what it can do and what it will continue to do to the best of its ability to make air power a true force for peace.[82]

RESHAPING THE BOLT

General George Kenney had not been among the inner circle of Air Corps leadership. He was not from West Point, and his name infrequently appears in accounts of the great air events of the interwar years. He did not participate in air refueling demonstrations, long-range flights to Alaska and South America, or air races, or write inflammatory articles from a desk at Maxwell Field. Nevertheless, he was an excellent officer with a solid combat record in World War I who had served as chief of staff of the GHQ Air Force under General Frank Andrews. Soon after Lewis Brereton's fleet was destroyed on the ground at Clark Field in December 1941, Kenney became the chief airman in the Pacific theater. The aged warrior with the corncob pipe soon grew fond of the garrulous Kenney, who remained in the Pacific until the end of the war.

There was recurring talk of General MacArthur's political ambitions, to which Kenney allowed himself to be a party. In April 1943, the airman returned to Washington and met with Senator Arthur Vandenberg to discuss MacArthur's presidential aspirations.[83] It is probable that such political dabbling was frowned upon by Arnold, and Kenney was never completely trusted. When B-29s became operational in 1944 and were deployed to the Pacific, Kenney fully expected his Far East Air Forces to receive them as replacements for the B-17s and B-24s. However, Arnold would not relinquish control; instead, he personally directed the bombers from Washington. After Germany's defeat, Spaatz left for Asia and took command of the B-29s. The implication of Spaatz's arrival in his theater was not lost on Kenney, and he resented it.[84]

When the war ended and the victors returned home, it was apparent that, upon Arnold's retirement, Spaatz—Kenney's junior in rank—would command the AAF. However, the United Nations was in its formative stages, and one proposal envisioned a UN military force to act as world policeman. Kenney was told he would lead its Air Force, and this assignment assuaged his pride. In February 1946, Spaatz reorganized the AAF into three combat commands, with Kenney receiving the Strategic Air Command. Surprisingly, Kenney did not relinquish his UN post, but instead wore two hats. What was even more surprising, Spaatz allowed him to remain in New York for the next six months, even though SAC headquarters was located at Andrews Field near Washington.[85]

The Strategic Air Command was in deplorable condition at the time. Only one of its groups, the 509th, was considered combat-ready in May 1946, and the rest of the command had a "very low" capability.[86] Some historians have made much of "atomic diplomacy," suggesting that the United States used its new weapon to club allies and adversaries into line. This interpretation is difficult to accept when one examines the facts.

There were still very few SADDLETREE bombers available in the Air Force.

In March 1948, the commander of the 43rd Bomb Group, which was supposed to be atomic-capable, complained that his B-29s had not yet been modified.[87] In July, soon after the start of the Berlin Airlift, Vandenberg wrote AEC chairman Lilienthal urgently requesting that more aircraft be modified; an additional eighty-two SADDLETREE bombers were necessary to carry out the atomic mission.[88]

In addition, SAC was deficient in trained atomic aircrews, having only six available in January 1948.[89] The number of atomic weapons was similarly small, with only thirteen devices in the American stockpile on June 30, 1947. Moreover, the bomb canisters and their atomic cores needed to be joined in a highly complex and time-consuming operation. Exercises in early 1948 demonstrated that one assembly team, consisting of thirty-nine persons, could prepare one weapon in approximately two days. Once the new mark IV bombs became available in late 1948, the preparation time was cut to between sixteen and twenty-four hours.[90] Unfortunately, there were no military assembly teams in 1947, and only three partially trained teams at the start of the Berlin crisis in March 1948. (It took six months to train an assembly team.) It was estimated, therefore, that it would take five days to get the first bomb assembled and delivered to the 509th at Roswell Field. In thirty days it was doubtful that even twenty bombs could be built.[91] Putting this data together it becomes clear that the United States possessed a very small atomic punch in the immediate postwar era, and it was certainly not able to react quickly. An atomic strike would have taken weeks and would have consisted of only a few dozen weapons. Unfortunately, Kenney said he would need at least two hundred bombs, delivered simultaneously, in order to carry out a successful strike. Thus, SAC would have been hard pressed to defeat a potential enemy in 1948.[92]

These difficulties were not the fault of General Kenney. The Army Air Force did not control the atomic stockpile and had little voice in determining its size and type. The Manhattan District and its successor, the Atomic Energy Commission, infrequently solicited the views of the military regarding the size and composition of the atomic stockpile. Moreover, very few military leaders were even privy to that information. The president himself was not regularly briefed. Under the procedures worked out during the war and continued until mid-1947, General Leslie R. Groves reported to his superior—the Army chief of staff—and he in turn reported to the secretary of war. There was no provision that any other military or civilian leaders be briefed. In February 1947, Navy Secretary Forrestal and Admiral Chester Nimitz were asked for recommendations on future atomic production. Neither knew anything about the matter, but each assumed the other did; consequently, they recommended that "the current production rate" be maintained.[93] When General LeMay, as deputy chief of the Air Staff for Research and Development, attempted to ascertain information regarding the size of the atomic stockpile in April 1947, General Groves told him: "That information is quite complicated and is based on many factors, I cannot answer your question because I force myself to forget the numbers involved."[94] It is likely that General Kenney, as SAC commander, was not told how many atomic bombs would be available for use in the event of war.

There were, however, SAC deficiencies that could have been corrected.

Kenney's deputy was his former logistics chief in the Pacific, Major General Clements McMullen, and it was he who actually ran the command for the next two years. McMullen was an uncompromising and difficult man; nicknamed "Concrete" and "Cement-head" because of his intractability, he soon alienated most of his subordinates with a disastrous personnel experiment involving cross-training. The effects of demobilization, which had left the AAF devastated, were still being felt, and McMullen's cross-training plan was designed to insulate SAC from its recurrence. He endeavored to train all pilots as navigators, bombardiers, flight engineers, and radar operators, and they were also to become familiar with the gunner's duties; all bombardiers were to be proficient navigators, flight engineers, and radar operators. In fact, all crew members were to be trained at different positions. McMullen reasoned that such a scheme would make SAC invulnerable to personnel fluctuations. A shortage of navigators would be solved by excess pilots or bombardiers filling in until the shortage was rectified. It would take four years for the average pilot to complete this scheduled training, with less time expected for the other crew positions.[95]

The result of this unusual experiment was predictable. Aircrew members were spending so much time learning how to do someone else's job they forgot how to do their own. Proficiency in the primary mission of SAC plummeted, but wily and fearful subordinate commanders labored to cover such shortcomings. High-altitude bombing made accuracy difficult owing to increased winds, air pressure differential, and equipment limitations; but because accurate bomb scores were required, crews flew training missions at fifteen thousand feet. Although that altitude would have spelled suicide in combat, it made for good scores. Radar bombing was also difficult and required long hours of experience and training to differentiate the radar returns made by buildings, weather, and ground features. The crews, therefore, relied upon visual identification, trusting they would go to war only on a clear spring day. When radar bomb drops became required, special radar reflectors were installed near the Texas Gulf Coast to be used as "targets." Even cross-trained pilots could locate the reflectors on a cluttered radar scope. In short, McMullen's theories and the lack of realistic training made SAC incapability a scandal.[96]

There were also problems with the commander. General Kenney loved to make speeches; his crusty personality and turns of phrase made him an especially popular guest speaker. Moreover, he was initially encouraged in such actions because the airmen were attempting to nurture grass roots support for a separate Air Force. But Kenney did have a tendency to get carried away. A former director of Air Force public relations, Steven Leo, remembered Kenney as his "problem child":

> George . . . used to think that the way to promote air power was to make speeches before the largest possible audience in which he could forecast that as soon as the enemy bombers dropped a bomb on New York City, radioactive taxicab fenders would be found out beyond Danbury, Connecticut.[97]

Leo told Kenney that he gave too many speeches and should spend more time at his headquarters. Kenney's former deputy in the Pacific, Lieutenant General

Ennis Whitehead, echoed these warnings: "If anything should happen and units of the Strategic Air Command be called upon for combat operations, the only thing which people would remember would be that George Kenney was the commander."[98] Such cautions were not heeded.

As the Berlin crisis began to heat up in the spring of 1948 and there was talk of war with the Soviet Union, the ability of SAC to carry out its mission was questioned. Although General Vandenberg was favorably impressed by a SAC exercise of early June, there were still nagging doubts in his mind. General Norstad recalls that Defense Secretary Forrestal inquired whether SAC was ready for war; Norstad stated that the reports said they were. Forrestal responded that he did not give a damn what the reports said, were they ready? Vandenberg decided to look into the situation more deeply and sent Major General Frederic H. Smith to evaluate the SAC personnel situation. Smith reported that it was very bad; in some units one-quarter of the personnel had turned over in one two-month period.[99] Digging further, Vandenberg asked an old friend, Charles Lindbergh, to serve as his special assistant, visit SAC bases around the country, study their operations, and report back on performance. Lindbergh was chosen for several reasons: he was unquestionably one of the greatest pilots in the world and would know better than anyone else how proficient crew members actually were; he had enormous prestige and commanded respect wherever he went; his name opened doors and mouths that would have been closed to most others; as a civilian, he had no fear of what impact such a study would have on his career; and finally, Lindbergh was honest and straightforward. He would tell Van the truth.[100]

After several weeks and over one hundred flying hours with SAC crews at six different bases, Lindbergh returned to Washington and reported to Vandenberg on September 14, 1948. His conclusions were largely negative: "Average pilots' proficiency is unsatisfactory, teamwork is not properly developed and maintenance of aircraft and equipment is inadequate. In general, personnel are not sufficiently experienced in their primary mission." Because of the atomic mission's importance, crews should be the best available, but instead, their skills were below those of the average airline pilot. Accident rates were too high. The cross-training program was especially singled out for criticism because it interfered with the primary mission of atomic training. The foolishness of radar bombing using reflectors and visual drops at low altitude was also noted. Overall, Lindbergh thought that SAC was seriously deficient.[101] At the same time that Lindbergh was evaluating SAC performance, Vandenberg directed Colonel Paul W. Tibbetts, pilot of the *Enola Gay* and first commander of the 509th, to inspect SAC headquarters. Tibbetts reported his findings at the same time as Lindbergh, and the results were similar: "There isn't anybody out there that knows what the hell they are doing. The crews don't know how to fly an airplane. The staff officers don't know what they are doing."[102]

A few days before the reports from Lindbergh and Tibbetts, Vandenberg had also received word that the JCS wanted a briefing on atomic readiness. Nerves were frayed by the Berlin crisis; President Truman had made his melancholy reference to war on September 10, and now the Joint Chiefs wanted to examine their readiness posture. Vandenberg notified Kenney of the required briefing on September 15. General Norstad later recalled that Kenney's subsequent presentation was not well received; the SAC commander seemed ill-prepared and uninformed. It is possible that this incident was the last straw for Vandenberg. Several days later, he spoke with Norstad and his vice chief, General Muir Fairchild, about "certain command changes about to take place." On September 21, Vandenberg summoned Kenney to his office and notified him that he was being transferred to Maxwell Field to become commander of the Air University. His replacement at SAC was to be Lieutenant General LeMay. That same day Vandenberg directed that the cross-training program be scrapped.[103]

LeMay said later that he had no inkling of the proposed change; he was immersed in his own problems in Berlin. He thought that perhaps Vandenberg had been impressed by the recent visit to Europe, leading to his choice.[104] LeMay was being modest. By all accounts, the man who had directed the B-29s over Japan was not the obvious choice to replace Kenney; he was the only choice. Vandenberg wrote President Truman on October 5, requesting approval for the proposed change.[105]

This was one of Vandenberg's most important decisions as chief of staff. The downward spiral that had gripped SAC since its inception had never been arrested. Unquestionably, there were many things beyond Kenney's control: demobilization had devastated his command, and he had been given little support in his efforts to secure atomic energy information so that his crews could receive better training. His command also had a higher-than-average personnel turnover that necessitated constant training of new people. There was more to it than that, however. After more than two years Kenney had been unable to make his troops combat-ready. His frequent absences from headquarters and failure to keep a firm rein on the overzealous McMullen, whose cross-training program had become an obsession, were largely to blame for his fall. Kenney had been warned. The stakes were simply too high to allow failure. Vandenberg's action was probably overdue because SAC's defects had been manifest for some months.

General Whitehead was shocked upon hearing news of the transfer and expected that he would be next. Although realizing Kenney's deficiencies, he thought sinister forces were at play:

Sep 24, 1948
Dear George,
I was shocked at your new assignment; shocked over your leaving SAC. You are the only USAF officer who has even a chance to be a theatre commander in event war comes. You and I have seen the position of the Army and Navy strengthened because their generals and admirals commanded theatres in World War I and World War II.
Without any dope I G-2 it this way:
a. Navy to Forrestal to Symington.
b. One USAF three star general had a hand.
c. Van acquiesced.
d. Santy [Fairchild] could do nothing.
e. LeMay is a pawn in the game; will lose his job in a year or two to make way for the guy who wants to complete his build-up to succeed Van in 1952.[106]

Whitehead was wrong. Van did not "acquiesce," and strings were not pulled by Whitehead's anonymous three star general—probably Norstad. Those who had thought the young chief would be passive and easily placated were shocked into realizing the error of their thinking. Vandenberg meant to *command* the Air Force, and he expected results.

Although General LeMay would later acquire many detractors because of his overemphasis and favoritism toward SAC, his lack of tact, his position on the Vietnam War, and his abortive political career, there are few who fail to acknowledge his stunning transformation of the derelict command he had inherited. After talking to his new subordinates he realized they were not aware that they "weren't worth a goddamn."[107] They needed to be shown. The story of his "lesson" is well known: He announced a special exercise that had the entire SAC fleet carry out a simulated attack on Dayton, Ohio—from high altitude, at night, in marginal weather, and using a radar bomb drop. As he expected, not a single aircraft completed the mission as directed.[108] Having proved his point, LeMay began to rebuild. Vandenberg had given him no specific directives, just to reshape SAC and make it ready for war. LeMay appreciated that kind of leadership; he had full authority to accomplish a mission without someone telling him how to do it.[109] The results were remarkable. Within two years, SAC became a "cocked weapon"—combat-ready and able to carry out its war plan rapidly and effectively. This improvement was owing partly to LeMay and partly to new bomb designs that allowed faster development and assembly, thus solving the crucial shortage that had plagued Kenney. It was also a result of General Vandenberg's emphasis on the importance of the atomic mission and his single-minded resolve to put the right man in charge to ensure that that mission was viable.[110] A deterrent force that is not credible is not a deterrent; it is an invitation.

Hoyt as a teenager growing up in Lowell, Massachusetts. (Vandenberg, Jr., Collection)

West Point graduation photo, 1923. (Vandenberg, Jr., Collection)

The handsome young officer, father, and husband in 1930. (Vandenberg, Jr., Collection)

Glad with Sandy and Gogo while stationed in Hawaii in 1930. (Vandenberg, Jr., Collection)

Van as an instructor pilot at Randolph Field, Texas, in 1932. (Vandenberg, Jr., Collection)

Maj Gen Vandenberg when deputy commander in chief of the AEAF. *Left to right:* Field Marshal Jan Christian Smuts, Van, Winston Churchill, King George VI, and Air Chief Marshal Sir Trafford Leigh-Mallory. (Vandenberg, Jr., Collection)

The youthful major general as commander of the Ninth Air Force in 1944. (USAF Photo)

Van, Reich Marshal Hermann Goering, and Gen Carl Spaatz in May 1945. (Vandenberg, Jr., Collection)

Lt Gen Vandenberg with Gen "Hap" Arnold in September 1945. (Vanden-berg, Jr., Collection)

Van, Spaatz, and Air Force Secretary Stuart Symington in early 1948. (Vandenberg, Jr., Collection)

Still trim, the chief—cigarette firmly in place—tees off at Burning Tree. (Vandenberg, Jr., Collection)

The Joint Chiefs—Adm Louis E. Denfeld, Van, and Gen Omar N. Bradley—with Defense Secretary James Forrestal. (Vandenberg, Jr., Collection)

Vandenberg and his major commanders in April 1949. *Seated, left to right:* Lt Gen George Stratemeyer, Far East Air Forces; Gen George C. Kenney, Air University; Vandenberg; Lt Gen Ennis C. Whitehead, Continental Air Command; Lt Gen Joseph K. Cannon, US Air Forces, Europe. *Standing, left to right:* Gen Muir S. Fairchild, vice chief of staff; Brig Gen Frank Armstrong, Alaskan Air Command; Maj Gen William Kepner, Air Proving Ground; Lt Gen Benjamin W. Chidlaw, Air Materiel Command; Brig Gen Robert Travis, Pacific Air Command; Maj Gen Gordon Saville, Air Defense Command; Maj Gen Robert M. Lee, Tactical Air Command; Maj Gen Willie Hale, Caribbean Air Command; Maj Gen Laurence S. Kuter, Military Air Transport Service; Maj Gen Robert Harper, Air Training Command; Lt Gen Curtis E. LeMay, Strategic Air Command; Maj Gen Leon Johnson, Third Air Division, England; Col Sydney Grubbs, Bolling Air Force Base. (USAF Photo)

Gen Nate Twining, Bradley,
and Van on a fishing trip to Alaska
in 1950. (Vandenberg, Jr., Collection)

Sandy, Glad, Gloria, and a
proud father at Sandy's graduation
from West Point in 1951. (Vandenberg, Jr., Collection)

Glad's favorite picture of Van. She thought it made him look "grandfatherly." (USAF Photo)

The exhausted chief trying to regain his stamina while testifying before the Senate for the last time in June 1953. (USAF Photo)

Van, relaxing with a beer in July 1953, soon after his retirement. (Vandenberg, Jr., Collection)

Glad and her beloved Van, out fishing in Colorado. This was the last photo taken of the chief. Despite his happy and robust appearance, his health failed rapidly and he soon entered Walter Reed Hospital. (Vandenberg, Jr., Collection)

The end of the world will be when some
enormous boiler shall explode and blow
up the globe. And they [the Americans]
are great boilermakers.

Jules Verne

V | War Plans and War Planes

A soldier should be sworn to the patient
endurance of hardships, like the ancient
knights; and it is not the least of these
necessary hardships to have to serve with
sailors.

Bernard Montgomery

STRATEGIC PLANNING

General Vandenberg had taken a decisive step toward preparing the Air Force
and the nation for war, but was war likely, and if it did occur, how would it be
fought? General Omar Bradley commented that America was "lucky" the Berlin
crisis did not become violent. Why did he feel so? Was there something more
than the deeply embedded fear of war that abides in all soldiers? The answer is
yes; Bradley and the other Joint Chiefs were aware that in 1948 the nation was
not prepared for war, either mentally or materially. Not only was the Strategic
Air Command in shambles, but demobilization and budgetary restraints had taken
their toll on all the services. Moreover, there was no coherent national war plan
to implement in the event war did break out.

Soon after World War II ended, the political situation between the United
States and the Soviet Union deteriorated rapidly. As a consequence, the Joint War
Plans Group began tentatively to address the question of what a future war with
the Soviet Union would entail. Air power was seen as a crucial ingredient of the
American response in the form of a major strategic air offensive against twenty
urban targets that would severely cripple Soviet industry. The use of atomic
bombs, 196 to be exact, was assumed and considered essential to the success of
the strike. The losses sustained by the attacking B-29s would be high, but they
would nonetheless accomplish their mission.[1]

Soon after, the Joint Strategic Plans Group was formed to devise a war plan,
and in early 1946 wrote PINCHER, a rudimentary outline for use in an emergency.
PINCHER assumed that the Soviet Union had launched an aggressive war of con-

quest for Western Europe and the Middle East. The plan predicted that most of continental Europe would be quickly overrun but thought that a toehold could be maintained in either the Italian or Iberian peninsula. The American response would unfold in six stages: first, the United States had to ensure the defense of the Western Hemisphere. Second, it needed to secure bases in Britain, the Middle East, and possibly China, which would be necessary for step three: the start of air operations against the war-making capacity of the Soviet Union. Fourth, the Navy would institute a blockade and destroy Soviet naval forces and shipping. Fifth, the Army would seize the Dardanelles and the oil fields in the Caucasus. Finally, the United States would carry on "as resources permit."[2]

Beyond this rough sketch, little detail was provided on how the war would actually be fought. Although annexes outlined the size of Allied and Soviet forces, there were no targeting data. The intelligence available on the Soviet Union was so limited that it was deemed impossible to list specific targets, other than to note that the majority of Soviet industry was located in urban areas. Again, the use of atomic bombs was assumed, but it was acknowledged that the number available, though unknown, was small. As an emergency war plan, PINCHER was deficient. The Joint Chiefs refused to approve it because of its limitations but did eventually allow its use as a planning document for further studies.[3] This was a very short and hesitant step. It appeared that the outbreak of peace had returned war planning to the dismal status it had held under the old Joint Board. It has been suggested that the Navy was deliberately stalling on the completion of a joint plan. Until the atom bomb went to sea, the Navy had only a minor role in a future conflict (blockade and commerce raiding), and that was unacceptable. The Navy, therefore, worked to develop more diverse capabilities so that it could then insist that a war plan be written to incorporate those new abilities. Until then, however, it would have to block agreement on a joint plan or else be constrained to a minor role and thus be prevented from expanding.[4]

In November 1947, Vandenberg wrote Secretary Symington in frustration that there was no agreed-upon joint war plan and that the planners were severely handicapped by the lack of a definite statement of the country's long-range objectives as well as a reasonable estimation of the nation's industrial and manpower mobilization capabilities.[5] Thomas K. Finletter, chairman of the President's Air Policy Commission, was also apprised of this deficiency by General Eisenhower.[6] Something had to be done. As the political situation deteriorated in Europe in 1948, the need for action became compelling. In March, the National Security Council declared unequivocally that "the ultimate object of Soviet-directed world communism is the domination of the world." To counter this threat, the United States must have an aggressive, offensive plan that incorporated military, economic, and political factors.[7]

It had been hoped that the National Security Act of 1947 would remedy this shortcoming because, for the first time, the Joint Chiefs were specifically tasked to prepare war plans. Initially, this appeared to be true when in May 1948 staffers presented a short-range emergency plan, codenamed HALFMOON, that envisioned war launched by Soviet ground forces against Western Europe. Heavily outnumbered, the West would retreat, retarding the onslaught by an atomic air offensive from bases in Britain and the Middle East. While the air campaign was in progress, the West would mobilize, secure control of the Atlantic and Mediterranean, and march eastward until Europe was once again liberated.[8] The emphasis placed on forward bases from which to launch the air offensive is important. For the next several years, overseas bases were an important goal of American foreign policy. B-29s could not reach Soviet targets from the United States and return home; they either had to fly one-way missions (presumably suicidal), increase their range, or obtain airfields closer to enemy territory. Within two years, this problem was solved through a combination of foreign bases, long-range bombers, and aerial refueling. Air crews would no longer have to plan on crash-landing in enemy territory.[9]

It is also significant that the JCS did not anticipate air power alone bringing victory. The air campaign was to be the first step, but both the Army and the Navy would be necessary to bring the Soviets to their knees; on this point Air Force doctrine was consistently and unequivocally clear. Even a devastating atomic strike "could guarantee neither a military victory nor the accomplishment of our National Policy objectives."[10] General Vandenberg publicly affirmed this stance on numerous occasions: "We do not expect, of course, that our initial air assault will win the war. Its primary objective will be to delay the enemy as much as possible" (May 12, 1948). "Air power alone and unassisted is scarcely capable of winning a complete victory. . . . We need an effective Army and Navy" (May 1, 1949). "Mr Symington has said, I have said, and many other representatives of the Air Force have said many times that to win a war or to maintain peace this nation must have adequate land forces and sea forces, as well as an adequate force in the air" (July 2, 1949).[11] These statements are important because the Air Force, and the JCS, would later be charged with "putting all their eggs in one basket" and relying solely on an "atomic blitz."

HALFMOON was a flimsy compromise. There was no agreement between the services on exactly how the war could or should be fought. As a result, in the tradition of World War II, everyone had a major role: the Air Force would have a strategic air offensive, the Navy its fast carrier task forces, and the Army dozens of divisions slugging their way toward Moscow. None of the chiefs was pleased with HALFMOON, especially Admirals Leahy and Louis E. Denfeld (chief of Naval Operations), but all reluctantly agreed to approve the document. One glaring defect involved the lack of provision for operations beyond the first year; in reality, HALFMOON was just an introduction to war, the details had not yet been worked out. Although it was barely feasible, military leaders had finally agreed, however tentatively, to a joint war plan three years after the end of hostilities.[12]

In early 1949 this basic plan was improved, expanded, and renamed TROJAN. The importance of this revision lay in its detailed annex, which gave flesh to the skeleton of an atomic attack. Specific targets, seventy Soviet industrial centers, were slated for vaporization by the SAC fleet of B-29, B-50, and B-36 bombers. The seventy designated targets included urban industrial centers, POL facilities, submarine bases, and the transportation system. To destroy these targets would require 133 atomic weapons.[13] General LeMay had been especially concerned about the lack of detailed target data in earlier war plans. He commented that, previously, the JCS had only provided general guidance like "take the high ground around Gettysburg," but he wanted specific objectives in specific locations. TRO-JAN was the first such attempt.[14] It was also stressed by the JCS planners that "not the slightest doubt can be allowed to creep into Soviet minds that we will use the bomb, or they may miscalculate and start the war we are trying so hard to avert."[15] Vandenberg concurred, adding that in the event of war and if national survival was at stake, we would certainly use atomic weapons. He therefore resisted suggestions that the United States renounce their employment or include provisos. Either admit that the bomb would be used or remain silent; do not send complicated mixed signals.[16]

In order to improve SAC's targeting information, Vandenberg engineered a clever operation. Communications intelligence (COMINT) had proven extremely valuable during World War II as evidenced by the Ultra operation. It will be remembered that Vandenberg well realized the importance of this intelligence source, and as early as February 1945 he pushed strongly for an Air Force COMINT capability. Because of budget limitations, however, these hopes had not been realized. In 1948, an opportunity presented itself when James Forrestal formed a board headed by Rear Admiral Earl F. Stone to study the issue of COMINT. Stone concluded that in the interests of unification and efficiency, an agency should be established to handle all COMINT for the three services. Vandenberg objected and sided with the Navy in opposing the merger. After haggling over the issue for the next year, the chief offered a compromise: he would agree to the new Armed Forces Security Agency—eventually to become the National Security Agency—if the Air Force was permitted to develop further its own COMINT capability for SAC targeting purposes. Secretary of Defense Louis Johnson, Forrestal's successor, agreed. But Vandenberg was not quite through. When the Armed Forces Security Agency's charter was written, it was stipulated that all "mobile collection facilities" would remain under the control of their respective services. Vandenberg then promptly defined all Air Force collectors—from reconnaissance aircraft to stationary intercept sites—as "mobile collection facilities." The Air Force had its cake and ate it too—a COMINT capability for SAC, with no strings attached. It was a very clever piece of work.[17]

Getting the three services to agree on a basic war plan, though a step forward, did not resolve all problems. The exact conduct of the strategic air campaign was ambiguous, stipulating that Navy aircraft would destroy the "other elements of the Soviet war-making potential as part of the coordinated air offensive against the Soviet . . . will to fight." It was made clear, however, that Navy air would "supplement and support" the Air Force, who had primary responsibility for the air offensive, and only after its required naval tasks were completed.[18] How could naval air best "supplement and support"? There were two quite different schools of thought on that subject.

ROLES AND MISSIONS

The term "roles and missions" was far more than a question of doctrine—it was the life blood of the military services. The breathtakingly rapid demobilization after the war left all the services devastated. The Army Air Forces went from a strength of 2,253,000 on V-J Day to 303,000 by the end of May 1947. The aircraft situation was equally grim, with the number of combat-ready groups falling from 218 to 2 by December 1946.[19] To make matters worse, there was little order or logic used in returning the warriors to mufti. The primary and overriding concern of the American people was to "bring the boys home." Those who had served the longest, and were therefore the most experienced, were the first to obtain discharges. The insidious aspect of such a system was that numbers told only part of the story. If a unit lost 50 percent of its manpower, it could easily lose 75 percent of its combat capability if those departing were centered in a particular job specialty.[20]

The nation was weary of wartime rationing and shortages, and the president knew he must dramatically curtail military spending and shift priorities to the domestic scene. Although there were already disturbing events in Eastern Europe, the euphoria of peace was such that Americans could not be induced to continue tightening their belts. General Marshall's words were painfully apt: "For the moment, in a wide-spread emotional crisis of the American people, demobilization has become, in effect, disintegration, not only of the armed forces, but apparently of all conception of world responsibility and what it demands of us."[21]

Faced with such a climate, the services clamored for funds to maintain their combat capability. This period is often depicted as a time of selfish, childish parochialism orchestrated by a group of uniformed Colonel Blimps bent on undermining civilian authority, but such an indictment is far too harsh. These men were self-confident and accomplished professionals; they had not risen to the top during the war by being passive and pliable. They sincerely believed they were right and that the desires of their service were in the best interests of the country. As Admiral King pontificated: "Any step that is not good for the Navy is not good for the Nation."[22] It was assumed that unification would clearly delineate roles and missions, but such was not the case. The National Security Act had made only broad and vague references to these matters. An executive order from the president attempted to clarify the act, but this was still not satisfactory. The services needed clear-cut guidance because the limitations on funds and resources made it essential to resolve ambiguities for the purpose of sound planning.[23] The two issues causing greatest argument among the services were the Navy's "private air force" and its "private army." Generals Bradley and Vandenberg maintained that these large Navy and Marine forces were an unnecessary and wasteful duplication of effort, and they pushed to have them reduced.

In an effort to resolve this disagreement, an ad hoc committee was appointed, but it failed to reach agreement; and so in March 1948, Secretary Forrestal gathered his chiefs to Key West, Florida, to effect a compromise. A result of these meetings was a statement of "primary" and "collateral" functions. A primary function was one in which a particular service had a clear-cut responsibility; whereas, in a collateral function, a service supported and supplemented the service that was primary in that area.[24] Forrestal realized that overlap was inevitable—some missions simply defied neat categorization—but he tried to make it clear that a service claiming collateral responsibility in a given mission could not use such a claim as a basis for establishing an additional force requirement. In other words, when a service was preparing its budget and the composition of its forces, it would plan on the basis of its primary responsibilities; if these were adequately covered and there were forces or funds remaining, they could then be allotted to collateral functions. Who would determine if the primary responsibilities were adequately met? The JCS; if they were unable to agree, then the matter would be decided by the secretary of defense.[25]

At Key West, the JCS agreed to assign twelve primary functions to the Navy; unfortunately, the wording in some of them was sufficiently vague to perpetuate, not solve, problems:

- To establish and maintain local superiority (including air) in an area of naval operations.
- To conduct air operations as necessary for the accomplishment of objectives in a naval campaign.

Those primary functions assigned to the Air Force included:

- To gain and maintain general air superiority.
- To defeat enemy air forces.
- To be responsible for strategic air warfare.

This last term was then supplied with a definition:

Strategic Air Warfare—Air combat and supporting operations designed to effect, through the systematic application of force to a selected series of vital targets, the progressive destruction and disintegration of the enemy's war-making capacity to a point where he no longer retains the ability or the will to wage war. Vital targets may include key manufacturing systems, sources of raw material, critical material, stock piles, power systems, transportation systems, communications facilities, concentrations of uncommitted elements of enemy armed forces, key agricultural areas, and other such target systems.[26]

Even this was not good enough, however. What was "an area of naval operations" and which air operations were necessary "for the accomplishment of objectives in a naval campaign"? If such air strikes were against power or transportation systems, did they then come under the aegis of strategic air warfare, and hence the Air Force? The more such questions were addressed and "clarified," the more complex they became.

Although it was not included in the written text, Forrestal noted in his diary that an oral understanding between the Joint Chiefs was somewhat tighter. The Marines would be limited to four divisions, and the Air Force recognized the "right of the Navy to proceed with the development of weapons the Navy considers essential to its function, but with the proviso that the Navy will not develop a separate strategic air force."[27]

This last decision appeared to be important. The Air Force was responsible for strategic bombing; the Navy could assist, but only after its primary missions were fulfilled and then under the direction of the Air Force. Unquestionably, the Navy wanted the mission of strategic bombing. In December 1947, Vice Admiral Daniel V. Gallery had written a memorandum stating that the Navy was "the branch of the National Defense destined to deliver the Atom Bomb." Gallery admitted that the next war would not be like the last. He thought this fortunate because if it were like the last, the Navy was obsolete. No, he predicted a war dominated by atomic weapons. Gallery wanted the Navy to control those weapons.[28] Given this type of thinking in the Navy, it is not surprising that Denfeld immediately tried to alter the delicate balance just agreed to at Key West, submitting a memorandum to Forrestal that sought to clarify the agreements outlined in the Secretary's communique. Denfeld thought targeting for the atomic air offensive should be a joint responsibility—the Navy should not have to take directions from the Air Force but should be permitted to attack any targets it thought necessary, "inland or otherwise." Denfeld wanted his clarification accepted as official policy. The other chiefs protested: Denfeld was attempting to change the entire thrust of the Key West decisions. If the Navy were allowed to develop any weapons it wished and employ them against any targets, regardless of their relevance to the primary mission as defined in the war plan, the chiefs were back to square one. Forrestal listened to the opposing arguments and agreed with the majority (which included Admiral Leahy); Denfeld's ploy was brushed aside, but disagreement did not abate.[29]

The next major argument to erupt among the services was the old thorn of atomic weapons control. Now that the Air Force had apparently gained clear jurisdiction in strategic bombing, Vandenberg moved for the next step: control of the development and targeting of atomic weapons. This proposal met with expected resistance from the Army and Navy, which feared being frozen out of this crucial area. Quite rightly, Denfeld reasoned that strategic bombing and atomic weapons were not synonymous; the devices could be used for other purposes. It may appear that Vandenberg was making a power grab, but in truth, his argument held much logic for that time. The rapid growth of the atomic stockpile that resulted from improved weapon design had not yet occurred. A very limited amount of fissionable material was available, and the weapon stockpile was small. It made sense to consolidate the control of that valuable resource to ensure its most effective use. In later years thousands of atomic warheads were in the American arsenal, and although planners never seem satisfied, there were enough weapons to allow all the services to build an atomic capability. In 1948, this luxury could not be afforded. Even so, the Joint Chiefs were not convinced. When Forrestal called his quarrelsome chiefs together again at Newport, Rhode Island, in October, this question was the main item on the agenda. A compromise was reached by which Vandenberg agreed not to deny the use of the atomic weapon to the Navy, nor to interfere with its strategic planning. In return, Denfeld agreed to place the atomic arsenal under Air Force control in the event of war.[30] Vandenberg considered USAF control over atomic bomb production as crucial. In February 1948, Brigadier General Roscoe Wilson wrote him concerning the forthcoming retirement of Major General Leslie Groves. Wilson argued that the USAF could not allow Groves's replacement to be a naval officer: "The Navy has not attempted to conceal its ambition to control the military atomic bomb program, including a major portion of its strategic air aspects." Wilson feared the Navy would use its position to outmaneuver the Air Force. Vandenberg penciled on the memorandum that he concurred with Wilson's reasoning. The result was a compromise; another Army officer, Major General K. D. Nichols, was chosen to head the Special Weapons Group.[31]

Overall, the meetings at Key West and Newport were disappointing displays of interservice squabbling. Admiral Leahy disgustedly wrote in his diary: "All parties fought vigorously for the interest of their own group and not for the interest of national defense."[32] Forrestal had been working himself into a state of exhaustion and was already beginning to evidence signs of the strain that would eventually bring about his suicide. In his annual report to the president, he mentioned the conflict among his subordinates and stated the key problem tersely: "What is to be the use, and who is to be the user of air power?"[33]

Open warfare over the issue of strategic missions broke out in 1949 when the new secretary of defense, Louis Johnson, canceled the order for the Navy's first "supercarrier," the U.S.S. *United States*. This ship, whose keel had already been laid, was designed as a flush-top 65,000-ton aircraft carrier that would be capable of launching and recovering heavy, multi-engined aircraft—bombers. Vandenberg was consistently opposed to the supercarrier as an infringement on what was an Air Force primary mission as defined at Key West and Newport. The resulting furor over Johnson's action led to a remarkably vicious and dangerous fight.

MUTINY BETWEEN DECKS

As early as July 1947, Vandenberg had expressed his thoughts to Secretary Symington on the proposed supercarrier. To his mind aircraft carriers were relatively poor weapons because they lacked mobility and flexibility. The aircraft they carried had short range and poor altitude performance caused by the weight of their arresting mechanism and heavy-duty landing gear, necessary for carrier deck landings. Vandenberg asserted that the carriers would be so busy defending themselves against air attack that they would have little time to do anything constructive. (If the carrier was as valuable as the Navy claimed, then it would be a prime target for enemy attacks.) He maintained further that this vulnerability, coupled with the limited range of its aircraft, would relegate the carrier to attacks against relatively safe, and therefore inessential, coastal targets. Looking back to the war, he said: "Not until the Japanese Air Force was pounded into impotency did our carriers dare to venture sufficiently close to the Japanese main islands or strike at shore installations." Moreover, Allied carriers had never been able to operate in the Mediterranean for fear of the Luftwaffe; Soviet land-based aircraft would make the ships just as vulnerable.[34] The Navy disputed such opinions and historical conclusions.

The supercarrier had been under discussion in the JCS for some time. At the Key West conference in March 1948, Forrestal, who believed the Navy should have one such ship, though not an entire fleet, reported that he would support its development, "if so decided by the Joint Chiefs of Staff."[35] Admiral Louis Denfeld ignored the qualification and joyfully announced that the JCS had approved the ship. General Spaatz angrily denied this claim and stated in a letter to Senator Chan Gurney that at Key West he had been informed the supercarrier was part of the president's defense program. When asked if such a program was acceptable to him, Spaatz replied yes, he would never presume to contradict the commander in chief. Spaatz maintained that such a deferral to the president's wish was not an expression of support for the carrier.[36] To clear up the confusion this denial caused, Forrestal asked the JCS in May for a formal opinion. Denfeld and Bradley supported construction, but Vandenberg (who had recently replaced Spaatz) stated: "I have not felt, nor do I now feel, that I can give my approval to the 65,000 ton carrier project."[37] Congress, not aware of the Spaatz letter or the Vandenberg memorandum, had the public assurances of Forrestal and Truman that there was no opposition to the program; the funds were approved.

Verbal jabs between the Navy and Air Force continued during the next few months. The Navy organized a special office within the Pentagon called OP-23, a classified planning group led by Captain Arleigh Burke, whose purpose was to carry the fight for the *United States* to Congress and the public. Burke had pleaded with Denfeld to fight for the supercarrier, claiming melodramatically that if the ship was scrapped, the next step would be the transfer of all Navy and Marine air units to the Air Force. Denfeld was sufficiently swayed by such arguments to authorize OP-23; unfortunately, he neglected to notify his civilian superiors of the secret office, and when Secretary of the Navy John L. Sullivan discovered its existence, he was irate. He ordered the OP-23 office raided and its files impounded. The Naval personnel working there were arrested and held incommunicado for the next three days. The office was permanently closed.[38] It appeared there were stormy seas ahead.

Sensing that this matter was far from concluded, Vandenberg, in turn, brought in a Harvard law professor and former AEAF staff member during the war, Barton Leach, to prepare a similar public relations effort. One of the first fruits of this program was the stunning around-the-world flight of the B-50, "Lucky Lady II," on March 2, 1948. For the first time, an aircraft had used aerial refueling to circle the globe nonstop. Vandenberg exuberantly compared the achievement to that of Kitty Hawk and Lindbergh's 1927 solo flight; "our bombers," he reported, were now "virtually invulnerable to enemy interception."[39] The implications of such a feat for a strategic air offensive were not lost on the Navy. The following month it mounted an experiment: a Lockheed Neptune took off from the deck of the U.S.S. *Coral Sea,* flew two hundred miles, and dropped a load equivalent to ten thousand pounds of bombs (the weight of an atomic weapon).

Admiral Denfeld emphasized that "it is not the Navy's intention to make strategic bombing a major Navy mission. But the Navy could do that type of bombing if requested."[40]

On April 18, 1949, the keel of the *United States* was laid amid much fanfare; it appeared the admirals had won their fight. Secretary Forrestal, however, had resigned the month before. The pressures of his office had become too burdensome, and it was apparent to everyone, including the president, that he was becoming mentally unbalanced; in two weeks he would be dead. His successor was Louis Johnson, a brash, abrasive businessman who believed in controlling people with an iron fist. It was said that he had been running for president for nearly a decade and looked upon the Department of Defense as his last stepping stone. A contemporary account said that he was "used to being sworn at. Big, two-fisted, and tough-skinned, Johnson has been hitting hard and getting his way for most of his life."[41] It was rumored that when choosing a Navy secretary, Johnson had originally favored Jonathan Daniels, son of Josephus Daniels, but when the prospective appointee asked who would actually run the department, Johnson replied: "I will." Daniels declined such a sinecure, and the seemingly more pliant John L. Sullivan was selected instead.[42] President Truman, Dean Acheson (then secretary of state), and General Bradley all came to believe that Johnson was mentally ill; his operation for a brain tumor a few years later seemed to confirm this view.[43] Upon taking office, Johnson stated that he had no preconceived notions about the supercarrier, but the dissension it was causing concerned him. He asked the JCS for their opinion once again. The chiefs remained hopelessly divided and therefore submitted separate memoranda.

Denfeld justified the carrier with the following arguments:

1. It could operate heavier aircraft capable of carrying "the more complex armament and electronic equipment presently available."
2. It could operate larger numbers of smaller aircraft.
3. It could provide for more defensive armament and radar.
4. It could carry more fuel for prolonged operations.
5. It could carry more armor to withstand attacks.

Denfeld stated that the *United States* was a logical progression in carrier development and was not designed simply for strategic air warfare, although it would indeed be capable of such a mission if so directed.[44]

Vandenberg argued that the ship was simply not necessary, and was therefore a waste of money. The Navy maintained that it would cost $190 million; Vandenberg thought the figure more like $500 million, and even that amount was for the ship itself, without aircraft or a supporting destroyer squadron. When added together, the total was $1.265 billion.[45] The carrier was also vulnerable to three types of attack: aircraft, surface vessel, and submarine. Vandenberg reckoned that the Navy was basing its plans for carrier operations on its Pacific War experience, circumstances that would not exist in a future conflict with the Soviet Union, which had a very small surface fleet. The Soviets did, however, have many submarines. Since primary Navy missions were protection of sea lanes and antisubmarine operations, supercarriers were unnecessary; small escort carriers would be more efficient. Let the Air Force attend to strategic bombing.[46]

Both these responses were predictable—that of General Bradley was not. Earlier, he had approved the project; now he reversed himself with a line of reasoning similar to Vandenberg's. "The Navy's mission as agreed to by the Joint Chiefs," he declared, "was to conduct naval campaigns designed primarily to protect lines of communication leading to important sources of raw materials and to areas of projected military operations." The *United States*, however, was being programmed for strategic air operations, and that task fell to the Air Force. The only conceivable enemy was the Soviet Union; the existing fleet of eight large carriers was ample to carry out the Navy's role in war. The supercarrier was too expensive.[47] General Eisenhower, filling in for the ailing Admiral Leahy, was also queried by Johnson regarding the new ship. Like Bradley, Eisenhower had originally supported the construction of one prototype vessel, but again like Bradley, had changed his mind. Money was crucial, and the Navy's arguments were illogical. Eisenhower confided to his diary in January 1949 that the seamen continually claimed Air Force planes could not penetrate Soviet airspace, but that for reasons inexplicable to him, carrier planes would be able to do so. In April, when Johnson asked his opinion on the *United States*, Eisenhower said scrap it. Johnson then called Millard Tydings and Carl Vinson, chairmen of the Senate and House Armed Services committees, respectively, and the two men approved the proposed cancellation.[48]

After conferring with President Truman, Secretary Johnson sank the supercarrier. The Navy was livid; Sullivan resigned in protest. The acting secretary then asked Johnson if the money thus saved could at least be used to remodel two conventional carriers. The secretary of defense asked the JCS for their opinion, and the verdict was once again two to one. Vandenberg said the proposed conversion program was simply another attempt to build carriers capable of handling bombers, and that was unacceptable. He proposed instead that the funds be used to increase the Navy's antisubmarine capability. Failing that, the money should be returned to the "national economy." Bradley concurred.[49] Even though Johnson overruled the majority and agreed to the conversion, Navy supporters had had enough.

The sailors felt outnumbered and surrounded, and had even begun referring to themselves as "the water division of Johnson's Air Force." No doubt because of anger and frustration, anonymous individuals began circulating rumors that cast shadows on Johnson, Symington, the Air Force, and the new intercontinental bomber they supported, the B-36. The Navy saw villainy at work, and one of their favorite bogeymen was the Air secretary.

Symington, a naturally aggressive individual, had often attracted naval gunfire in the past. In March 1948, Sullivan had written an angry and accusatory letter to Forrestal charging Symington with attacking the Navy and trying to undermine its position. Symington riposted that the Air Force was faithfully adhering to the unification agreements and had made no attempts to absorb naval aviation. The Navy, on the other hand, had repeatedly tried to infringe on the strategic bombing mission and Admirals Chester Nimitz and Dan Gallery had even called for the elimination of SAC to be replaced by carrier-borne bombers. Symington concluded angrily that Sullivan's charges were a smoke screen to mask his own evil intentions. Army Secretary Kenneth Royall, who had also been smeared in the Sullivan missive, replied more stoically that the Navy's charges were unfounded, outrageous, and tiresomely typical.[50]

In October, Vice Admiral Arthur W. Radford was called before the Hoover Commission that was examining reorganization of the Executive Department. Although asked to address Navy capabilities, Radford used the hearings as a platform to attack the Air Force and the new B-36 bomber. Once again Symington saw duplicity and complained to Forrestal that although he objected strenuously to the naval tactics, he would not sink to their level and engage in an unseemly public brawl.[51]

With the cancellation of the supercarrier, however, a public brawl is exactly what ensued. Rumors of impropriety became so frequent and damning that the House Armed Services Committee announced that it would hold hearings concerning those disturbing reports. Noted newspaper columnist Hanson Baldwin (Annapolis, class of 1924) hinted darkly of fraudulent airplane contracts and "financial high jinks."[52]

When the hearings began, Congressman James E. Van Zandt (commander, USNR, "with thirty-two years of naval service and proud of it") reiterated the charges of fraud and misdoings that had been circulating for weeks. Referring to an anonymous document, he stated that reports had reached him linking Symington and Johnson with Floyd Odlum, president of Consolidated-Vultee Corporation, builder of the B-36. (Johnson had been a director of that company before taking office.) It was claimed that contracts with four other aircraft companies had been unfairly canceled in order to transfer funds to larger B-36 orders. It was then suggested that plans were afoot for Symington to resign from government office and head Consolidated. Van Zandt called for a full investigation. Symington was quick to respond; he not only welcomed an investigation, he demanded it.[53]

The B-36 hearings were a squalid affair. It was soon clear that Van Zandt had little more to offer in proof than his infamous "anonymous document." The innuendo and barroom gossip that he attempted to pass as fact finally riled Symington to dare Van Zandt to drop his congressional immunity and make his allegations public so that he could take "proper recourse."[54] Van Zandt declined the offer. A host of Air Force witnesses then took the stand and swore that the B-36 had been chosen on its merits and was the best aircraft available; there was no pressure from anyone at any time. Vandenberg defended his superior forcefully and convincingly: "I raise my voice . . . as any man might who hears a friend unjustly accused." It was "utterly unthinkable" and "absolutely fantastic," he maintained, that Symington would have bought planes for political motives when men's lives were at stake. Vandenberg said that General LeMay knew more about strategic bombing that any man alive, and if he said the B-36 was a good airplane, then it was. As for the charge that the B-36 was a "sitting duck," the chief replied that, if so, it had a healthy sting to it.[55] Admiral Radford admitted ruefully that Vandenberg's testimony was very good. All attacks on the Air Force, its leaders, and its weapons were effectively parried.[56]

The authorship of Van Zandt's secret document was quickly becoming a crucial issue; if the charges were so demonstrably false, where did the congressman get the information, and why did he believe it was accurate? Demands were made on Chairman Vinson to reveal the anonymous accusers; the committee's counsel threatened to resign if they were not. At last relenting, Vinson called Cedric Worth to the stand on August 24. Worth was a former Hollywood script writer who held a top secret clearance as an aide to Assistant Secretary of the Navy Daniel A. Kimball. When asked if he knew the author of the document, Worth responded that he had written it himself, but then admitted that he had no proof as to its accuracy. Kimball later claimed under oath that he was not aware Worth had been up to such activities. In fact, because Kimball was curious about the authorship of the document, he had directed his assistant to try to find out, but the assistant was unable to solve the mystery. His assistant was Cedric Worth.[57] After some very hostile questioning, Worth admitted that it was all a "tragic mistake," and that he had no intention of impugning the integrity of honorable men like Secretaries Johnson and Symington.[58] *Newsweek* called this admission a "knockout blow" and concluded: "If the Air Force fights with the B-36 the way it fights for it, heaven help America's enemies."[59] Even Hanson Baldwin was forced to conclude that the hearings were "an impressive Air Force vindication," and that its opponents had not displayed "perspicacity or judgment" in the matter.[60]

Worth's testimony brought the hearings to a conclusion, with the committee stating that there was not one iota of evidence to substantiate any of the charges made by Van Zandt. Within days, the Navy launched a court of inquiry to determine if Worth had received assistance from members of the Navy Department in composing his fable. The account of this investigation is even more melancholy than the congressional hearings.[61] Testimony before the court of inquiry made clear that Worth indeed had had help—a great deal of it—although many who admitted passing "rank gossip" claimed they never expected it to be used.[62] In fact, it would not be an exaggeration to say that a small group of willful men, in and out of uniform, had deliberately conspired to smear the Air Force and its leaders. It was an astonishing display of insolence and insubordination to civilian authority, but the episode was far from over.

When Vinson recessed the hearings in August, he announced that they would reopen in October, not to investigate more charges of wrongdoing, but to examine the entire issue of unification, national defense, and strategy. Once the Navy's court of inquiry began turning into a fiasco, however, Secretary Francis Matthews (Sullivan's replacement), Admiral Denfeld, and Vinson quietly decided to postpone the hearings, perhaps indefinitely. Such was not to be; certain officers had a definite case to make, and although the Worth affair was an embarrassment, it did not detract from their overall theory of the primacy of naval warfare. Consequently, a much decorated war veteran, Captain John C. Crommelin, threw himself into the breach by releasing a classified document to the press that revealed wholesale discontent in naval ranks. He said it was "necessary to the interests of national security" that he make the report public. He wanted a public airing of the issues.[63] Barely closed wounds immediately reopened as a group of high-ranking admirals, led by Admiral Arthur Radford, jumped to Crommelin's defense. Although Denfeld was loath to wash more dirty linen, Radford insisted that the October hearings be used as a platform to debate defense priorities.

When Vinson's gavel fell on October 5, most of the Navy hierarchy was primed for battle. Admiral Radford, commander in chief, Pacific Fleet (CINCPAC), had been recalled from Hawaii to "give advice and otherwise help to strengthen the Navy's case." Captain Arleigh Burke was also available to prepare testimony for "less articulate officers."[64] The admirals' arguments fell into three main categories: the concept of an "atomic blitz" was a poor strategy in the event of war; the B-36 was a substandard aircraft that could not successfully carry out the "blitz" even if it were an acceptable strategy; and the Navy was being treated as an unequal partner in the defense establishment as evidenced by the cancellation of the *United States*.

It was the Navy's contention that the Air Force was deluding the American public with promises of a "cheap victory" won by an atomic air strike. The Navy maintained that strategic bombing would never win a war, and reliance on it would only result in the loss of valuable time and allies. In an effort to clear the air, the JCS appointed Air Force Lieutenant General Hubert R. Harmon to chair a committee to evaluate the effect of the strategic air offensive on the war-making capability of the Soviet Union. In order to complete this evaluation, Harmon visited SAC headquarters near Omaha, Nebraska, and asked for briefings on targeting plans, aircraft availability, crew training, and performance. LeMay was irritated and called Fairchild complaining that he did not like the depth and specific nature of the questioning. Vandenberg responded firmly that he expected LeMay's unqualified support given to Harmon's staff: "We cannot afford to be hypersensitive when we are questioned about our capabilities." He concluded with a faint warning: "please give careful consideration to the matter of [your] attitude."[65]

Perhaps LeMay was sensitive for good reason. He had only been the SAC commander for six months and had not yet been able to correct all of his command's deficiencies. The conclusions of the Harmon Report were not a ringing endorsement of SAC. It acknowledged that the planned atomic offensive, which envisioned 133 bombs dropped on seventy Soviet cities, would reduce Soviet industrial capacity by 30 to 40 percent and kill 2.7 million people while wounding 4 million more. Although such destruction was massive, it would not cripple the Soviet economy and might even harden the population's will to resist. In addition, the atomic offensive would not prevent the Soviets from overrunning Western Europe. Nevertheless, the report concluded somewhat ambiguously that the air offensive was still the only way of rapidly inflicting shock and serious damage on the Soviet Union; moreover, "every reasonable effort should be devoted to providing . . . for prompt and effective delivery of the maximum numbers of atomic bombs to appropriate target systems."[66] In other words, Harmon seemed to be saying that although the air offensive would not win a war under present conditions, it might in the future if more bombs were used. Vandenberg was not pleased with these findings. Although in truth the report was similar to what current war plans postulated and what Vandenberg had been saying publicly, it is possible that the chief had been deliberately understating his case in order to sound reasonable and measured. He hoped that the Harmon board would more resoundingly ring SAC's praises. The Navy was a bit more pleased with the report's findings, but was also concerned with its ambiguities. In short, the Harmon Report was a mixed bag that neither satisfied nor offended. Perhaps because of this, neither the Air Force nor the Navy made much of the findings, and, miraculously, the report was not leaked to the press.[67]

Although the August hearings had destroyed all charges of wrongdoing in the selection of the B-36, the Navy still maintained that the leviathan was substandard technically and virtually obsolescent. Radford said that the B-36 could easily be detected, intercepted, and destroyed by fighter aircraft then available. "I can sincerely say to you," he remarked, "that I hope the enemy bombers which may attack our country in any future conflict will be no better than the B-36." What was worse, Radford maintained, the Air Force was concentrating on the bomber to such an extent—"putting all its eggs in one basket"—that other vital missions, such as transport and close air support, were deficient.[68]

Finally, the Navy claimed that it was not an equal partner in the defense setup because the Army and Air Force consistently united against it. The admirals claimed that their budget had been cut so drastically that it threatened to reduce them to impotency. The cancellation of the supercarrier was the symbol of this discrimination. They believed that the carrier would prove to be an effective and efficient weapon system, tailored to the needs of modern war. The abrupt, and in their minds arbitrary, cancellation of the ship dealt a severe blow to Navy morale of all ranks.[69]

The Air Force trade magazine referred to this performance as a "revolt against the Law of the Land." JCS Chairman General Bradley later wrote that he was aghast and could scarcely believe the Navy's actions. "Never in our military history," he asserted, "had there been anything comparable—not even the Billy Mitchell rebellion of the 1920s, a complete breakdown in discipline occurred. Neither Matthews nor Denfeld could control his subordinates . . . Denfeld . . . allowed his admirals to run amok. It was utterly disgraceful." Admiral Denfeld, whom Bradley described as an "affable glad-handing Washington bureaucrat with only minimal naval combat experience and no grasp at all of large-scale land warfare," bore the brunt of his ire. Bradley charged Denfeld with complete dishonesty regarding Navy claims pertaining to American war plans. He also said that the admirals had deliberately skewed data from atomic bomb tests to support their claims against the Air Force.[70] From retirement General Spaatz snorted: "The Navy is having a miscarriage—in public."[71] It was all very unsettling.

Vandenberg rose to defend his service against these various charges. In Bradley's words, he was "icily cool and precise" and "utterly demolished" the testimony of the "crybaby [Navy] aviators." Reading the transcript of the hearings even forty years after the event, one cannot help but agree. Vandenberg's testimony was remarkably dispassionate and logical. It was often said by contemporaries that he was at his best in situations of this type; as things grew hotter, he became cooler and quieter. The effect was devastating.

Vandenberg began by describing the organization of the Joint Chiefs, who by law were charged with formulating strategic war plans. They were assisted in that task by a Joint Staff, composed of an equal number of officers from the three services, which at that time was headed by an admiral. The Joint Staff was advised by two important groups: the Research and Development Board and the Weapons Systems Evaluation Group, both led by distinguished civilian scientists. After many months of study and debate, these diverse groups presented a war plan (TROJAN) that was officially approved by all members of the JCS. The claim that strategic bombing was an Air Force plan was simply not true; it was the *national* plan. The tool of the air offensive called for in the war plan was SAC, under the direct control of the JCS—not the Air Force—and whose targets were selected by the JCS. The purpose of the strategic air campaign was not to win the war; only surface forces could ensure that. Rather, its purpose was to serve as an equalizer to the hordes of enemy troops that greatly outnumbered our own. What was the alternative? Vandenberg asked. "Is it proposed that we build and maintain a standing Army capable of meeting the masses of an enemy army on the ground in equal man-to-man, body-to-body, gun-to-gun combat?"

As for the effectiveness of the B-36, Vandenberg stated that although the airplane was not perfect, it was the best bomber of its type in the world, and it would get through. It had already flown ten thousand miles, dropped a ten-thousand-pound bomb, and returned to its base, all at an altitude of forty-two thousand feet. When questioned about Navy claims that it could be detected, intercepted, and destroyed, the general replied that radar and fighter aircraft were not new; the bomber would get through. When asked if escort fighters should be provided, perhaps supplied from aircraft carriers, Vandenberg responded that such aircraft had insufficient range. Escort was desirable but not necessary. The bomber would still get through.

Concerning the issue of overemphasis on bombers to the detriment of other air arms, Vandenberg noted that of the forty-eight combat groups in the Air Force, only four were equipped with the B-36. If current plans to expand to seventy groups were fulfilled, still only four groups would operate the B-36. When all aircraft (including the reserves) available on M-Day (the hypothetical date for the outbreak of war) were counted, the B-36 comprised only 3 percent of the total. Moreover, as commander of the Ninth Air Force during World War II, he fully realized the crucial importance of close air support. General Bradley did not dispute the point.[72]

As for the *United States* and claims that the Air Force was trying to absorb naval and Marine Corps aviation, Vandenberg stated once again that such was not the case. He objected to the supercarrier because the ship was not needed for the Navy's primary mission. Funds were too scarce to buy weapons not directly supportive of the nation's war plan. Perhaps the carrier was a good weapon, but was it necessary? TROJAN called for specific tasks to be accomplished by specific forces; that was what unification was supposed to be all about. That the Army agreed with him on this issue did not suggest a conspiracy; rather, the Army also thought the Navy was mistaken.[73]

Reading the testimony, one is also struck by the lack of vitriol in Vandenberg's statement. Considering the emotional, sometimes personal and vicious charges that had been levied against him, his secretary, and his service, Vandenberg's mild remarks are amazing. To ensure that the rest of the Air Force remained similarly low key, he had press officers assigned to handle all public statements by his two most rambunctious generals—Kenney and LeMay—so that intemperate remarks would not cause an incident.[74] After Cedric Worth's charges were proved fraudulent, the chief must have realized that the tide was flowing in his direction; he could now afford to be reserved and subtle, attempting to soothe bruised egos rather than exacerbate a split. Revenge was an unjustified luxury.

As a result of the hearings, few heads rolled in the Navy. Worth resigned; Vice Admirals William Blandy and Gerald Bogan were nudged into retirement; and Captain Crommelin was eventually reassigned and given a letter of reprimand, although not without one last bit of controversy. Secretary Matthews ordered Crommelin transferred as punishment, but when told this had been done, the Secretary discovered the "banishment" had been to a rear admiral's billet! Crommelin was reassigned once again.[75] Admiral Denfeld was not so fortunate. When the "revolt of the admirals" began, Matthews and he had fought a losing battle to maintain order within the bulkheads. When Denfeld testified, however, he "defected" to the enemy and joined the Radford group; Matthews stood alone in condemning the actions of those in uniform, and he did not like it. Denfeld was relieved, and in his message to the president, Matthews gave his reasons. The chief of naval operations did not accept unification. What was far worse: "A military establishment is not a political democracy. Integrity of command is indispensable at all times. There can be no twilight zone in the measure of loyalty to superiors and respect for authority existing between various official ranks."[76]

The Navy had fought unification from the beginning, ostensibly because it threatened civilian control of the military—the fear of "the man on horseback." How ironic that the sailors would then deliberately slander their civilian superiors. In truth, the admirals were not repentant, steadfastly maintaining that their astonishing display of insubordination was justified in order to protect naval interests. Those few who suffered for their conduct were considered martyrs. Even three decades later, the revolt was considered by the Navy hierarchy as a glorious chapter in their history.[77] In contrast, General Vandenberg ran a very tight ship indeed.

In the long term, the effect of the incident was small. Within two years increased defense spending would permit the Navy to build supercarriers, and one of the individuals most responsible for the clash, Admiral Radford, would four years later be chosen by President Eisenhower as chairman of the Joint Chiefs of Staff. In the short term, however, the affair had more significance. Observers on both sides of the Atlantic were shocked by the whole incident; one called it a display of "pettiness, inconsistency and hatred." The London *Economist* asked: "What faith can the United States have in Chiefs of Staff who behave like children? What faith can the powers who signed the North Atlantic Treaty have when their strongest partner shows much internal weakness?"[78] Of far greater significance, relations between the services were at their nadir, and in less than a year there would be war.

Vandenberg never forgot the affair. Three years later he still kept a thick dossier in his safe that documented Navy criticism of the Air Force together with his projected responses to such charges. Although he never was required to defend himself again, he was ready if it became necessary.[79]

Vandenberg's performance in this entire controversy was an eloquent response to those critics who thought he was too soft and agreeable for the job of chief of staff. When put to the test, he proved a sturdy and determined spokesman for Air Force and national interests. He resolutely defended unification and the principle of civilian control, and he demanded that his subordinates do so as well.

In the aftermath, Secretary Johnson told his troops to shake hands and forget it; he recommended that they all go golfing together. Johnson congratulated the victors: "My informants stated General Vandenberg sank three fantastic fifty-foot chip shots, and General Norstad constantly played over his head."[80] It is reported that Van and Larry won two dollars each.

There is no present to aviation—only a
past and a future. And, no man can properly develop aviation who cannot change
his mind every twenty-four hours.
                              Italo Balbo

VI | Economics and Atoms

Youk'n hide de fier, but w'at you gwine do
wid de smoke?
                              Uncle Remus

THE BUDGET BATTLES

Money was the underlying cause of the B-36/supercarrier controversy and
the main factor that would lead to the resignations in 1950 of Secretaries Johnson
and Symington and nearly of Generals Vandenberg, Bradley, and Collins. Disagreements between the services were unavoidable given the magnitude of the
issues and the aggressive personalities of the individuals involved. What made
the clashes so violent was the frustration, almost desperation, caused by budget
cuts that left each service feeling it was ill-prepared to carry out its mission. Soldiers, sailors, and airmen fought bitterly because they believed they were fighting
for their institutional lives. Had more funds been available for defense, then each
service could have had the weapons and forces it thought necessary to carry out
its mission; but more funds were not available, and so the budget fights became
particularly heated.

When the Air Force gained independence in 1947, its strength, like that of
the other services, was far below what it considered sufficient for safety, but budget cutting was paramount. After much urging, the president and Congress decided to look into the issue of air power, because advocates had long held that
"winged defense" was the most economical method of protecting the nation. In
mid-1947, President Truman appointed a blue-ribbon panel, the Air Policy Com-

mission, led by Thomas K. Finletter, to study the question. Symington and Vandenberg were called to testify, and both pushed strongly for a more powerful Air Force. Vandenberg called for 131 groups, 70 of which would be active. These 70 would consist of 21 heavy bomb groups, 22 fighter groups, and the rest attack, reconnaissance, and transport aircraft. At that time, the Air Force had only 40 groups but was hoping to expand. Vandenberg's testimony was so frank as to be shocking. *Aviation Week* called his candor an "astonishing break with military policy" because it extensively detailed Air Force capabilities. This candor was deliberate. Vandenberg wanted the American public to know the state of its Air Force, and that state was not good.[1]

The Finletter commission continued its examination and after interviewing over 150 witnesses, released a report in January 1948 that caused a stir. "Survival in the Air Age" stated boldly that "this Military Establishment must be built around the air arm. . . . our military security must be based on air power." It stressed the necessity of being powerful enough not only to defend the country, but capable of "dealing a crushing counter offensive blow on the aggressor." The report added that, unfortunately, the Air Force was not then strong enough to ensure such a deterrent. A seventy-group Air Force composed of 12,400 modern aircraft, of which 700 were atomic-capable heavy bombers, should be immediately available for war. These were almost the exact numbers that Vandenberg had suggested the previous month. The naval air arm was also deficient and had to be increased; 5,793 front line planes were required, with another 5,100 in support.[2] Such findings were a welcome encouragement to both the Air Force and the Navy. The touchstone of the seventy-group Air Force had been a major goal of airmen even before the war had ended. Vandenberg and other air leaders continuously emphasized the necessity for maintaining a force of that size to assure national defense.[3]

Aviators received more good news two months later when the House, which had also been studying the question of air power, released its findings in the form of the Hinshaw-Brewster Report, which concluded that air power was the weapon most likely to discourage an aggressor from attacking, and that it was also the most effective method of thwarting such an attack if it were launched. It too called for a seventy-group Air Force.[4]

These two reports coming in rapid succession seemed to augur well for the nascent Air Force. In addition, the public also admired the airmen: a Gallup poll revealed that 74 percent of those surveyed thought the Air Force would be the most important factor if another war broke out.[5] The Air Force and the Joint Chiefs began immediately to estimate what the proposals called for by the commission and the board would cost and how long they would take to implement. Problems quickly arose. Under existing budget ceilings, an Air Force buildup could only occur at the expense of the Army and Navy, and the sister services were in no mood to be generous. Secretary Forrestal felt similarly that the Defense dollar must be shared, warning that the expansion of one service at the expense of the others would be dangerous.[6] Tension increased further when President Truman made it clear that, reports and surveys notwithstanding, budgetary restraint was the order of the day. It was an election year, and increasing taxes to finance a defense buildup was not feasible. The budget was as much a political question as an economic one; at times the services forgot that simple truism, but President Truman did not.

On May 13, 1948, the president informed the secretary of defense that: "Unless world conditions deteriorate . . . it is my purpose to hold the 1950 budget . . . to a level which can be supported on a continuing basis and which will not undermine our economy." He added it was his desire that "increased emphasis be placed . . . on efficiency, economy and getting a dollar's worth of value for each dollar expended." In order to ensure there was no misunderstanding, Truman sent memoranda to each of his chiefs with the admonition: "There are still some of you who are thinking more of representing the interests and objectives of your individual service than of interpreting the broad national program and its requirements to your subordinates and to the Congress."[7] The president was of the opinion that healthy economies in America and Europe were the best guarantee of success in war, and thus launched the European Recovery Program (the "Marshall Plan") largely to shore up European economies to better withstand Soviet pressures. Truman believed that the enormous capacity of American industry would be able to generate victory in a future conflict just as it had in the world wars. This theory necessarily postulated that war was not imminent and that existing force levels were sufficient to deter Soviet aggression. In his message to Congress the president put it this way:

> This Nation's military security should rest on a nucleus of highly trained and mobile forces . . . backed by ready reserves of trained men, standby equipment and production facilities, and an integrated mobilization plan which relates our national security requirements to the tremendous productive capacity of American industry.[8]

Vandenberg questioned this logic; in the future, a lengthy breathing spell allowing gradual mobilization might not be available. All American war plans called for three basic goals in the event of attack: defense of the United States; the launching of a strategic air offensive; and preparation for the "later phases of war." The first two steps were largely the responsibility of the Air Force and would have to be taken with forces in being; the third phase allowed time for mobilization. Vandenberg reasoned that the Air Force's duties required the bulk of its capability constantly available for battle, but the forces of the Army and Navy could be relatively inert until the outbreak of hostilities.[9]

The president was insistent that the military hold its fiscal year (FY) 1949 budget to $15 billion, fearing a higher figure would generate inflation and necessitate unpopular wage and price controls. (The figure of $14.4 billion is usually used because $600 million was to be skimmed off the top for stockpiling; hence, the services were left with $14.4 billion to spend.) After studying the limitations this budget would place on the Air Force, Symington remonstrated with the president, asking him to reconsider, but to no avail. Symington then wrote Forrestal that the president's directions were unrealistic and that "vital objectives in our program of national security are jeopardized." The seventy-group program mandated by Congress could not be achieved with such a budget ceiling.[10] Forrestal was sympathetic, but events would prove him no more successful at changing Truman's mind.

The JCS attempted to meet the president's spending limit, but were unable to decrease projections below $30 billion—twice what the president had ordered. In an effort to break the logjam, the JCS agreed to appoint a committee to concentrate on the budget. This group, referred to as the McNarney board after its senior member, General Joseph McNarney, labored for weeks to resolve the budget impasse, but had only partial success.[11] Most arguments were between the Navy and the Air Force. An indication of the seriousness of these disagreements can be gained by reading the transcript of one such budget meeting:

ADMIRAL RADFORD: I doubt if your bombers will get through.

GENERAL VANDENBERG: If we can't get in there with a 300 knot bomber, how are you going to exist in there with a 30 knot task force?

RADFORD: We will have fighter protection. You won't be able to conduct successful bombing operations in World War III without fighter protection and not with 300 knot bombers.

GENERAL GRUENTHER: Then you would cast considerable doubt on the air offensive conducted from Great Britain?

RADFORD: I would go further than that. In my opinion it is almost certain to fail.

VANDENBERG: The Russians have poor air defenses and they are not centrally controlled.

RADFORD: That reminds me of the 30s when you were putting forth the thesis that you could do bombing without fighter protection. It certainly fell flat during the war.

VANDENBERG: It was done during the last war.

RADFORD: Yes, but at great cost.

VANDENBERG: They bombed their objectives and destroyed them. That is all you have to do with the A-bomb.

RADFORD: You have got to get an entirely different type of A-bomb carrier to make A-bomb delivery more satisfactory. I think the Air Force has to develop high-speed bombers that can go in and have a fair chance of success.

VANDENBERG: We think the Navy ought to develop an anti-submarine force.

GENERAL BRADLEY: I don't think this is getting us anywhere except to bring out our weaknesses.[12]

Secretary of the Army Kenneth Royall grew impatient with the incessant bickering and advised Forrestal to end the squabbling once and for all; either give all the airplanes to the Navy and abolish the Air Force, or give all the planes to the Air Force and let the sailors run the ships.[13] Others also believed that Forrestal was exerting insufficient control over the JCS. Director of the Budget James Webb told David Lilienthal of the Atomic Energy Commission that Forrestal was being "bulldozed" and was not carrying out the president's wishes in budgetary matters. Webb concluded that the defense secretary's lack of control was a "very disturbing" situation. Truman agreed, confiding to his diary that Forrestal "can't take it. He wants to compromise with the opposition."[14]

After two months, McNarney's committee decreased estimates to $23 billion, still far too high. On October 6, Forrestal prodded his chiefs once again: "I want it clearly established . . . that I am expecting a definite recommendation from you, as an entity, under a ceiling of $14.4 billion."[15] While directing his chiefs to decrease their figures, Forrestal visited the president once again in an effort to convince him to raise his, but was unsuccessful. In exasperation, General Vandenberg wrote Forrestal that the Navy's proposals were "out of balance in relation to the estimated strength and capabilities of our only possible potential enemy." He therefore suggested the following split: Army, $4.9 billion; Navy, $4.4 billion; Air Force, $5.1 billion.[16] Bradley concurred, arguing that the Navy said it needed carriers in the Mediterranean to help stop a land invasion. Why? asked Bradley. Naval air had never stopped an army movement before, and that was not their mission anyway: "The Navy should have whatever air force is necessary to carry out its *naval* mission but when there is a limited amount of money available I think we must consider primary missions first." Admiral Denfeld disagreed with the generals and offered the following division: Army, $4.9 billion; Navy, $4.9 billion; Air Force, $4.6 billion.[17]

Forrestal sent his Chiefs back to their desks; he did not want split decisions, he wanted consensus. Finally, on November 8 an agreement of sorts was reached and forwarded to the secretary: Army, $4.8 billion; Navy, $4.6 billion; Air Force, $5.0 billion.[18] However, there was still dispute about what weapon systems should be purchased; specifically, how many carriers would be authorized for the Navy? Denfeld wanted nine, Vandenberg offered four, and Bradley compromised at six. Vandenberg argued that the Navy's figure anticipated a carrier task force in the Mediterranean. He pointed out that no such mission was projected in the war plan (HALFMOON); therefore, four carriers were sufficient. All were in agreement on one point: $14.4 billion was "insufficient to implement national policy in any probable war situation that can be foreseen." Forrestal once again wrote the president, asking him to raise the Defense budget to $16.9 billion, contending that the Joint Chiefs did not believe national security could be adequately safeguarded with the lower ceiling. He had tried to enlist the support of Secretary of State George Marshall by asking him to assert that higher defense spending was needed because of the hazardous political situation. Marshall would not bite, however; he was pushing his own European Recovery Program and did not want funds diverted to a military expansion. The most he offered Forrestal was the bland assurance that a bigger military budget would provide a state of readiness that would help negotiations and reassure European allies. The president remained obdurate.[19]

Forrestal reluctantly accepted his lot and the fund split recommended by the Joint Chiefs of the $14.4 billion; he then resolved the carrier issue by settling on a total of eight. Although the secretary breathed a sigh of relief, he realized the battle was not over and a struggle in Congress would probably be inevitable. He reminded his subordinates that it was their responsibility to support the budget if called upon to testify. This was far from a "gag order," but Forrestal clearly foresaw that nerves had been rubbed raw during the prolonged budget discussions and an attempt by the services to "take their case to court" was a possibility.[20] Eugene M. Zuckert, then assistant secretary of the Air Force, remembers Forrestal asking Symington pointedly if he would support the budget before Congress.

Symington replied that he would be under oath and could not lie; Forrestal agreed. The president later asked Symington the same question and received the same response. Truman then asked for Symington's word that he would not "originate any questions" before the committees. When the secretary agreed, the president told him to answer all questions honestly.[21]

Vandenberg was disgusted by the constant arguing. He and Admiral Denfeld did not see eye to eye, and it was doubtful that they ever would (the B-36 hearings were going on at that same time). Writing Forrestal in November 1948, he deplored the powerlessness of the JCS to reach a timely decision even on elementary issues; something must be done.

> Specifically, there is a difference of opinion as to whether the JCS, as a body, should determine the strategic concept for future war and establish the major elements of forces required to carry out such a concept. I firmly believe that law and precedent make this, together with the strategic direction of such forces in the event of war, the primary function of the JCS.

He strongly recommended that a Chairman of the Joint Chiefs be appointed to *force* a decision if unanimity was impossible.[22] To his mind, a definite decision, even if wrong, was preferable to weakness and vacillation. In a lengthy and strongly worded memorandum to Secretary Forrestal in January 1949, Vandenberg expanded on the ideas he had presented in November. Citing provisions in the National Security Act, the president's executive order of 1947, and the Key West Agreement of 1948, he reasoned that it was imperative for the JCS to take charge of military strategy. It seriously concerned him that the chiefs refused even to acknowledge that such was their function. He concluded: "In the face of the failure of the Joint Chiefs of Staff to either recognize or discharge their collective responsibilities, this memorandum constitutes my unilateral opinion concerning that advice which I strongly believe should properly be provided the Secretary of Defense by the Joint Chiefs of Staff."[23]

Ironically, Secretary Forrestal, who had been one of the main architects of his virtually powerless position, finally realized his error, and in the month following Vandenberg's first memorandum pushed for increased authority. In addition, the Commission on the Organization of the Executive Branch of the Government, led by former President Herbert Hoover, also studied the problems of the Defense establishment and agreed that changes were necessary. Vandenberg was called to testify before the commission and repeated his opinions regarding the inadequacy of the Defense secretary's position and the need for a JCS chairman.[24]

The president concurred with the Hoover commission's conclusions and wrote Congress in March 1949 asking for amendments to the National Security Act. The changes, which took effect in August 1949, were an improvement but did not go as far as Vandenberg had wanted: the service secretaries were demoted below cabinet level rank and placed directly under the Defense secretary, and the posts of one deputy secretary and three assistant secretaries of Defense were added to help administer the newly named "Department of Defense." The role and composition of the National Security Council were more clearly defined. The Joint Chiefs were specifically authorized to present to Congress, "on their own initiative, after first so informing the secretary of Defense, any recommendation relating to the Department of Defense, that [they] may deem proper." In addition, the post of chairman of the Joint Chiefs was established; unfortunately, he had no vote and thus was denied the authority which Vandenberg thought so crucial. Split decisions would continue. General Bradley was named the first chairman and his place as Army chief was taken by General J. Lawton ("Lightning Joe") Collins.[25]

Finally, an entirely new section was added to the act that detailed a new budgeting process, centering more decision making in the Defense secretary's office. This provision especially rankled Vandenberg. The budget had always been, quite properly, a largely civilian affair—proposed by the president on the advice of the service secretaries and the Bureau of the Budget, and then debated and decided by the Congress—but now even technical details regarding force structures and weapon systems were being taken out of the hands of the Joint Chiefs. To make matters worse in Vandenberg's opinion, Wilfred J. McNeil, the Department of Defense Comptroller, was a particularly unsatisfactory choice to be making such decisions. McNeil, an officer in the Naval Reserve, was seen as an opponent of the Air Force, and this interpretation was not tempered when he was promoted to rear admiral at the height of the budget fights in 1949—reputedly just after deciding the Air Force did not need an extra twenty-two groups, but the Navy did need an extra carrier. One reporter commented that McNeil was the man in Washington whom Vandenberg hated the most.[26]

Another reason for disliking McNeil was because he and his staff did not seem to appreciate what Vandenberg regarded as the superior efficiency of the Air Force budget process, which he maintained was more economy-minded than those of the Army and Navy because of the organizational efforts of successful businessmen like Symington and Zuckert. Cost analysis and modern management techniques implemented by the secretaries helped ensure that fat was trimmed from the budget before it ever reached McNeil's office. In October 1947, the Air Force had created the position of air comptroller and appointed a Harvard Business School graduate to the post, Lieutenant General Edwin Rawlings; his job was to oversee the entire Air Force budget process. One of his first moves was to purchase the military's first computer, the UNIVAC 1, to more efficiently manage finances. Rawlings then introduced into the Air Force organization the modern business methods he had learned at Harvard, and executives from Sears, Roebuck and Company were called in to study the Air Force supply and inventory system in an effort to improve efficiency. Moreover, Vandenberg insisted that all officers be annually rated on their ability to manage resources and personnel.[27] Because of the rapid obsolescence of aircraft, a close association with industry was a necessity. It was believed this symbiotic relationship helped keep the Air Force running smoothly and efficiently. As Vandenberg put it: "It is our theory that as long as we are using taxpayers' money we should employ as many as possible of the methods and techniques that enabled the taxpayers to make the money."[28] Nevertheless, "the admiral" slashed Air Force estimates anyway, assuming they were as bloated as those of the Army and Navy. Vandenberg and Symington complained frequently, charging that the other services were guilty of bad management and of padding their personnel and cost figures. McNeil and his superiors, Forrestal and later Johnson, were not receptive to Air Force claims.[29]

When the proposed budget for fiscal 1949 went before Congress and the Joint Chiefs were called to testify, their words were hardly a ringing endorsement. Vandenberg was the most vocal. Although careful not to attack the overall budget ceiling, and thus the president, he did disagree with the division of funds. He maintained that an adequate defense could be purchased for $15 billion, but if Congress was serious about its previous pledges to build the Air Force to seventy groups, then the Air Force needed a total of $7 billion.[30] Symington expressed similar opinions, and this especially rankled Forrestal. There was some thought of Symington being asked for his resignation, but Forrestal realized he did not have sufficient clout with the president to risk such a confrontation. Even so, the relationship between the two secretaries was never the same. Forrestal considered Symington insubordinate and thought he was maneuvering for the position of secretary of Defense. Eugene Zuckert later stated that he also thought Symington was given too much rein and that was ironic, because Symington would never have tolerated such actions by a subordinate.[31]

Symington and Vandenberg were alike in many respects, and their opinions were often the same. The two men were exceedingly self-confident and poised. Perhaps because they did not look upon each other as a threat—as was so often the case in the Navy and would be in the Air Force when Symington resigned— the two worked together closely, loyally, and smoothly. Their offices were close together in the Pentagon, and Symington was always invited to Air Staff meetings. The two became close personal friends and this relationship continued after their professional one was severed. Not surprisingly, Vandenberg and Symington thought similarly on the budget problem, and the secretary wrote in late 1948:

> It is our earnest desire to support the administration's budget, because we realize that economic disaster could be equivalent to military disaster. That, however, does not change the position of the Air Force; namely, from a purely military standpoint, 70 groups, or its equivalent (now 67 groups) is necessary for the minimum peacetime security of the United States.[32]

What had put the services even more on edge in the budget struggle was the realization that President Truman intended to hold the Department of Defense to the same funding levels for the following year. The anguished arm-twisting necessary to commit a fiscal plan to paper was barely completed, and it was time to begin anew. No doubt aware of how difficult the prospect was, at Forrestal's urging Truman recalled General Eisenhower to active duty and made him "presiding officer" of the JCS in January 1949. (This was before the NSA amendments passed later in the year that resulted in Bradley becoming chairman.) Forrestal had become chary of the Navy hierarchy's constant carping, telling

Eisenhower he no longer trusted most of them. He hoped Ike would "unify the services."[33] Although he had no power to compel agreement, it was hoped that Eisenhower's enormous prestige would smooth conflicts. Such hopes were not fulfilled, and Eisenhower soon found himself frustrated. Nevertheless, Eisenhower began his task optimistically. He saw the first hurdle as being the need for an agreed upon strategic war plan. Once such a document was officially approved, then the services could determine what forces were necessary to carry out their primary missions as defined in the plan. It was anticipated that these forces, which Eisenhower called "red bricks," would absorb about 80 percent of the budget. The remaining 20 percent would be used for secondary missions—"blue bricks." On February 28, Eisenhower directed the chiefs to push ahead with war plans and budgetary projections and be prepared to meet together to discuss these matters the following week.[34]

When the requested plans were unveiled on March 2, 1949, it was clear that the problems of the previous year had returned with a vengeance. Projections for the Army were similar among the three services and thus presented little controversy. Regarding the Air Force, Vandenberg once again proposed an expansion to seventy groups while the Navy repeated that forty-eight were sufficient. Even so, the strategic bombing forces in both plans were comparable; it was the tactical air units that were deleted by the Navy. When one remembers that the Navy was at the same time in the B-36 hearings charging the Air Force with overemphasizing strategic forces and neglecting the tactical, this fact is ironic and significant. The forces rejected consisted of six medium bomber groups (B-50s for the strategic air offensive), four light bomber groups (close air support aircraft), three reconnaissance, five tactical fighter, and four troop carrier groups. In other words, if the Air Force had been expanded to seventy groups as desired, sixteen of the additional twenty-two groups would have been earmarked for use with the ground forces. It was precisely in this area that the Air Force was deficient when war came the following year.[35] The Air Force was unbalanced, and Vandenberg knew it, but he could do little to redress the problem. In a major war with the Soviet Union, the United States could be defeated unless it had an adequate atomic strike force, but the lack of a sizable conventional capability would only delay victory in a minor war. If funds were available, then Vandenberg wanted both; his plans for the composition of the seventy groups clearly prove this. But funds were not available, and so Vandenberg had to set priorities. Total war was more dangerous and must be provided for first. He did not like it, but there was nothing to be done —not yet.

It was the radical difference of opinion regarding naval forces that was to precipitate the most conflict in the budget process. In the first place, both the Army and the Air Force proposed the elimination of all Marine aviation units. Two independent air forces were undesirable but acceptable, three separate air arms were not. As for aircraft carriers, Vandenberg threw down the gauntlet: there were insufficient funds and reason to justify *any* fleet carriers, although he agreed to twelve escort carriers for use in an antisubmarine role. Eisenhower disagreed and thought the Navy needed large carriers; Vandenberg told him he was "nuts."[36] The Air Force commander argued that the naval function of paramount importance in the war plan was the maintenance of the sea lines of communication; this required the elimination or containment of the Soviet submarine menace. Fleet carriers were inefficient in such a role. When Denfeld countered that the four large carriers originally conceded by Vandenberg were too few to be of use, the general, no doubt with a twinkle in his eye, quickly agreed: it would be best if *no* large carriers were built.[37] Vandenberg stated that the United States already had the largest navy in the world and was allied with Britain, the second greatest naval power. There was only one major enemy; that enemy had neither a surface fleet nor a strategic air force. It did, however, have an enormous army, great tactical air strength, and a sizable submarine fleet. Aircraft carriers would not survive in the Mediterranean because of Soviet air power; if the carriers remained well off-shore in the Atlantic, the short range of their aircraft would make them useless in a major land campaign. Besides, the Navy's mission did not include strategic bombing. The Department of Defense was "out of balance"; the Air Force and Army should be enlarged and the Navy decreased in order to restore equilibrium.[38] Bradley generally agreed with this line of reasoning, and so did Eisenhower, at least privately.

Upon assuming his duties, Eisenhower had discussed basic military strategy and budgetary considerations with the president, and the two had agreed that the Air Force should be strengthened and the Navy cut back. In July, he reiterated this position to Johnson, stating his "inescapable conclusion" that the Air Force, and especially its atomic strike force, be reinforced, even if that meant "cutting into other features of our program more than we believe desirable or wise." By November, Eisenhower seemed fully to accept the thrust of Vandenberg's arguments, writing to an old friend and naval officer that the Navy should worry more about Soviet submarines and less about strategic bombing. The naval mission was first and foremost the control of the seas, and Eisenhower was not convinced that the admirals were sufficiently concerned with that mission.[39] Publicly, however, the general had to maintain a much more even keel.

In his quest for reconciliation, Eisenhower showed commendable innovation. He devised one formula after another in an attempt to draw the estimates of the three services closer together and within presidential guidelines. But all such attempts—"red bricks," the "four estimates," and "Ike I and Ike II forces"—ended in failure. The problem about which Vandenberg had railed the previous December was still painfully apparent: Eisenhower could suggest formulas, but if any one of the services refused his overtures, deadlock resulted. Even so, there was some progress made until July 1949, when things erupted once again. At that point, President Truman reevaluated the nation's fiscal balance sheet and decided the defense budget would have to be trimmed still further, to $13 billion. Secretary Louis Johnson quickly and energetically endorsed the cut.[40] It would seem that if Johnson's political ambitions were as lofty as reported, he looked upon the economy as a major campaign issue, feeling that this concerned the American public more than potential Soviet aggression. Johnson hitched his wagon to the star of thrift and hoped it would carry him closer to the executive mansion.

It was thought by many and hoped by some that Johnson would be partial to the Air Force because of his previous association with Consolidated-Vultee Aircraft Corporation, but in truth the Air Force fared no better than under Secretary Forrestal. A phrase bandied about by the budgeteers at that time was "balanced forces." All wanted balance, but like many catchwords it meant different things to different people. Because the Navy considered itself as having world-wide commitments that it thought the other services did not, it moved for the lion's share of the funds. Eisenhower had suggested at one point an even three-way split. Bradley thought balanced forces meant "effective forces equal to the tasks that modern warfare may thrust upon this military." Vandenberg suggested that funds should be balanced against the proposed enemy's capabilities; weapons projected for use in war plans should have precedence over all others.[41] Whose definition was to be used?

Although the services argued and fumed that the new cuts were totally unrealistic, Johnson remained impassive. The final figures submitted to the president on September 20 were: Army, $4.0 billion; Navy, $3.8 billion; Air Force, $4.3 billion.[42] This budget would permit the Air Force forty-eight groups, of which four were heavy bombers; the Army would have nine divisions, and the Navy six carriers. Johnson realized that not everyone would be happy with such a decision, but he was certain that the economy measures he had instituted would soon bear fruit and save millions of dollars. Of greater concern, Johnson believed that: "The Department of Defense recognizes the overriding necessity of keeping military costs within limits which will not endanger the fundamental soundness of our economy—one of our primary military assets."[43] When questioned about this allocation, Vandenberg refused to toe the line and replied as he had the previous year: he supported the president's budget; the secretary's was another matter: "The Air Force believes that it can perform its responsibilities in the national defense with an establishment usually described as the '70-group Air Force.' It does not feel that it can take responsibility for the military risks involved in any lesser force."[44]

Congress was also in an economizing mood, but not to the same degree as Truman and Johnson, and it was especially favorable to the Air Force. In a surprising transformation, the Navy's erstwhile legislative supporter, Carl Vinson, became a strong advocate of air power and pushed for seventy groups. In April 1948, he had expressed the opinion that the United States could not compete with 175 Soviet divisions, but it could compete in air power.[45] Congressman Clarence Cannon voiced this same feeling more colorfully: "We will not necessarily have to send our land army over there in the next war, as in the last war. Let us equip soldiers from other nations and let them send their boys into holocausts instead of sending our own boys. That is what long-range planes mean."[46] Even so, President Truman remained unconvinced. The crisis atmosphere of mid-1948 that had led to a modest attempt at military buildup had cooled by early 1949 and with it all thoughts of rearmament. Moreover, the president's surprise reelection probably emboldened him to carry on with his policy of fiscal restraint. The people had apparently spoken. The previous year, Congress had defied the president and had added $615 million to a supplemental Air Force budget—the House vote was 306–1. When Truman vetoed the bill, Congress overrode him by a wide margin. The president then said the extra money was "inconsistent with a realistic and balanced security program" and would "interfere with orderly planning." He therefore directed the Defense secretary to "place in reserve" the additional funds appropriated for the Air Force.[47] As a result, Vandenberg held little hope for relief, even with a sympathetic Congress. What later proved especially ironic was the deteriorating world situation, which seemed to dictate increased defense spending. China had fallen to the Communists in 1949 and with it much of American foreign policy in the Far East. The coup in Czechoslovakia followed by the Berlin Blockade had shown the aggressive intentions of the Soviets, and there were still fears for the stability of Western Europe. Of far greater significance, however, were the events in Siberia.

JOE I AND THE SUPER

In April 1947, Lewis L. Strauss of the Atomic Energy Commission, concerned over the dearth of intelligence regarding foreign atomic research, asked his colleagues if there was any agency tasked to monitor the level of radioactivity in the atmosphere. Strauss thought this the best means of detecting an atomic test conducted by another nation. When told there was none, Strauss approached Vandenberg, then head of the Central Intelligence Group, and requested that a long-range detection system be established. Vandenberg agreed and wrote the secretaries of War and Navy, suggesting a meeting to discuss the matter, but the initial response was negative. Many American experts believed that the Soviets were so far behind in atomic energy development that a monitoring program would be a waste of time and effort. Eventually, however, Army Secretary Royall became convinced of the program's necessity and directed Spaatz to take action.[48]

Events moved slowly, but by mid-1948 the Air Force's monitoring system consisted of seismic and sonic listening posts at various points around the globe and periodic flights by specially equipped aircraft to sample the atmosphere at high altitude for signs of radioactivity. The system was in full operation by July 1948, when the United States conducted atomic tests at Eniwetok Atoll in the Pacific. The blast data collected by the Air Force at numerous locations as the radioactive cloud drifted across the globe were examined, and proved conclusively to David Lilienthal that the detection methods were a success. He wrote in his diary that the results were "quite remarkable and beyond our expectations." Unless it happened in a cave, an atomic detonation occurring anywhere in the world would be picked up by Air Force sensors.[49]

On the morning of September 3, 1949, an Air Force WB-29 weather reconnaissance aircraft registered an unusually high concentration of radioactivity over the North Pacific, east of the Kamchatka Peninsula. Later that day, other aircraft began reporting the same phenomena farther to the south, so the data were sent to Washington for further analysis. Vandenberg appointed Vannevar Bush to head a committee to study the evidence. After two weeks, Bush and the other top scientists, including J. Robert Oppenheimer, met with Vandenberg to discuss the results of their investigation. Upon reviewing the facts, it was clear that an atomic detonation had occurred in Siberia between August 26 and 29. More importantly, the Soviets had engineered an advanced plutonium bomb—the type used at Nagasaki—and had bypassed the cruder uranium device dropped on Hiroshima. It was also quite powerful—six times larger than the first American blast.[50] When Secretary Johnson was briefed the following day, he was highly skeptical, suggesting instead that the Soviet detonation was probably an accident and not a true bomb at all. Nevertheless, it was decided that the president should be notified.

The next day, September 21, Lilienthal, Johnson, the Joint Chiefs, and Bush met at the White House, with Vandenberg briefing the president on the detonation. The president was stunned, and, like Johnson, expressed doubt, but after repeated assertions by Vandenberg and Bush, Truman finally understood. Even so, the president ruminated for two more days on the news. Finally, on September 23, President Truman went before the nation and announced: "We have evidence that within recent weeks an atomic explosion occurred in the USSR." He called for calm and assured the public that everything was under control.[51] Somewhat melodramatically, the next issue of the *Bulletin of the Atomic Scientists* had a new cover. It had always featured a clock showing the time at eight minutes to midnight—Armageddon. After the announcement of the Soviet blast, the *Bulletin* moved its chronometer up to three minutes before midnight.

Administration officials quickly announced that the Soviet explosion was not a surprise and had been anticipated for some time, pronouncements that Lilienthal labeled "bunk."[52] In truth, there had been a plethora of estimates as to when Red Atom Day would occur, and many would-be prophets changed their views over time. In 1946, Major General Lauris Norstad had briefed the president that 1949 would be the most likely date for the Soviets to develop a bomb; but by 1949 the Air Force had officially endorsed the 1951 date as most probable, while the other services and the CIA predicted 1953. Major General Leslie Groves and Vannevar Bush had also originally prophesied a date of 1949 or 1950, but in August 1949, Groves had changed his estimate to twenty years in the future and Bush to ten years hence. In truth, events in the Soviet Union were so hidden that an assessment of their atomic capabilities was little better than guesswork. Air Force officers have since maintained that their predictions for Joe I—the name given to the first Soviet blast—were always more conservative, and thus more accurate, than those of the CIA, AEC, or other military services. However, General Charles P. Cabell, chief of Air Force intelligence in 1949, later admitted that although he had a hunch the Soviets would detonate by 1949, he was not certain enough to put his feelings on paper.[53]

Whether or not anyone in America was caught by surprise, everyone was certainly caught unprepared. Vandenberg admitted as much and wrote LeMay that the event had "serious implications on plans for the national security."[54] It now became necessary to build air defenses for the United States, which at that time were virtually nonexistent. A radar fence had to be constructed to warn of a possible Soviet attack, and Vandenberg diverted $50 million from other Air Force projects for that purpose.[55] He then wrote a sobering memorandum to the Joint Chiefs stating that Joe I had occurred four years earlier than estimated and that there was no guarantee the Soviets had exploded the first completed bomb; they might have been stockpiling weapons for the past two years (as the Soviets themselves claimed). If such a stockpile did exist, and American intelligence could hardly claim authoritatively that it did not, then a Soviet air strike could be catastrophic.

> With the United States defenses against air attack in the state they are today, almost any number of Soviet bombers could cross our borders and fly to most of the targets in the United States without a shot being fired at them and without even being challenged in any way. Moreover, implementation of the program of air defense which we have approved will not suffice to correct this situation.

Vandenberg therefore called for a "Manhattan Project" to build American defenses and "reduce this peril" to the United States.[56]

War plans also had to be modified and the atomic stockpile examined; the slow, almost leisurely expansion of the American atomic arsenal had to be accelerated. In early October, the Joint Chiefs pushed strongly for an expansion of the atomic energy program. The Eniwetok tests had demonstrated methods of using fissionable material more efficiently, so that the precious uranium 235 and plutonium 239 could be used to build more bombs. The chiefs also noted that the "continuing refusal of the Soviet Union to become a cooperating member of the world community" was likely to become even more pronounced as a result of Joe I. Truman agreed, and the AEC budget was immediately boosted by $300 million.[57] Of greater importance, the new thermonuclear weapon—the so-called "super bomb" that still only existed in theory—needed to be addressed.

The theory of the super, or hydrogen, bomb had been discussed as early as the 1920s when a scientist described the evolution of the sun as a continuous series of massive explosions caused by the conversion of hydrogen into helium. These explosions resulted from the *fusion* of atomic nuclei; however, only incredibly high temperatures could cause such fusion to occur—far higher than anything produced by man. With the detonation of the atomic bomb—which was a result of *fission,* or the splitting of an atomic nucleus—scientists realized they now had a method of generating the tremendous heat necessary to induce fusion in light elements such as hydrogen. Potentially, thermonuclear weapons could be thousands of times more powerful than atomic bombs, but the technical obstacles were formidable. Even so, Vandenberg realized the significance hydrogen bombs would have for an atomic air offensive and pushed steadily for their development. A debate over targeting was going on within the Air Force at the time, and the projected super bomb could quickly resolve the conflict.

The strategic bombing doctrine of the United States since the days of Billy Mitchell had emphasized precision bombing of selected military and industrial sites. During the European campaign, the AAF had resisted attempts to switch this doctrine to the city-busting tactics of RAF Bomber Command. The Pacific Theater was a different matter. Unique problems of weather and distance prompted Curtis LeMay, commander of the XXI Bomber Command, to scrap precision doctrine and opt for mass incendiary bombing of Japanese cities. These tactics seemed at least as successful as those employed against Germany. After the war, the debate over precision versus area bombing did not disappear. Vandenberg advocated the former and directed that the enemy's industrial capacity—specifically the petroleum and electrical facilities—be prime targets. When LeMay became SAC commander, he disputed this policy, claiming that the Pacific war experience had demonstrated the superiority of an area bombing strategy. To help crystallize the issue, Vandenberg invited noted historian Bernard Brodie to study the matter.[58]

Brodie had gained prominence with the publication of *The Absolute Weapon*, a discourse detailing how the atomic bomb had changed the world. This work caught the attention of General Norstad, who suggested to Vandenberg that Brodie might be useful to the Air Staff. Characteristically, the chief concurred; he had relied on such civilian expertise in the past, and would continue to call on the services of men like Jimmy Doolittle, Charles Lindbergh, Theodore Von Karman, and Barton Leach in the years ahead. Brodie, according to his own account, made few friends at SAC headquarters when he reviewed their targeting procedures and offered "heretical" advice. He utterly rejected the LeMay thesis, arguing that a massive air offensive designed to leave the Soviet Union in ashes was not a viable military or political strategy. Brodie urged restraint and precision strikes. Rather than lessening the debate over targeting, Brodie's views fanned the flames.[59] Fortuitously, the prospect of the thermonuclear weapon offered a way out of this heated controversy. The destructive power of the projected super was so massive—predicted at one thousand times more powerful than existing atomic bombs—that questions of precision became meaningless. Whether a hydrogen bomb was aimed at Moscow's city center or at an electrical plant several blocks away would make little difference to the several hundred thousand people who would be killed in either event.

There was, however, strong opposition to the super bomb from noted scientists J. Robert Oppenheimer and Leo Szilard. Many of the leading scientists who had helped build the atomic bomb began to develop moral scruples. In March 1948, Oppenheimer, the intellectual doyen of the atomic scientists, uttered his famous apologia: "In some sort of crude sense which no vulgarity, no humor, no over-statement can quite extinguish, the physicists have known sin; and this is a knowledge which they cannot lose."[60] Many of his colleagues at the Los Alamos laboratory shared these sentiments, frequently baring their souls in their trade journal, the *Bulletin of the Atomic Scientists*. One of their members, however, was not similarly afflicted. Harold Agnew, a director at Los Alamos, later described his coworkers: "There were remnants of this feeling that we shouldn't pursue these endeavors [thermonuclear development]. I was not in sympathy with these individuals; in fact, I thought they were nuts. . . . they even got into religious matters. They would quote the Bible. I thought they were quite off their rockers, frankly."[61]

When the General Advisory Committee to the AEC studied the issue of the super's development during the month following Joe I, they opposed it unanimously. The committee, composed of such luminaries as Oppenheimer, Enrico Fermi, James Conant, and Isaac Rabi, not only doubted the technical feasibility of the device but decried its construction on moral grounds: "We base our recommendations on our belief that the extreme dangers to mankind inherent in the proposal wholly outweigh any military advantage that could come from this development." The scientists said that employment of the hydrogen bomb would be akin to genocide; therefore, it should never even be built.[62]

David Lilienthal, the chairman of the AEC, was strongly opposed to super experimentation, and thought it would be a waste of precious radioactive material. In truth, however, Lilienthal was opposed to atomic weapons in principle. When General Groves retired in 1948, his replacement as chief of the Armed Forces Special Weapons Group was Major General K. D. Nichols. Lilienthal and Nichols had known each other for some time and were not friends. When appointed as chief of the Special Weapons Group, Truman called both him and Lilienthal to the White House and sat them down in front of his desk. Nichols remembered the incident.

> After we sat down, as I recall it, the president said to both of us, "I know you two hate each other's guts." Then looking me squarely in the eyes, he said, "Nichols, if I instruct Mr. Lilienthal that the primary objective of the AEC is to develop and produce atomic weapons, do you see any reason why you cannot cooperate fully with Mr. Lilienthal?" I replied: "There is no problem if that is the primary objective." Then the president turned to Lilienthal and said: "Dave, I am signing the letter appointing Nichols a major general and he is to be chief of AFSWG and a member of the MLC [Military Liaison Committee to the Atomic Energy Commission]. You will have to forgo your desire to place a bottle of milk on every doorstep and get down to the business of producing atomic weapons."[63]

Lilienthal's opposition to thermonuclear development was, therefore, not unexpected. Writing to the president, the AEC chairman said that he opposed the new weapon because it was a tool for mass destruction. He feared that the administration's constant calls for world peace would ring hollow if such a device were built. Moreover, even testing the weapon could release large amounts of dangerous radioactivity into the atmosphere, polluting the world. Finally, a decision to build the super would merely cause another round in the arms race, which would not enhance American security.[64] Lilienthal was so opposed to the very idea of the super that when Louis W. Alvarez, a leading physicist at Los Alamos who favored the weapon, came to argue the question with him, Lilienthal turned his back on Alvarez, looked out the window, and refused to discuss it.[65] Lilienthal's views were shared by Commissioners Henry Smythe and Sumner Pike.

The other two commissioners disagreed. Gordon Dean stated simply that retiring from the thermonuclear lists would leave the Soviets a monopoly, thereby inviting aggression.[66] Lewis Strauss was more emphatic, arguing that the super was indeed technically feasible and that the atheistic Communists would not desist from building it on moral grounds. In fact, he suspected they were already hard at work on its development. If the United States refrained from building the new bomb, then the Soviets would almost certainly gain a monopoly. "I am unable to see any satisfaction in that prospect," he remarked soberly. Responding to Lilienthal's arguments, Strauss scoffed at the suggestion of atmospheric pollution, claiming it would take hundreds of thermonuclear detonations to wreak the havoc envisioned by Lilienthal. As for the claim that super development was incompatible with a peace offensive, Strauss said simply that unilateral renunciation by the

United States would probably be seen by the Kremlin as a trick. The United States should build the bomb.[67]

Vandenberg strongly supported thermonuclear development. Soon after Joe I, Edward Teller, a leading physicist in the atomic program, approached Major General Roscoe Wilson, deputy chief of the Special Weapons Group. Teller detailed to Wilson his thoughts on the hydrogen bomb, suggesting that the matter be broached to the Air Force hierarchy. Wilson concurred, and Vandenberg was briefed on Teller's ideas. The chief was impressed. That afternoon, October 13, he informed the JCS of these developments and the following day testified before the Joint Committee on Atomic Energy. Vandenberg spoke forcefully concerning the new weapon, warning that it was essential for the United States to acquire it before the Soviets did. Senator Brian McMahon, the committee chairman, agreed wholeheartedly with Vandenberg's assessment and soon after wrote an impassioned letter to President Truman advocating thermonuclear development.[68]

It appears, however, that the JCS were not overly enthusiastic about the hydrogen bomb. A possible reason may have concerned interservice rivalry. The super, if it could be built, was expected to be a massive device, weighing perhaps fifty thousand pounds. The equally massive B-36 was capable of carrying such a load, as were the new B-47 and B-52 jet bombers then undergoing development; but the Air Force appeared to be the only service that would have a delivery capability for the new weapon in the foreseeable future. On the other hand, if scientists concentrated on atomic development, soon there would be small, tactical warheads available for Army and Navy weapon systems. Before the Eniwetok tests, all attempts to build small atomic weapons had ended in failure. Three or four bombs could be assembled for the amount of fissionable material it took to build one artillery shell. Until energy production was drastically increased or a method was discovered to use existing uranium and plutonium more efficiently, Vandenberg was adamantly opposed to the excessively wasteful tactical weapons.[69]

Writing his JCS colleagues in March 1951, Vandenberg argued forcefully that the future security of the United States depended upon air power: "The first nation which gives full recognition to the potential of Air Power and as a consequence acts to secure and maintain a controlling military position in the air will dominate the next chapter of military history. I feel that we must and will be that nation." Vandenberg went on to state that there were so many strategic targets to strike in the event of war with the Soviet Union, and not enough bombs yet available to cover them, that it would be foolish to begin production of weapons for secondary, tactical targets. He asked that Air Force requirements for fissionable material be "primary and over-riding."[70]

Although eventually thermonuclear warheads would also be miniaturized, the other services may have been reluctant to surrender their now attainable atomic status in return for an Air Force armlock on supers. Nevertheless, in late November, the Joint Chiefs did agree that Soviet monopoly of the super would be "intolerable." Although stopping short of calling for all-out nuclear development, the chiefs did stress the necessity of not being left behind by the Soviets.[71] They reiterated this somewhat ambivalent stand in a lengthy memorandum to Secretary Johnson on January 13, 1950.[72]

The arguments of Vandenberg regarding the danger of a Soviet breakthrough in thermonuclear research were given ominous credence when in January 1950 the atomic scientist Klaus Fuchs confessed to spying for the Soviets. Fuchs had worked at Los Alamos during the war; more importantly, he had been involved in early thermonuclear experimentation in 1946. After his arrest, Fuchs confessed proudly that his efforts had saved his Soviet masters several years of hard work in their atomic program. He was able to detail which avenues *not* to explore, thus saving steps that the Americans had mistakenly trod. Edward Teller agreed gloomily with this assessment; the Soviets were no doubt well on their way to a thermonuclear device.[73]

Although it is clear that the president was leaning toward development, he was concerned about the lack of consensus among his advisors and thus decided to appoint a three-man panel to study the matter: Secretaries Acheson and Johnson and Chairman Lilienthal. Johnson was an early and vocal advocate of the super, stating in his own inimitable way: "There is but one nation in the world tonight that would start a war that would engulf the world and bring the United States into war. . . . We want a military establishment sufficient to deter that aggressor and sufficient to kick the hell out of her if she doesn't stay deterred."[74] In a rare circumstance, Acheson agreed with Johnson. Oppenheimer had argued fervidly against the super, but Acheson was unmoved, commenting: "You know, I listened as carefully as I know how, but I don't understand what Oppie was trying to say. How can you persuade a paranoid adversary to disarm by example?"[75]

On January 31, the three presented a split decision to the president, with Acheson and Johnson opting for development of the super: "Possession of a thermonuclear weapon by the USSR without such possession by the United States would constitute a situation fraught with danger to the United States, and must be avoided." The report went on to state that such a weapon would have a powerful deterrent effect on the Soviets. Besides, just because the United States renounced development did not mean that the Soviets would.[76]

Lilienthal's heart was heavy. He disagreed fervently with Acheson and Johnson and tried to articulate these fears to the president. Truman cut him short; people had predicted the end of the world when he decided to support Greece in 1948. Nothing happened, and he was certain things would be all right now as well. The bomb would be built.[77] Two weeks later, Lilienthal was no longer at the AEC, replaced by Gordon Dean, a staunch advocate of the super. In 1954, President Eisenhower remarked on this momentous decision: "If the Soviets had beaten us to the hydrogen bomb, Soviet power would today be on the march in every quarter of the globe."[78] The cold war plummeted several more degrees.

Although the president's decision seemed clear, there still existed a certain amount of inertia within the JCS regarding the urgency of the situation. Such lethargy evaporated the following month. Brigadier General Herbert B. Loper, a member of the Military Liaison Committee to the AEC, wrote a lengthy memorandum that shocked the Department of Defense hierarchy. Loper had reviewed the facts regarding the Soviet atomic energy program; and based on the availability of fissionable material, production capabilities, technical expertise, and the fruits of recent espionage operations (Fuchs), he concluded that it was possible that the Kremlin already had a super.[79] Louis Johnson was obviously startled. His earlier scoffing at Joe I was forgotten, and he wrote the president on February 24 that he too feared the possibility of an already existing Soviet super. Referring to "the limitlessimpli cations to our national security" of such a situation, Johnson asked that an all-out program of thermonuclear development be instituted forthwith.[80]

The president agreed, but even so, friction remained among the atomic scientists. Over the next eighteen months, Teller became increasingly unhappy with the AEC and the personnel at Los Alamos who seemed to be hindering as much as helping his research. In November 1951, Teller approached Oppenheimer suggesting that a second laboratory be built, independent of Los Alamos, that would concentrate on thermonuclear experimentation. Oppenheimer demurred, maintaining that such a lab would lower morale among the personnel at Los Alamos and would also be a wasteful duplication of effort. Teller was unconvinced and turned to the Air Force for help. After talking to Jimmy Doolittle—often seen by civilian scientists as a bridge to the military leadership because of his extensive engineering background plus his high military rank—Teller informed Vandenberg of the slow progress on the super. Vandenberg was concerned and immediately took Teller to see Secretary Finletter. Their solution was not subtle, but effective. The Air Force officially proposed that an entirely new laboratory be established under Teller's direction at the University of Chicago to pursue thermonuclear research. It would be independent of the AEC and Los Alamos. Seeing the danger, Gordon Dean, the new head of the AEC, suggested a compromise—the new laboratory would be built under Teller's leadership, but under AEC auspices. This plan was approved (although the new laboratory was actually built at Livermore, California). Teller's sobriquet, "Father of the H-Bomb," is an exaggeration, but the first thermonuclear detonation of November 1952 was in great part owing to his efforts and those of the staff at Livermore, which had been established only at Vandenberg's insistence.[81]

ON THE EVE

The budget process for FY 1951 was a repeat of the previous two years. The Air Force and Navy continued to haggle over the relative merits of bombers versus aircraft carriers, with Vandenberg's staff providing numerous studies "demonstrating" the inefficiency of naval air operations during and after World War II. These studies were lengthy and detailed, but the conclusions were usually similar: the Air Force could deliver a strategic air offensive at one-tenth the cost it would take the Navy: "The cost of naval operations is a luxury which the country can ill afford with the present budgetary limitations."[82]

Once again the Defense Secretary tried to keep his subordinates in line. General Eisenhower continued his efforts at reconciliation and compromise, but the debilitating B-36 hearings of late 1949 made agreement nearly impossible. The president's budget cuts in July had also caused consternation when it became clear that even more reductions were likely in the years ahead. These fears seemed confirmed when in his Annual Budget Message of January 1950, Truman boasted that fiscal efficiency would allow continued reductions in defense overhead and the elimination of low priority activities. The final figures he submitted to Congress were: Army, $4.0 billion; Navy, $3.9 billion; Air Force, $4.4 billion.[83] The Air Force sum included the funds impounded previously, and although the total was greater than that of either the Army or Navy, it would still permit only forty-eight groups.[84]

The chiefs were extremely discouraged by these events. Generals Bradley and Collins admitted later that they came close to resigning in protest over the budget issue, but stopped short upon realizing that the American people supported the president's fiscal policies; resignation would have been an empty gesture.[85] Symington did not feel similarly constrained. When a soldier ends his career, he is indeed retired and must begin anew; but a politician can leave one position for another and continue to work effectively toward his goals. In March 1950, Symington resigned as secretary of the Air Force to demonstrate his disagreement over the administration's defense policies.[86] He would later return to Washington as chairman of the National Security Resources Board and after that as a senator from Missouri.

When the budget went before the Senate, Johnson defended it staunchly, admitting that more money would be useful, but not necessary. He listed the benefits gained from his tightened management practices that cut fat, but not muscle. When asked by Senator William Knowland how he could possibly advocate a cut in defense spending in light of events in China, Europe, and Siberia, Johnson responded with optimism and assurance.[87]

General Bradley followed his superior, but was not as sanguine in his view of the future and stated bluntly: "It is truly understood that our Forces—Air, Army and Navy—are not sufficient now to fight a major war. Nor do we expect them to be sufficient for such a calamity by the end of fiscal year 1951." He then claimed that the budget was prepared before the Soviet atomic explosion had occurred, and that it was now clear more funds should be added.[88]

Vandenberg echoed the statements of Bradley and reminded the senators that the determination of whether there would be an atomic war was no longer the sole decision of the United States. The nation must rebuild its defenses and that was expensive. The proposed budget was adequate for peacetime operations, but not for war. More than ever the Air Force needed a large force in being to deter enemy attack and defend the nation; current plans for forty-eight groups were insufficient for that purpose. He was quick to add that it was not his job to determine the overall budget and he would wholeheartedly support whatever the civilian leadership decided, but in his military opinion the Air Force needed an additional $2 billion.[89]

Although members of Congress sounded sympathetic, they made few changes in the president's requests. As a result, just as the military was gaining new responsibilities in the North Atlantic Treaty Organization, the Military Assistance Program, and thermonuclear weapons development as a consequence of Joe I, it was simultaneously having its capabilities progressively lowered. Columnist Stewart Alsop viewed this contradiction with puzzlement. It seemed that the president and the government were gripped with a "curious euphoria" in the early months of 1950. Truman expressed the opinion as late as May 1950 that the international situation was improving all the time.[90] Vandenberg did not agree with such an optimistic appraisal. At a Pentagon meeting in March 1950, he listened to Secretary Johnson tell a group of congressmen that the Soviets were not interested in expansion, but would rely instead on subversion and covert operations to advance their goals. Congressman Clarence Cannon disputed the secretary's statement, asking for proof that the Soviets had mollified their actions or temperament in recent months. Vandenberg agreed with Cannon: "I want to stand up and be counted as one who admits there will be a war—and soon."[91]

Three months later the much pared budget for FY 1951 was approved by the House, only days before North Korean forces exploded across the 38th Parallel.

You will usually find that the enemy has
three courses open to him, and of these he
will adopt the fourth.

Moltke the Elder

VII | The War for Asia

For it's Tommy this, an' Tommy that, an'
'chuck him out, the brute!
But it's "Savior of 'is country" when the
guns begin to shoot.

Rudyard Kipling

THE ONSLAUGHT

"Korea hung like a lumpy phallus between the sprawling thighs of Manchuria
and the Sea of Japan." That is how William Manchester picturesquely describes
the geographical location of Korea. Another more conventional metaphor limns
the Hermit Kingdom as a dagger pointed at the heart of Japan. The meaning of
both these depictions is that events on the Korean peninsula have always been
of great interest to all three of its neighbors, Japan, China, and the Soviet Union.
Although the roots of crisis were buried in centuries past, the events of 1950 are
directly traceable to World War II.

Since Japan occupied Korea, its liberation was discussed by Churchill, Roosevelt, and Chiang Kai-shek at the Cairo Conference of December 1943. The three
leaders proposed that Korea endure a period of trusteeship, then gain its independence; Stalin agreed at Yalta in February 1945. With the defeat of Japan, however,
problems immediately arose as the Soviet troops occupying the northern portion
of Korea installed a strong Communist, Kim Il Sung, as leader. In the American-
occupied South an equally strong anti-Communist, Syngman Rhee, soon gained
the upper hand, and all attempts at negotiating a unification scheme between the
two factions were fruitless. American Secretary of State George Marshall therefore decided to turn the problem over to the United Nations, and in November
1947 the new organization agreed to assume responsibility for Korean unification.

The UN commission sent to Korea was ignored by the Communists, who did
not acknowledge its authority or permit its access to the North. Nevertheless, the

commission decided to hold elections throughout the peninsula as a means toward unification under one government. When Kim Il Sung refused to participate, the elections were held anyway, but only in the South. Rhee won, and the United Nations proclaimed him president of a unified Korea. Not to be outdone, Kim Il Sung then staged elections in which he was victorious, proclaiming himself president of the entire country also. In late 1948, the Soviet Union withdrew its occupation troops from Korea; and by June 1949, the United States followed suit. But the removal of foreign forces did not solve the basic political problems of Korea, and because diplomacy had failed to achieve unification, force was the obvious next step.[1]

When North Korea attacked on June 25, 1950, the United States was profoundly surprised, both strategically and tactically. Defense Secretary Louis Johnson and General Omar Bradley, who had left the Far East only the day before, had no inkling that invasion was imminent. The CIA had been highly suspicious of Soviet designs, stating categorically in April 1950 that the Kremlin was bent on world domination and would use any means to achieve it. The study continued that the Soviets were expansionist, as evidenced by Stalin's article, "Problems of Leninism," which called for capitalism's overthrow through violence and war. The CIA concluded that World War I had brought communism to Russia; World War II had brought it to Eastern Europe and China; and the Soviets probably expected that World War III would bring communism to the rest of the globe. Even so, the study concluded that the main danger area was Europe, not Asia.[2] When it is recalled how often the specter of Pearl Harbor had been raised to justify a reorganization of the intelligence function, the Korean shock is remarkable. In truth, things could have been worse. In late April, Dean Acheson had pushed hard for the conclusion of a peace treaty with Japan. Vandenberg, however, argued against an agreement because it would reduce American occupation troops to a token force, unable to protect Japan in the event of Soviet attack.[3] The occupation forces, such as they were, remained, and upon them fell the initial burden of South Korean defense. Although MacArthur's intelligence staff had also been caught by surprise, it appeared the CIA had blundered badly by not predicting the North Korean attack. In August, the CIA director, Rear Admiral Roscoe Hillenkoetter, was replaced by General Walter Bedell Smith.

When reports of the invasion began arriving in Washington, the president returned from vacation and called his chief advisers to Blair House on the evening of June 25 to discuss the situation. Interestingly, these men included neither a CIA representative nor a Soviet expert, such as George Kennan or Charles Bohlen, although all present assumed it was the Kremlin that had instigated the attack. (Bohlen was in Paris and Kennan, as was his wont, had taken his family on a secluded weekend vacation in the country where he had no telephone, newspapers, or radio.) Secretary of State Dean Acheson began the conference by advancing two suggestions: that the United States furnish the Republic of Korea (ROK) with arms and equipment; and that American personnel be evacuated from Seoul. He also recommended that the Seventh Fleet be positioned so as to protect Formosa from mainland attack. Acheson was fearful that the events in Korea might signal a wholesale Communist offensive in Asia. General Bradley said that the line had to be drawn somewhere and suggested that United States air and naval forces be used to stem the enemy advance and shore up ROK morale. He did not recommend introducing ground units, "particularly if large numbers were involved."[4]

All the chiefs were fairly bellicose: Admiral Forrest Sherman stated that the North Korean attack was a "valuable opportunity" for the United States to act decisively. Vandenberg agreed that the North Koreans must be stopped, but worried about Soviet intervention. He was confident that American air power could handle the North Korean air force and blunt its tanks, but if the Russians intervened with air, he thought the situation would be radically altered. When Truman asked if the Soviet air bases could be "knocked out," Vandenberg said yes, but that would take time and require atomic weapons. The president did not pursue the matter. The others present expressed their views, and all agreed that something had to be done but thought that the use of American ground forces was inadvisable. In any event, Sherman and Vandenberg thought that air and sea power alone could stop the North Korean attack—a serious miscalculation.[5]

After listening to the discussion, Truman announced the following decisions:

1. General Douglas MacArthur, commander in the Far East with headquarters at Tokyo, was to send supplies to the ROK.

2. A survey team was to be sent to Korea to assess the military situation.

3. The Seventh Fleet would leave the Philippines and position itself between Formosa and the Chinese mainland.

4. The Air Force should make plans to "wipe out" all Soviet air bases in the Far East but take no action for the time being except to cover the evacuation of American personnel from South Korea.

5. Careful calculation should be made about where the Soviets might strike next.

Vandenberg then asked if his aircraft could attack North Korean tanks if it were necessary. The president said yes, and finished the conference by stressing that in order to maintain international support, all American efforts must be linked to the legitimacy of the United Nations.[6] Bradley said later that the shadow of the appeasement policies of the 1930s colored the discussion at Blair House that night. No one was willing to be cast in the role of a Chamberlain.[7]

The commander of the Far East Air Forces (FEAF) under MacArthur was Lieutenant General George Stratemeyer. "Strat" was a West Point graduate and classmate of Eisenhower and Bradley (1915). Predominantly a bomber pilot throughout his career, he had met Vandenberg at Fort Leavenworth when he was an instructor and Van a student there in 1935. The two attended the Army War College together in 1938, then served on the Air Staff for the next three years under General Arnold. For the last year of the war Strat had commanded the AAF forces first in the India-Burma Theater, then in China. After the war, Stratemeyer headed the Air Defense Command until April 1949, when he was reassigned to Tokyo. He was an amiable, avuncular-looking gentleman who had always provided steady, reliable service. He loved to play golf and enjoyed taking a nap every afternoon. Vandenberg would soon worry about his lack of tactical air experience.

Stratemeyer's chief subordinate was Major General Earle Partridge, commander of the Fifth Air Force, also based in Japan. At the time of invasion, Stratemeyer was out of town, and Partridge acted in his stead. "Pat" was Vandenberg's company mate at West Point, although a year ahead. A fighter pilot initially, he had served with Van in the 3rd Attack Group at Brooks Field, followed him as instructor in fighter tactics at the Air Corps Tactical School, and, like Van, had served on the staff of the Northwest African Air Forces in 1942–43. By the end of the war, Partridge had commanded a bomb group, a bomb division, and finally the Eighth Air Force, succeeding Jimmy Doolittle. He had assumed command of the Fifth Air Force in October 1948. Of great importance, the Fifth's mission was the air defense of Japan, so its pilots were not trained for close air support; their aircraft—F-51s, F-80s and F-82s—were obsolescent. This deficiency had been noted before, but little had been done about it. Major General Edward Almond, MacArthur's chief of staff, said later that the lack of training in air-ground cooperation was a costly error. Before June 1950, however, the mission of the American army in Japan was occupation duty, and it was too busy acting as a police force to train for war. The airmen and soldiers stationed in Japan had to learn cooperation through trial and error while in actual combat, and it took several weeks.[8]

Upon hearing of the invasion, Partridge directed a deployment of fighter-bombers to cover the evacuation, and the following day the first wing left for Korea. Soon after arrival on station over Seoul, a flight of F-82s was attacked by enemy fighters. Not knowing if they should fight back, the American pilots took evasive action, and the enemy aircraft withdrew. When he was informed of the incident, Vandenberg was irritated and told Partridge to be more aggressive and to have his men defend themselves if attacked: "no interference with your mission will be tolerated."[9]

On the evening of June 26, the president once again called his advisers to Blair House. Vandenberg began the meeting by announcing that the Air Force had shot down its first "Yak" (a Soviet-made fighter plane). Truman retorted that he hoped it was not the last; he then authorized the Air Force to take whatever action necessary to stem the invasion. When asked if this included operations north of the thirty-eighth parallel, Truman said, "Not yet."[10] Possible diplomatic moves were then discussed, and it was again made clear that UN support was essential before each escalatory step was taken. General Collins said the military situation in South Korea was bad: "The Korean Chief of Staff has no fight left in him." The president appeared melancholy and remarked that he had done everything he could for five years to prevent this kind of situation. He did not want to go to war.

Following the meeting, the Joint Chiefs sent a directive to MacArthur authorizing him to attack all North Korean forces below the thirty-eighth parallel, but not to commit ground troops.[11] According to Partridge, when MacArthur received this directive he was "astonished" and muttered: "I don't believe it; I can't understand." He had not expected to fight for South Korea; there were no war plans for that contingency, and he had been specifically told by the administration that Korea did not fall within his area of responsibility.[12]

The following day, both Congress and the United Nations Security Council approved the American response and labeled the North Koreans as aggressors. The Soviet Union, boycotting the United Nations over the question of the admittance of the People's Republic of China, was powerless to stop the proceedings. Even so, the Joint Chiefs were still reluctant to commit themselves to an Asian war and hoped that air and sea power alone would be sufficient to prevent South Korean collapse. They especially did not want to provoke a war with the Soviet Union.[13] By the twenty-ninth, however, it was clear that American ground forces would be necessary to prevent a Communist victory. Seoul had fallen, and ROK forces were streaming southward in ever-increasing numbers. MacArthur visited the front and reported to Washington that the ROK Army was in confusion, had not fought tenaciously, and was incapable of counterattack. He recommended the immediate dispatch of an American regimental combat team, to be followed by a buildup to two divisions. Collins, who received this communication in his capacity as Army chief of staff and therefore MacArthur's immediate superior (even though he wore only four stars to MacArthur's five and was twenty years junior in rank), reluctantly agreed with the assessment and passed the request to the president. Truman approved, and none of the Joint Chiefs protested the decision. At the same time, Vandenberg was authorized to strike military targets in North Korea, although he was warned not to violate Manchurian or Soviet air space.[14] The police action was beginning in earnest.

On July 3, Vandenberg explored the possibility of sending two B-29 groups to Britain. He, as well as most other political and military leaders, believed the Korean invasion was a diversion and that the real threat was still to Europe. At the time of the Berlin crisis two years previously, the bombers had also been sent to England as a signal to the Soviets, but the aircraft had not been atomic-capable. This time they would be. Because such a step had serious political implications, Air Chief Marshal Arthur Tedder, chief of the Royal Air Force, took the request to Prime Minister Clement Attlee. The British government was reluctant to approve the deployment for fear the Soviets would look upon it as an "unfriendly act." Within a few days the prime minister acquiesced, but stressed that the operation must look normal and not be advertised as a show of strength.[15] Atomic bombs, minus their nuclear cores, accompanied the B-29s, and the SAC crews conducted numerous assembly and loading exercises while in England.

On July 3, Vandenberg also ordered two B-29 groups to the Far East for use in a strategic bombing campaign against targets in North Korea. "While I do not presume to discuss specific targets," he asserted, "it is axiomatic that tactical operations on the battlefield cannot be fully effective unless there is a simultaneous interdiction and destruction of sources behind the battlefield."[16] To command the strike force, Vandenberg sent Major General Emmett "Rosie" O'Donnell, an experienced and colorful bomber pilot who was then commanding SAC's Fifteenth Air Force. The vigorous training program and high standards introduced by LeMay were evident in this deployment; within five days of being notified of their move, the B-29s were established in Japan and carrying out air strikes against North Korea. It was O'Donnell's intent to strike the enemy hard and fast. The day of his arrival in Tokyo, O'Donnell briefed MacArthur and suggested a "fire job" (incendiary attack) on the five industrial centers of northern Korea. O'Donnell argued that the bombing of airfields, tanks, bridges, and "Koreans on bicycles" was useless; he wanted to go after "sources of substance." MacArthur said no; only high explosive bombs were to be used and then only against bona fide military targets. O'Donnell ordered three thousand tons of incendiaries to be shipped to the Far East anyway—in the event MacArthur changed his mind.[17] Soon, however, the bombers found themselves in a tactical role, hitting targets in support of the hard-pressed 24th Division. Stratemeyer apologized to Vandenberg for this diversion, but said that it was necessary because of the critical ground situation.[18] The 24th's commander, Major General William F. Dean, was appreciative of the aid: "Without this continuing air effort it is doubtful if the courageous combat soldiers . . . could have withstood the onslaught of the vastly numerically superior enemy."[19] It was soon evident that the two divisions estimated by MacArthur would not be enough—by July 9 he was seeking eight divisions.

In order to gain a better impression of the rapidly changing situation, Collins and Vandenberg decided to observe things firsthand. Arriving in Tokyo on July 13, the two chiefs met with MacArthur for a situation briefing. Collins recalled the old warrior as displaying his typical coolness, poise, and élan. The situation was serious, but not desperate; he no longer underestimated the ability of the North Koreans, but was certain he could smash them. He told his audience (although only a handful were present, Collins said he always spoke as if he were lecturing to a packed auditorium) that he would soon stabilize the battlefront, and the reinforcements en route would be used for an amphibious counterstroke that was already forming in his mind. He did not wish merely to repulse the invaders, but to destroy them. The ultimate goal of his enveloping movement would be "to compose and unite Korea." Presciently, Vandenberg asked if, in the event of Chinese intervention, MacArthur would need to advance into Manchuria. MacArthur said that since Korea was a cul-de-sac, he could effectively choke off the peninsula from either Chinese or Soviet supplies: "I see here a unique use for the atomic bomb—to strike a blocking blow—which would require a six month repair job. Sweeten up my B-29 force—(we'll give them back)—perhaps by a rotational feature, and we can isolate the Korean peninsula."[20] In any event, he wanted two more B-29 groups; O'Donnell's bombers were proving extremely valuable. Against MacArthur's wishes, Vandenberg flew to Korea to confer with Partridge and talk to his troops. He returned to Washington guardedly optimistic and briefed the president and secretary of Defense. Plans were made to dispatch the air and ground reinforcements requested by MacArthur.[21]

The UN commander had been extremely tight-lipped about his proposed amphibious assault. For security reasons, he declined to provide the JCS with a detailed plan for his intended landing at Inchon—a stance Bradley later recalled as "insultingly evasive."[22] In order to ascertain these plans, General Collins and Admiral Sherman flew to Tokyo and on August 21 were treated to the famous MacArthur oratorical talents that left his audience "spellbound." Although the chiefs were not enthusiastic about the risky venture, they were unwilling to reject it. MacArthur's staff worked out the details, but although specifically asked by the JCS to do so, once again refused to send a detailed plan to Washington, fearing a security leak. Instead, a courier was dispatched to brief the JCS personally. The messenger left Tokyo on September 10 with MacArthur's injunction: "Don't get there too soon." By the time the chiefs were thoroughly informed on September 14, it was too late to cancel the assault—scheduled for that afternoon—even if they had wanted to.[23] Control over MacArthur was beginning to slip from the hands of the Joint Chiefs.

The story of Inchon needs no retelling, but as a result, the North Korean army retreated as quickly as it had advanced. Ironically, MacArthur's victory— and it can be attributed to no one else—was so total that it destroyed him. The words of one historian are so powerful that they deserve to be quoted in full:

> Inchon, then, could not have happened under any other commander but MacArthur. It sprang from his overpowering personality and his self-confidence, and his plan was supported by no one else for it looked back to an age of warfare unencumbered by specialist objections and peripatetic Joint Chiefs. It remains an astonishing achievement precisely because it was a triumph not of military logic and science, but of imagination and intuition. It was justified on no other grounds, but the most overwhelming, most simple; it succeeded and remains a Twentieth Century Cannae ever to be studied.[24]

Inchon put MacArthur beyond the orbit of the Joint Chiefs, and that was unfortunate because only they had the expertise and experience to offer him sound military advice.

As the widening conflict swept into North Korea, Vandenberg increasingly unleashed his aircraft on targets beyond the thirty-eighth parallel. The North contained most of Korea's industry, just as the South had the agriculture and greater population density. At first there were many lucrative targets for the B-29s. Even so, some areas were kept off-limits: the city of Rashin near the Soviet border, the hydroelectric plants that supplied power to China, and the capital city of Pyongyang. Aircraft were also prohibited from violating the Soviet and Chinese borders—not even reconnaissance flights were permitted north of the Yalu River.[25] Vandenberg warned Stratemeyer of this repeatedly, so when two pilots inadvertently flew sixty miles into Soviet territory and attacked the airfield at Vladivostok, destroying several Yaks, the chief was irate. He ordered Stratemeyer to court-martial the two pilots and relieve their commander within forty-eight hours. There were enough difficulties without precipitating a war with the Soviet Union.[26]

There was, however, another problem that was troubling the Air Force chief—the control and capability of tactical air power.

THE CLOSE AIR SUPPORT CONTROVERSY

The question of whether tactical air power should be commanded by soldiers or airmen had raged for decades. By the end of World War II the answer seemed to favor the airmen; Vandenberg's Ninth Air Force was an independent unit that effectively coordinated its efforts with Bradley's 12th Army Group. Almost immediately after the war, however, demobilization and confusion led some Army officers to return to the old arguments for air power being controlled from the ground. They suggested that when the Air Force gained independent status it should consist only of strategic units; tactical air power should remain with the Army. This argument threatened to erupt into a major confrontation until General Eisenhower intervened to settle the dispute.

In November 1947, Eisenhower, then Army chief of staff, wrote Forrestal a clear and unequivocal memorandum expressing his views. The general's experience proved to him that tactical air power must be under the command of a single individual to ensure flexibility and concentration of force. During the last war, tactical air power had been unified and controlled by airmen, and this system worked: "effective support of the front-line fighting units *was* provided and proved an essential element in the achievement of the Army objectives."[27] The proposal that tactical air units should be developed within the Army was misguided: "The Army does not belong in the air—it belongs on the ground." The resources necessary for a tactical air force complete with its support functions, base facilities, and research and development organizations would result in a wasteful duplication of effort. The entire issue had been thoroughly explored by Congress and decided by the National Security Act: air power belonged to the Air Force. Eisenhower concluded that he had full confidence that the airmen could provide the close air support so vital to the Army mission, and he recommended adherence to that proven concept.[28] Perhaps to ensure Eisenhower's support, General Spaatz had formed three major combat commands in mid-1946: the Strategic, Defense, and Tactical Air commands. The formation of TAC served as clear evidence that air leaders intended to take close air support seriously and regard it as a primary mission.

When Vandenberg took over as chief of staff in April 1948, he directed his staff to reevaluate close air support owing to budgetary pressures necessitating economy measures. As a consequence, a young colonel, William Momyer, wrote a study in August 1948 that called for a diminution in the importance of TAC. Momyer reasoned that tactical air power would only be useful in a major war if the atomic offensive failed, and the conflict degenerated into a conventional air-surface action. He estimated that such a situation would take as long as two years to develop after the outbreak of hostilities; therefore, the only missions for fighter aircraft during the initial phases of a major war were air defense and escort. The Tactical Air Command should be assigned a lower priority.[29]

Partly as a result of this study and partly because of financial constraints caused by the Berlin Airlift and presidential budget limits, Vandenberg decided to downgrade TAC. In December 1948 he directed that TAC and ADC be combined into a Continental Air Command (CONAC). This would consolidate the dwindling tactical resources of the Air Force into one organization that could allocate personnel and aircraft to whatever mission was most pressing. All pilots were to be trained in both air defense techniques and close air support. Because of guidelines determined by the Joint Chiefs, air defense had a greater priority, so TAC, commanded by Lieutenant General Pete Quesada, was relegated to a "planning headquarters, charged with writing joint doctrinal manuals and organizing joint training exercises."[30] Quesada resented the change, viewing it as a violation of the trust between Spaatz and Eisenhower to maintain tactical air support as a major function of the Air Force.[31] Vandenberg disagreed, arguing that it was a financial necessity because of the JCS decision that the two primary missions of the Air Force were air defense and the atomic offensive, with close air support a distant third. The perennial budget fights over the forty-eight versus seventy-group Air Force made it plain that tactical air power was a pawn to be bartered. As long as JCS priorities remained constant, forty-eight groups would not permit sufficient tactical strength. CONAC was an attempt to do more with less. The detonation of Joe I in late 1949 accelerated the emphasis on air defense at the expense of tactical air.

Vandenberg may have had another motive for the formation of CONAC. Quesada had never been a close friend, but he could hardly be removed as George Kenney had been; by all accounts TAC was in excellent condition, given its severe budgetary restraints. But if TAC were downgraded, its three-star commander would either have to suffer the resulting embarrassment or be transferred. Quesada was reassigned, becoming Air Force Reserves chief; the following year he moved to the Joint Staff and served as commander of the Eniwetok atomic bomb tests of 1950. In February 1951, Quesada wrote Vandenberg an extremely stiff and formal letter stating his desire to retire; the offer was accepted.[32]

The formation of CONAC was not well received by the Army, and rumblings of discontent were heard throughout 1949. In April of that year, an Army study concluded that the United States had no tactical air force "worthy of the name." It hastened to add, however: "In stating these facts we ascribe no fault. We know that the Chief of Staff of the Air Force, the outstanding tactical-air Commander the U.S. produced during the war, has recognized this need and has repeatedly sought resources to meet it."[33] The following month General Jacob Devers, commander of the Army Field Forces, commented that Army–Air Force cooperation was unsatisfactory and that the lack of dedicated tactical air support would seriously hamper the ground mission in war. In response, CONAC's commander, Lieutenant General Ennis Whitehead, suggested that the Fourteenth Air Force be specifically designated as a tactical unit to support the Army, that its commander be of two-star rank, and that his headquarters be located with General Devers at Fort Bragg, North Carolina. It was hoped that this solution would lessen Army complaints, but it was still short of what was necessary.[34] Although the Air Force had increased the number of training missions it conducted in support of the ground forces by over 30 percent since 1947, fund shortages continued to limit such cooperation below what was desired.[35]

Vandenberg also directed his Air Board to review close air support. In November 1949, the board (of which Quesada was a member) determined that the number of groups designated for close air support (seven) was adequate for the Army's ten divisions. There were still not, however, enough joint training exercises to remove the "recurring suspicion that the USAF was placing inadequate emphasis on tactical air operations." The report recommended that CONAC be disbanded and the two commands of TAC and ADC be reestablished. The board concluded gloomily:

If the Air Force continues its present relatively negative tactical air policies for a period of four to six more years, the Army will have compiled a dossier of facts which will completely justify its requisitioning a budget for its own air force on the grounds that the USAF has neither been able to meet nor has it physically discharged its responsibilities for providing support to the ground forces.[36]

For fiscal reasons, Vandenberg still resisted an increased emphasis on tactical air power at the expense of air defense and strategic air, but the controversy continued. In early 1950, Congressman Carl Vinson "jokingly" remarked that the Air Force must pay more attention to support of the Army or else the job would be given to the Marines.[37] Such comments increased in number after the Korean War broke out.

As the American and ROK troops retreated southward to Pusan, reports began reaching Vandenberg in July that the close air support provided by Stratemeyer's forces was not satisfactory. Turning to an old friend, Vandenberg asked Jimmy Doolittle to visit the Far East and study the problem. Vandenberg believed and trusted his subordinate commanders, but he well realized the necessity of having advisers who could step back and monitor events objectively. Doolittle's reputation, popularity, and expertise made him ideal for the task. The balding war hero visited Korea during July and reported that the Air Force had already eliminated the enemy air force and thus enjoyed almost total air superiority. He was impressed by the interdiction campaign against North Korean supply lines that forced the enemy to travel only at night. He was, however, concerned about inadequate coordination between the services and the lack of tactical expertise among the top FEAF planners.[38] Realizing that neither Stratemeyer nor Partridge had recent tactical experience, Vandenberg decided to send an expert to the Far East to assist. Major General Samuel Anderson was initially considered for the mission. Anderson, who had led Vandenberg's IX Bomber Command during World War II, would have been an excellent choice, but he had just received orders for a new assignment in Texas, so Vandenberg looked elsewhere. The man sent was Major General Opie Weyland, Patton's comrade, who had led the XIX TAC in Europe.[39] Stratemeyer welcomed the assistance and immediately put Weyland to work straightening out the close air support tangle.

The first problem noted by Weyland was that tactical air operations were being directed from Tokyo by MacArthur's staff. This procedure was inadequate for two reasons: Tokyo was too far from the battle area, and MacArthur's staff was heavily weighted with ground officers who did not understand tactical air. MacArthur's Far East Command was theoretically subdivided into the three services: Far East Air Forces, Naval Forces Far East, and Army Forces Far East, each under a separate commander reporting to MacArthur. The Army component's headquarters was never formed, however; MacArthur's staff performed that function along with its duties as General Headquarters Far East. In addition, MacArthur never relinquished his responsibilities for the Japanese occupation. His staff, nearly all Army personnel, was therefore heavily burdened and unable to manage the air war. Under Weyland's prompting, Stratemeyer gained control over air operations; Partridge moved to Korea, and established Fifth Air Force headquarters near that of Major General Dean.[40]

Weyland also had to resist the traditional efforts of Army commanders who desired "their own personal air force." Claiming the situation was critical, Generals Dean and Walton Walker (commander of the Eighth Army) requested that air power, including the B-29s, be placed under their direct control until the emergency passed. Major General Almond, leading the X Corps, was especially insistent on this arrangement, stating that he believed in unity of command and concentration of force, but in the hands of the ground force commander. Almond wanted tactical air under his control to strike targets of his choosing.[41] Weyland reiterated to all these men the lessons learned during the Second World War and refused to parcel out his airplanes. MacArthur concurred, and Army efforts to control air power were deflected for the next two years.[42]

Weyland's third problem concerned coordination with Navy and Marine air units, but in this area he was largely frustrated. The Task Force 77 commander, Vice Admiral Turner Joy, used Navy and Marine aircraft as he thought necessary to assist the war effort. Because of deck handling procedures necessitating a mass launch of aircraft, the Navy could not fly on-call close air support missions, which usually required one or two aircraft to strike specific targets. In addition, since the fleet usually maintained radio silence at sea, it was difficult to plan USAF strikes when it was not clearly known where the Navy planes would be operating. In one instance, a B-29 strike had to be canceled when it was discovered at the last moment that carrier aircraft would be operating in the same area.[43] Stratemeyer was irritated and asked MacArthur to place all Navy and Marine air under his command to ensure effective coordination. Admiral Joy objected, saying that Air Force control of his aircraft would interfere with fleet defense. Although the North Koreans possessed no air force or navy to threaten the American fleet, Joy was concerned about denuding his ships of air protection. Stratemeyer compromised, and it was agreed that he would assume "coordination control" of land-based Marine aircraft and carrier-based Navy planes when they were operating over Korea. Unfortunately, the new term held little meaning, and Stratemeyer remained largely in the dark in regard to Navy intentions. When asked if there was a special office established to coordinate USAF and Navy air operations, General Partridge later replied, "If there was one I never found it."[44]

Eventually, the Navy was assigned a specific geographic area where it held exclusive responsibility for conducting air operations. This area, located in northeastern Korea, permitted the Navy to conduct an air war without having close air support responsibilities or contesting air superiority with the Chinese jet fighter planes that in late 1950 began operating in "Mig Alley" to the west.[45] This arrangement irked Weyland; he did not want the Navy "roaming around North Korea" fighting a strategic war, when at the same time, he was being told the ground situation was so critical that his B-29s were needed to strike battlefront targets. Because of the unbalanced headquarters at the theater level, however, the only person who could compel unity was MacArthur. Perhaps believing that it was more important not to precipitate inter-service rivalry than it was to run an efficient air war, MacArthur never took this step.[46]

To exacerbate matters further, a United Press International (UPI) correspondent visiting Korea, Robert Miller, wrote a sensational news story in August 1950 that highly lauded Marine air and ground units while denigrating efforts of the Army and Air Force. The article stated that Marine pilots operating propeller-driven aircraft conducted air strikes within yards of friendly troops and inflicted massive enemy casualties. On the other hand, the report continued, Air Force jets had such high fuel consumption they were unable to loiter in the battle area long enough to be effective. (At that point in the war there were no airfields in South Korea with runways long enough to accommodate the jets; they therefore had to launch from bases in Japan, which left little loiter time over the Korean battlefield.) Moreover, the story added, because the jets were inaccurate, strikes were not permitted within three miles of friendly forces. Miller concluded that inferior training and doctrine kept the Army bogged down while Marine ground units supported by Marine air surged ahead.[47]

Vandenberg was flabbergasted and immediately fired off a message to Stratemeyer demanding an explanation. Equally irate, Stratemeyer responded that the article was "one of the most reprehensible pieces of carefully contrived propaganda and untruths that I have ever read in my military career. It is my opinion and that of my PIO [public information officer] that this was not only stimulated by Navy sources, but was ever [sic] prepared by them in detail." Stratemeyer listed several factual inaccuracies in the article and said that he had already complained to General MacArthur; he urged Vandenberg personally to discuss the matter with Admiral Sherman.[48]

To dig further, Vandenberg asked a distinguished civilian professor, Robert Stearns from the University of Colorado, to visit Korea and evaluate Air Force performance. Upon arriving in Korea, Stearns, a lawyer and historian who had served in the Operations Analysis Division of the Twentieth Air Force during World War II, interviewed MacArthur and asked him to comment on the support given by the FEAF. MacArthur said it was outstanding and, referring to Generals Stratemeyer and Partridge, stated: "no Air Commanders in history have been more superb." Stearns then asked for MacArthur's opinion on the controversial news item by Miller; the general's remarks were surprisingly strong. He began by stating that the Marine was an outstanding fighting man when hitting the beaches in a brief, intense assault, but was wholly inadequate when inserted into a protracted ground struggle like that in Korea. He lacked staying power. As for Marine air, yes it was very good, but that was because of several unusual factors peculiar to Korea. First, the Air Force had achieved air superiority, which allowed the slow, propeller-driven Marine aircraft to operate unimpeded. Second, Marine pilots had no responsibility other than that of close air support so they should be experts at such tasks. But such specialization was highly inefficient and necessitated that air power be used as a substitute for heavy artillery, which Marine ground forces did not possess. Finally, MacArthur stated that the Marines were at least 20 percent overmanned, whereas all Army and Air Force units were under-strength.[49]

Judging from MacArthur's unusually cutting remarks, it would appear that he also had felt the sting of the ill-advised newspaper column. Stearns heard much the same from the other Army commanders in Korea. He told Vandenberg that FEAF operations at the beginning of the war were relatively ineffective, but countered that *all* operations in Korea, both air and ground, were ineffective during the first month. Initially, FEAF had neither the training nor the equipment necessary to perform the Close Air Support (CAS) mission. The Marines were indeed more accomplished than the Air Force because they were overmanned, but Stearns maintained that this advantage had quickly evaporated. The USAF was now every bit as able as their Navy and Marine counterparts. Stearns concluded: "I want you to understand that the Air Force has a good system which can be improved in detail, not a bad system that must be scrapped and replaced."[50]

Although the Marines were short of heavy artillery by design, the Army was short by accident, since the Eighth Army's occupation duties had not required such equipment. As a result, Army commanders were apt to call for air strikes to compensate for their lack of canon. Although there never seemed to be enough air cover during the frenetic weeks of July and August when American and ROK troops were ever in retreat, senior ground commanders were loud in their praise of Partridge's pilots. General Walker told Collins and Doolittle: "If it had not been for the air support that we received from the Fifth Air Force, we would not have been able to stay in Korea."[51] Walker also acknowledged the excellent work of the Marines, but, echoing MacArthur, noted that Marine air was proportionally much larger and thus more inefficient than the Army-Air Force team.[52]

As for the question of propellers versus jets, the opinion of ground and air officers on both sides (based on prisoner interrogations), confirmed that the jet was far more effective at close air support. In the first place, the slower, piston-engined aircraft were more vulnerable to ground fire and suffered far greater losses than the jets. The F-51 was especially vincible because of its liquid-cooled engine—one round in the radiator and the plane was down. Indeed, the Mustangs suffered losses at twice the rate of the more durable and quicker F-80s.[53] Vandenberg's discussions with his pilots in Korea confirmed this fact. As the chief himself later phrased it when questioned about the matter by a congressman: "You can slow down an F-80 for a strafing run, but you can't speed up an F-51 to fight a MIG."[54] As soon as F-80s and F-84s became available, the old F-51s were phased out. Once airfields were built in South Korea with runways long enough to handle the jet fighters and they were transferred from Japan, the only factor working in favor of the aged Mustangs—range—was removed. As one member of the 8th Fighter-Bomber Group said: "A lot of pilots had seen vivid demonstrations of why the F-51 was not a ground-support fighter in the last war and weren't exactly intrigued by the thought of playing guinea pig to prove the same thing again."[55]

What was most unfortunate about the UPI editorial was that it caused serious ill will between the services just when the police action was about to enter a new phase.

THE NEW WAR

The Inchon victory sent the North Korean Army reeling back north of the thirty-eighth parallel. Flushed with confidence, MacArthur was granted permission by the president on September 30 and the United Nations on October 7, 1950, to destroy the remnants of the North Korean Army and, more significantly, to unify the country. Thus, the political objective changed from the initial goal of merely restoring the status quo ante. Like MacArthur, political leaders were optimistic. Although the abrupt reversal of Allied fortunes enormously enhanced the supreme commander's reputation, two events occurred almost simultaneously that eventually served to check his independence.

On September 22, Omar Bradley was elevated to the rank of general of the army (five stars), allowing him to deal with MacArthur on a more equal basis. The disparity between the UN commander and his titular superiors, the Joint Chiefs, must be understood to appreciate fully why MacArthur was given so much free rein. Bradley and Collins had been instructors at West Point and Vandenberg a plebe when MacArthur was superintendent in 1920. A decade later, MacArthur became Army chief of staff and was promoted to full general at a time when Bradley was still a major, Collins and Vandenberg both captains, and Forrest Sherman a Navy lieutenant. (Even the illustrious Dwight Eisenhower had been only a major and one of MacArthur's aides during the 1930s.) It was not uncommon for exceptional officers to advance more rapidly than their peers and have former superiors become subordinates, but the MacArthur-JCS situation was unprecedented. The man was a living legend, and although the chiefs have been criticized for not controlling their subordinate in Tokyo, their reticence, especially after Inchon, is understandable.

The day after Bradley's promotion, another change took place when George Marshall, called from retirement once again, was made secretary of Defense. Louis Johnson had been deeply discredited by the events in Korea. He had fully embraced the president's economic policies and had constantly boasted that he was merely trimming fat from the defense budget, not muscle. Although persistently warned by the Joint Chiefs and service secretaries that this was not so, Johnson persevered. In April 1950, Johnson had lectured Vandenberg: "I *know* that Russia does not plan to try to conquer the United States by force or by war. They intend to do it by pushing us into an economic collapse and a depression so that the discontents and the agitators and others can take us over in the confusion."[56] Johnson insisted that, in any event, the United States could easily deal with the Soviet military threat, boasting that "he wanted Joe Stalin to know that if he starts something at four o'clock in the morning, the fighting power and strength of America will be on the job at five." As is often the case, silly words came back to haunt the speaker; after the North Korean invasion and initial American defeats, one wag commented that when Johnson promised we could lick the Russians, he did not say anything about the North Koreans.[57]

By early September, Truman had decided to fire Johnson and replace him with George Marshall. On the morning of September 11, President Truman summoned Johnson to the White House and asked for his resignation. Startled, the secretary nearly fainted, but recovered and tried to reverse the president's decision. He had, he thought, merely been carrying out the president's wishes to cut the budget; he had not set the funding limits, just enforced them. Johnson wept and begged the president not to fire him. His efforts were futile; the president's mind was made up. Truman later explained: "He is the most ego maniac I've ever come in contact with—and I've seen a lot. . . . Potomac fever and a pathological condition are to blame for the fiasco at the end. . . . He offended every member of the cabinet."[58] In his letter of resignation, Johnson referred bitterly to the many enemies he had made in attempting to achieve unification of the Armed Forces. He admitted the Korean War required a Defense secretary who was not hampered by such a past.[59]

Dean Acheson and Bradley thought that an underlying cause of Johnson's dismissal was his repeated political maneuverings behind the president's back. On the morning of September 11, Averell Harriman was in Johnson's office while the secretary spoke on the telephone with Republican Senator Robert Taft. Johnson told Taft: "We've got Acheson on the run at last," then turned to Harriman and said: "Averell, I think I can assure you—you're in." Harriman left and went straight to the White House; Johnson was fired that afternoon. Consorting with the enemy was an unforgivable sin.[60]

George Marshall was a welcome choice to Acheson and the Joint Chiefs. More importantly, he was the only military man in the nation who had the confidence and prestige to deal with MacArthur.

There had been evidence throughout October that Chinese troops were infiltrating into Korea. Nevertheless, warnings from Peking leaders through the Indian government went unheeded, and intelligence agencies both in Washington and Tokyo discounted the possibility of large-scale Chinese intervention. Perhaps because China was seen as a pawn of the Soviet Union and Moscow was not making similar threats, the signals from Peking were disregarded. Even so, MacArthur was directed to employ only ROK troops near the Manchurian border. On November 1, the first MIG-15s crossed the Yalu River into Korea and attacked US aircraft. After disengaging, the MIGs flew back to their airfields in Manchuria. The next day, Stratemeyer asked MacArthur for permission to pursue the enemy across the border. Stratemeyer argued that the Chinese Air Force had about three hundred aircraft, including MIGs, which if employed en masse could seriously hinder UN ground operations. MacArthur too was concerned and pressed the JCS for permission to pursue. Vandenberg was initially inclined to grant such authority but, after extended talks with Marshall and Finletter, decided against such a widening of the war.[61] On November 7, however, MacArthur was sufficiently concerned about Chinese infiltration that he ordered Stratemeyer to destroy the bridges spanning the Yalu River. MacArthur had not sought JCS permission for this air strike, thinking it was not applicable to his limiting directives. Stratemeyer wired his intentions to Washington, but Vandenberg balked. The chief, realizing that MacArthur's order was not in keeping with previous JCS directives, informed Secretary of the Air Force Finletter. After several hours, the situation percolated upward to the president, who directed cancellation of the proposed air strikes. MacArthur was angry, and wrote passionately to Washington that his command was threatened with ultimate destruction unless the bridges were struck. This message shocked the Joint Chiefs, who had had no inkling that doom was impending.[62] After consulting with the president, the JCS informed Tokyo that if the situation was sufficiently serious, the bridges could be hit, but only on the Korean side. Manchurian airspace could not be violated by the attacking aircraft.

When the Chinese struck in full force on November 25, 1950, and the UN forces were nearly trapped and destroyed, tempers flared and jaws tightened among military leaders. Plans were made for evacuation, under the umbrella of atomic bombs if necessary. Stratemeyer wired for more fighter planes immediately in the event Japan was attacked. Vandenberg appreciated the seriousness of the situation and placed SAC on a worldwide full alert.[63] Stratemeyer suggested that, because of the possibility of war with China, two more B-29 groups, armed with atomic bombs, should be sent to the Far East. Vandenberg instructed him to prepare for their use and designate suitable targets. Stratemeyer complied, listing the following objectives: Antung, Mukden, Peking, Tientsin, Shanghai, and Nanking. Strat then added that if we got "in the big one," he would strike Vladivostok, Khabarovsk, and Kirin.[64]

On 3 December, Vandenberg argued with his JCS colleagues that China should be punished and that targets in Manchuria should be struck. He maintained that a limited series of attacks involving only two B-29 groups would not jeopardize the defense of Europe.[65] At the same time, LeMay was alerted to sharpen his spear; the SAC commander responded quickly that he was ready and, if the deployment order was given, would personally leave for the Far East.[66] On December 6, the Joint Chiefs sent a warning to all commanders: "The JCS consider that the current situation in Korea has greatly increased the possibility of general war. Commanders addressed take such action as is feasible to increase readiness without creating atmosphere of alarm."[67] This warning gained credence when intelligence revealed in early January that the Soviets had hastily withdrawn their personnel from Mukden in anticipation of US atomic strikes in Manchuria.[68] Meanwhile, the CIA reported pessimistically that both China and the Soviet Union seemed willing to "risk a showdown with the West at an early date." Admiral Sherman admitted later that he thought a major war was imminent.[69] When President Truman was asked at a press conference if atomic weapons might be used to stop the enemy in Korea, he replied: "that includes every weapon that we have."[70] The world seemed very close to another global war.

In March 1951, Vandenberg requested that nine atomic bombs *plus* their atomic cores be transferred to the Air Force. There was evidence that Soviet troops were massing north of the Yalu. More ominously, it was reported that some seventy Soviet submarines had gathered near Vladivostok. It was feared that the Soviets were about to attack, pushing the United Nations out of both Korea and Japan. On April 6, 1951, Vandenberg visited the White House and convinced the president to authorize the transfer. This was a momentous decision. For the first time, the custody of atomic weapons slipped from the hands of the AEC. It had taken five years, but Vandenberg had finally unlocked the atomic door.[71]

It seems that Vandenberg was in a bellicose mood in the month following the Chinese invasion. When the North Koreans first attacked back in June, Vandenberg had been one of the primary advocates of limiting the war. Although he had taken steps to increase Air Force readiness for global war—ordering his atomic weapons storage facilities to remain on "battery alert"—he maintained a tight rein on rambunctious subordinates. When Major General Orvil A. Anderson, commandant of the Air War College, made intemperate remarks to reporters regarding the desirability of a preemptive atomic strike on the Soviet Union, Vandenberg relieved him.[72] But after the massive Chinese attack in November and as reports of reverses continued to roll in from the Far East, the chief looked for ways to react quickly and decisively. It would soon become apparent, however, that the situation in Korea was not as bleak as was being painted.

When American ground forces were struck by the Chinese onslaught, their leaders once again revived complaints about the lack of air cover. In late November, General Collins wrote a pointed memorandum to Vandenberg stating that close air support requirements were "currently not being met satisfactorily." He recommended the by then traditional position that control of tactical air operations be given to the ground commanders.[73] At the same time, Collins wrote MacArthur advocating that the Army be given operational control of CAS units as far down as army or corps level. He added, however, that he was not suggesting that the Army control all tactical units or form their own tactical air force. Collins recognized that budgetary restraints imposed over the previous two years were largely responsible for the deemphasis on tactical air—a deemphasis that the JCS had concurred in—but the time had come to change directions.[74] Vandenberg, expressing surprise at his colleague's charges, asked for clarification:

> My impression of the reports from the Far East—other than certain press comments of dubious origin [a probable reference to the Miller article of August]—is that the tactical air effort has been effective. However, if the close support picture is unsatisfactory, I want to know it, and I also want to know exactly the respect in which it has failed, so that corrective measures can be aimed at the specific difficulty.[75]

In a move that some thought overdue, Vandenberg reestablished Tactical Air Command and chose General Joe Cannon as the new commander. The war had brought a great expansion in the Air Force, and claims that austerity prohibited a separate tactical command were no longer valid. Indeed, the first ten Reserve groups activated for combat were tactical units. The elevation of the new TAC commander to the rank of full general was a sign to the Army, and perhaps even to the tactical people within the Air Force, that Vandenberg had miscalculated and now wanted to mend fences.[76]

General MacArthur was also on edge as he watched the fruits of Inchon slip through his fingers. As Chinese forces continued to push south, he became increasingly vocal in demands for assistance. On November 30, in a response to JCS queries concerning force dispositions, he sent a message to Washington that Bradley later remembered as particularly insulting: "He treated us as if we were children."[77] The situation in Korea continued to deteriorate; and on December 2, MacArthur sent his famous "entirely new war" message with its insistence on new political decisions and plans. The following day, the Joint Chiefs met with Secretaries Acheson and Marshall to discuss the crisis. Lieutenant General Matthew Ridgway, also present at the meeting, approached Vandenberg, whom he had known since West Point, asking him why the Joint Chiefs did not simply order MacArthur to do what they wished:

> Van shook his head. "What good would that do? He wouldn't obey the orders. What can we do?" At this I exploded. "You can relieve any commander who won't obey orders, can't you?" I exclaimed. The look on Van's face is one I shall never forget. His lips parted and he looked at me with an expression both puzzled and amazed. He walked away then without saying a word.[78]

General Collins flew to Tokyo to confer with MacArthur and tour the battle area. Returning on December 8, he reported the situation as serious, but not desperate. At the same time, the president and the United Nations reverted to their original goal: the repulse of the invading forces. All talk of unifying Korea was ended.[79] Nevertheless, as the days passed and the situation failed to improve, MacArthur continued to ask for reinforcements. On December 19, at a meeting with Secretary Marshall and Assistant Secretary Dean Rusk (Acheson was in Europe), Vandenberg suggested that withdrawal of American ground forces from Korea, with continued air and sea operations, would be preferable to the debacle of being pushed back to Pusan again. If Korea was merely a diversion preparatory to a Soviet move into Europe, then Vandenberg thought it wise to avoid a lengthy war of attrition in Asia.[80] MacArthur had said that if conditions persisted, then he would be forced to evacuate. So be it. Focusing on the global situation, Vandenberg, as was the case two years previously in Berlin, was growing impatient with the entangling morass of a peripheral conflict. The JCS had reacted to the Chinese attack with confusion, produced by conflicting reports from Tokyo, Korea, and Europe, on the nature, focus, and extent of Communist actions. Vandenberg was caught up in this mood, hence his desire to step back from the Korean smoke and look for the real fire elsewhere. As it became apparent that a worldwide conflagration was not imminent, Vandenberg refastened his attentions on the Far East.

As Chinese attacks continued, MacArthur withdrew south; on January 4, Seoul fell once again to the enemy. One week later, MacArthur wrote angrily that political indecision was leaving the initiative to the enemy. Under the "extraordinary limitations" placed upon him, the position of his command was becoming untenable. During the months of December and January, MacArthur's emotions rode a roller coaster from optimism to despair. Bradley later referred to many of the messages from the Far East as "hysterical." Although that term is too strong, MacArthur did seem to be losing the poise and self-confidence displayed in July when the situation was also grim. Talk of abandoning Korea was continually discussed. Collins decided to return to Korea, with Vandenberg accompanying him to review Air Force evacuation plans. The Air Force chief had wanted General LeMay to make the trip as well so that he could meet with the B-29 personnel and prepare for possible future contingencies, but Acheson vetoed the idea; LeMay was known as "Mr. Atom Bomb," and his presence in Korea would "excite people unduly."[81]

Vandenberg later told an aide that, upon arriving in Japan, they found

MacArthur in a "dramatically tragic mood." Fearing the worst for his forces in Korea, MacArthur insisted that the chiefs give him an order either to evacuate or to "stand and die."[82] Vandenberg was taken aback, but upon visiting Korea found the situation less serious than depicted in Tokyo. After touring the frontline units and conferring with General Ridgway (the replacement for General Walker, who had died in an auto accident), Collins and he determined that the front had stabilized and that there was no cause for alarm. To confirm the optimistic reports of Ridgway, Vandenberg flew twelve miles past the front line in a helicopter, landed, and participated in a ground patrol. One American soldier, astonished to see a four-star general—and an airman at that—on the front lines, commented: "Hey General, we say a prayer of thanks for your flyboys every night, sir." Vandenberg was much impressed with what he saw regarding the resiliency and high morale of the American troops.[83]

In an official report to Secretary Marshall, General Collins concluded that unless the Soviet Union intervened, the Eighth Army could continue operations in Korea.[84] As for bombing Manchuria to stop the Chinese, Vandenberg now argued that it would be ineffective. The majority of war supplies and equipment being used by the enemy were coming from the Soviet Union. In order to interdict Communist supplies, it would thus be necessary to strike Siberia as well as Manchuria. Vandenberg was "not in any sense urging that we do this."[85] The January visit was the beginning of the end for MacArthur; his influence was ebbing rapidly with the chiefs, who were growing weary of his incessant carping. It had now become clear to Vandenberg that disaster in Korea was not imminent, atomic strikes against China were not necessary, and the limited war would remain limited—with the tacit consent of all parties involved.

As weeks passed, it became clear that neither the United States nor the United Nations was willing to expand the war in Asia; both wanted stability and peace. As MacArthur realized this, he became ever more outspoken in his criticism of administration policy. He was not accustomed to losing and was too old to learn new habits. His string of intemperate speeches and remarks finally culminated in a letter to Congressman Joseph E. Martin, the House minority leader, made public on April 5, 1951. The president was incensed, and later said that it was then he decided to fire the general. First, however, he asked his advisers for their opinion. On Friday afternoon, April 6, Truman met with Secretaries Acheson and Marshall, Averell Harriman, and General Bradley to discuss what action should be taken regarding the Martin letter. Acheson and Harriman recommended immediate relief, but Marshall and Bradley counseled restraint and deferment of any action until after the weekend. The following day the same five men met again for over an hour, with the same results, although Bradley and Marshall had weakened somewhat on their call for restraint.

Because the president wanted to hear the opinions of the other Joint Chiefs, Bradley gathered them to his office on Sunday afternoon. The four discussed the matter for over two hours, then met with Marshall to talk further. Finally, all agreed that MacArthur should be relieved for two reasons. First, the general "was not in entire sympathy with the policies being followed by the government" regarding the Far East. Moreover, as Bradley wrote, the chiefs were afraid that

MacArthur might make a "premature decision" and attack targets in Manchuria without specific authorization. (The JCS had drafted an emergency order authorizing such strikes as a retaliatory measure if the Communists made a major attack against UN forces. Because they did not trust MacArthur, however, the order was kept in JCS files and not sent.)

Second, the chiefs were concerned that if MacArthur were not relieved, "a large segment of our people would charge that civil [ians] no longer controlled the military."[86] The chiefs never really addressed the question of whether MacArthur had disobeyed orders. In the memoirs published after his death, Bradley stated that the question of disobedience was raised, but not pursued. To charge MacArthur with such an offense would have required a court-martial—a trial that would have been worse than the Billy Mitchell episode of the 1920s or the revolt of the admirals in 1949. The chiefs wanted MacArthur removed, not martyred.[87]

The following morning, April 9, President Truman listened as his chief counselors unanimously recommended relief. Agreeing, Truman told Bradley to draw up the necessary orders. When asked afterwards what his personal feelings were about the matter, Vandenberg replied that he had enormous respect for General MacArthur and thought him a truly great man, but that he was wrong.[88] The storm that erupted over the president's decision culminated in the dramatic Senate hearings of May and June 1951 when the Old Warrior and key leaders testified on American policy in the Korean War.

THE OLD SOLDIER FADES AWAY

The importance of the MacArthur hearings was not lost on Vandenberg. He knew that Congress would address more than the removal of a famous general; the administration's entire foreign and military policy was to be on trial, and there were numerous senators who were standing ready to draw blood. Before testifying, Vandenberg called in Barton Leach, the Yale-educated lawyer who had helped during the B-36 hearings, and asked for guidance. Leach staged a trial run of what the senators' questioning would be like. He queried the chief about his personal feelings toward MacArthur: "Well, I admire him," said Vandenberg, "I recognize him as a great strategist; I recognize his abilities." Was there any criticism he could levy against the former UN commander? "Yes, I think he is pompous; he is egotistical; he's not as sharp as he used to be in that he made some serious errors here in the war, and I think he has almost openly defied the President, which is foolish." Leach cautioned him that he must not allow personal criticism or animosity to creep into his testimony; he must stick to the facts and remain dispassionate.[89]

Vandenberg took the stand on the morning of May 28 and was questioned closely by twenty-six senators over the next two days. There were three major topics addressed: did he concur in the relief of MacArthur; did he agree with MacArthur's plans to widen the war in the Far East; and what were the global capabilities of the Air Force?

Vandenberg was emphatic that he concurred in the relief of General MacArthur, but sidestepped the question of disobedience; that was a complex legal question, and it was not of major importance in his decision. Vandenberg supported dismissal because MacArthur's views on the conduct of the war were not in consonance with those of the Joint Chiefs and the president. Such disagreement could be dangerous given the power of MacArthur as a theater commander with enormous forces at his disposal. A man in MacArthur's position had to be given great latitude and independence, and it had to be hoped he would use that power wisely; Vandenberg no longer trusted MacArthur to do so. Vandenberg's reasoning was far more sobering than that of Secretary Marshall and the other chiefs, who hung their rationale on the pegs of MacArthur's failure to clear speeches in advance and differences in his strategic outlook.[90] The Air Force chief strongly implied that he feared MacArthur would precipitate World War III; and because his Air Force would bear the initial brunt of operations against China and the Soviet Union in the Far East, he did not want to fight that war. As cautioned, he spoke of the general as "brilliant" and a man for whom he had great personal admiration, but one who was too narrow-minded in his outlook. The Air Force had global responsibilities that MacArthur's Far East Command did not.[91]

The question of whether Vandenberg thought the war in Asia should be expanded to include the bombing of Manchuria brought a definite no. That such an air effort would be successful in compelling China to negotiate a truce he did not doubt, but it would also weaken the Air Force so that it could no longer fulfill its other responsibilities.

> The fact is that the United States is operating a shoestring air force in view of its global responsibilities . . . we cannot afford to peck at the periphery. . . . While we can lay the industrial potential of Russia today waste, [sic] in my opinion, or we can lay the Manchurian countryside waste, as well as the principal cities of China, we cannot do both, again because we operate a $20 million business with about $20,000.[92]

In further testimony deleted by the censors, Vandenberg went on to state that 80 percent of the USAF's tactical strength and 25 percent of her strategic forces were tied up in Korea. An expansion of the air war to involve China would severely strain Air Force resources. Recounting the enormous Soviet air strength available for use in the Far East, Vandenberg was even less sanguine. The Air Force would be extremely hard pressed if forced to take on both the Chinese and the Soviets. In that regard, Senator Russell raised again the question of "hot pursuit." Vandenberg was not in favor of such actions because it would signal a potentially dangerous escalation of the war. Yes, the Communists had "privileged sanctuaries," but so did the United States. American air bases in Japan had never been attacked; therefore, both sides appeared to be tacitly limiting the war.[93]

Vandenberg's stance on the issue of hot pursuit is significant because he had been under increasing pressure from the Far East since early November 1950 to sanction such retaliation. In late December, Stratemeyer had sent a personal, "your eyes only" letter to Vandenberg pleading for a reevaluation of the no-pursuit policy. Strat said his pilots were loyal, devoted, and efficient, "but are becoming rebellious against being used as *sacrificial expendables*."[94] When Van once again said no, Strat was disappointed and angry.

The FEAF commander was coming increasingly under MacArthur's spell and was also moving for a widening of the war. Stratemeyer's affection for MacArthur was evidenced when he awarded him a Distinguished Flying Cross for merely riding along on a routine reconnaissance patrol. In November, Stratemeyer recommended his commander for an oak leaf cluster to his Medal of Honor. (Vandenberg dismissed the request out of hand.) When MacArthur began to go over the edge in April 1951 Stratemeyer followed, waxing rapturous in his diary concerning the brilliance and patriotism of the old general. On April 6, MacArthur and Stratemeyer met with a visiting delegation of congressmen at which time the UN commander lectured his visitors on the "fantastic" restraints placed upon him by his enemies in Washington. MacArthur thought the Soviet "bluff" should. be called. Stratemeyer stood by admiringly during this display, noting in his diary that MacArthur's performance had left the lawmakers "speechless." Indeed. It is possible that Vandenberg was aware of Stratemeyer's psychological drift, for after MacArthur was relieved, Strat was issued strict orders to desist from any public comments regarding the politics or strategy of the Korean War. The week before the MacArthur Senate hearings began, Stratemeyer suffered a severe heart attack while on the golf course.[95] It is not unlikely that Vandenberg would have soon replaced him in any event.

When Vandenberg was asked at the Senate hearings what should be done to ensure that the Air Force could carry out its global commitments and also win the war in Korea, he stated, as he had for the previous three years, that forty-eight groups were inadequate. With the advent of the Korean War, the Air Force was finally beginning to expand and had an interim goal of ninety-five groups. Such strength would be adequate to cope with the Soviet menace and Korea, but, as the Soviet atomic stockpile increased, ninety-five groups would also be insufficient because air defenses, hitherto neglected, must now be built as well.[96]

At several points during his testimony, Vandenberg was able to expound on his theory of air power and its role in war. This testimony is of great importance because it constitutes the largest single body of Vandenberg's ideas on the subject. These were his own words, not those of a speech writer, spoken for the record to a group of distinguished officials. Vandenberg stated the basic military strategy of the United States in the event of World War III with the Soviet Union as follows: first, to defend the United States and the Western Hemisphere; second, to launch an atomic air strike against Soviet industry; and third, to liberate Europe, which would have been overrun soon after the outbreak of hostilities, through the use of a combined air-land-sea campaign reminiscent of World War II. That was the war plan approved by the Joint Chiefs and the secretary of Defense.

The Air Force's role in the war plan was also agreed to by military leaders. Vandenberg preached that the best defense was a good offense; American strategic air power was the most important factor in keeping the peace. His aim was not to fight and win World War III, but to prevent it from ever happening with a strong deterrent force. Therefore, the first two tasks of the war plan required a strong strategic Air Force in being at all times. The third phase of the war, liberation, would require strong tactical air power. But phase three, though crucial to ultimate victory, was a longer-range task. Tactical air power could wait. The Soviets would not be deterred from major aggression through fear of our fighter bombers but because they feared our strategic bombers. Vandenberg even opined that if the Air Force had been up to strength (seventy groups) when the Korean War broke out, China might not have dared to enter the fray.[97] Yes, he wanted tactical air power as well, but forty-eight groups were insufficient to provide it, as he had stated many times before. Nevertheless, the Air Force had done an excellent job of close air support in Korea, even with its meager resources. All the talk of poor air support for the Army was grossly exaggerated; virtually every commander from MacArthur and Ridgway down to the regimental level had said on numerous occasions that it was air power that had prevented the Army from being pushed off the peninsula. Vandenberg was proud of the Air Force effort in Korea, though he had often warned that more was needed.[98]

This theory of air power employment, though most fully articulated here, had been evident in Vandenberg's words and actions ever since he had taken over as chief of staff. Whether arguing over the budget, jousting with the Navy over the B-36 and the supercarrier, pushing for a more realistic war plan, forming CONAC, or selecting General LeMay as SAC commander, Vandenberg had consistently and single-mindedly sought to establish strategic air power as the cornerstone of American defense policy. He was rapidly approaching that goal because an increasing number of civilian and military leaders were being swayed by the logic of his arguments.

It is easy to criticize Vandenberg's seeming shortsightedness in focusing too intently on World War III while ignoring the possibilities of limited war, but he was not alone in this myopia. Few military leaders were yet speaking of "brush fire wars" or those of "national liberation." His colleagues were no more prescient than he. More to the point, Vandenberg would no doubt have claimed that such arguments missed the mark. Defeat in Korea would not result in the destruction or subjugation of the United States; defeat in World War III most certainly would. Prepare for the worst case, and then deal with the lesser alternatives as resources permit.

Typically, Vandenberg's performance under tough questioning was smooth and precise. He consistently refused to tumble into the snares laid by wily legislators. He would not comment on whether MacArthur should have traveled to Washington rather than the president flying to Wake Island for their famous conference. He had no opinion regarding the method by which MacArthur had been relieved. When asked who was at fault for the Air Force not expanding to the promised seventy groups, he replied that there were political factors at play that were beyond his expertise. When pressed and told that the funds for expansion had been appropriated by Congress but were impounded by the president, the general once again refused to bite; the commander in chief had multiple concerns that far transcended military opinion. In fact, he even declined to state at that time how large an Air Force he deemed necessary, lest his statement be misconstrued and he be accused of using the hearings as a "sounding board" for service interests.[99] When asked if he had ever been restrained in his public statements on military policy, he said no, giving several instances when he had publicly disagreed with his civilian superiors on military matters. It was his duty to advise the civilian leadership and to tell the truth.[100]

General Vandenberg did, however, make one serious blunder. In an exchange with Senator Styles Bridges over the objective of the UN forces in Korea, the chief stated: "I believe our objective is to kill as many Chinese Communists as is possible without enlarging the war at the present time in Korea."[101] Bridges let the statement slide, but the following day Senator Guy Gillette said he was "tremendously perturbed" by the remarks: "Now, if there is that uncertainty in the mind of a member of the Joint Chiefs of Staff, and a great United States Senator, what can we expect from the general public that is committing their resources and their sons to this conflict?"[102] A good question, and Vandenberg beat a hasty retreat, stating that besides killing Communists, it was the UN objective to restore freedom to the South Koreans and push the aggressors back. Senator Gillette was assuaged by the response, but others were not. That afternoon, when it was Senator Bourke Hickenlooper's turn to ask questions, he went straight to the mark: "I have been under the impression, General, our objective is to terminate that war and save American lives, and to win the victory against aggression, . . . and not to kill as many Chinamen as we can." Once again Vandenberg waffled, acknowledging that killing Chinese was "incidental" to the *main* objective of "stopping aggression." The embarrassing incident then passed and the questioning took a different tack.[103] By this point, the hearings were already beginning to lose widespread interest, and although more testimony would follow, the fireworks were over.

Chairman Richard Russell thanked Vandenberg for his help, candor, and usefulness; he had enunciated "some mighty good old American doctrines." After two months of extensive testimony, the hearings anticlimactically shuddered to a halt. A new soldier fended and an old soldier faded, while the police action continued. The total wars of an earlier era were passing; limited wars of circumscribed objectives fought with restrained means were now in the ascendancy. Vandenberg realized this change in the nature of war. MacArthur did not.

STALEMATE AND TERMINATION

With MacArthur gone and Ridgway the new United Nations commander, the chiefs were assured of a subordinate who was obedient to their will and a staunch advocate of the administration's limited war policy. Ridgway launched no war-winning offensives, made no provocative speeches, and threatened no attacks on China.[104] For the next two years, the Korean War stabilized into a static war of trenches and dug-in gun emplacements, faintly resembling the First World War. A major difference was the effect of air power. Although arguments over the control of close air support did not disappear, they were muted. Since there was little maneuvering, there was also less need for tactical air strikes. Moreover, as the Communist forces dug in ever deeper such strikes became less productive. As a result, FEAF and Navy fighter-bombers were able to concentrate more firepower on interdiction targets in North Korea.

In mid-1951, FEAF planners devised a massive interdiction campaign, operation STRANGLE, designed to dry up supplies to the enemy's front line. One of General Weyland's first recommendations upon arriving in the theater had been to launch such a campaign, arguing that attempting to rely solely on close air support was like trying to dam a river at the bottom of a waterfall. It was far more productive to stop enemy supplies before they reached the front.[105] Vandenberg, well remembering the effects of Ninth Air Force efforts during World War II, needed no convincing on this score. He often stated that the most efficient way of preventing an enemy bullet from killing an American soldier was to destroy the factory that produced the bullets; that would save hundreds of American lives. Because the enemy factories were located in China and the Soviet Union, however, Vandenberg advocated an alternative: hitting the railroads and trucks that were delivering the shells to the front lines. STRANGLE was intended to do that.[106]

The choice of codename for the air campaign was unfortunate. Although FEAF planners hoped the interdiction campaign would force the Chinese back to the Yalu, Vandenberg was more realistic. He maintained repeatedly that it was not possible to halt the flow of all supplies, but only to slow them down and make their delivery highly expensive. He knew the Chinese would not retreat because of STRANGLE, but he hoped they would be unable to attack. The air campaign was successful in attaining that goal; the Chinese were unable to launch a sustained attack, and losing seven thousand trucks per month had much to do with that failure.[107]

To avoid the jet fighter-bombers that roamed North Korea striking roads, bridges, railroad lines, and trucks, the Communist forces were compelled to travel at night. Unfortunately, night operations were an Achilles heel of the FEAF, as Vandenberg realized early in the war. Writing Stratemeyer in August 1950, he urged that no stone be left unturned in an effort to improve night interdiction strikes; new tactics must be devised to deny the enemy the security of darkness.[108] Numerous solutions were attempted: flare drops, spotlights, radar, pathfinders, and so forth, but each innovation was countered by Chinese ingenuity. The rugged and dangerous terrain exacerbated the problem. The Fifth Air Force was never able to throttle the enemy's night movements to any appreciable extent.[109]

In addition, another method was devised to retard the American interdiction campaign. The two hundred aircraft of the North Korean Air Force had been neutralized within the first month of the war, and the small Chinese Air Force seldom contested American air superiority. In September 1951, that situation changed dramatically when Soviet-made MIG-15 jet fighters began appearing south of the Yalu in great numbers. By October, it was estimated that at least seven hundred MIGs were stationed at a string of airfields just inside the Manchurian border. The MIG-15 was an extremely good airplane. Smaller, lighter, faster, more maneuverable, and with a higher altitude capability than most American fighters, its appearance augured ill. The only aircraft in the American inventory that could compete with the MIG, barely, was the F-86 Sabre.[110] The fact that the MIGs seldom strayed far from their bases, whereas the Sabres were usually at the limit of their range, gave the Communists an advantage. Moreover, because US aircraft were prohibited from pursuing the MIGs into Manchuria, the Chinese retained the initiative in air battles by attacking only under advantageous conditions. Worse, there were only seventy-nine F-86s in the Far East, and Vandenberg had to refuse Weyland's request for more; the Sabres were also needed for American air defense and in Europe.[111]

As mentioned earlier, the area of northwest Korea where the MIGs ventured forth to challenge the Sabres was known as "Mig Alley." Given the comparability of the two jets, it is remarkable that American pilots achieved such results. By the end of the war, there were 792 confirmed MIG kills at the cost of seventy-eight F-86s—a ratio of over ten to one.[112] This incredible statistic is usually credited to the superior skill of the American pilots. Most of the MIG aviators were clearly inferior in air-to-air combat and seldom offered a challenge, but there were a number of excellent enemy flyers, dubbed "honchos," who usually flew apart from the main formations. The nationality of these honchos has always been in question. The bodies of two Soviet officers were recovered from MIG crashes, and a Polish pilot who defected in Europe stated that several of the Soviet instructor pilots in his unit had fought in Korea. Vandenberg testified unequivocally before the Senate that enemy pilots were Soviets, East Germans, and Chinese.[113] Fortunately, there were only a few honchos in Mig Alley.

When reconnaissance revealed that three major airfields were being built one hundred miles south of the Yalu, however, there was much concern. If the MIG range was thus extended, they could interfere with the ground struggle near the thirty-eighth parallel. The FEAF launched dozens of air strikes to destroy these fields, and the MIGs rose by the hundreds to stop them. Consequently, the massive air battles of late 1951 were of great importance. Vandenberg believed that air superiority had been the decisive factor preventing American defeat; without it, the Eighth Army would have been pushed off the peninsula. Too often this was overlooked by Army officers who saw the air battles as glamorous and interesting, but largely insignificant. To Vandenberg this view was naive; the numerically superior foe, operating on shortened supply lines, was virtually prohibited from traveling or operating in the daylight, while UN forces had complete freedom of movement. What if these conditions had been reversed? To his mind, the struggle in Mig Alley was as crucial and decisive as the Battle of Britain had been in World War II—whoever controlled the skies controlled the ground beneath.[114]

It concerned Vandenberg that, although Sabres were defeating MIGs at a wondrous rate, it was still not enough. The swarms of enemy fighters did more than just dogfight with their American counterparts: they went after far bigger game—the B-29s. One purpose of the Chinese air assault was to disrupt STRANGLE, and in this they were successful. The B-29s were no match for the MIGs, and the escorting Sabres were too few. After three of the big bombers were shot down and five others were damaged on one raid, Weyland made the difficult decision to use them only at night using radar bomb drops. The new tactics were not nearly as accurate or effective as daylight operations, but were necessary to prevent decimation of the bomber force.[115]

As the military stalemate continued into 1952 and the armistice negotiations begun the previous June proved fruitless, command changes provided new ideas for the air war. General Stratemeyer who, as mentioned earlier, had suffered a serious heart attack in May 1951, returned home. After filling in for a month, Partridge was also transferred to a new assignment, with Weyland taking over FEAF. In early 1952, Weyland had his planners thoroughly reevaluate the objectives and assumptions of the air war. Interdiction as understood by the STRANGLE operation, though a good concept, had outlived its usefulness. Weyland wanted to apply pressure to the Communists so that they would negotiate more seriously. He did not want to *disrupt* enemy movements and supplies but to *destroy* enemy resources. The war had to be made too costly for the enemy—especially the Soviets—to continue.[116]

The most obvious targets were the eleven hydroelectric plants of North Korea, which supplied not only the North but a large portion of Manchuria as well. The plants had been suggested for attack before, but the JCS had denied permission because of their political implications. In April 1952, Vandenberg asked his colleagues to reconsider this decision; the glacial pace of the armistice negotiations led the chiefs to approve the request.[117] However, General Ridgway now balked, saying he did not wish to jeopardize negotiations unless absolutely necessary. When Ridgway was replaced by General Mark Clark the following month, Weyland reintroduced the question of the hydroelectric plants. Clark assumed his new command understandably eager to produce tangible results, and he approved the strikes immediately.[118]

The eleven generator complexes were hit by USAF and Navy fighter-bombers between June 23 and 27. The strikes were successful, blacking out all of North Korea for two weeks, reducing power to 10 percent of its former capacity for the remainder of the war, and, more significantly, reducing the electricity supplied to Manchuria by 23 percent.[119] Unfortunately, the impact of these strikes was diluted by the international uproar that followed. The British government was particularly upset by what it perceived as a widening of the war, especially since it had not been consulted in advance. The furor caused Secretary of Defense Robert Lovett (Marshall had once again retired) to announce that there had been no change in UN policy; the air strikes did not signal an increasing of pressure on the Communists. In fact, increasing pressure was precisely what the attacks were all about, but Lovett's official denial probably sent a mixed signal to Chinese leaders that undercut the value of the strikes.[120]

Clark and Weyland, still determined to raise the price of the war to the enemy, suggested additional targets previously off-limits: the oil refineries at Rashin near the Soviet border, the North Korean capital of Pyongyang, and the earthen dams that kept the numerous rivers of North Korea in check. Having learned his lesson, Clark cleared the attack on Pyongyang through Washington, which in turn notified the Allies.[121] The capital was hit in August, the oil refineries in September. Although the attacks were militarily successful, they failed to produce a political breakthrough. The major stumbling block in the negotiations—the disposition of prisoners—was not yet resolved. The Communists insisted on forced repatriation of all captives on both sides. The American position was that repatriation should be an individual choice.[122]

In an attempt to lever the American position on the issue, the Chinese introduced a new wrinkle. On March 8, 1952, Chou En Lai declared that the United Nations was using chemical and bacteriological weapons against the Korean people. This was genocide and captured American pilots were not, therefore, prisoners of war, but rather common criminals. Vandenberg responded vehemently that such charges were false. He saw it as a propaganda trick by the Chinese and warned that the United States would hold the Communists responsible for the treatment of captured pilots.[123] There is no question that the USAF had a chemical and bacteriological capability. Hundreds of such weapons were in the American stockpile and were deliverable by a variety of aircraft. One such weapon was described as a converted leaflet bomb that contained ten pounds of feathers dusted with a toxic agent that could destroy up to 75 percent of the entire Soviet wheat crop.[124] There is no evidence, however, that such weapons were ever used in Korea. Moreover, JCS orders to Clark in September 1952 specifically prohibited their use.[125] The entire question did serve, however, to further aggravate Vandenberg and the Joint Chiefs.

As stalemate limped into 1953, plans were being discussed in Washington for an even greater escalation than that witnessed by the powerplant and oil refinery strikes. One of Dwight Eisenhower's campaign promises had been to end the war in Korea. After his inauguration, therefore, he directed the Joint Chiefs to study possible courses of action to end the war, including the use of atomic weapons. On May 19, 1953, the Joint Chiefs presented their proposal, which stated in part:

> It is the view of the Joint Chiefs of Staff that the necessary air, naval, and ground operations, including extensive strategical and tactical use of the atomic bombs, be undertaken so as to obtain maximum surprise and maximum impact on the enemy, both militarily and psychologically. If undertaken piecemeal—for example, starting with a naval blockade, followed by gradually increasing air operations, and finally followed later by ground operations—we would minimize the chance of success of the course of action outlined.[126]

Two days later, Secretary of State John Foster Dulles met with Prime Minister Jawaharlal Nehru in New Delhi and implied strongly that American patience had reached an end:

> I agreed with his estimate [Nehru's], stating that if the armistice negotiations collapsed, the United States would probably make a stronger rather than a lesser military exertion, and that this might well extend the area of conflict.[127]

It has been commonly assumed that Dulles warned Nehru that if the Chinese did not become more amenable at the peace table, an air attack on Manchuria, to include atomic bombs, would be the next step. This message was passed to Peking. At the same time, Vandenberg secured the transfer of atomic weapons to Okinawa in the event they were to be used.

Vandenberg's views on the conduct of the war evolved considerably from 1951 to 1953. As noted, he was strongly opposed to a widening of the war at the time of the MacArthur hearings—both his public and his private remarks confirm this. After the Chinese intervention, Vandenberg seriously considered a withdrawal from Korea rather than risk a major war. As it became clear that the Communists also intended to fight a limited war, his fears subsided. With STRANGLE's auspicious beginning, Vandenberg's attitude began to harden. He advised against an armistice while the enemy was on the run; pressure should be tightened, not relaxed.[128] The initial air victories in Mig Alley tended to strengthen this hawkish position. But as the MIG threat continued to build, the B-29s began to suffer losses, the interdiction campaign petered out, and negotiations remained stalled, Vandenberg began to question the value of attrition warfare. By December 1951, he was once again weighing the option of withdrawal; in February 1952, he urged an armistice, and by September, he was obviously growing exasperated.[129] At a meeting between representatives from State, Defense, and the JCS, Vandenberg listened to desultory debate concerning peace negotiations and finally asked if anyone had considered what steps should be taken if the talks failed:

> There has been no real thought as to what we should do if this thing is going on indefinitely. You have to have a new tack sometime. . . . The people in Michigan and Ohio and out there across the country where I have been are red-headed about this. They want something done. The people here in Washington don't realize that. It is going to affect the elections. . . . the lid will blow off.[130]

As the months dragged on without progress, Vandenberg grew increasingly restive and became a prime mover in the campaign to step up the air pressure on North Korea and China. In May 1953, he gained authorization to bomb the North Korean dams. The initial raids were even more devastating than had been predicted as thousands of acres of rice fields were flooded, roads and rail lines were washed away, and whole villages inundated. Thus, by mid-1953, Vandenberg's attitude had hardened considerably. Speaking before the Air War College, he advanced proposals from which he had shrunk two years earlier.

> We ought to put on a very strong blockade of the Chinese coast; we ought to break her rail lines . . . we ought to mine her rivers . . . and we ought to destroy those small industrial installations that are contributing either toward her welfare or toward her war-making capacity.[131]

Vandenberg thought that atomic bombs were neither necessary nor desirable; he did not wish to "fritter away" the limited atomic stockpile unless a truly strategic target presented itself. He suggested Mukden.

This was a remarkable speech, but another given to a different audience the same day was substantially the same. He had had time, therefore, to retract his previous statements, but did not. Why had his views changed so markedly? Why was he now advocating the major war he had so dreaded earlier? It is apparent that the months of attritional warfare took their toll on him emotionally. The frustration and anger felt at the intractable Communist leaders were mounting in him. Like American leaders two decades later, his patience finally expired; Vandenberg wanted to lash out and end the source of so prolonged an agony. The war was draining men, material, and money in what seemed a never-ending ordeal. The war was a cancer that needed to be excised.

The Chief of Staff was due to retire at the end of June. For the previous three years he had been fighting this apparently interminable war. He must have wanted to end it before leaving his post, to tie up the loose ends, and present a clean slate to his successor. The desire to escalate the war was perhaps an attempt to end it—once and for all.

It is also possible that Vandenberg had a need to feel that this war was something within his control, something that a man of action and decisiveness could influence. The chief was dying of cancer, and he was powerless to stop it; but perhaps he could stop the war. It was a great disappointment to General Vandenberg that the armistice was not signed before his retirement on June 30, 1953. He was content to realize, however, that air power had saved American forces from defeat in the dark days of 1950 and had been instrumental in compelling an agreement at the negotiating table in July 1953.

Our splendid arguments concerning the
cost of war and the expense of defense
have influenced no one but ourselves.
Hoyt S. Vandenberg

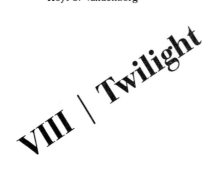

Who living had no note,
when death approached,
unlocked her silent throat.
from "The Silver Swan"

FIRST WARNINGS

The relationship between General Vandenberg and Secretary Symington had always been extremely cordial; they were an effective, complementary team that worked well together. When in 1950 Symington resigned in protest over administrative fiscal policies, his place was taken by Thomas K. Finletter, a successful New England lawyer who had chaired the President's Air Policy Commission in 1947. Finletter, not a businessman or manager as Symington had been, was more interested in the abstract, philosophical aspects of his position. Leaving the management of the Air Force to Vandenberg, Finletter dwelt often on the most effective method of air power employment, and eventually decided that strategic bombing was the most important mission of the Air Force. He was a strong admirer of General LeMay.[1]

Although their personalities were dissimilar, the relationship between Finletter and Vandenberg went smoothly at first. An unfortunate event then occurred, seemingly insignificant, that was to cause hard feelings between the two men. At a social function attended by the wives of the secretary and the chief, Glad, for whatever reason, was seated at the head chair. Mrs. Finletter, insulted, informed her husband, who in turn chastised Vandenberg. The chief immediately drove home to speak with Gladys. An aide recalled that the ensuing argument was the stormiest they had had in years. Although Vandenberg apologized for his wife's faux pas, his relations with the secretary were severely strained thereafter.[2] And there were other difficulties.

Secretary Finletter had a drinking problem. On one occasion both he and General Vandenberg were scheduled to speak in New York City. Upon taking the podium, the secretary muttered a few incoherent words about the power of SAC, and then collapsed. After helping Finletter from the room, Vandenberg told the astonished audience that the man was ill. He said that if an enemy were aware of his condition they might try to take advantage of the situation. In the interest of national security he begged their indulgence and discretion concerning the incident. From that point on, the two men seldom spoke to each other, and virtually all communication was in writing or through intermediaries.[3]

Finletter also tried to split Vandenberg from his staff by calling certain members directly to his office without going through the chain of command. On one occasion, he even gathered several deputy chiefs of staff to his vacation lodge for a week while Vandenberg was out of the country and attempted to wean them from their superior. He was not successful. As General Kuter later explained: "This was a case of a 'civilian mind' not being able to understand organizational loyalties, organizational discipline, and military structure."[4] No way to run an air force.

The ill will between the two men reached public attention by mid-1951, when questions arose concerning Vandenberg's retirement. The general's four-year tour as chief of staff was due to expire in April 1952, and although he would have been eligible to retire at that point, it was clear that he preferred to serve a full, thirty-year career. The difficulty was what to do with a full general who, by law, could no longer act as chief, but who, though there were whispers of a "big civilian job" awaiting him, wished to remain active for the fourteen months before his thirty-year retirement date. One solution was to ask Congress for a waiver, allowing Vandenberg to remain in office for the additional fourteen months. Rumors and speculation regarding the situation became widespread, forcing the chief to write all his commanders that retirement talk was untrue—he would remain in uniform until June 1953.[5] Stories then surfaced that Vandenberg would be elevated to JCS chairman at the expiration of Bradley's tenure, but this possibility faded, reputedly owing to the opposition of Finletter. The secretary wanted Vandenberg retired, not promoted, with LeMay becoming the new chief of staff. State Department officials quickly objected to a man of LeMay's personality and temperament being placed in such a delicate position; it was said that the SAC commander "lacked tact."[6]

As a compromise, Defense Secretary Robert Lovett decided that Vandenberg would be extended as chief for an additional fourteen months, LeMay would become vice chief, and Nate Twining would move to SAC. In order to effect this plan, President Truman, a firm supporter of Vandenberg, asked the Senate to approve the general's extension, telling the lawmakers that he wanted to ensure that "General Vandenberg has the opportunity to round out his full 30 years of military service as Chief of Staff." He did not wish the general to be in a "subordinate command" before his retirement.[7]

Some members of the Senate Armed Services Committee balked at the president's proposal. Senator Harry P. Cain objected that the stated rationale for extension was "about as meaningless and inconsequential as any reason I have ever heard." Senator John Stennis also questioned the move, saying that he had nothing personal against Vandenberg, but it was a "bad precedent." Other members of the committee were solid Vandenberg backers: Senators Richard B. Russell, Harry F. Byrd, Styles Bridges, and Wayne L. Morse all expressed support for the extension and spoke of Vandenberg in laudatory terms.[8] In the event, the nomination hearings lasted six weeks; Vandenberg was not confirmed until April 28.[9] This embarrassing episode made it apparent that relations within the Air Force hierarchy were far from smooth, but before the compromise that had been hammered out over the previous three months could take effect, crisis struck.

On May 6, 1952, Vandenberg visited the flight surgeon to check on an ailment that had been troubling him for some time. Perhaps expecting bad news, or perhaps because he was too busy, the chief had not had a physical examination in years. His fears were confirmed—prostate cancer; an operation was scheduled for the following morning. That Vandenberg had cancer was not released to the public, not even former Secretary Stuart Symington was told at first; reports said merely that the general had had abdominal surgery.[10] When Vandenberg entered the hospital, the plans for Twining and LeMay to switch positions were scrapped; Twining immediately became acting chief of staff, and Major General Larry Kuter, the ranking deputy, automatically became acting vice chief.[11]

Vandenberg spent two months in Walter Reed Hospital, was given flowers during visits by, among others, President Truman and General Eisenhower, and quickly grew tired of lying in bed. By early July, he was back on the golf course, eager to return to work. (His game wasn't yet up to par, but one golf partner noted it was far better than his singing—which he still inflicted upon family and friends alike.) The operation appeared successful; by late August he was back in the office, and in early September Norstad wrote him that he was looking better than he had in years.[12] In December Van wrote to a seven-year old boy dying of Hodgkin's Disease. The general hoped Santa would be good to him and encouraged him to keep fighting; illness could be overcome. Such optimism was short-lived.

NSC-68 AND REARMAMENT

The difficulties between Vandenberg and his secretary were particularly unfortunate because they coincided with the nation's attempts to rearm while fighting a war. Even before the North Korean invasion, there were indications that American foreign and military policy needed reassessment. The "fall of China" and the detonation of Joe I pointed to heightened external threats, while the B-36 hearings revealed serious disagreements within the uniformed hierarchy.

Consequently, on January 31, 1950, President Truman directed Secretaries Acheson and Johnson to undertake a "reexamination of our objectives in peace and war."[13] The Joint Chiefs then appointed the Joint Strategic Survey Committee (JSSC) to collaborate with a State Department team headed by Paul Nitze in carrying out the president's wishes.[14] Initially, the JSSC wrote plans assuming that current budget limits would remain in effect; Nitze, on the other hand, elected to ignore fiscal strictures for his projections. The Defense team soon agreed to State's method; and the result was a study, NSC-68, which painted a somber picture of the world situation that required a massive military buildup in America.[15]

NSC-68 is a stark document, written in shades of black and white. The Soviet Union is "animated by a new fanatic faith, antithetical to our own," the study avers, "which seeks to impose its absolute authority over the rest of the world." It continues that "the issues that face us are momentous, involving the fulfillment or destruction not only of this Republic, but of civilization itself."[16] The State-Defense authors then listed the relative strengths and weaknesses of the United States and the Soviet Union, pointing out that the enemy had substantially greater forces in being, as well as greater manpower reserves. Soviet atomic capability also boded ill. Faced with this menace, the United States was presented with four courses of action: continuation of present policies; isolation; war; or a military buildup "to better defend ourselves in the event that the free world is attacked."[17]

Taking each of these options in turn, the authors of NSC-68 projected probable outcomes, concluding that only the last strategy was viable. America must rearm. The report conceded that this program would be costly, but asserted that the United States could routinely devote up to 20 percent of its gross national product for defense while not lowering the American standard of living; in an emergency, it could devote up to 50 percent, as it had during World War II.[18]

The Joint Chiefs unanimously endorsed NSC-68, sending it to the president on April 17, 1950. Truman, however, was reluctant to support its conclusions and instead sent the document to the Bureau of the Budget for analysis. Not surprisingly, the accountants severely criticized NSC-68 and stated the nation's economy could not support rearmament.[19] Debate continued within the administration between opponents and proponents of NSC-68, with the president remaining above, neither accepting nor rejecting the study that he had commissioned. It appeared that his inclinations remained on the side of fiscal restraint, for on May 4 he expressed the hope that the defense budget could actually be lowered the following year.[20] It was this prospect that had led Generals Bradley and Collins to consider resignation. This was the climate when war broke out in late June. Dean Acheson remarked candidly in his memoirs that those in favor of retrenchment were in charge, and only the Soviets "being stupid enough to have instigated the attack against South Korea" enabled rearmament to take place.[21]

In June 1950, the Air Force consisted of forty-eight wings and 411,000 personnel, numbers that Vandenberg had often stated were insufficient. Within days of the Communist invasion, however, increased estimates were being projected to deal with the crisis. On July 6, the Air Force requested 25,000 more people and then doubled that amount the following week. On July 17, Secretary Johnson approved a JCS request for ten more combat wings.[22] Communist victories in Korea continued, prompting the JCS to revise their requirements once more. The chiefs now requested an additional six divisions, forty ships, and twelve wings. Once again, President Truman assented. The Air Force was finally to achieve its magical seventy-wing strength; moreover, this increase was to take place by June 1951, only nine months distant.[23] It was further stated that the entire military establishment should continue to expand until mid-1954, with the Army receiving an extra division, the Navy seventy-five more ships, and the Air Force a total of ninety-five wings. Although Vandenberg welcomed the increased emphasis on air power, thinking it long overdue, he disagreed with the timing. He suggested that instead of 1954, "wherever possible . . . we [should] bend every effort to telescope existing target dates in the direction of the 1952 date." His suggestion was rejected.[24]

As MacArthur's "war winning" offensive swept forward during October 1950, it appeared the other chiefs had been correct: there was no need to institute a rapid buildup; in fact, by November there was already talk of halting rearmament.[25] Korea had demonstrated that some expansion was necessary, but on a limited scale. Such fancies evaporated two weeks later when Chinese forces savaged two American divisions near the Manchurian border. By early December, JCS estimates once again called for ninety-five Air Force wings and stated that goals previously advanced for 1954 should be met no later than mid-1952. Vandenberg's proposal of two months before had been resurrected.[26]

As the seriousness of the Chinese intervention became apparent, the JCS pressed for more troops and weapons. Talk of global war prevalent in December 1950 and January 1951 suggested massive rearmament. In addition, the tenets of NSC-68, which seemed confirmed by events in Korea, also begged for military expansion. The MacArthur hearings of May and June provided a forum for the chiefs to state their case directly to Congress. Vandenberg's claim that the nation possessed a "shoestring air force" was the opening salvo in an attempt to establish air power as the first line of American defense. In May 1951, Vandenberg submitted plans calling for a buildup to 140 wings by mid-1955. This proposal met with predictable responses from the Army and the Navy, as debate over force levels raged for several months. Admiral William Fechteler (chief of Naval Operations—Admiral Sherman had died of a heart attack in July 1951) maintained that not only was the 140-wing figure too high, it was also out of balance, placing too much emphasis upon strategic air power. General Collins tended to agree.[27] Vandenberg responded that rapidly changing technology affected the Air Force more than the other services: the Army had reserve divisions and the Navy put ships into mothballs, but rapidly obsolescent jet aircraft made similar options unavailable to the Air Force. Vandenberg defended the emphasis placed on SAC, using arguments he had employed for the previous three years: the war plan demanded it.[28]

It is apparent that a fundamental shift in opinion had occurred among American leaders. President Truman and Secretary Marshall had become enamored with strategic air power; JCS thinking did not lag far behind. By the end of October 1951, the Joint Chiefs had unanimously agreed to an Air Force consisting of 143 wings, nearly half of which were programmed for the strategic air offensive. Even more amazing, although the Air Force would continue to grow until 1957, the Army and Navy would shrink by 13 percent.[29] The reasons for this dramatic about-face are unclear. One historian lists three primary explanations: a traditional American love for air power and complex machinery; the likewise traditional American yearning for simple solutions to complex problems; and economic conservatism.[30] The hydrogen bomb was on the horizon, promising enormous destruction at relatively low cost. General Twining later claimed that nuclear air power was one-tenth as expensive as previous methods of defense.[31] Although the "new look" and "massive retaliation" are terms ordinarily associated with the Eisenhower administration, the roots of such policies were buried in America's response to the Korean War.[32] Vandenberg's arguments on the supremacy and efficiency of air power for defense had finally taken root, and it appeared the momentum was at long last flowing irresistibly in air power's direction. It was now up to Vandenberg to maintain that trend.

THE LAST BATTLE

Shortly after President Truman approved the new force levels, he began to retreat in the face of high budget figures—there was a shortage of $26 billion to cover the FY 1953 rearmament program.[33] His solution was to stretch out the buildup. Even so, the new budget presented to Congress on January 21, 1952, called for defense spending totaling $48.1 billion distributed as follows: Army, $14.2 billion; Navy, $13.2 billion; Air Force, $20.7 billion.[34] Testifying before Congress, Defense Secretary Lovett admitted that the stretch-out was a "calculated risk" because it assumed that the Soviets would not attack in 1953.[35] The Joint Chiefs felt more strongly, contending that "any appreciable delay in attaining the air force levels . . . which may be dictated by reasons other than military, will result in a force structure inadequate to perform the survival tasks for a period at least equal to the period of deferment." The chiefs concluded glumly that a stretch-out would result "in a relatively low order of readiness to meet major aggression in late 1953 and 1954."[36] Nevertheless, Congress, also in a gambling mood, cut the president's budget a further $2 billion but actually increased the Air Force percentage of the defense pie: Army, $12.2 billion; Navy, $12.8 billion; Air Force, $21.1 billion.[37]

In actuality, the figures do not truly indicate the primacy given to air power, since much of the appropriations earmarked for the Army were based on Korean War needs. The Air Force, however, would build to 143 wings even without a war for justification. Vandenberg had sought 168 wings but consented to the lower figure. Now, however, the congressional appropriations would delay the expansion further. At that time the Air Force had but ninety-five wings operational.[38] Debate continued throughout the remainder of 1952 concerning the size of the Air Force. Vandenberg continued to press for expansion, warning of the Russian bear that had been outproducing the United States in aircraft since 1945 by a factor of five. Such a situation could not be allowed to continue.[39] At the same time, he took a heavy swipe at an old antagonist—the aircraft carrier.

In October 1952, Vandenberg wrote a lengthy and detailed memorandum to his JCS colleagues questioning the persistent emphasis within the Navy on fleet-sized aircraft carriers. Over the previous four years, Vandenberg's position had not changed: "I am convinced that the capabilities of Carrier Task Forces for use in a war with the Soviet Union are limited; that they do not justify investment of national resources; that all tasks . . . which a Carrier Task Force can perform can be performed with greater effect and at less cost by land-based air power." Carriers were useful in the Pacific during World War II, but would be useless in a European war. Looking over his shoulder at the Korean Conflict, Vandenberg added that the mission of close air support as performed by carriers would also be highly inefficient and expensive in a European war. As for the atomic offensive, land-based fighter aircraft like the F-84 were now atomic capable, and, from bases in Europe, had far greater range than similar planes floating on carriers in the Mediterranean. Besides, the ships were hopelessly vulnerable to submarine and air attack. Moving along in a similar vein for some twenty pages, Vandenberg concluded by scoring the Navy for continuing to waste money on fleet carriers when they should be concentrating on their antisubmarine capability.[40] Vandenberg's ire over the revolt of 1949 had obviously abated little. He proposed other uses for the defense dollar.

Next to launching the atomic offensive, air defense was officially stated to be the most important mission of the USAF. As early as December 1947, Vandenberg had expressed his concern over the lack of an air defense system for the United States.[41] Because of budget constraints, however, little money could be diverted to this area until the explosion of Joe I in late 1949. After that event, Vandenberg had called for a "Manhattan Project" to beef up the nation's air defense system. The USAF Research and Development Board, examining the problem over the next year, concluded that the air defense system was totally inadequate and made tentative suggestions on what should be done to correct the situation. In December 1950, Vandenberg contacted the president of the Massachusetts Institute of Technology (MIT) and proposed that a laboratory be established at the school which would study problems of interest to the Air Force, specifically, air defense. The offer was accepted.[42]

The first product of the MIT lab was Project Charles, a comprehensive study of the problems of detecting enemy aircraft and the control of friendly aircraft to intercept them. The Charles scientists confirmed the belief that American air defenses were inadequate. A radar fence was necessary to detect incoming planes, and more interceptors were required. To control the enormous defense system envisioned, the scientists suggested a much greater reliance on computers—at that time still in their infancy.[43]

To continue investigations into the matter, Vandenberg directed MIT to launch another study, Project Lincoln. In mid-1952 the first tentative reports on air defense began issuing from Lincoln.[44] Contrary to what air leaders had been saying for several years, the MIT scientists suggested that a near total defense against air attack was possible, if sufficient funds were earmarked for that purpose (estimates varied from $20 billion to $150 billion). Vandenberg and others had stated repeatedly that even the best defense would stop only 30 percent of an attack force—and experience in World War II had produced a figure far less than that. Now, however, Lincoln was claiming that a 90 percent destruction rate could be achieved.[45] Vandenberg disputed such a theory.

At the same time Lincoln was in progress, the Air Force established ties with Cal Tech to provide similar research. Cal Tech's effort, Project Vista, examined the conduct of tactical air operations.[46] This broad subject was soon narrowed in a way that was not to Vandenberg's liking. Vista concentrated on the efficacy of tactical nuclear weapons, arguing that such weapons could and should be developed to "take the battle back to the battlefield." Implicit in such a proposition was that tactical weapons would be more effective in deterring war, and also in winning a war if deterrence failed, than would strategic weapons.[47] Vandenberg rejected these findings as he had those of the Lincoln study. Both projects tended to denigrate the importance and effectiveness of strategic air power: Lincoln because it stated that there *was* an effective counter to air attack; Vista because it recommended an increased emphasis on tactical air power at the expense of SAC. Vandenberg sniffed a plot. One of the key participants in both projects was J. Robert Oppenheimer. This scientific genius, instrumental in atomic weapons development, had since 1949 vocally expressed his opposition to thermonuclear experimentation, the super bomb coveted by the Air Force. Now Oppenheimer seemed to be once again undermining the foundations of Air Force doctrine. Vandenberg questioned his motives. After Vista, the chief directed that Oppenheimer be banned from participating in all future Air Force projects.[48] Vandenberg wanted open discussion—he continued to support research studies similar to Charles, Lincoln, and Vista—but he suspected there were deeper forces at work in Oppenheimer's persistent and long-standing opposition to Air Force goals. When Oppenheimer's loyalty was publicly called into question in 1954 and his security clearance officially removed by the Atomic Energy Commission, it appeared that Vandenberg's deep-seated distrust had at least some foundation.[49]

Shortly before his retirement, Vandenberg himself elaborated on his feelings toward the controversial issue of air defense: "Unfortunately, some people got hold of Project Lincoln and saw an opportunity for directing or controlling national thinking, and it developed into a sort of columnist debate in the public press, and then later it got to the point of putting pressures of various types on the Congress and the Defense Establishment. And it got out of hand." Vandenberg then added: "Air defense . . . is not a panacea to all our troubles. It is not a preventative of atomic warfare. . . . Space is too big, speeds are too high, altitudes are too high, and they are constantly going up. . . . I will be very happy, gentlemen, on the day when you can intercept 30 percent of an attacking force."[50]

Not surprisingly, the conclusions reached by the Lincoln and Vista projects were used by the Army and Navy as ammunition in the budget fights of 1953. The Navy wanted more aircraft carriers and veiled their request as a plea for more tactical support in the event the strategic air offensive failed. In the same vein, the Army argued increasingly for atomic artillery and similar battlefield weapons. Congress, though ever economy-minded, still seemed to favor the Air Force. President Truman advocated a stretch-out. The new president's view was more radical.

One of Dwight Eisenhower's campaign pledges had been to reduce taxes and balance the federal budget. Upon taking office in January 1953, he knew that achieving those two goals required heavy budget cuts, largely from Defense. Robert Taft, Senate majority leader, readily endorsed such plans and actually insisted on far more than Eisenhower proposed. The new Secretary of Defense, Charles Wilson, was alarmed at such talk, but the new chief executive was insistent—at least $10 billion had to be cut from Truman's projections. Eisenhower rejected talk of 1954 as the year of "maximum danger"—when the Soviets were expected to possess the hydrogen bomb—and labeled it "rot." Wilson was told to get his house in order and control the recalcitrant Joint Chiefs. Wilson was only partially successful and Eisenhower was forced to step in and subdue his restless military leaders. His greatest difficulties came from the Air Force.[51]

Wilson informed Vandenberg on February 4 that the Air Force civilian personnel ceiling would be held at 1952 limits, a cut of 93,000 from what had been planned. By March, Wilson was asking what effect a cut to $11.6 billion—a reduction of nearly 50 percent—would have on Air Force capabilities. Vandenberg responded that this figure would limit the Air Force to seventy-nine wings and force cancellation of nearly 9,500 aircraft from the production program. Vandenberg raised a strong protest before the National Security Council, chaired by Eisenhower, but it was to no avail. The JCS echoed this warning, stating somewhat surprisingly that 143 wings were essential; *any* reduction would increase the risk to national security.[52] Nevertheless, in May Eisenhower submitted a revised budget to Congress for FY 1954: Army, $13.7 billion; Navy, $9.8 billion; Air Force, $11.3 billion—a total of $34.8 billion. Whereas the Army's share actually increased, the Air Force budget had been cut nearly $10 billion from the previous year, and an "interim goal" of 120 wings was substituted for the 143 wings previously authorized. Moreover, those 120 wings would not be formed until FY 1956, a year after the 143 wings were to have been completed.[53]

Stuart Symington, now a senator from Missouri, remained one of air power's staunch supporters in Congress, but the real fight for 143 wings was to be carried on by Vandenberg. The chief was scheduled to retire at the end of June, and Senate hearings on the new budget were to be held earlier that month. These hearings were to be Vandenberg's last, and were also among the most important of his career. He was deeply opposed to Eisenhower's budget cuts, but how could he publicly criticize the policies of his superior and old friend?[54]

Before testifying, Vandenberg gathered several close friends and advisers to his quarters one evening to discuss his forthcoming Senate statement. An aide recalled that Vandenberg was obviously in great pain; the cancer discovered the year before had grown far worse and would soon kill him. Those present that night, especially Senator Symington, urged the chief to make a strong and unequivocal condemnation of the president's defense policies. Suggestions were offered on what should be said before Congress. Vandenberg listened for several hours until finally Glad entered, saw the weariness in her husband's eyes, and asked the visitors to go home. Vandenberg motioned his speech writer aside as the men were leaving and said sadly that the discussion had bothered him. He was a team player and now it was suggested that he publicly attack a man whom he liked and respected. He just could not do it. He told his scribe to prepare a statement that was more moderate than that suggested by Symington and the others.[55]

When Vandenberg appeared before the Senate Appropriations Committee on June 3, 1953, he began by reviewing the Soviet threat. Since 1948, the communist powers had become increasingly belligerent. Coupled with this overt animosity was an enormous military buildup which far outstripped that of the United States.

More worrying still, although the Soviet Air Force was already larger than the American, it was also constructing atomic-capable light bombers. These aircraft, IL-28s, could devastate all of Europe and Asia.[56] Vandenberg was a true cold warrior. His experience in Moscow during the Second World War, his tenure as DCI in 1946, and his confrontations with the Soviets thereafter convinced him that the Kremlin leaders were aggressive and untrustworthy. He was unable to view things from their perspective.

In addition to this specific threat, there were four events that had convinced the Joint Chiefs unanimously to recommend Air Force expansion to 143 wings by the end of 1954: the exploding of the Soviet atomic bomb; the invasion of South Korea; the decision to assist in the defense of Europe; and the determination that by 1954 the Soviet Union would be able to launch an all-out attack against the United States. The Air Force strength needed to counter these dangers had fallen victim to the stretch-out imposed by the Truman administration. The policy of the new government was even more dangerous; expansion to only 120 wings by 1957 would increase the risk to national security "beyond the dictates of national prudence." Vandenberg did not approve of the reduction to 120 wings and had formally protested that decision to the new Air Force Secretary, Harold Talbott. In addition, the JCS felt similarly and had so reported, in writing, to Defense secretary Wilson.[57] When asked if there were any strategic factors that would make 143 wings no longer necessary, Vandenberg replied:

> There are no such factors known to me. I know of no change in the strategy which the 143-wing Air Force was designed to enable us to carry out. Nor do I know of any alternate strategy designed to protect the security of the United States and its people which would not require an equal or greater Air Force than the 143-wing force toward which we have been building for two years.[58]

What was worse, not only were funds and force levels being reduced, but so were authorizations for personnel and base construction. An adequate Air Force required planes, people, and bases; the administration was curtailing all three and not providing cogent logic for its action. This resulted in start-and-stop planning that was causing enormous confusion to military planners, civilian industry, and allies.[59] Vandenberg was not satisfied with the strength of the Air Force. He admitted that it was the best and most efficient fighting organization in the world; but as the Soviet menace grew, it would increasingly become a "one shot" air force. If major war occurred, the entire fleet would be committed at the outset, and nothing would be left in reserve. He reiterated that anything less than 143 wings would be a "calculated risk" to the security of the United States and the free world.[60] After three days of testimony, Senator Margaret Chase Smith thanked Vandenberg: "I compliment you on the courage and candor of your answers. I wish the committee could always get such lucid answers."[61] His Air Force colleagues were similarly pleased with his toughness before Congress. Said the *Air Force Times*: "He can now hang up his jet helmet with satisfaction. He has done his full and complete duty."[62] Others did not share this opinion.

Secretaries Wilson and Talbott were irritated at Vandenberg's testimony, at variance with their own, and there was talk of disciplinary action.[63] Although this censure never materialized, it was apparent that Vandenberg's retirement was none too soon for administration officials. Before that last day in uniform, however, the chief had one more round to fire. In a speech to the National Press Club on June 22, he restated his arguments against the stretch-out. Once again railing against the confusion caused by changing requirements levied by superiors, Vandenberg exclaimed: "If it had been the deliberate intention of members of the Office of the secretary of Defense to hamper and delay the Air Force program, they could scarcely have taken actions which would better have served such a purpose."[64] Vandenberg intended to leave uniform with a bang, not a whimper.

On June 30, 1953, General Hoyt S. Vandenberg retired; Secretary Talbott pinned an oak leaf cluster to his Distinguished Service Medal as a flight of new B-47 jet bombers roared overhead. Neither President Eisenhower nor Secretary Wilson attended the ceremony.[65] As his successor, Nate Twining, was being sworn in, the bar of four stars slipped from Vandenberg's shoulders and fell to the floor. Everyone laughed uneasily and made comments about the finality of retirement.[66] Two days later, Congress voted to approve the administration's budget, which included the Air Force stretch-out. The chief had lost. Although his service was more than twice as large and powerful as when he took office and had become the dominant military service in the nation, it was still not what Vandenberg thought sufficient. In his final message to senior commanders, the retiring chief said:

> Five years of duty as the Chief of Staff and my military career as well end at a time when the security of this Nation is threatened as never before. I regret that I shall no longer have the privilege that is still yours of working actively towards the lessening of this threat.[67]

DARKNESS

It had been Van and Glad's intention to retire in Colorado Springs where Gloria and her husband were stationed. Accordingly, the Vandenbergs' furniture and goods were shipped west in anticipation of a leisurely retirement near the mountains. Houses were viewed and building plans were examined. Van wrote Shedd that he intended to do nothing but play golf for two months and then become a "tycoon." He had been offered the position of chairman of the board of two companies and also a lucrative airline position. Van's illness was never discussed. But disease was relentless, and the chief was growing weaker. His old comrades had given him a new shotgun as a retirement gift, and in a stubborn attempt to pretend all was well, Vandenberg went on a week's hunting trip to try out the new weapon. He returned home exhausted. Sandy, now a fighter pilot, visited his parents in Colorado on his way to San Antonio, Texas. The severe leg injury suffered in the earlier auto accident needed to be tended. Perhaps sensing that his illness was becoming worse, Vandenberg decided to accompany Sandy to Texas and spend some time with his son.

Soon after arriving in San Antonio, they were watching the World Series on television and Sandy noted that his father was in obvious pain. Sandy then suggested that the doctor working on his leg examine him as well. Van trusted Doc Spitler, and agreed. After the examination, Spitler called Sandy aside. The cancer had spread throughout the body; he recommended the general be hospitalized and his remaining weeks made as comfortable as possible. Sandy called Nate Twining in Washington and the new chief immediately sent an aircraft down to pick up his comrade. On October 3 Vandenberg checked into Walter Reed Hospital. Ike, dismissing recent disagreements over the budget, saw to it that he was given the presidential suite.[68]

Glad remained at his side for the final months, but watching her beloved Van "die by centimeters" took a heavy toll. Glad would soon become a total recluse, living out her life in solitude in a quiet Washington apartment. Van continued to waste away, and there was nothing the doctors could do to prevent it. During one visit, he grabbed the hand of his son and begged him to please do something; nothing seemed to help; could he please speak with the doctors about attempting new remedies? Sandy was desperate. He talked to the physicians and although the situation was hopeless, it was suggested that the bottle of yellow glucose that was feeding the general intravenously be changed. Food coloring was added to produce red glucose. This seemed to hearten Van considerably, and he thanked his son for helping.[69]

Death came on the morning of April 2, 1954, ten months after retirement. The day before, President Eisenhower had signed a bill authorizing establishment of the Air Force Academy at Colorado Springs. When completed, the cadet dormitory was named in honor of the late Air Force chief of staff who had done so much for the cause of air power. An air base in California was also named in his honor, and even the Navy forgot the past and christened one of its new ships the U.S.S. *Vandenberg*.

Vandenberg's funeral was held at the Washington Cathedral. The service was conducted jointly by the cathedral's dean and the West Point chaplin. The pallbearers were George Marshall, Robert Lovett, Stuart Symington, Carl Spaatz, Omar Bradley, and Bernard Baruch. Most of the Washington hierarchy attended, including President Eisenhower. A parade was held in his honor, and at Glad's request, it featured the West Point cadets from A-1 and L-2 companies, the units that her husband and son had belonged to.[70]

General Vandenberg was buried in Arlington Cemetery on a small knoll near the Robert E. Lee mansion. On the gravestone were carved four stars and a set of pilot's wings. Glad returned to his side in 1978.

CONCLUSION

Hoyt Vandenberg's career was marked by a consistent ability to get the job done effectively, quietly, and diplomatically. Beginning with his first assignment after being commissioned, Vandenberg endeavored to achieve technical competence as an aviator and junior officer and soon developed into an outstanding fighter pilot whose reputation was known throughout the small cadre of Air Corps officers. Unlike the Army and Navy, the Air Corps had never placed a great deal of importance on formal education; experience was the key. Air was a new medium with its own laws and its own logic. Air pioneers seldom looked backward for tradition and legitimacy but emphasized the future. One of the early doctrinal manuals written at the Air University during Vandenberg's tenure as chief expressed it succinctly: "The principles of air warfare stem from Mitchell, Arnold, and Knerr more notably than from Frederick or Napoleon, and Air Force thinking needs no Old Testament text for justification."[71]

Because air power was new and unique, airmen consciously tried to break away from the thinking and traditions of the past; one of Billy Mitchell's most significant achievements was the inculcation among his followers of the feeling that they were different. The brash, self-confident, and flamboyant personalities of Mitchell, Arnold, Spaatz, Doolittle, Kenney, Chennault, and Vandenberg were not atypical in the Air Corps; they were expected, perhaps even cultivated. It would be wrong, however, to conclude that aviators were men of limited intellect or vision who were mere manipulators of machines. Most of these men were highly intelligent and thoughtful; but in order to establish credibility as a leader in this environment, one first and foremost had to be technically able; he had to be a good pilot. Almost without exception, air leaders were men with thousands of flying hours who knew the sky. It was normal for commanders at the two-star level to fly combat missions and perform the same physical duties as men half their age. That was the way respect was won. Vandenberg had established his credentials in this area during the 1930s; his insistence on flying combat during World War II and then maintaining his pilot skills as chief confirmed it.

Such ideas made good theory, but in practice the Air Force is a large and complex organization requiring administrative efficiency. All bureaucracies run on paper. As Vandenberg put it: "The 50-mission stuff is great, but we must have people to do the planning as well as the flying."[72] As chief of staff, he frequently called attention to the fact that the Air Force was a complex and technical profession that drew heavily on the practices of modern business. To be a fully competent senior Air Force officer, it was essential to become a manager. Although airmen complained about the drudgery of attending service schools and flying desks, most of them realized the importance of such activities, even though some could not make the mental shift. Vandenberg was able to adapt to such demands. There has been much debate in recent years regarding the relative merits of the manager versus the leader. Individuals tend to become advocates in this debate, stressing the importance of one trait over the other. Vandenberg demonstrated no such ambivalence. In his view, it was essential that both characteristics be strengths, not weaknesses. His own experience had shown conclusively that one must *lead* men into combat. But his experience also informed him that the new Air Force was a large organization that depended heavily on advanced technology. In addition, in the postwar era of budget austerity, Vandenberg realized the necessity of sound fiscal policy and procedures. As a consequence, Vandenberg was the ideal blend of leader and manager. One of the great heroes of World War II, Dwight Eisenhower, was well aware of these issues:

[I]n the higher positions of a modern Army, Navy and Air Force, rich organizational experience and an orderly, logical mind are absolutely essential to success. The flashy, publicity-seeking adventurer can grab the headlines and be a hero in the eyes of the public, but he simply can't deliver the goods in high command. On the other hand, the slow, methodical, ritualistic person is absolutely valueless in a key position. There must be a fine balance—that is exceedingly difficult to find.[73]

Vandenberg struck that delicate balance and his numerous assignments at the staff level made him adroit at dealing with other services and allies and at tackling difficult and multifaceted problems. In a series of tours on the Air Staff, Vandenberg had proven to be remarkably flexible and effective.

More importantly, Vandenberg had the self-confidence to delegate authority. In 1950, he realized that the rapid expansion of the Air Force owing to the Korean War, combined with his onerous responsibilities as a member of the JCS, necessitated a new organizational structure. Consequently, Vandenberg established a deputy chief of staff system that relied heavily on the ability and maturity of the Air Staff; orders from these officers were to be obeyed throughout the Air Force as if they were issued by the chief himself. On one occasion he chided General Norstad for not impressing this fact sufficiently on his staff in Europe.[74]

When delegating authority to a subordinate, he expected it to be used; on one occasion a commander asked him for advice, prompting Vandenberg's comment: "He's a major general and I expect him to operate like one. I'm not going to do his thinking for him. I'd a damn sight rather have men make mistakes than sit quietly and not do anything."[75] When appointing a new commander he seldom gave detailed directives but told his men to accomplish the mission as they saw fit, the only caveat being that all actions must be legal and ethical.[76] One of his senior commanders noted that the chief was an expert at recognizing a job's requirements and a person's capabilities, and then matching the two.[77] Vandenberg knew when to decentralize power and when to garner it. Also important, he understood his own limitations, remarking once that he knew there were several members of his staff who were more intelligent than he; that did not concern him; it was only important that they all worked together and toward the same goal.[78] Vandenberg was a master at achieving that type of teamwork.

Besides his technical and managerial ability, Vandenberg possessed the intangible and amorphous quality of leadership. To say that someone is a born leader is a cliché; nevertheless, it may still be true. Vandenberg's leadership was a combination of those qualities just mentioned and his personality. He made few enemies and had the ability to get along, even with adversaries. Remarkable self-control prevented him from losing his temper or acting precipitously. He well realized that one of the keys to effective leadership is loyalty to both superiors and subordinates. Throughout his career superiors trusted him and found him utterly dependable. His tenure as Leigh-Mallory's deputy at the AEAF in 1944 is perhaps the clearest example of his ability to serve a difficult master without becoming either recalcitrant or a sycophant. He was never anyone's yes-man. On the other hand, loyalty must also extend downward. Men will seldom follow someone they do not trust. In all my research, interviews, and correspondence, I came across none who felt Vandenberg had treated them unjustly or with duplicity. Even those with whom he disagreed strongly respected his honesty and integrity.

Perhaps one of the most crucial reasons for his success as a leader was his obviously sincere concern for his men. Even as a junior officer, he displayed such compassion, a quality that did not diminish as he advanced in rank and responsibility. When as chief three members of his staff developed heart ailments, he called in one of the nation's top heart specialists to examine everyone over forty.[79] When an emergency required that a senior officer be transferred back to Washington from Europe on short notice, Vandenberg flew the officer's family and goods back in his own plane.[80] General Ben Chidlaw, a friend since West Point, had worked particularly hard as commander of the Air Materiel Command. Van was grateful for his service, wrote Chidlaw that he did not want to "ride a good horse to death," and suggested a quiet command that would allow him to relax for several months while hunting and fishing.[81] Significantly, such concern was not merely for his generals.

While Sandy recovered from his auto accident in Walter Reed Hospital, he made the acquaintance of Captain Clinton Summersill, an Air Force pilot shot down over Korea during the winter who, while escaping back to American lines, had suffered severe frostbite, necessitating the amputation of both feet. Equipped with artificial limbs, Summersill had impressed Sandy with his determination to the degree that the chief was told of the young pilot's plight. There were no double amputees in the Air Force, but after meeting with Summersill and being similarly impressed by the man's courage, Vandenberg arranged for him to work on the Air Staff so that he could remain on active duty. Eventually, Summersill even returned to the cockpit.[82]

Vandenberg was not, however, soft. Fears that he would not have the fortitude for the duties of chief proved unfounded. His numerous and intense confrontations with the other services, Congress, the service secretaries, and even the president conclusively demonstrated that Vandenberg had the courage of his convictions but the dignity and grace to accept defeat, as in the budget battles of 1948 and 1949. Several months after Van's retirement, Larry Kuter, whom many considered an adversary, wrote a moving letter. Addressing Van as "Chief"—a sobriquet Kuter had previously reserved for Arnold—he wrote: "I know that you are a very great guy. You were never greater than in your last couple of months as Chief of Staff. You and your service should be very proud of your period of leadership"[83]

Although Vandenberg was not usually considered an intellectual, General Twining and others noted the depth of his intelligence and knowledge, which allowed him to think through even the most difficult problems in a logical and systematic fashion. He comprised the ideal blend of thinker and activist. Once deciding on a particular course of action, he was immensely persuasive in discussion.[84] Though one should be wary of testimonials, the London *Times* described Vandenberg in unusually strong terms: "Though modest and unassuming in private conversation, the clarity and power of his mind, his great natural force, and his gifts of leadership were unmistakable." The obituary then listed his qualities of force, articulateness, and courage, "yet no word of criticism was ever voiced against his integrity, disinterestedness, and sense of public good."[85] By the completion of his tour as chief of staff, he had convinced the other chiefs and civilian leaders that air power was the most important element of national defense.

Despite all Vandenberg's efforts, however, when war broke out in Korea, the Air Force, like the entire military establishment, was unready. Budget cuts had left Vandenberg's forces barely able to perform their primary, atomic mission. With only restricted funds available under the bare-bones policies of Harry Truman and Louis Johnson, the air power needed for the specific conditions of Korea's limited, conventional war were simply not available. Vandenberg wanted a powerful tactical force, but priorities had to be set and decisions made. The result was what he termed a "shoestring air force."

What is somewhat surprising is the emphasis that Vandenberg increasingly placed on the Strategic Air Command. Although he was criticized for this decision when the Korean War revealed deficiencies in tactical air power, his explanations were consistent and logical. In an era of fiscal restraint, first things must come first; defense of the United States and the atomic air offensive were his top priorities. Less understandable—especially considering his operational background in the tactical sphere—was Vandenberg's continued stress on strategic air power while rearmament was in progress. The chief believed that such air strength would not only deter major war but minor conflicts as well. He was wrong, but his logic was not puerile. Vandenberg's arguments made a great deal of sense to American leaders; he convinced the Joint Chiefs and the majority of civilian leaders that air power was not only decisive, but economical. The doctrine of "massive retaliation" espoused by John Foster Dulles and President Eisenhower was based on principles advocated repeatedly by Vandenberg since 1948. The chief was trusted and his opinion respected. Before his fatal illness, there was talk of a fifth star and elevation to chairman of the Joint Chiefs upon the retirement of General Bradley. In addition, Vandenberg's aide thought his commander had political ambitions and contemplated running for the Senate in Wisconsin after retirement.[86] A bright future was cut short.

Just getting the air arm through its teething years was an important and challenging task. In this, Vandenberg was a great success. A myriad of decisions regarding organization, structure, and doctrine had to be made. Vandenberg's measured judgment has stood the test of time. His ability to pick quality subordinates—LeMay at SAC, Norstad at USAFE, Weyland in Korea, and Tunner in the Airlift—guaranteed a competence and professionalism that was recognized worldwide. Vandenberg was also instrumental in moving the new Air Force into modern technology. He pushed hard for rocket development, computer proliferation, thermonuclear experimentation, and the transition to an all-jet inventory. A man of exceptional vision, Vandenberg proved the ideal choice for building the independent Air Force.

In one of his last public appearances before the War College, Vandenberg offered air power as the lodestar for aspiring Air Force officers:

When you leave here, you should understand air power, and you *must* preach the doctrine. You will be on staffs where you are going to meet people who do not understand air power, and you are *going to have to educate*. . . . You have got to go out and preach the doctrine of air power and never give an inch on it.[87]

By his retirement in 1953, the air arm was confirmed as the dominant tool of American military policy.

NOTES

PREFACE

1. Sidney Shalett, "Man on a Hot Seat," *Saturday Evening Post*, May 28, 1948, p. 138.

I. THE LEARNiNG YEARS

1. Shedd Vandenberg, ltrs. to the author, May 15 and Jun 3, 1984; C. David Tompkins, *Senator Arthur H. Vandenberg: The Evolution of a Modern Republican, 1884–1945* (Lansing: Michigan State University Press, 1970), pp. 1–3.
2. Shedd Vandenberg correspondence; personal interview with Maj Gen Hoyt S. Vandenberg, Jr., Feb 21–23, 1984; undated news clipping in family scrapbooks, Hoyt S. Vandenberg, Jr., collection, Tucson, Az.
3. Ltrs., Collins to VandenBergs, Sep 19 and Nov 7, 1899, Vandenberg, Jr., collection.
4. Undated news clipping, Vandenberg, Jr., collection.
5. Ibid.; Maj Gen Sidney P. Spalding, ltr. to the author, Jul 28, 1984. (Spalding was also from Lowell and a West Point graduate.) Later, both VandenBerg and F. B. Shedd would have city parks in Lowell named in their honor.
6. Shedd Vandenberg correspondence; Col Carroll F. Sullivan, ltrs. and tape to the author, Sep 13 and 24, 1984, and Feb 27, 1985. (Sullivan was a boyhood friend of Vandenberg's from Lowell who also attended West Point, graduating in 1921.) Cadet records of Hoyt S. Vandenberg, US Military Academy, West Point, N.Y., copy in possession of the author; undated news clipping, Vandenberg, Jr., collection.
7. Shedd Vandenberg correspondence; telephone interview with Mrs. Gloria Miller (née Vandenberg), Jun 24, 1984.
8. Sullivan correspondence.
9. Ernest H. Abbot, "The Plum Island Idea," *National Service*, Aug 1917, p. 352; John G. Clifford, *The Citizen Soldiers: The Plattsburgh Training Camp Movement* (Lexington: The University Press of Kentucky, 1972), pp. 186–90; Col William R. Burt, ltr. to the author, Feb 7, 1985.
10. Ernest H. Abbot, "The Boys of Plum Island," *The Outlook*, Aug 23, 1916, p. 951.
11. Shedd Vandenberg correspondence; Vandenberg, Jr., interview.
12. Ltr., Brown to Mrs. VandenBerg, n.d., Vandenberg, Jr., collection.
13. Tompkins, pp. 6, 28.
14. Douglas MacArthur, *Reminiscences* (New York: McGraw-Hill, 1964), p. 77. MacArthur, with his two Distinguished Service Crosses and seven Silver Stars, was in 1919 one of the most decorated and illustrious soldiers in the country.
15. Ibid., p. 82; William A. Ganoe, *MacArthur Close-Up* (New York: Vantage Press, 1962), pp. 86–87.
16. Personal interview with Lt Gen Joseph Smith, Jul 11, 1984. (Smith was one of Vandenberg's roommates at West Point, and the two remained close friends for life.) The cadet magazine of that time, *The Bray*, chastened the Corps about its conduct at hops. Cadets should remember who and what they were; they must remain proper and dignified. *The Bray*, Feb 17, 1920, p. 3. Nevertheless, a medical doctor stationed at West Point at the time noted darkly that there was a significant problem within the Corps of "auto-erotism." Maj Harry N. Kerns, "Cadet Problems," *Mental Hygiene*, Oct 1923, p. 693.

17. Lucius H. Holt, "An Educational Institution," *Infantry Journal*, 24, No. 5 (May 1924), pp. 559, 562.

18. Ibid.; Ganoe, p. 88.

19. Ganoe, p. 30; D. Clayton James, *The Years of MacArthur*, vol. I (Boston: Houghton Mifflin, 1970), pp. 267–73. The Academic Board consisted of the superintendent, commandant, and faculty department heads. The MacArthurs and Danfords would come and go; professors stay until age sixty-five. See also Roger H. Nye, "The United States Military Academy in an Era of Educational Reform, 1900–1925," diss. Columbia University, 1968, passim.

20. Ganoe, p. 106; James, I, p. 278.

21. James, I, p. 265.

22. Ganoe, p. 31.

23. Stephen E. Ambrose, *Duty, Honor, Country: A History of West Point* (Baltimore: Johns Hopkins University Press, 1966), p. 271.

24. Ibid.; *The 1921 Howitzer: The Yearbook of the United States Corps of Cadets* (West Point, N.Y.: USMA Printing Office, 1922), pp. 104–109.

25. Ambrose, p. 277; Ganoe, p. 106.

26. Ambrose, pp. 282–83; Ganoe, p. 160. The official reason given for the transfer was that MacArthur was next in line for an overseas assignment (he was posted to the Philippines), but this was questioned because he had just returned from Europe in 1919. Another popular rumor held that the general's new bride, whom he had married in Feb 1922, had also been courted by Army Chief of Staff General John J. Pershing. It was speculated that MacArthur was shipped out as a punishment for stealing the boss's girl. Ambrose, p. 282; Frazier Hunt, *The Untold Story of Douglas MacArthur* (New York: Devin-Adair Co., 1954), p. 111. James irately refutes this theory, I, pp. 290–93. Maj Gen Fred W. Sladen, "Foreword," *Infantry Journal*, May 1924, p. 523.

27. *Official Register of the Officers and Cadets, United States Military Academy, for 1920* (West Point, N.Y.: USMA Printing Office, 1920), p. 35; same publication for 1921, p. 30; for 1922, p. 35; Gen Earle E. Partridge, interview by Lt Col Jon Reynolds, Maj Robert Bartanowicz, and the author, United States Air Force Academy (USAFA), Feb 16, 1978, pp. 33–34. It was typical to lose 40 percent of a cadet class to academic deficiency. Lt Col F. H. Hicks, "The Story of West Point," *The Mentor*, Sep 1924, p. 14. Vandenberg's best subjects were history and foreign language, in which he was near the upper portion of the bottom half of his class.

28. Smith interview; Maj Gen Alfred L. Johnson, ltr. to the author, Jun 17, 1984.

29. Partridge interview, pp. 33–34; Sullivan correspondence.

30. Vandenberg cadet records.

31. *Official Register for 1922*, p. 35.

32. Ganoe, p. 122.

33. Col R. E. M. des Islets, ltr. to the author, Jun 20, 1984.

34. Vandenberg, Jr., interview; ltr., Vandenberg to Sandy, n.d. but during World War II, Vandenberg, Jr., collection; *The 1923 Howitzer: The Yearbook of the United States Corps of Cadets* (West Point, N.Y.: USMA Printing Office, 1924), p. 64. Interestingly, Vandenberg's name was mispelled in all four yearbooks.

35. Sullivan correspondence.

36. As a plebe, Van wrote home requesting that his father look up twenty funny stories for him. It was his responsibility to entertain the upper classmen at the dinner table and without a fresh supply of jokes, he would be in trouble. Ironically, twenty-five years later Hoyt, Jr., was in a similar predicament. Unfortunately, the upper classmen chose the entertainment: whenever an article appeared in the newspaper concerning General Vandenberg, Air Force chief of staff, the lowly plebe had to memorize and recite it to his superiors—backward! Ltr., Hoyt to parents, n.d., but probably 1919, Vandenberg, Jr., collection; Hoyt Vandenberg, Jr., interview.

37. Sullivan correspondence; Col Milo G. Cary, ltr. to the author, Sep 20, 1984; Col

Morris H. Marcus, ltr. to the author, Sep 12, 1984; Col R. B. Evans, ltr. to the author, Jul 8, 1984. This feeling was not unanimous; others stated that no pressure whatsoever was applied to them. Incidentally, cadets did not then graduate with a bachelor's degree as is presently the case; hence, accreditation was not the problem it would be today if a college decided to cut its curriculum by one-fourth. (In 1937, Congress passed a law retroactively granting a B.S. degree to all West Point graduates.) Whether those choosing early graduation suffered in their Army careers is moot. In fact, the class of 1921 was actually promoted to first lieutenant on its graduation day! Had those seventeen remained with their class, it would have taken them four more years to attain that rank. Promotions to general officer were about equal between those who left and those who stayed. Two individuals stated that Col Danford placed uncomplimentary letters reflecting their graduation decision in their *officer* personnel files, and that this proved detrimental to their careers. Sullivan and Marcus correspondence.

38. Joseph Smith interview.

39. *1921 Howitzer*, p. 52.

40. Vandenberg cadet records; *1923 Howitzer*, pp. 327–28. His name was not mentioned in the recaps of the hockey or polo games, nor was he even present for the hockey team picture during his senior year.

41. Vandenberg cadet records. In order to ensure they would not be a social embarrassment, all cadets were required to take dancing classes before attending their first hop. They practiced with their roommates. Vandenberg "qualified" on Jul 31, 1920. Vandenberg cadet records; Joseph Smith interview.

42. Alfred L. Johnson correspondence. Over a dozen other ltrs. from former cadets describe him in similar terms.

43. Vandenberg, Jr., interview; Evans correspondence. He then goes on to relate that he saw Glad many years later and approached her to say hello, but she did not remember him—a crushing blow.

44. Alfred L. Johnson correspondence; Col Wendell Johnson, ltr. to the author, May 30, 1984; Hoyt Vandenberg, Jr., and Joseph Smith interviews.

45. *1923 Howitzer*, p. 73.

46. Col William S. Triplet, ltr. to the author, Jun 9, 1984. Similar sentiments were expressed by Brig Gen Ernest V. Holmes, ltr. to the author, Jun 14, 1984; Col Raymond T. Beurket, ltr. to the author, Jun 24, 1984; Col B. S. Mesick, ltr. to the author, Jun 29, 1984; and des Islets.

47. George W. Cullum, Biographical Register of the Officers and Graduates of the U.S. Military Academy at West Point, New York, Supplement Vol. VII, 1920–30 (Chicago: Lakeside Press, 1930), pp. 1721–1806.

48. Vandenberg, Jr., and Joseph Smith interviews; *The Bray*, Dec 9, 1919, p. 4.

49. As usual, the most popular branch was the Corps of Engineers; fourteen of the first sixteen graduates took the only such slots available. The Signal Corps was next in popularity, followed by the Cavalry. Cullum, pp. 1721–1806.

50. Jon A. Reynolds, "Education and Training for High Command: General Hoyt S. Vandenberg's Early Career," diss. Duke University, 1980, pp. 20–23; Alfred L. Johnson and Evans correspondence; Col Ralph M. Neal, ltr. to the author, Jun 23, 1984.

51. *Roster of Students of Air Corps Primary Flying Schools, September 1922–October 1932*, pp. 9–11, 45, 84–85. Located in Maj Gen Jarred V. Crabb papers, USAFA Archives. Actually, Vandenberg's class did better than most: 54 percent graduated and won their wings, whereas most classes had only a 40 percent completion rate.

52. Vandenberg, Jr., interview.

53. Ibid.; Miller interview; Shedd Vandenberg correspondence. Actually, Van and Glad almost did not make it to the altar. A few months before the wedding, they were involved in an auto accident that destroyed their car, but they both escaped without a scratch. *Rockland County Messenger*, Aug 23, 1923, n.p., Vandenberg, Jr., collection. Van's relationship with his mother-in-law was excellent. Gramma Rose was a large, comfort-

able looking woman with snow-white hair and a perpetual smile on her face. Most family photos show her either cuddling her grandchildren or wearing an apron in the kitchen. Van adored her, as did the children.

54. This tradition endures even today as, for example, in the cocksure arrogance displayed by the fighter pilots in *Top Gun* and the test pilots-turned-astronauts in *The Right Stuff*, both modern motion pictures.

55. Jim Greenwood and Maxine Greenwood, *Stunt Flying in the Movies* (Blue Ridge Summit, Pa.: Tab Books, 1982), pp. 44–49; undated news clipping, Vandenberg, Jr., collection; *Air Corps Newsletter*, Mar 31, 1927, p. 98.

56. Sidney Shalett, "Man on a Hot Seat," *Saturday Evening Post*, May 29, 1948, pp. 36–38. In 1927, Vandenberg also participated in a sequel to *Wings* called *Legion of the Condemned*, Gary Cooper's first major role. Greenwood and Greenwood, p. 49; Cullum, p. 1799.

57. In 1925, Vandenberg finished eighth overall, and in 1926 a very close second. Reynolds, pp. 63, 80.

58. Transcript of story told to Hoyt S. Vandenberg, Jr., by Lt Col Rudy J. Baros, Jul 14, 1972, Vandenberg, Jr., collection. Vandenberg relates that while he was a colonel stationed at Randolph Air Force Base in 1972, Baros walked into his office and told him he had known his father many years before. Vandenberg called in his secretary who took notes as Baros told the story related in the text.

59. Partridge interview, p. 30.

60. Gen Orval R. Cook, interview by Hugh N. Ahmann and Richard Emmons, Air Force Historical Office (AFHO), Jun 4–5 and Aug 6–7, 1974, p. 107; George H. Beverley, *Pioneer in the U.S. Air Corps* (Manhattan, Kans.: Sunflower University Press, 1982), p. 21.

61. Reynolds, p. 114.

62. Ltr., Nathan F. Scudder to Vandenberg, Mar 28, 1929, Vandenberg, Jr., collection.

63. Edgar F. Puryear, Jr., *Stars in Flight: A Study in Air Force Character and Leadership* (Novato, Calif.: Presidio Press, 1981), p. 104.

64. Vandenberg, Jr., interview.

65. Ibid.; undated card in Vandenberg, Jr., collection.

66. Vandenberg, Jr., and Miller interviews.

67. Ibid.

68. Puryear, p. 106; Reynolds, pp. 126–27. Today it is prohibited by Air Force regulations for an unpressurized aircraft to fly above ten thousand feet without the entire crew being on oxygen.

69. In fact, Vandenberg's assignment was actually cut short one year. Reynolds, pp. 129–30; *Air Corps Newsletter*, Jul 2, 1930, p. 197; Vandenberg, Jr., interview.

70. Reynolds, p. 154.

71. Ibid., p. 148.

72. Vandenberg's Form 51s (Flight Records) show that he had flown the DH-4, PT-1, 2, 3, and 11; BT-1, 2, and 3; P-6 and 12; A-3, 10, and 11; O-2, 19, and 25, and the C-7. In the next few years he would fly most aircraft in the Air Corps inventory. Of his 3,012 flying hours in 1934, 821 were in attack, 611 in pursuit, and 990 in trainers. Hoyt S. Vandenberg papers, Library of Congress (LOC), Box 81.

73. Norman E. Borden, Jr., *Air Mail Emergency: 1934* (Freeport, Maine: Bond Wheelwright Co., 1968), p. 37; John F. Shiner, *Foulois and the U.S. Army Air Corps, 1931–1935* (Washington: Government Printing Office [GPO], 1984), Chapter V passim.

74. Borden, pp. 135–36; Aeronautical Chamber of Commerce of America (ACCA), *The Aircraft Yearbook for 1934* (New York: ACCA, 1935), p. 440.

75. The incident occurred at South Fork, Pa.; the man with the lantern was one Warren Rugh. Col William R. Burt, ltr. to the author, Oct 20, 1984. Burt and Vandenberg worked in the same office on the Air Staff from 1941 to 1943. "General Vandenberg Steps In," *Air Force*, May 1948, p. 46; Shalett, p. 136; undated news clipping, Vandenberg, Jr., collection. Actually, Vandenberg survived at least four other aviation mishaps in his career:

he taxied into a parked truck—embarrassing but no injuries; while landing in dense fog with ceiling and visibility both "zero," he ran over a runway light and ripped out the bottom of the plane's fuselage; and on two occasions his engine quit at low altitude, necessitating forced landings. In both these instances the aircraft were totaled, but Vandenberg walked away unharmed. He was a very lucky pilot. "Aircraft Accident Reports," Feb 5, 1934; Aug 9, 1936; Feb 19, 1937; and May 14, 1938. Air Force Simpson Historical Research Center (AFSHRC), File 200.3912–1.

76. Individuals who instructed at the Air Corps Tactical School and later attained high rank were as follows: Gens J. T. McNarney, G. C. Kenney, H. S. Vandenberg, M. S. Fairchild, E. E. Partridge, and L. S. Kuter; Lt Gens L. H. Brereton, H. L. George, and M. F. Harmon; Maj Gens O. Westover, R. Olds, D. Wilson, C. Bissell, C. Chennault, H. S. Hansell, F. Bradley, R. Stearley, G. Gardner, B. E. Gates, J. E. Palmer, W. H. Frank, C. C. Chauncey, J. F. Curry, and G. P. Saville. Virtually every other officer destined for high rank in World War II—with the notable exceptions of Hap Arnold and Jimmy Doolittle—attended as students. Robert T. Finney, *History of the Air Corps Tactical School, 1920–1940.* USAF Historical Study: No. 100. (Maxwell AFB, Ala.: Air University, 1955), pp. 53–65.

77. William Mitchell, *Skyways: A Book on Modern Aeronautics* (Philadelphia: J. B. Lippincott, 1930), pp. 255–70. Michael S. Sherry, in his *Rise of American Air Power: The Creation of Armageddon* (New Haven: Yale University Press, 1987), has done an excellent job of pointing out that American air leaders, as well as the public, viewed air power with a strange ambivalence. On the one hand, bombardment was portrayed as horrible and utterly devastating, but on the other hand, because it was so terrible, most nations would undoubtedly keep the peace to avoid such a cataclysm. Air power was, therefore, benign and horrifying at the same time. Mitchell, for example, opined that air war was "a distinct move for the betterment of civilization." He foresaw "a few gas bombs" in cities such as New York and Chicago compelling a short, and therefore relatively bloodless, war. Mitchell, p. 262.

78. Alfred F. Hurley, *Billy Mitchell: Crusader for Air Power* (New York: Franklin Watts, 1964), p. 101.

79. Maj Gen Donald Wilson, interview by Hugh N. Ahmann, AFHO, Dec 10–11, 1975, pp. 58–60. Actually, since there were also ground force officers and naval officers on the school faculty, Wilson's contention is questionable.

80. Claire Chennault, *Way of a Fighter* (New York: Putnam's, 1949), pp. 22–28. The curriculum also included lessons dealing with air defense artillery, cavalry, chemical warfare, coast artillery, engineering, field artillery, intelligence, signals, and naval warfare. "Curriculum Schedule for Class of 1934," Scrapbook no. 2, p. 27, Gen Laurence S. Kuter collection, USAFA Archives, Colorado.

81. Boyd L. Dastrup, *The U.S. Army Command and General Staff College: A Centennial History* (Manhattan, Kans.: Sunflower University Press, 1982), pp. 71–75; "The Command and General Staff School Schedule for 1935–36," pp. 3–18, Fort Leavenworth Archives.

82. Ltr., Brett to Spaatz, Jan 31, 1935, Spaatz papers, LOC, box 7; "Annual Report of the Command and General Staff School, 1935–36," p. 12, Fort Leavenworth Archives.

83. Donald Wilson interview, p. 74; Joseph Smith interview; Gen Earle E. Partridge, interview by Tom Sturm and Hugh N. Ahmann, AFHO, Apr 24–25, 1974, pp. 243–44, 256. A dissenting voice: Maj Gen Edmund C. Lynch enjoyed the program, and although admitting that air power was covered sparingly, thought he learned an enormous amount and was qualified to command an Infantry division when he had completed Leavenworth! Maj Gen Edmund C. Lynch, ltr. to the author, Aug 26, 1984.

84. Maj Ira C. Eaker, "Now It Can't Be Told," *Air Corps Newsletter*, Jul 15, 1937, pp. 1–3. Actually, because Vandenberg had been a horseman since youth and had been on the polo team at West Point, he probably enjoyed this aspect of the course more than his brethren.

85. "Annual Report," pp. 2–7.

86. Ltr., Spaatz to Arnold, Feb 5, 1935, Spaatz papers, LOC, box 7.

87. Finney, pp. 38–39; Thomas H. Greer, *The Development of Air Doctrine in the Army Air Arm, 1917–1941*, USAF Historical Study No. 89 (Maxwell AFB, Ala.: Air University, 1955), chapter 4 passim. Lt Gen Elwood R. Quesada had a colorful description of Chennault: "He was a pain in the ass to a lot of people. He did turn out to be quite right, as many people who are pains in the ass do." Quoted in Richard H. Kohn and Joseph P. Harahan, eds., *Air Superiority in World War II and Korea* (Washington: AFHO, 1983), p. 17; ltr., Maj Gen Haywood S. Hansell, Jr., to the author, May 13, 1974. Claire Chennault was an interesting study. He had nine children and lived on a farm near Montgomery. His wife was a very large and plain-looking woman. The Vandenbergs visited them often; Sandy enjoyed catching frogs and fishing with the Chennault brood. In 1937, however, Claire left his wife and children to start a new career and a new life in China. Although his efforts there later earned him much fame, culminating in the Flying Tigers, his Air Corps colleagues never forgave him for leaving his family behind, destitute, to be cared for by the other officers at Maxwell. This story was told to me by two of Chennault's contemporaries who wish to remain anonymous.

88. Cook interview, pp. 102–103; Joseph Smith interview; Col Harry E. Wilson, ltr. to the author, Aug 2, 1984.

89. Ltr., Wilson to Vandenberg, Aug 26, 1936, AFSHRC, File 248.2806.

90. Air Corps Tactical School, "Lectures on Pursuit Aviation," Oct-Nov, 1936, AFSHRC, Files 248.2806–1 through 248.2806–9. One would be hard pressed to find much difference between Vandenberg's lectures and those given by his predecessor.

91. Capt Hoyt S. Vandenberg, "Pursuit Flying Angles," 1938, AFSHRC, File 168.7045-28; Hoyt S. Vandenberg, "Pursuit," *Flying and Popular Aviation*, 29, No. 3 (Sep 1941), pp. 54–60. This type of attitude was later proven wrong over the skies of Germany. The Luftwaffe was not defeated until the American escorts deliberately left the bomber stream to seek out and destroy the enemy interceptors. Vandenberg was correct in stating that for escort to remain with the bombers was unacceptably defensive. His solution—to simply ignore escort altogether—was, however, absolutely wrong.

92. Puryear, p. 107; Ethel Kuter, ltr. to the author, Aug 11, 1984.

93. Partridge AFHO interview, p. 228; Maj Ira C. Eaker, "The Air Corps Tactical School," *Air Corps Newsletter*, Apr 15, 1936, pp. 9–10.

94. Vandenberg, Jr., interview; personal interview with Gen Lauris Norstad, Feb 22, 1984; personal interview with Gen Leon Johnson, Feb 21–23, 1984.

95. Reynolds, p. 193; Maureen Mylander, *The Generals* (New York: Dial Press, 1974), p. 89.

96. Reynolds, pp. 194–95; Harry P. Ball, *Of Responsible Command: A History of the US Army War College* (Carlisle Barracks, Pa.: Alumni Association of the Army War College, 1983), p. 251.

97. Ball, p. 245; George S. Pappas, *Prudens Futuri: The U.S. Army War College, 1901–1967* (Carlisle Barracks, Pa.: Alumni Association of the Army War College, 1967), pp. 93, 137.

98. "Organization and Command," Student Committee Report (STC), Oct 12, 1938; "Manpower Mobilization in the Continental United States," STC, Oct 28, 1938, both in Army War College (AWC) Files, Army Historical Institute (AHI), Carlisle Barracks, Pa.

99. "Policies of the United States in the Americas," STC, Feb 25, 1939, AWC Files, AHI; Ball, pp. 240–41.

100. Ball, p. 240.

101. "War Plans—Green," STC, May 17, 1939, AWC Files, AHI.

102. "War Plans—Philippine Department," STC, Apr 8, 1939, AWC Files, AHI. Significantly, the report was classified "secret" at the time it was written.

103. "Command Post Exercise," STC, Jun 7, 1939, AWC Files, AHI.

104. J. Lawton Collins, *"Lightning Joe": An Autobiography* (Baton Rouge: Louisiana State University Press, 1979), pp. 89–92. Collins was an instructor, but he and Vandenberg played squash together regularly and became good friends.

105. Vandenberg, Jr., interview. Besides Collins, with whom he would work very closely for most of the next fifteen years (Collins became Army Chief of Staff in 1949), other classmates included: John R. Deane, Oliver Echols, Lawrence Gerow, Leslie R. Groves, Alfred Gruenther, Vic Strahm, George Stratemeyer,and Robert Eichelberger.

II. THE WAR FOR EUROPE

1. Robert R. Russell, *Expansion of Industrial Facilities Under Army Air Force Auspices, 1940–1945.* USAF Historical Study No. 40 (Maxwell AFB, Ala.: Air University, 1946), pp. 4–13; Wesley F. Craven and James L. Cate, eds., *Plans and Early Operations, January 1939 to August 1942*, vol. I of *The Army Air Forces in World War II* (Chicago: University of Chicago Press, 1948), pp. 104–106. The previous assistant secretary had been F. Trubee Davison, who served from 1926 to 1931.

2. Irving B. Holley, Jr., *Buying Aircraft: Materiel Procurement for the Army Air Forces* in *United States Army in World War II* series (Washington: GPO, 1964), p. 210.

3. Ibid., p. 186.

4. Reynolds, p. 210; William R. Burt, unpublished manuscript, 1986, pp. 102–12. Burt, then a captain, was an associate of Vandenberg's in the Plans Division and later in Europe.

5. Craven and Cate, I, pp. 126–35; Holley, pp. 196–208; memo for record (MFR), by Arnold, Mar 13, 1941, Arnold papers, LOC, box 223. Although Arnold did begin to "play ball," President Roosevelt still eyed him warily. Gen Marshall later told Secretary of War Stimson that a promotion list was being held up because Arnold's name was on it and the president wanted him to retire, not be promoted. Marshall backed Arnold. Memo, Marshall to Stimson, May 16, 1941 located in Larry I. Bland, Sharon R. Ritenour, and Clarence E. Wunderlin, Jr., eds., *The Papers of George Catlett Marshall, Vol 2: "We Cannot Delay," July 1, 1939–December 6, 1941* (Baltimore: Johns Hopkins University Press, 1986), pp. 508–10.

6. Reynolds, p. 215; Citation to the Distinguished Service Medal, for Brig Gen H. S. Vandenberg, Sep 1942, AFSHRC, File K141.2421.

7. I. B. Holley, Jr., "General Carl Spaatz and the Art of Command," in *Air Leadership*, Wayne Thompson, ed. (Washington: AFHO, 1986), pp. 31–32.

8. Ray S. Cline, *Washington Command Post: The Operations Division* in *United States Army in World War II* series (Washington: GPO, 1961), pp. 68–69, 250; Craven and Cate, I, p. 146.

9. Memo, Spaatz to Arnold, Sep 1, 1939 (S), p. 2. The (S) denotes that the memo was originally classified secret. Although it has since been declassified, such notations will be used to give an indication of the relative importance attached to a document at the time it was written. I am indebted to Col William R. Burt for providing me with a copy of this memo.

10. Ibid., p. 7.

11. Ibid., pp. 10–11. Aircraft totals are approximate.

12. Henry H. Arnold, *Global Mission* (New York: Harper and Bros., 1949), p. 208; Stetson Conn and Byron Fairchild, *The Framework of Hemisphere Defense* in *United States Army in World War II* series (Washington: GPO, 1960), pp. 10–11.

13. Conn and Fairchild, pp. 128–32; Craven and Cate, I, p. 141; Henry L. Stimson and McGeorge Bundy, *On Active Service in Peace and War* (New York: Harper and Brothers, 1948), pp. 388–89.

14. Memo, Marshall to Arnold, Jul 16, 1941 (C), located in Bland et al., II, p. 580.

15. Craven and Cate, I, pp. 178, 182; Louis B. Morton, *The Fall of the Philippines* in *United States Army in World War II* series (Washington: GPO, 1953), p. 42.

16. Memo, Sherrod to Hulburd (re. Gen Marshall's press conference), Nov 15, 1941, located in Bland et al., II, pp. 676–79. The authenticity of this document has been held in question. Sherry discusses the controversy and concludes firmly that the account is accurate. Sherry, pp. 108–12.

17. Col William R. Burt, ltrs. to the author, Oct 20 and Nov 12, 1984.
18. Morton, pp. 37–45.
19. Arnold, p. 209.
20. Maurer Maurer, "A Delicate Mission: Aerial Reconnaissance of Japanese Islands Before World War II," *Military Affairs*, 26, No. 2 (Summer 1962), pp. 66–75.
21. Reynolds, pp. 222–23; Burt manuscript, pp. 47–48.
22. Arnold, p. 308; Reynolds, pp. 219–22; Burt correspondence.
23. Vandenberg wrote over a dozen such memos in Jan and Feb 1942. Arnold papers, LOC, box 184. Of interest, Vandenberg also directed that eighteen B-25s be modified for Lt Col J. H. Doolittle's "special project." He later ordered that three of these planes be sent to Norfolk, Va., to determine their take-off characteristics from aircraft carriers. In Apr 1942, these aircraft were launched from the deck of the U.S.S. *Hornet* on their Tokyo raid. Memos, Vandenberg to air staff, Jan 13 and 30, 1942 (S), Arnold papers, LOC, box 184. See also ltr., Vandenberg to Combined Chiefs of Staff, Apr 29, 1942 (TS), AFSHRC, File 143.04N.
24. Burt manuscript, pp. 12–13, 57.
25. Ltr., AFDOP to Arnold, Aug 27, 1941, copy supplied by Col Burt.
26. Burt correspondence. Burt has also sent me copies of two letters he received from Daniel P. Davison, son of the late F. Trubee Davison, dated Jun 7 and 13, 1983. Trubee Davison had been the assistant secretary of War for Air from 1926 to 1931 and joined the Army Air Forces after Pearl Harbor. He was commissioned a colonel and served on the Air Staff in 1942 and 1943 along with Vandenberg and Burt. Allegedly, Davison was also deleted from the brigadier general's list in Jun 1942 and blamed FDR for the ill-treatment. The younger Davison's ltrs. to Burt confirm this story based on his own memories and those of his mother. Actually, Burt insists the incident occurred in Jun 1941, but since Vandenberg was only a major at the time, this seems unlikely. A stronger case for Davison's rejection on political grounds could be made, but there is still little evidence to support it.
27. Personal interview with Gen Lauris Norstad, Feb 22, 1984.
28. Vandenberg, Jr., interview. Vandenberg went on to say that it was believed within the family that his father's name had been removed from the list by FDR because of the president's animus toward Uncle Arthur.
29. Distinguished Service Medal citation for H. S. Vandenberg, Jul 3, 1943, AFSHRC, File K239.293.
30. Personal diary of Gen Carl M. Spaatz, Jul 17, 1942, Spaatz papers, LOC, box 8; "Memorandum of Agreement Between Arnold-Towers-Portal," Jun 22, 1942 (TS), located in "Records of the Joint Chiefs of Staff (JCS), Part I, 1942–45: Strategic Issues" (Frederick, Md.: University Publications of America (UPA), 1980), microfilm reel 8.
31. Sorting out World War II codenames is always a confusing chore. The buildup in 1942 for a potential cross-channel assault was termed BOLERO; the actual cross-channel attack, scheduled for late 1943, was called ROUNDUP; a more limited invasion for late 1942 was SLEDGEHAMMER. The initial plan for a landing in North Africa at Casablanca was GYMNAST; when landings were proposed instead at Dakar, Casablanca and Tunisia, the operation was termed SUPER-GYMNAST. The final plan that called for landings at Casablanca, Oran, and Algiers was TORCH.
32. Spaatz diary, Aug 12, 1942; Wesley F. Craven and James L. Cate, eds., *Europe—TORCH to POINTBLANK: August 1942 to December 1943*, vol. II in *The Army Air Forces in World War II* (Chicago: University of Chicago Press, 1949), pp. 61–62.
33. George F. Howe, *Northwest Africa: Seizing the Initiative in the West*, in *United States Army in World War II* series (Washington: GPO, 1957), pp. 12–14; Forrest C. Pogue, *George C. Marshall: Ordeal and Hope, 1939–1942* (New York: Viking, 1966), pp. 333–36.
34. Spaatz diary, Jul 17–25, 1942.
35. Ltrs., Spaatz to Arnold, Jul 23, 1942 (S); Arnold to Spaatz, Jul 30, 1942 (S); Spaatz to Arnold, Aug 11, 1942 (S), all in Spaatz papers, LOC, box 8.
36. Memo, Arnold to Marshall, Aug 19, 1942 (S), Arnold papers, LOC, box 39. Empha-

sis in original. "Relationship Between TORCH and the Air Operations from the Middle East and the United Kingdom," Sep 11, 1942 (S), located in "JCS Records: Strategic Issues," reel 8. Cable, Eisenhower to Marshall, Aug 13, 1942 (S), located in Alfred D. Chandler and Louis Galambos, eds., *The Papers of Dwight David Eisenhower: The War Years*, 11 volumes (Baltimore: Johns Hopkins University Press, 1970), I, pp. 464–65.

37. Ltrs., Spaatz to Arnold, Aug 11, 27, and 31, and Oct 31, 1942 (S), Spaatz papers, LOC, boxes 8 and 9. Maj Gen Ira C. Eaker, commander of the Eighth Air Force, was also bitterly opposed to the diversion, saying it "almost immobilized us." Lt Gen Ira C. Eaker, interview with Donald Shaughnessy, Columbia University, 1960, p. 178.

38. Ltr., Spaatz to Arnold, Oct 31, 1942 (S), Arnold papers, LOC, box 273.

39. Ltr., Eisenhower to Marshall, Jul 29, 1942 (S), located in Chandler and Galambos, I, pp. 426–27; Lowell Thomas and Edward Jablonski, *Doolittle: A Biography* (Garden City, N.Y.: Doubleday, 1976), pp. 207–209.

40. Norstad interview. Quentin Reynolds, *The Amazing Mr. Doolittle* (New York: Appleton-Century-Crofts, 1953), p. 258.

41. *Air Phase of the North African Invasion*, USAF Historical Study No. 105 (Maxwell AFB, Ala.: Air University, n.d.), pp. 8–37; "TORCH in the Sky," Oct 21, 1942 (S), AFSHRC, File 650.430–1; "Outline Plan for Operation TORCH," Aug 21, 1942 (S), "JCS Records: European Theater," reel 2.

42. Memos, Clark to Eisenhower, Aug 15, 26, 29, and Sep 8, 17, 1942 all (S) and all in Gen Mark Clark's papers, The Citadel, Charleston, South Carolina; Captain Harry C. Butcher, *My Three Years with Eisenhower* (New York: Simon and Schuster, 1946), p. 78.

43. Spaatz diary, Sep 11, 1942; Arnold, p. 327; Monro MacCloskey, *TORCH and the Twelfth Air Force* (New York: Richards Rosen Press, 1971), pp. 53–55. MacCloskey was the assistant operations officer of the Twelfth AF throughout the campaign. Interestingly, the pilots were taught how to make carrier takeoffs, but not carrier landings. In fact, their landing training even on land was not very good. Of the seventy-seven P-40s launched from the carriers, one promptly went into the sea, one disappeared, and seventeen others were destroyed when they crashed upon landing in Morocco.

44. Ltr., Doolittle to Arnold, Oct 21, 1942 (S), Arnold papers, LOC, box 41.

45. Msg., Eisenhower to Marshall, Nov 7, 1942 (S), located in Chandler and Galambos, I, p. 669.

46. "The Outline Plan for Operation TORCH," Sep 11, 1942 (S), located in Maj Gen George McDonald papers, USAFA Archives, box 7.

47. Howe, p. 37; MacCloskey, p. 56. One wonders whether Doolittle, the Shell Oil Company executive, chose the Standard Oil Building deliberately.

48. Ltr., Doolittle to Arnold, Nov 19, 1942 (S), Arnold papers, LOC, box 11; Craven and Cate, II, pp. 59, 72, 159–63; MacCloskey, pp. 28, 135; *Air Phase of North African Invasion*, p. 79.

49. "US Tactical Air Power in Europe," *Impact*, May 1945, p. 7.

50. Ltr., Doolittle to Arnold, Nov 19, 1942 (S), Arnold papers, LOC, box 11; Brig Gen Bruce Johnson, *The Man with Two Hats* (New York: Carlton Press, 1968), pp. 112–18; ltr., Vandenberg to Sandy, Nov 15, 1942, Vandenberg, Jr., collection. Interestingly, Van had not been able to notify his family of his whereabouts, and it was not until Nov 8 that Glad was told where he was located. Ltr., Cabell to Gladys, Nov 8, 1942, Vandenberg, Jr., collection.

51. [Arthur] Lord Tedder, *With Prejudice* (Boston: Little, Brown, 1966), pp. 371–75.

52. Ltrs., Arnold to Spaatz, Nov 18, 1942 (S) and Spaatz to Arnold, Nov 23, 1942 (S), both in Spaatz papers, LOC, box 9; Craven and Cate, II, pp. 107–10.

53. Tedder, p. 380; cable, Eisenhower to Marshall, Dec 31, 1942 (S), located in Chandler and Galambos, II, pp. 878–79; Sqdn Ldr J. N. White, "Air Command in the Mediterranean in Nov 1942," n.d., James Parton papers, USAFA Archives, box 1.

54. General Order No. 1, Hq Mediterranean Air Command, Feb 18, 1943 (S), Spaatz papers, LOC, box 10; Craven and Cate, II, pp. 115–16; "Air War: Official Report of the

Commanding General of the Army Air Forces to the Secretary of War," Jan 4, 1944, p. 25. The other components of Tedder's organization were the Malta Command and the Middle East Command (Egypt).

55. MacCloskey, pp. 147, 159. Close air support operations were handled by the Northwest African Tactical Air Force commanded by Air Vice Marshal Arthur Coningham, a distinguished New Zealander with the nickname of "Maori," usually pronounced and spelled "Mary." Van would serve beside him again in Europe.

56. Craven and Cate, II, p. 150. MacCloskey, p. 159; ltr. Spaatz to Arnold, Mar 7, 1943 (S), Spaatz papers, LOC, box 11.

57. Ltr., Stratemeyer to Spaatz, Aug 25, 1942, Spaatz papers, LOC, box 8.

58. Ltr., Doolittle to Arnold, Nov 19, 1942 (S), Arnold papers, LOC, box 11; ltr., Eisenhower to Marshall, Nov 22, 1942 (S), located in Chandler and Galambos, II, pp. 755–56.

59. Vandenberg flight records, Vandenberg papers, LOC, box 81; Sholto Douglas, *Years of Command* (London: Collins, 1966), p. 183; decoration citations for medals indicated, H. S. Vandenberg, AFSHRC, File K239.293; undated news clipping, Vandenberg, Jr., collection.

60. R. Ernest Dupuy, *Men of West Point: The First 150 Years of the United States Military Academy* (New York: William Sloane, 1951), p. 429.

61. Shalett, "Man on a Hot Seat," p. 138; Norstad interview; "General Vandenberg Steps In," p. 46; *London Daily Express*, Aug 10, 1948, n.p.

62. Thomas and Jablonski, pp. 219, 255. This, by the way, was also Doolittle's first inkling that he had been nominated for a second star.

63. "Staff Meeting Notes," Feb 22, 1943, AFSHRC, File 65.01–1, p. 51.

64. Ltr., Spaatz to Arnold, May 24, 1943, Spaatz papers, LOC, box 9. The quote is from Vandenberg's Legion of Merit citation, AFSHRC, File K239.293.

65. Craven and Cate, II, p. 137; ltr., Spaatz to Arnold, Mar 7, 1943 (S), Spaatz papers, LOC, box 11.

66. Bernard Montgomery, "Some Notes on High Command in War," Sep 1943, in Leigh-Mallory papers, RAF Museum, Hendon, box 7.

67. Ltr., Spaatz to Wilson, May 8, 1943, Spaatz papers, LOC, box 11.

68. "Command and Employment of Air Power," Army Field Manual (FM) 100–20, 1943, p. 1.

69. James Gould Cozzens, *Guard of Honor* (New York: Harcourt, Brace, 1948). For the revelation that Nichols was patterned after Vandenberg, see the ltr. from Cozzens to Peabody, quoted in James Gould Cozzens, *A Time of War: Air Force Diaries and Pentagon Memos, 1943–1945* (Columbia, S.C.: Buccoli Clark, 1984), p. 14.

70. Winston Churchill, *The Grand Alliance*, vol. III in *The Second World War* (Boston: Houghton Mifflin, 1950), pp. 462–63.

71. Memo, Marshall to Stimson, Aug 1, 1941 (S), located in Bland et al., pp. 581–82; Richard C. Lukas, "Aircraft Commitments to Russia," *Air University Review*, 16, No. 5 (Jul-Aug 1965), p. 47. The British were particularly upset by the Soviet requests, fearing that any aircraft sent to Moscow would be deducted from their own allotment. "Report to Air Staff of RAF Delegation to Washington," Oct 21, 1941 (S), Air 45, File 13, Public Records Office (PRO), London.

72. Memo, Leahy to Roosevelt, Dec 30, 1942 (S), Arnold papers, LOC, box 39; Richard C. Lukas, "The VELVET Project: Hope and Frustration," *Military Affairs*, 28, No. 4 (Winter 1964–65), pp. 146–50; Winston Churchill, *The Hinge of Fate*, vol. IV in *The Second World War* (Boston: Houghton Mifflin, 1950), pp. 64–65, 79–82.

73. Lukas, "VELVET," pp. 156–57; Maurice Matloff and Edwin Snell, *Strategic Planning for Coalition Warfare, 1941–1942* in *United States Army in World War II* series (Washington: GPO, 1953), pp. 331–36; msg., Roosevelt to Stalin, Jan 8, 1943 (S), Arnold papers, LOC, box 39.

74. Memo, Arnold to Marshall, Feb 26, 1943 (S), Arnold papers, LOC, box 39.

75. Ltr., Spaatz to Arnold, Apr 16, 1943 (S), Spaatz papers, LOC, box 11; Maurice

Matloff, *Strategic Planning for Coalition Warfare, 1943–1944* in *United States Army in World War II* series (Washington: GPO, 1959), pp. 498–500; Wesley F. Craven and James L. Cate, eds., *Europe: ARGUMENT to V-E Day, Jan 1944 to May 1945*, vol. III of *The Army Air Forces in World War II* (Chicago: University of Chicago Press, 1951), pp. 308–309.

76. Memo, Marshall to Bundy, Dec 12, 1941 (S), located in Bland et al., II, p. 690; Arnold, p. 307.

77. Burt correspondence; Thomas A. Julian, "Operation FRANTIC and the Search for American-Soviet Military Collaboration, 1941–1944," diss., Syracuse University, 1968, p. 112.

78. Ltr., Vandenberg to parents, n.d., Vandenberg, Jr., collection; Maj Gen Sidney P. Spalding, ltrs. to the author, Jul 28 and Aug 26, 1984; Adm Harry D. Felt, ltr. to the author, Aug 11, 1984; RAdm Kemp Tolley, ltr. to the author, Jul 21, 1984. U.S. Cong., Senate, Hearings before the Armed Services and Foreign Relations Committees, *The Military Situation in the Far East*, 82nd Cong., 1st sess. (Washington: GPO, 1951), p. 1486. Spalding, Felt, and Tolley were all members of the Military Mission to Moscow. Interestingly, Gen Spalding, though a decade older than Vandenberg, was also from Lowell and a West Point graduate. The two shared a bedroom in Moscow and reminisced about their hometown and the lovely women they knew there. Van was not impressed by his stop-over in Persia; it contained an "open water supply where they drink—wash faces—pis [*sic*] and sweep the streets into it."

79. Tolley and Spalding correspondence. Spaso House did not have central heating.

80. Tolley correspondence.

81. Msg., Deane to AGWAR, Oct 24, 1943 (S), NA, RG 334, box 50; John R. Deane, *The Strange Alliance: The Story of Our Efforts at Wartime Co-Operation with Russia* (New York: Viking, 1946), pp. 19–20; Charles E. Bohlen, *Witness to History, 1929–1969* (New York: W. W. Norton, 1973), p. 243.

82. Msgs., Deane to AGWAR, Oct 26 and 31, Nov 1, 1943 (S), NA, RG 334, box 50; msg., JCS to MILATTACH, Moscow, Oct 26, 1943, NA, RG 334, box 63; Deane, p. 22; W. Averell Harriman and Elie Abel, *Special Envoy to Churchill and Stalin, 1941–1946* (New York: Random House, 1975), p. 239.

83. John R. Deane, "Negotiating on Military Assistance, 1943–1945," in Raymond Dennett and Joseph E. Johnson, eds., *Negotiating with the Russians* (Boston: World Peace Foundation, 1951), pp. 6–8.

84. Msg., Deane to AGWAR, Nov 13, 1943 (S), NA, RG 334, box 50. Although told on several occasions this would be arranged, there is no evidence Vandenberg was ever allowed to visit the front.

85. Msg., AGWAR to MILMIS, Moscow, Nov 20, 1943 (S), NA, RG 334, box 34; "Papers and Minutes of the Sextant and Eureka Conferences," p. 223, Spaatz papers, LOC, box 99; *Foreign Relations of the United States, 1943: The Conferences at Cairo and Teheran* (Washington: GPO, 1961), p. 136; Deane, *Strange Alliance*, p. 45.

86. Msgs., Spalding to AGWAR, Dec 3, 1943 (S); Deane to AGWAR, Dec 19 and 21, 1943 (S), both in NA, RG 334, box 50.

87. Msgs., Harriman to AGWAR, Dec 28, 1943 (S), and Harriman to AGWAR, Jan 16, 1944 (S), both in NA, RG 334, box 50; Harriman and Abel, p. 291.

88. Msg., Deane to AGWAR, Feb 2, 1944 (S), NA, RG 334, box 50.

89. Ltr., Deane to Slavin, Jan 31, 1944, NA, RG 334, box 63; Deane, *Strange Alliance*, pp. 107–10. I was unable to determine the exact date of Vandenberg's departure from Moscow; his official vita lists simply "Jan 1944." In his msg. of Feb 2, Deane asks Spaatz to send another qualified airman to work out the details of the agreement, which implies that Vandenberg had already left. However, since the replacement did not arrive until Mar 6, it is obvious that arrangements had been largely completed by Vandenberg before he left for London.

90. Deane, *Strange Alliance*, p. 121.

91. For a detailed though very anti-Soviet account of this raid, see Glenn B. Infield,

The Poltava Affair: A Russian Warning: An American Tragedy (New York: Macmillan, 1973). The worst day of the war for the AAF was the Schweinfurt-Regensburg raid of Oct 17, 1943, when sixty B-17s were lost.

92. The Warsaw Uprising is discussed in Winston Churchill, *Triumph and Tragedy*, vol. VI in *The Second World War* (Boston: Houghton Mifflin, 1950), pp. 133–45; Herbert Feis, *Churchill-Roosevelt-Stalin* (Princeton: Princeton University Press, 1967), pp. 385–90; Marvin W. McFarland, "Air Power and the Warsaw Uprising," *Air Power Historian*, Oct 1956, pp. 189–95; Harriman and Abel, pp. 340–48.

93. Paul L. Kesaris, ed., *Ultra and the History of the United States Strategic Air Force in Europe vs. the German Air Force* (Frederick, Md.: UPA, 1980), pp. 103, 127.

94. Matloff, p. 500. A contemporary official report termed the operation "a failure." Rpt., McDonald to Anderson, Aug 21, 1944 (TS), Spaatz papers, LOC, box 157. In a personal interview with Lt Gen Ira Eaker on Mar 30, 1978, he concluded that FRANTIC was "completely unsatisfactory."

95. Tolley correspondence. Similar feelings were expressed several times in the memoirs of Harriman and Deane and in ltrs. received from General Spalding and Admiral Felt.

96. Tolley correspondence.

97. Gen Carl Spaatz, obituary notice in West Point alumni magazine, 1954, p. 54. Vandenberg related similar feelings to the United States Senate in 1951. *Far East* hearings, p. 1486.

98. The headquarters of the Allied Expeditionary Air Force was at Stanmore, north of London. Eisenhower's headquarters was supposed to be at Bushy *Heath*, near Stanmore. Unfortunately, the American engineers tasked to remodel the supreme commander's accommodations misread their maps and built a new headquarters at Bushy *Park*, ten miles west of London. Eisenhower elected to remain at Bushy Park, and communications between the headquarters suffered as a consequence. Lt Gen Sir Frederick Morgan, *Overture to Overlord* (London: Hodder and Stoughton, 1950), pp. 257–59.

99. Undated news clipping, Dec 5, 1942, in Leigh-Mallory papers, RAF Museum, Hendon, UK, box 5.

100. David Irving's *War Between the Generals* (London: Allen Lowe, 1981) is largely a description of these personality conflicts. Virtually every history or memoir of the war that mentions Leigh-Mallory speaks of him in similar terms. Perhaps one anecdote will suffice, provided by an American officer on the AEAF staff: "I have just returned from a meeting with our British Commander-in-Chief. The rascal held the meeting in a room which was cold as outdoors—no fire at all—but he, the devil, sat there wrapped in a wooly rug which he constantly adjusted to keep snug and warm. My hands were like ice and my nose was cold and dripping." E. C. Langmead, private diary, Oct 7, 1943, AFSHRC, File 168.7011–1.

101. Ltr., Eaker to Portal, Sep 6, 1943 (S), Parton papers, USAFA Archives, box 1; Charles Webster and Noble Frankland, *The Strategic Air Offensive Against Germany, 1939–1945*, 4 volumes (London: Her Majesty's Stationery Office, 1961), III, p. 15.

102. Memo, Eisenhower to Tedder, Feb 29, 1944 (S) and MFR, by Eisenhower, Mar 22, 1944 (S), both in Chandler and Galambos, III, pp. 1755 and 1784–85; E. J. Kingston-McCloughry, *The Direction of War* (New York: Praeger, 1958), p. 122.

103. Irving, p. 68. By the end of the war, Bomber Command would lose nearly sixty thousand crewmen killed in action. Webster and Frankland, III, pp. 286–87.

104. Charles Messenger, *"Bomber" Harris and the Strategic Bombing Offensive, 1939–1945* (London: Arms and Armour Press, 1984), p. 157; Kenneth Young, ed., *The Diaries of Robert Bruce Lockhart, Vol. 2: 1939–1965* (London: Macmillan, 1980), p. 330.

105. Ltr., Spaatz to Leigh-Mallory, Mar 15, 1944 (S), Spaatz papers, LOC, box 14; Tedder, pp. 564–65; Kingston-McCloughry, p. 121.

106. Ltr., Eisenhower to Tedder, Mar 27, 1944 (S), Spaatz papers, LOC, box 14; MFR, by Eisenhower, Mar 22, 1944 (S), in Chandler and Galambos, III, pp. 1784–85; Solly Zuckerman, *From Apes to Warlords* (New York: Harper and Row, 1978), p. 230; Kingston-McCloughry, pp. 116, 135; Webster and Frankland, III, p. 17. Not all Americans were

pleased with this. Maj Gen Hugh Knerr, a member of Spaatz's staff, confided bitterly to his diary: "Today the Air Forces of Gen Spaatz passed under control of Supreme Comdr theoretically—actually Spaatz was instructed to take orders from Tedder—the Supreme Comdr's Deputy. Result—another Britisher controls American forces. If they ever demonstrated the ability to command better than Americans there might be some excuse. Aside from Montgomery they have a long record of glorious defeats. Again the bedazzled FDR has sold us out to his friend Winston." Maj Gen Hugh Knerr, personal diary, Apr 14, 1944, USAFA, box 6.

107. Ltr., Giles to Spaatz, Mar 16, 1944 (S), Spaatz papers, LOC, box 14; ltr., Eisenhower to Marshall, Dec 17, 1943 (S) and ltr., Eisenhower to Arnold, Jan 23, 1944 (S), both in Chandler and Galambos, III, pp. 1604, 1677; Butcher, pp. 498–99.

108. Omar Bradley and Clay Blair, *A General's Life* (New York: Simon and Schuster, 1983), p. 229. Incidentally, Bradley had been one of Vandenberg's math instructors at West Point.

109. Ltr., Spaatz to Arnold, Mar 6, 1944 (S); MFR, by Spaatz, Mar 24, 1944 (TS), both in Spaatz papers, LOC, box 14; Zuckerman gives a highly spirited defense of his position in *From Apes to Warlords*, while Walt W. Rostow, who was a member of Spaatz's staff and thus an oil man, presents a critique of Zuckerman and a brief of his own views in *Pre-Invasion Bombing Strategy: General Eisenhower's Decision of March 25, 1944* (Austin: University of Texas Press, 1981). Though dated, the best and most balanced account remains Webster and Frankland, which gives a highly illuminating, though somewhat depressing, account of the Tedder/Harris/Spaatz/Leigh-Mallory squabbles.

110. "Comments by Air Marshal P. Wigglesworth on the draft of RAF Narrative of the Liberation of North West Europe," n.d., pp. 32–33, located in Air Vice Marshal E. J. Kingston-McCloughry papers, Imperial War Museum (IWM), London, box P417.

111. Ltr., Churchill to Eisenhower, Apr 29, 1944 (S), Kingston-McCloughry papers, IWM, box P416; Tedder, p. 516.

112. "French and Belgian Reaction to Bombing of Railway Targets," Joint Intelligence Committee (JIC) Report, Apr 4, 1944 (TS), McDonald papers, USAFA Archives, box 12; "The Employment of the Night Bomber Force in Connection with the Invasion of the Continent from the UK," Jan 20, 1944 (MS), Air 37, File 752, PRO; Vandenberg diary, Jul 4, 1944; ltr., Spaatz to Eisenhower, Apr 24, 1944 (TS), Spaatz papers, LOC, box 14; Harris's memoirs, written in 1947, mention the controversy only briefly, and the civilian casualty issue not at all. In the event, there were approximately twelve thousand civilian casualties.

113. Ltr., Eisenhower to Churchill, May 2, 1944 (TS), in Chandler and Galambos, III, pp. 1842–44; Winston Churchill, *Closing the Ring*, vol. V in *The Second World War* (Boston: Houghton Mifflin, 1950), pp. 466–68, 529–30; Tedder, pp. 526–31. Actually, Harris caved in to the rail plan fairly quickly. One historian suggests the reason for Harris's somewhat halfhearted resistance was the severe losses Bomber Command had been suffering throughout March. The Lancasters needed a respite, and the rail plan seemed to offer one. Sherry, p. 164.

114. Memo, by Tedder, no addressee, Mar 24, 1944 (TS); "Minutes of SHAEF Meeting," Mar 25, 1944 (TS), both in Kingston-McCloughry papers, IWM, box P414; Vandenberg diary, Jun 2 and 3, 1944; Tedder, pp. 526–31.

115. Craven and Cate, III, pp. 77–79.

116. Ltrs., Arnold to Spaatz, Mar 15, 1944 (S); Spaatz to Arnold, Mar 26, 1944 (S), both in Spaatz papers, LOC, box 14; msg., Giles to Eisenhower, Mar 4, 1944 (S), NA, RG 165, File 210.31, box 6; Maj Gen E. C. Langmead, "A Report on the AEAF," Jun 1, 1967, pp. 4–5, AFSHRC, File 168.7011–1. Two days before his relief, Butler had written a report stating that the main reason for the difficulties between the British and Americans was Leigh-Mallory. He recommended that the Air Marshal be fired and replaced by Spaatz. Butler was removed instead. Butler, "Staff Study," Mar 23, 1944 (S), AFSHRC, File 50517–10.

117. Vandenberg diary, May 23, 1944. The month before, Vandenberg had written Arnold that there were too few Americans on the AEAF staff. What few there were, Leigh-

Mallory soon removed. Memo, Vandenberg to Arnold, Apr 6, 1944 (S), AFSHRC, File 50517-10.

118. Irving, p. 228; Zuckerman, pp. 250–53; Burt correspondence.

119. Vandenberg diary, Mar 24, 1944.

120. Lord Solly Zuckerman, ltr. to the author, Sep 24, 1984; Kingston-McCloughry, p. 172. Leigh-Mallory died in a plane crash in Nov 1944, en route to a new command in India.

121. Directive from Supreme Commander to United States Strategic Air Forces USSTAF), Apr 17, 1944 (TS), Spaatz papers, LOC, box 14; Messenger, pp. 161–63; Rostow, p. 5.

122. Vandenberg diary, Apr 3 and 15, May 11, 1944.

123. Rostow, p. 148.

124. Air Chief Marshal Trafford Leigh-Mallory, personal diary, Jun 27, 28, 1944, Air 37, File 559, PRO; Craven and Cate, III, p. 174; Messenger, p. 166.

125. Kesaris, pp. 109, 127; Max Hastings, *OVERLORD: D-Day and the Battle for Normandy* (New York: Simon and Schuster, 1984), p. 43; interview with Albert Speer conducted by Army intelligence personnel, Jul 11, 1945, in *Defeat* (Washington: Headquarters Army Air Forces, 1946), p. 10.

126. Ltr., Vandenberg to parents, Jul 7, 1944, Vandenberg, Jr., collection; Vandenberg diary, Jun 6 and 7, 1944. "Minutes of Allied Air Commanders Conference," Jun 7, 1944 (TS), AFSHRC, File 505.25–8. Irving gives a more colorful account, pp. 157–58.

127. He got it. Burt correspondence. Vandenberg diary, Jun 13, 1944; "Minutes of Allied Air Commanders Conference," Jun 8, 1944 (TS), AFSHRC, File 505.25–8.

128. Ltr., Vandenberg to parents, Jul 7, 1944, Vandenberg, Jr., collection.

129. Leigh-Mallory diary, Jun 15, 16, 19, 26, Jul 2, 4, 16, 1944; "Minutes of Allied Air Commanders Conference," Jun 14, 16, 27, 1944 (TS), AFSHRC, File 505.25–8.

130. Leigh-Mallory diary, Jul 19, 21, 1944.

131. Vandenberg diary, Jul 19, 1944; Bradley and Blair, pp. 346–48; Craven and Cate, III, pp. 228–34. Zuckerman says he warned Bradley personally about the possibility of friendly casualties, and the general replied that that was tolerable as long as the bombers were successful in blowing open a hole in the German lines. Zuckerman, p. 280.

132. Vandenberg diary, Jul 25, 1944; memo, Vandenberg to Anderson, Jul 26, 1944 (TS), Vandenberg papers, LOC, box 77; Bradley and Blair, pp. 279–80. Lt Gen James H. Doolittle, interview with Lt Col Robert M. Burch, Maj Ronald R. Fogelman, and Capt James P. Tate, Sep 26, 1971, USAFA, p. 55. Once again, Irving's account is the more colorful, if not the more accurate, pp. 211–25. Gen Joe Collins later stated that McNair had visited the front in violation of Bradley's orders; he never should have been that close to the front line. Gen J. Lawton Collins, interview with Lt Col Charles C. Sperow, 1972, AHI, pp. 193–96; Chester B. Hansen, personal diary, Jul 25, 1944 (S), Hansen papers, AMHI, box 1.

133. Spaatz diary, Jul 26, 1944; "Report of Investigation [COBRA]," Aug 14, 1944 (S), Spaatz papers, LOC, box 168.

134. "P/W Interrogation of General-Leutnant Fritz Bayerlein," May 29, 1945 (S), McDonald papers, USAFA Archives, box 2; Butcher, p. 617.

135. Cable, Eisenhower to Marshall, Aug 2, 1945 (S), in Chandler and Galambos, IV, p. 2051; "Notes of meeting at SHAEF headquarters, Dec 5, 1944 (TS), Spaatz papers, LOC, box 16; Vandenberg diary, Jul 29, 1944. In a classic case of understatement, an Army historian mused on the short bombs: "the morale of our troops. . . is greatly diminished if our bombs fall within their lines and kill some of their comrades." J. W. Perkins, "Use of Heavy Bombers on Tactical Missions," *Military Review*, 26, No. 2 (May 1946), p. 19.

136. Memo, Eisenhower to Smith, Jun 23, 1944 (TS), in Chandler and Galambos, III, pp. 1946–47; msgs., Arnold to Spaatz, Jul 7, 1944 (TS), Eisenhower to Marshall, Jul 8, 1944 (TS), both in Spaatz papers, LOC, box 18; cable, Eisenhower to Arnold, Jul 13, 1944 (S), in Chandler and Galambos, III, p. 2001. Of some interest, Browning was married to the noted authoress, Daphne DuMaurier.

137. Msgs., Marshall to Eisenhower, Jul 10, 1944 (TS) and Eisenhower to Marshall, Aug 2, 1944 (TS), both in Spaatz papers, LOC, box 18; cable, Eisenhower to Marshall, Jul 15, 1944 (S), in Chandler and Galambos, III, p. 2008. It was probably fortunate for Vandenberg that he did not receive the Airborne Army because, in the same message, Marshall explained that he foresaw the position largely as an administrative one: "He would not command troops actually fighting on the ground, but would be responsible for providing them all logistical support." Moreover, the major campaign conducted by the Airborne Army occurred in September during Operation MARKET-GARDEN, when the allies attempted to advance toward the enemy a bridge too far. Such a debacle would not have helped Vandenberg's career. In a rather melancholy letter to Arnold after that operation, Brereton complained that he was receiving no support, no staff assistance, and no sympathy. He had been forgotten. Ltr., Brereton to Arnold, Oct 24, 1944 (TS), NA, RG 341, DCS/Ops, box 7.

138. Lewis H. Brereton, *The Brereton Diaries* (New York: William Morrow, 1945), p. 325. Brereton was an interesting case. A Naval Academy graduate, he had been heavily involved in the war almost from the first day. He had been MacArthur's air commander in the Philippines whose planes had been destroyed on the ground Dec 8. He survived this embarrassment and in Jun 1942 was selected to command the Ninth Air Force throughout the African campaign.

139. Lt Gen Edward M. Almond, personal diary, Nov 26, 1944, Almond papers, AHI.

140. Hansen notes, "Bradley's Commentary/WWII," Hansen papers, AHI. Besides keeping a detailed diary, Hansen also sat down with Bradley shortly after the war, asked numerous questions, and recorded the answers. These notes are a valuable historical source. Hansen himself greatly disliked Brereton; see his diary entries for Aug 6, Oct 14, Nov 26, and Dec 7, 1944.

141. Vandenberg diary, Jul 16, 1944; ltr., Norstad to Vandenberg, Jul 4, 1944, Vandenberg papers, LOC, box 77.

142. Vandenberg diary, Jul 16 and 19, and Aug 15, 1944. Royce had been the base commander at Brooks Field when Vandenberg was a student pilot there in 1924.

143. Vandenberg diary, Aug 2, 1944.

144. The IX Troop Transport Command had officially been transferred to the First Allied Airborne Army; but because Brereton required its services infrequently, the transports usually remained with the Ninth, hauling gasoline and supplies. Personal interview with Gen Robert M. Lee, Aug 29, 1986. Lee was the Ninth Air Force chief of staff under Vandenberg.

145. Memo, Bradley to Eisenhower, Dec 1, 1944 (S), Hansen papers, AHI, box 26. At that point, Vandenberg was ranked a distant twenty-sixth on Bradley's list. There is no question Bradley's opinion of Van had improved dramatically by the end of the war, primarily because of Van's performance during the Battle of the Bulge. Unfortunately, when Bradley prepared a similar list in Jun 1945, he omitted all air officers because Eisenhower was only concerned with which *ground* officers should be promoted and retained in the Army after the war. Quesada even received an honorable mention from Ernest Hemingway, who in *Across the River and into the Trees* has the fictitious Col Richard Cantwell say, "But for ground support give me a man like Pete Quesada. There is a man who will boot them in," pp. 225–26.

146. Lt Gen Elwood R. Quesada, interview by Lt Cols Steven Long and Ralph Stephenson, May 12–22, 1975, AFHO, pp. 273–74; Butcher, p. 604. The P-51 is a single place airplane, but there is some room behind the pilot's seat if one squeezes in; Eisenhower must have been quite uncomfortable. There is no record of his asking for a rain check.

147. Quesada interview, p. 15.

148. George S. Patton, Jr., *War as I Knew It* (Boston: Houghton-Mifflin, 1947), p. 99.

149. Ltr., Vandenberg to Spaatz, Nov 9, 1944 (S), Knerr papers, USAFA Archives microfilm reel 15.

150. Craven and Cate, III, pp. 239–40; Lee interview.

151. Lee interview.

152. Langmead, p. 9.

153. IX TAC Memo 20–2, "Standing Operating Procedures for Air-Ground Cooperation Officers," Jan 28, 1945, Quesada papers, LOC, box 5; Gen Omar Bradley et al., "Effect of Air Power on Military Operations: Western Europe," 12th Army Group Study, n.d., pp. 40–67, Arnold papers, LOC, box 256; ltr., Weyland to Patton, Oct 14, 1944, Vandenberg papers, LOC, box 46.

154. "United States Third Army After-Action Reports," Aug 11, 1944; Patton, p. 113; Alan F. Wilt, "Coming of Age: XIX TAC's Roles During the 1944 Dash Across France," *Air University Review*, 36, No. 3 (Mar-Apr 1985), p. 74.

155. "Third Army," Aug 14, 1944.

156. Msg., Simpson to Weyland, Sep 16, 1944, Vandenberg papers, LOC, box 46; Craven and Cate, III, pp. 265–66; Patton, p. 129; Gen Otto P. Weyland, interview by Brig Gen Noel F. Parrish and James C. Hasdorff, AFHO, Nov 19, 1974, pp. 78–83. Patton anecdotes have become somewhat of an industry, but Weyland does relate one concerning Patton's interesting use of air power. The two had an arrangement whereby Patton would drive his highly polished and ostentatious jeep toward the front, passing the columns of his advancing troops. Upon reaching the limits of their penetration, he would park his jeep and jump into one of Weyland's light aircraft, which would return him to headquarters. When the Army had advanced sufficiently Patton would retrieve his jeep and repeat the procedure; hence, his men never saw him retreating, but always advancing toward the enemy. Incidentally, Vandenberg's pistol is now in the possession of his son.

157. Wilt, p. 77.

158. Ltr., Quesada to Vandenberg, Aug 25, 1944 (TS), Vandenberg papers, LOC, box 75.

159. Ltr., Patton to Vandenberg, Sep 1, 1944, Vandenberg papers, LOC, box 75.

160. Vandenberg, Jr., interview.

161. Shalett, "Man on a Hot Seat," p. 23; Col James M. Shelley, ltr. to the author, Feb 2, 1985. Perhaps one of the reasons Vandenberg wore such clothing was because he was always cold. He constantly complained about the damp and chilly weather in Europe. Whenever he moved to a new headquarters he insisted that the building have a good heating system and that his own office have a fireplace. Lee interview. After one visit, James F. Byrnes was so impressed he termed Vandenberg "one of the hottest military characters he had run into in Europe." Msg., McNaughton to Welch, Jan 3, 1945, McNaughton papers, Truman Library, Independence, Mo.

162. Lee interview; Burt correspondence; telephone interview with Col Edward C. Hitchcock, Jan 30, 1987; personal interview with Walter Pforzheimer, Jan 30, 1987.

163. "Leading Personalities in the British and American Air Forces," British intelligence document captured from the Germans, Nov 1944, Air 40, File 1497, PRO. The comment regarding commander of the Far East air forces is intriguing. I have found no evidence of such a proposal anywhere else. Possibly the Germans were referring to the planned American bases in Siberia, knowing that Vandenberg had spent time in Moscow working on such an arrangement. Incidentally, the Germans also thought highly of "Toughey" [sic] Spaatz, Ira Eaker, and Joe Cannon. They thought little of Doolittle and Leigh-Mallory, referring to the latter as "the flying sergeant."

164. Craven and Cate, III, p. 257.

165. "Third Army," Aug 27, 1944; Craven and Cate, III, p. 261.

166. *New York Times*, Mar 25, 1945, p. 6. Robert Lovett had also recognized the importance of publicizing tactical air power. In November, he remarked that he wanted a "Jeb Stuart Air Force" that roamed Germany shooting up targets of opportunity. Sherry, p. 183.

167. "Third Army," Oct 5, 1944; H. M. Cole, *The Lorraine Campaign* in *United States Army in World War II* series (Washington: GPO, 1950), p. 599; Craven and Cate, III, pp. 612–13.

168. Charles B. MacDonald, *The Siegfried Line Campaign* in *United States Army in World War II* series (Washington: GPO, 1963), p. 381.

169. Cole, p. 601.

170. MacDonald, p. 414.

171. "The Effectiveness of Third Phase Tactical Air Operations in the European Theater, 5 May 1944–8 May 1945," Aug 11, 1945, p. 28, Vandenberg papers, LOC, box 93; Craven and Cate, III, pp. 631–34; Bradley, "Effects of Air Power," pp. 105–108, 185–87.

172. *New York Times*, Dec 16, 1944, p. 1.

173. Spaatz diary, Dec 6 and 9, 1944; ltr., Spaatz to Doolittle, Dec 13, 1944 (S), Spaatz papers, LOC, box 16; Patton, p. 183; H. M. Cole, *The Ardennes: Battle of the Bulge* in *United States Army in World War II* series (Washington: GPO, 1965), p. 485.

174. Quentin Reynolds, pp. 294–95. Vandenberg did have a problem attending these conferences. On another occasion he was traveling with Eisenhower in a B-25. On takeoff leg from Laval, France, they were almost rammed by an Army liaison aircraft. Continuing on, the right engine caught fire so they made an emergency landing at Granville. Van decided to drive home, but Eisenhower insisted on trying again. Transferring to a light plane, the supreme commander lifted off, but now the weather began to deteriorate so rapidly that the pilot elected to land on the beach rather than risk a crash. After an uneventful landing, the tide began to come in. Trying to pull the aircraft to higher ground, Eisenhower badly wrenched his knee. It was one of those days. Laurence J. Hansen, *What It Was Like Flying for "Ike"* (Largo, Fla.: Aero Medical Consultants, 1983), pp. 38–40.

175. Zuckerman, pp. 307–10; Lee interview.

176. "Meeting Notes at USSTAF Hq.," Dec 20, 1944 (TS), Spaatz papers, LOC, box 16; Knerr diary, Feb 1, 1945; *The Liberation of North West Europe, Vol V: From the Rhine to the Baltic*. Royal Air Force Historical Study, (London: Air Ministry, n.d.), p. 67; Maj Gen Sir Kenneth Strong, *Intelligence at the Top: The Recollections of an Intelligence Officer* (Garden City, N.Y.: Doubleday and Co., 1969), pp. 242–43.

177. Charles C. Wertenbaker, "Back in Stride," *Time*, Jan 15, 1945, p. 26; Craven and Cate, III, pp. 687–88; Bradley, "Effects of Air Power," p. 156.

178. Henry H. Arnold, "Third Report of the Commanding General of the Army Air Forces to the Secretary of War," Nov 12, 1945, p. 7, Arnold Papers, LOC, box 108.

179. "Interrogation of Reich Marshal Hermann Goering," by Generals Spaatz, Vandenberg et al., May 10, 1945 (TS), Spaatz papers, LOC, box 134.

180. MacDonald, p. 547; "Minutes of daily staff meeting," Dec 22, 1944 (TS), Spaatz papers, LOC, box 16.

181. Ltr., McAuliffe to Vandenberg, Jan 25, 1945, Vandenberg papers, LOC, box 93; James A. Huston, "Tactical Use of Air Power in World War II: The Army Experience," *Military Affairs*, 14, No. 4 (Winter 1950), p. 170.

182. *New York Times*, Jan 8, 1945, p. 7.

183. Wertenbaker, p. 28.

184. Ibid.

185. I am indebted to Prof Walt W. Rostow for providing me with a copy of the Hughes memoir. Rostow and Hughes had been on Gen Spaatz's staff together before December 1944. In a ltr. to the author on Jan 19, 1985, Prof Charles P. Kindleberger, another member of Vandenberg's staff, also sounded critical of his commander's ability, feeling that he supported the interdiction campaign longer than it was really useful to do so.

186. Hughes memoir, pp. 57–66.

187. Ltr., Vandenberg to Dixon, Jan 3, 1945, Vandenberg papers, LOC, box 77.

188. Report to USSTAF from SHAEF/G-2, "Proposed plan to isolate the Ruhr," Feb 10, 1945 (TS), Spaatz papers, LOC, box 146; Vandenberg diary, Feb 8, 10, and 15, 1944; ltrs., Bradley to Vandenberg and Vandenberg to Bradley, Feb 23, 1945 (TS), both in Vandenberg

papers, LOC, box 77; ltr., Eisenhower to Vandenberg, n.d., Vandenberg papers, LOC, box 47. There was apparently a good deal of animus between those who supported the rail plan and those who supported the oil plan on the USSTAF, AEAF, and Ninth Air Force staffs. Hughes, Rostow, and Kindleberger were dedicated oil men. It is possible that they resented Vandenberg's less than passionate support for their strategic point of view.

189. Quoted in D. Clayton James, *A Time for Giants: The Politics of the American High Command in World War II* (New York: Franklin Watts, 1987), p. 85.

190. Bradley and Blair, p. 488; ltr., Kuter to Arnold, Jan 28, 1945 (TS), Arnold papers, LOC, box 38.

191. Officer Efficiency Report on General Vandenberg, by General Spaatz, May 1, 1945, Spaatz papers, LOC box 17.

192. Ltr., Arnold to Vandenberg, May 31, 1945, Vandenberg, Jr., collection.

III. PREPARATIONS FOR COMMAND

1. Cable, Eisenhower to Marshall, May 8, 1945 (S), in Chandler and Galambos, ed., VI, pp. 21-22; Several undated news clippings in Vandenberg, Jr. collection.

2. Eisenhower considered Vandenberg for the job as military advisor to the United Nations, but eventually settled on Gen George C. Kenney instead. Chandler and Galambos, VI, p. 672. There is no evidence Vandenberg played any role in the targeting decisions regarding the atomic bombs used against Japan.

3. Spaatz Report, Oct 23, 1945, Spaatz papers, LOC, box 270, Chapter 4, pp. 6–10.

4. Ibid., pp. 7–10.

5. Spaatz Report, Nov 1945 (TS), AFSHRC, File 145.86–104. It is possible that the two-staged format was deliberate. The first report was fairly general and could be given wide dissemination. The second report noted that it dealt with such highly classified matters that not even the Air Staff would be privy to its contents.

6. "Minutes of Meeting," Oct 30, 1942 (S), Arnold papers, LOC, box 273.

7. November Spaatz Report.

8. Ibid.; memo, Arnold to Patterson, Oct 24, 1945 (TS), Arnold papers, LOC, box 38; R. D. Little and Lee Bowen, *The History of Air Force Participation in the Atomic Energy Program, 1943–1953.* 5 volumes. USAF Historical Study (Maxwell AFB, Ala.: Air Force Archives, n.d., II, part 1, pp. 125–28. LeMay's biographer does not reach the same conclusion, and he argues simply that no one in the Air Force was really qualified for such a position; LeMay was as capable as anyone. Thomas M. Coffey, *Iron Eagle: The Turbulent Life of General Curtis E. LeMay* (New York: Crown Publishers, 1986), pp. 251–57. Maj Gen Kenneth D. Nichols, Groves's successor as head of the Armed Forces Special Weapons Group, also disputes my theory. If the intent was to push LeMay into atomic development, then he should have been appointed to the Military Liaison Committee to the Atomic Energy Commission. Maj Gen K. D. Nichols, ltr. to the author, Dec 7, 1987.

9. Gen Curtis E. LeMay, interview with John T. Bohn, Mar 9, 1971, AFHO, pp. 1–2; memo, Spaatz to Brereton, Oct 31, 1947 (R), Spaatz papers, LOC, box 256; Gregg Herken, *The Winning Weapon: The Atomic Bomb in the Cold War, 1945–1950* (New York: Alfred A. Knopf, 1980), pp. 198–99.

10. Little and Bowen, II, part 1, pp. 123–40; Herman S. Wolk, *Planning and Organizing the Postwar Air Force, 1943–1947* (Washington: GPO, 1984), pp. 121–23; John T. Greenwood, "The Emergence of the Postwar Strategic Air Force, 1945–1953," in *Proceedings of the Eighth Military History Symposium*, USAF Academy, 1978 (Washington: GPO, 1979), p. 230.

11. Richard G. Hewlett and Francis Duncan, *A History of the Atomic Energy Commission,* 2 volumes, (University Park: Pennsylvania State University Press, 1969), II, p. 130.

12. Memos, Vandenberg to Eaker, Oct 30, 1945 (S), AFSHRC, File K143.519–1; Eaker to Norstad, Dec 3, 1945 (S), NA, RG 18, File 370.2, box 178.

13. Memos, Samford to Eaker, Dec 6, 1945 (S); Norstad to Eaker, Dec 14, 1945 (S), both in NA, RG 18, File 370.2, box 178.

14. An interesting anecdote concerning this period: General Vandenberg received a letter from General Groves in 1946 proposing that a B-29 group be assigned to the Manhattan District to become America's atomic strike force. This letter enraged most people at AAF headquarters; LeMay grabbed the letter and tore it up, much to the dismay of Brig Gen Roscoe Wilson, who was responsible for securing the top secret document. Quoted in Kenneth S. Moll, "Nuclear Strategy, 1945–1949: America's First Four Years," thesis, University of Omaha, 1965, pp. 82–83. I could find no copy of this letter, torn or otherwise.

15. Memo, Vandenberg to Eaker, Jan 2, 1946 (S), AFSHRC, File 179.061–34A. The standard combat unit of the AAF during World War II was the group, composed of three or four aircraft squadrons. After the war, the various support units—maintenance, supply, administration, transportation, etc.—were added and the new organization was termed a wing. Therefore, the postwar wing was appreciably larger than the group, but its capability was essentially the same. The atomic strike force was an exception: the 58th Bomb Wing was composed of three combat groups (one of which was the 509th).

16. Ibid.

17. W. H. Lawrence, "Regrouping of Army Airmen in 3 Commands Set by Spaatz," *New York Times*, Mar 6, 1946, p. 1; memo, Spaatz to Kenney, Mar 12, 1946, AFSHRC, File 416.01–46.

18. Ltr., Eisenhower to Patterson, Dec 20, 1945 (TS), in Chandler and Galambos, VII, pp. 665–67; memo, Patterson to Lovett, Nov 11, 1945 (S), AFSHRC, File 170.2204–3; Col Bruce W. Bidwell, *History of the Military Intelligence Division*, 8 volumes, Department of the Army Historical Study (Washington: US Army Historical Office, 1959–61), VI, pp. 117–20; Thomas F. Troy, *Donovan and the CIA* (Frederick, Md.: UPA, 1981), pp. 316–18. Note that Vandenberg sat on this committee at the same time that he was working on the Spaatz board. It is thus not surprising that the Spaatz Report forcefully emphasized the need for a strong intelligence function in the Air Force. His investigation into the G-2 morass must have been an eye-opener.

19. Ltr., Eisenhower to Patterson, Dec 20, 1945 (TS), in Chandler and Galambos, VII, pp. 665–67; ltrs., Vandenberg to parents, Jan 18 and 25, 1946, Vandenberg, Jr., collection.

20. The quote is from Thompson, p. 57; Col Edward C. Hitchcock, ltr. to the author, Mar 3, 1987. Perhaps the best and most authoritative account of how the enigma was broken can be found in F. H. Hinsley et al., *British Intelligence in the Second World War*, 4 volumes (London: HMSO, 1979–88), I, pp. 487–95. See also Aileen Clayton, *The Enemy Is Listening* (New York: Ballantine Books, 1980), pp. 66–70, 195, 320; Peter Calvocoressi, *Top Secret Ultra* (New York: Ballantine Books, 1980), pp. 44–51, 65–68. The TACs and IX Bomber Command also had Special Liaison Units for Ultra use. Group commanders, because they were expected to fly combat, were not briefed on Ultra. Similarly, on the Army side, Army commanders were privy to Ultra, Corps commanders were not.

21. "Synthesis of Experiences in the Use of Ultra Intelligence by US Army Field Commands in the European Theater of Operations," n.d., NA, RG 457, File SRH-006. To avoid arousing German suspicions, it was standard to confirm Ultra intelligence by visual means before acting upon that intelligence. More importantly, it was imperative the Germans realized they had been sighted before a strike was carried out; hence, the launching of several reconnaissance flights, one of which would fortuitously "discover" the German position.

22. "Reports of US Army Ultra Representatives with Army Field Commands in the European Theater of Operations," May 1945, NA, RG 457, File SRH-023, part II, appendix F; Hinsley, IIIA, pp. 320–22.

23. Ltr., McDonald to Vandenberg, Jan 7, 1945 (TS), McDonald papers, USAFA Archives, box 3; Vandenberg to Kuter, Feb 26, 1945, Vandenberg papers, LOC, box 77; memo, Amoss to Vandenberg, Apr 14, 1945 (S), Vandenberg papers, LOC, box 63. In the Pacific, most signals intelligence activities were controlled by the Americans, who then shared their information with the British. Thus, those serving in the Pacific were not usually as paranoid concerning signals intelligence as were their European-based counterparts.

24. Vandenberg diary, Feb 12, 1945, Vandenberg papers, LOC, box 81.

25. Memo, Donovan to Roosevelt, Nov 18, 1944 (S), AFSHRC, File 170.2204–3.

26. Tom Braden, "The Birth of the CIA," *American Heritage*, 27, No. 2 (Feb 1977), pp. 6–7. Braden says the memo was leaked by J. Edgar Hoover of the FBI, who was strongly opposed to Donovan's proposals. However, Walter Pforzheimer, legislative counsel for the Central Intelligence Group, maintains that the information was leaked by Stephen Early on the White House staff. Personal interview with Walter Pforzheimer, Jan 30, 1987.

27. Thomas Parrish, *The Ultra Americans: The U.S. Role in Breaking the Nazi Codes* (New York: Stein and Day, 1986), pp. 205, 231–32.

28. Carl Kaysen, *Notes on Strategic Air Intelligence in World War II (ETO)*, Rand Study No. R-165, Oct 1949 (S), (Santa Monica, Ca.: Rand Corporation, 1953), p. 30; Sidney Shalett, "Army Intelligence Being Reorganized, *New York Times*, May 16, 1945, p. 14; Hoyt S. Vandenberg, "The Objectives and Functions of the Central Intelligence Group," lecture to the Army War College, Dec 11, 1946 (S), AFSHRC, File K239.716246–34(S), pp. 2–3; General Charles P. Cabell, "Memoirs of an Unidentified Aide," unpublished memoir, n.d., AFSHRC, File 1025181, pp. 69, 454.

29. Bidwell, VI, p. I22. An interesting project that Vandenberg managed at G-2 was Operation Paperclip, the US exploitation of captured German scientists. The most famous of these was Werner Von Braun, who became one of the leading rocket scientists in this country. It is unknown what role, if any, Vandenberg played in sanitizing the past of certain former Nazi officials. Clarence G. Lasby, *Project Paperclip: German Scientists and the Cold War* (New York: Atheneum, 1971). See also Michel Bar-Zohar, *The Hunt for German Scientists* (New York: Hawthorn Books, 1967).

30. Bidwell, VI, pp. VI40–45; Maj Gen Clayton Bissell, "Report on Intelligence Matters," Oct 26, 1945 (S), AFSHRC, File 170.2204–5B; memo, Amoss to Vandenberg, Apr 14, 1945 (S), Vandenberg papers, LOC, box 63.

31. Kaysen, p. 26; "Synthesis of Experiences with Ultra," pp. 28–29.

32. U.S. Cong., Senate, *Final Report of Select Committee to Study Governmental Operations with Respect to Intelligence Activities*, IX Books, 94th Cong., 2nd sess. (Washington: GPO, 1976), I, p. 100. This report is usually referred to as the Church Report after the committee's chairman, Senator Frank Church; it will be referred to as such in future notes. Harry S. Truman, *The Memoirs of Harry S. Truman, Vol. II: Years of Trial and Hope* (Garden City, N.Y.: Doubleday, 1956), pp. 56–57.

33. Troy, appendix U, pp. 464–65.

34. Troy, pp. 346–51. "Minutes of NIA meeting," Feb 12, 1946 (TS), Leahy papers, NA, box 20.

35. Memo, Eisenhower to Nimitz, Dec 29, 1945 (TS); memo, Eisenhower to Vandenberg, Feb 13, 1946 (S), both in Chandler and Galambos, VII, pp. 696–97, 862–63; Church Report, I, pp. 20–21.

36. Troy, p. 267; Ovid Demaris, *The Director: An Oral Biography of J. Edgar Hoover* (New York: Harper's Magazine Press, 1975), pp. 107–108; Ralph de Toledano, *J. Edgar Hoover: The Man in His Time* (New Rochelle, N.Y.: Arlington House, 1973), pp. 242–43.

37. Harold Graves, "Intelligence Untangled," *Providence Bulletin*, Jun 11, 1946, n.p.; "Minutes of IAB Meeting," Apr 8, 1946 (C), NA, RG 353, box 96; Stewart Alsop, "U.S. Quietly Laying Foundation for Competent Secret Service," *New York Herald-Tribune*, Jun 30, 1946.

38. Braden, p. 10. The AAF intelligence chief, Gen Cabell, also commented at a meeting of the Air Board in July 1946 that Admiral Souers was too lethargic, but now that Vandenberg was in charge things should improve markedly. "Air Board Meeting Notes," Jul 17, 1946 (S), AFHO, p. 67; Pforzheimer interview. It is also possible that Admiral Souers was merely following the lead of the Navy Department that was opposed to the CIG's formation; if it had to exist at all, then it should remain innocuous. Indeed, Souers did not return home to Missouri; he remained in Washington eventually to become the first secretary of the National Security Council.

39. Troy, p. 546.

40. James Bamford, *The Puzzle Palace: A Report on America's Most Secret Agency* (Boston: Houghton Mifflin, 1982), pp. 309–10; Thomas L. Burns, unpublished manuscript titled, "History of the National Security Agency," NSA: Fort Meade, Md.,1987, chapter 4, passim.

41. Troy, p. 361; *U.S. News & World Report*, Aug 23, 1946, pp. 60–61; "Spy Master," *Newsweek*, Jul 22, 1946, p. 34; Constantine Brown, "New Central Intelligence Badly in Need of Funds," *Washington Star*, Jun 16, 1946.

42. Troy, p. 546.

43. Adm William D. Leahy diary, Apr 26, 1946, Leahy papers, LOC, box 5; memo, Leahy to Truman, May 9, 1946, Leahy papers, NA, box 20.

44. Ltr., Eisenhower to Truman, Apr 27, 1946 (C), in Chandler and Galambos, VII, p. 1037; memo, Truman to Patterson, May 16, 1946, Harry S. Truman papers, Official File, Truman Library. Navy Secretary James Forrestal wrote the president that he was pleased with Vandenberg's appointment because he had always given complete cooperation to the Navy and worked well with the ONI. Ltr., Forrestal to Truman, Jun 8, 1946, Harry S. Truman papers, Official File, Truman Library; Vandenberg daily appointment calendar, Vandenberg papers, LOC, box 6; ltr., Truman to Vandenberg, Jun 7, 1946, Vandenberg papers, LOC, box 90.

45. Charles J. V. Murphy, "The State of the Armed Forces," *Life*, Sep 2, 1946, pp. 197–98. Virtually all the newspapers welcomed the appointment. His outstanding war record made him a well-known figure; for example: "General Vandenberg's extraordinary record as a flyer and staff officer—as a tactician and strategist—in the late war shows that he possesses the qualities needed to insure success in his new assignment." *Washington Evening Star*, Jun 10, 1946.

46. Troy, p. 361; "Minutes of NIA meeting," Jul 17, 1946 (TS), Leahy papers, NA, box 20. One of his first moves was to replace the deputy director, Kingman Douglass, with one of his own men from G-2, E. K. Wright. Pforzheimer interview.

47. "Minutes of IAB Meeting," Mar 9, 1946 (TS), NA, RG 253, box 96; NIA directive no. 5, Jul 17, 1946 (TS), memo, Vandenberg to Leahy, Jul 14, 1946 (TS), "Minutes of 7th NIA Meeting," Sep 25, 1946 (S) all in Leahy papers, NA, box 20; Leahy diary, Jan 2, 1947, LOC, box 5.

48. Memoes, Leahy to Truman, Aug 21, 1946 (TS), and Vandenberg to Leahy, Sep 12, 1946 (TS); minutes of NIA meeting, Aug 21, 1946 (TS); NIA directive no. 9, Apr 18, 1946 (TS), all in Leahy papers, NA, box 20.

49. David Lilienthal, *The Journals of David Lilienthal, Vol. 2: The Atomic Energy Years, 1945–1950* (New York: Harper and Row, 1964), p. 104. The date of the briefing was Nov 11, 1946.

50. "Minutes of NIA meeting," Aug 7, 1946 (TS); memo, Leahy to Vandenberg, Aug 12, 1946 (TS), both in Leahy papers, NA, box 20; Leahy diary Aug 9, 1946; Hanson Baldwin, "Intelligence—II," *New York Times*, Jul 22, 1948, p. 2; Troy, p. 547; Sanford Ungar, *FBI* (Boston: Little, Brown, 1975), p. 225; Pforzheimer interview.

51. US Cong., House, hearings before the Committee on Expenditures. *The National Security Act of 1947*, 80th Cong., 1st sess. (Washington: GPO, 1982), p. 5. This testimony was given in executive session. See also Church Report, I, pp. 101–2; "Minutes of the 4th NIA Meeting," Jul 17, 1946 (TS), Leahy papers, NA, box 20.

52. Memos, Craig to Hull, Mar 14, 1946, and Weckerling to Hull, Mar 18, 1946, Vandenberg to Souers, May 1, 1946, all TS and all in NA, RG 165, File OPD 335.05 TS, box 75; John Loftus, *The Belarus Secret* (New York: Alfred A. Knopf, 1982), pp. 58–60. In a report of Oct 1946, Vandenberg admitted that all intelligence on Soviet development of war material and weapons was "meager." CIA Report, ORE 3/1, Oct 31, 1946 (TS), Declassified Documents Quarterly Index (DDQI), 1978, p. 20D.

53. Harry Rositzko, *The CIA's Secret Operations* (New York: Reader's Digest Press, 1977), pp. 14–15; William M. Leary, ed., *The Central Intelligence Agency: A History and Documents* (University: University of Alabama Press, 1984), p. 26. Gen Cabbel, then chief of Air Force intelligence, expressed similar views, unpublished memoir, p. 466.

54. Memo, Vandenberg to NIA, Jun 27, 1946 (C), and CIG Directive No. 9, May 9, 1946 (TS), both in Leahy papers, NA, box 20.

55. Rositzko, pp. 14–15; Church Report, I, p. 133. Vandenberg had even attempted to insert agents into the Vatican, but the State Department, with Truman's concurrence, rejected the idea. Memo, Truman to Byrnes, Nov 14, 1946, Myron Taylor papers, Truman Library. China was not overlooked. In February, Vandenberg directed his staff to begin drawing up a plan for collecting and evaluating information on China. NIA Directive No. 9, Feb 12, 1947 (TS), NA, RG 165, File P&O 350.05 (TS), box 76.

56. CIG Directive No. 15, Oct 1, 1946 (TS), Leahy papers, NA, box 20. Hoover strenuously objected to this practice, seeing it as an infringement on FBI turf. He was overruled. Ltr., Hoover to Vandenberg, Aug 23, 1946, Leahy papers, NA, box 20.

57. Vandenberg AWC speech, p. 14; Harrison E. Salisbury, *Without Fear or Favor: An Uncompromising Look at the "New York Times"* (New York: Times Books, 1980), p. 595.

58. Salisbury, pp. 595–603; Church Report, I, p. 195.

59. WARINTELSUM, various dates, Mar-Apr, 1946 (TS), NA, RG 319, File 219.25 G-2, box 151.

60. "Minutes of IAB Meeting," Jun 28, 1946 (TS), NA, RG 353, box 96.

61. "Coordination of Collection Activities," CIG Study 18/2, Nov 21, 1946 (C), NA, RG 353, box 95; Pforzheimer interview; Troy, p. 355; "President's Secret Newspaper," *The Senior Scholastic*, Sep 23, 1946, p. 9.

62. Troy, p. 365; Truman, II, p. 56; Vandenberg AWC speech, p 16.

63. Memo, Vandenberg to Truman, Aug 24, 1946 (TS); CIG Study: "Soviet Military Intentions," Sep 18, 1946 (TS); memo, Vandenberg to Truman, Oct 30, 1946 (TS); CIG Study: "Revised Soviet Tactics in International Affairs," Jan 6, 1947 (TS). All are located in "CIA Research Reports, 1946–1976: The Soviet Union" (Frederick, Md.: UPA, 1980), reel 1; Memo, Vandenberg to Truman, Sep 27, 1946 (TS), DDQI, 1981, p. 140C.

64. Vandenberg AWC speech, p. 17.

65. Pforzheimer interview.

66. Ibid.; Troy, pp. 367–73.

67. Pforzheimer interview. It is interesting, however, that Gen Vandenberg's appointment calendar does not record any visits to the Senator's office during the entire year at the CIG. Also, there are several pages missing from the general's calendar, including the entire week from Jan 23 to 31, 1947, the week following the climactic meetings at the White House with Clark Clifford, when the arguments over the proposal were most heated.

68. Pforzheimer interview.

69. Ibid.

70. US Cong., Senate, hearings before the Armed Services Committee. *The National Defense Establishment*, 80th Cong., 1st sess. (Washington: GPO, 1947), pp. 491–94.

71. Vandenberg's executive testimony before the House, Jun 1947, pp. 10–15. Covert activities were officially authorized by the National Security Council the following year. Phillip Knightly maintains that Vandenberg had actually begun covert operations as DCI. The confusion may be semantical. Vandenberg had indeed originated "clandestine activities," but by this he meant intelligence gathering, not sabotage or the like. Philip Knightley, *The Second Oldest Profession: Spies and Spying in the Twentieth Century* (New York: W. W. Norton, 1986), pp. 245–46, says Vandenberg originated covert operations before they were authorized by Congress, but the sources upon which he bases that allegation say no such thing. Memo, Vandenberg to Truman, Feb 25, 1947 (TS), Leahy papers, LOC, box 20. NIA Directive No. 3 authorized the CIG covertly to collect intelligence. "NIA Directive No. 3," Mar 21, 1946 (TS); "Minutes of the 4th NIA Meeting," Jul 17, 1946 (TS), both in Leahy papers, LOC, box 20.

72. Sidney Shalett, "General Vandenberg Set for New Post," *New York Times,* Feb 26, 1947, p. 18; Braden, p. 10; Leary, pp. 22–23, 36. Vandenberg's replacement was Rear Admiral Roscoe Hillenkoetter. From Missouri, Hillenkoetter was Admiral Leahy's choice and had been with him in Vichy, France, several years before. Pforzheimer thought "Hilly"

a smart, capable man who was simply too young and innocent for the Washington bureaucracy: "They ate him alive." Pforzheimer interview.

73. Nelson A. Rockefeller (chairman), *Commission on CIA Activities Within the United States* (Washington: GPO, 1975), pp. 20, 34, 37; Church Report, III, pp. 565–67, 681, 789.

74. Ltr., Truman to Vandenberg, Apr 30, 1947, Vandenberg papers, LOC, box 90.

75. Ltr., Eaker to Hester, Mar 5, 1947, Eaker papers, LOC, box 10; Lt Gen Ira C. Eaker, personal interview with the author, Mar 30, 1978. Spaatz had also wanted to retire, according to his wife, but had been prevailed upon by Vandenberg, Norstad, and others to remain. They said that Gen George C. Kenney, the most likely replacement for Spaatz at that time, was unacceptable; only Spaatz could hold the AAF together through the upcoming unification fight. Ruth Spaatz, interview by James C. Hasdorff, AFHO, Mar 3, 1981, pp. 35–36. Strangely, Gen Joseph McNarney, who outranked Kenney and Spaatz, was not mentioned as a possible candidate.

76. Ltr., Arnold to Spaatz, Apr 5, 1943, Vandenberg, Jr., collection.

77. Leahy diary, Jan 22, 1947, LOC, box 6; *Newsweek*, Jun 2, 1947, p. 13. Those generals who outranked Vandenberg at war's end in order of seniority were the following: H. H. Arnold (five stars); J. T. McNarney, G. C. Kenney, and C. M. Spaatz (four stars); D. C. Emmons, G. C. Brett, B. K. Yount, I. C. Eaker, J. H. Doolittle, L. H. Brereton, B. M. Giles, H. L. George, and J. K. Cannon (three stars). In 1947, the only lieutenant generals remaining on active duty were Emmons, Brereton, and Cannon. Incidentally, U. S. Grant made general at age forty-six. Lauris Norstad and Curtis LeMay, two of Vandenberg's protégés, received their fourth stars at ages forty-five and forty-four, respectively.

78. Ray S. Cline and Maurice Matloff, "Development of War Department Views on Unification," *Military Affairs*, 13, No. 2 (Summer 1949), p. 65.

79. Paul Y. Hammond, *Organizing for Defense* (Princeton: Princeton University Press, 1961), p. 162.

80. Cline and Matloff, p. 67. There was never a supreme commander in the Pacific Theater as there was in Europe (Eisenhower). MacArthur and Nimitz were equals, although within their own subtheaters they were supreme.

81. Robert G. Albion and Robert H. Connery, *Forrestal and the Navy* (New York: Columbia University Press, 1962), p. 271.

82. Speech and questions by Stuart Symington and Gen Carl Spaatz, June 17, 1946, Detroit, copy in Vandenberg papers, LOC, box 34, p. 11; Demetrios Caraley, *The Politics of Military Unification* (New York: Columbia University Press, 1966), pp. 70–71, 104–109; Wolk, *Planning*, pp. 90–94.

83. Wolk, *Planning*, p. 103; Edwin L. Williams, Jr., *Legislative History of the AAF and USAF 1941–1951*, USAF Historical Study No. 84 (Maxwell AFB, Ala.: Air University, 1955), p. 42.

84. Cline and Matloff, pp. 68–71.

85. Ibid.; Caraley, pp. 35–38. The findings of the Richardson committee were not unanimous; Adm Richardson filed a separate, dissenting opinion.

86. Hammond, pp. 203–13; Alfred D. Sander, "Truman and the National Security Council," *Journal of American History*, 59, No. 2 (Sep 1977), pp. 370–72.

87. Cline and Matloff, p. 71. One source maintains that Marshall struck a bargain with Robert Lovett during the war: if the AAF would remain loyal during the conflict, he would grant them autonomy, and after the war he would push for their independence. Walter Isaacson and Evan Thomas, *The Wise Men: Six Friends and the World They Made* (New York: Simon and Schuster, 1986), p. 206.

88. Robert F. Futrell, *Ideas, Concepts, Doctrine: A History of Basic Thinking in the United States Air Force, 1917–1964*, 2 volumes. USAF Historical Study No. 139 (Maxwell AFB, Ala.: Air University, 1971), I, pp. 171–72; Albion and Connery, p. 257. There was a significant exception to Navy solidarity. Adm Raymond A. Spruance, hero of Midway,

said at a press conference in Aug 1945 that the postwar Navy should be drastically reduced in size because the nation had no naval enemy with which to contend. Although the newspapers welcomed his "statesmanship," his Navy superiors severely reprimanded him for his intemperate candor. Thomas B. Buell, *The Quiet Warrior* (Boston: Little, Brown, 1974), pp. 272–73.

89. Albion and Connery, p. 257.

90. Secretary of War Henry L. Stimson had experienced difficulties with these men for many years and he referred to them simply as "the Admirals" who "retire from the realm of logic into a dim religious world in which Neptune was God, Mahan his prophet and the United States Navy was the only true church." He felt the problem with the Navy was that they had never had an Elihu Root to give the admirals their "comeuppance." Stimson and Bundy, p. 506.

91. Vincent Davis, "Admirals, Politics and Postwar Defense Policy: The Origins of the Postwar U.S. Navy 1943–1946," diss., Princeton University, 1961, pp. 315–22. The author notes that the percentage of naval aviators who attained flag rank jumped from 12 to 23 percent during the war.

92. Ibid., pp. 373, 406, 456, 466, 492. Early atomic bombs were extremely large and heavy, weighing over ten thousand pounds, so only large, multiengine aircraft could carry them.

93. U.S. Cong., House, hearings before the Select Committee on Post-War Military Policy, *Proposal to Establish a Single Department of Armed Forces*, 78th Cong., 2nd sess. (Washington: GPO, 1944), p. 50.

94. Caraley, p. 100.

95. Ibid. Spaatz said as late as 1965 that all naval aviation should have been given to the Air Force. Gen Carl Spaatz, interview with Arthur Goldberg, May 19, 1965, AFHO.

96. Caraley, p. 151; Walter Millis and E. S. Duffield, eds., *The Forrestal Diaries* (New York: Viking, 1951), p. 229. Armstrong's remarks were made at a dinner where naval officers were present. Predictably, Armstrong was in hot water for his indiscretion; and in a letter to Lt Gen Ira Eaker (deputy commander of the AAF), he apologized profusely, claimed it was just a joke, his words had been twisted, and that he had not been drinking as had been reported. He concluded indignantly: "I am sorry this incident occurred; however, I am delighted to find out at this stage what the Navy's true colors are and I shall remember their treatment of me to my last day." Ltr., Armstrong to Eaker, Feb 17, 1947, Eaker papers, LOC, box 10. Armstrong, incidentally, was reputedly the model for Gen Frank Savage in the popular motion picture and television series "12 O'Clock High."

97. Memo, Spaatz to JCS, Mar 15, 1946 (TS), in "Records of the JCS, Part 2, 1946–53: Strategic Issues, Section 2" (Frederick, Md.: UPA, 1981), microfilm reel 10.

98. Henry H. Arnold, "Third Report of the Commanding General of the Army Air Forces to the Secretary of War," Nov 12, 1945, p. 72. A book that captures the fear felt by Marines who saw themselves fighting for their institutional survival is Gordon W. Keiser, *The US Marine Corps and Unification, 1944–1947: The Politics of Survival* (Washington: National Defense University Press, 1982). Incidentally, in the same speech given by General Armstrong in Feb 1947, he allegedly referred to the Marines as "bitched-up Jarheads."

99. *A Concise History of the Organization of the Joint Chiefs of Staff, 1942–1978*, JCS Special Historical Study (Washington: JCS, 1979), pp. 11–16; Ernest J. King and Walter M. Whitehill, *Fleet Admiral Ernest J. King: A Naval Record* (London: Eyre and Spottiswoode, 1953), pp. 36–38.

100. Herman S. Wolk, "The Defense Unification Battle, 1947–1950: The Air Force," *Prologue*, 7, No. 1 (Spring 1975), p. 19; Harry S. Truman, "Our Armed Forces Must Be Unified," *Colliers*, Aug 26, 1944, p. 16.

101. "State of the Unification," *Economist*, Oct 22, 1949, p. 893.

102. *Chronology, Functions and Composition of the Joint Chiefs of Staff*, JCS Historical Study (Washington: JCS, 1979), p. 30; Wolk, *Planning*, p. 160.

103. Millis and Duffield, p. 161.

104. King and Whitehill, p. 421; William D. Leahy, *I Was There* (New York: McGraw-Hill, 1950), p. 222.

105. Caraley, pp. 222–24.

106. Albion and Connery, p. 271.

107. *New York Times*, Dec 16, 1945, p. 14; Millis and Duffield, p. 466; "Air Board Meeting Notes," Aug 27–28, 1946 (S), AFHO, p. 129.

108. Cable, Eisenhower to George, Jul 25, 1945 (S), Chandler and Galambos, VI, p. 790.

109. Memo, Vandenberg to Staff, Jul 31, 1947; "Minutes of Meeting," Aug 13, 1947, both in NA, RG 341, "Unification File," box 89; telephone conversation, Vandenberg to Symington, Aug 29, 1947, Vandenberg papers, LOC, box 1; memo, Eisenhower to Royall, Sep 15, 1947, Spaatz papers, LOC, box 267.

110. William R. Kintner, *Forging a New Sword: A Study of the Department of Defense* (New York: Harper and Bros., 1958), pp. 24–27; Marquis W. Childs, "The Battle of the Pentagon," *Harper's Magazine*, Aug 1949, p. 48.

111. W. Stuart Symington, interview with Hugh N. Ahmann and Herman S. Wolk, May 2 and Dec 12, 1978, AFHO, pp. 16, 52–53, 114.

112. Millis and Duffield, p. 295.

113. Laurence J. Legere, "Unification of the Air Forces," diss., Harvard University, 1950, p. 360; Wolk, *Planning*, p. 167.

IV. PREPARATIONS FOR COMMAND

1. Pforzheimer interview.

2. Personal interview with Brig Gen Godfrey McHugh, Jul 13, 1984; "Warning Siren," p. 23; *U.S. News & World Report*, Aug 19, 1948, p. 37; Robert J. Donavon, *Conflict and Crisis: The Presidency of Harry S. Truman, 1945–1948* (New York: W. W. Norton, 1977), p. 270.

3. Ltr., Col Richard E. Sims, to Maj Gen Hoyt S. Vandenberg, Jr., Aug 4, 1987, Vandenberg, Jr., collection.

4. Vandenberg, Jr., interview.

5. Most of this information derives from the interviews with Hoyt Vandenberg, Jr., perusals of the family scrapbooks and photo albums, and letters from Gloria Miller. The ending quote is from the *Miami Star Sun*, Apr 8, 1948, p. 28.

6. Vandenberg, Jr., interview.

7. John A. Giles, "General Van," *Flying*, Jul 1948, p. 27; Shalett, "Man on a Hot Seat," pp. 36–38. The comment concerning "Mr. America" is often referred to, but always out of context. In truth, he was given the title by a Boston anthropologist, Dr Alice Brues, because of his nondescript looks! "General Vandenberg has such a good, average American face that he probably would make as little permanent impression on the public mind as anyone in the country. If you were to pass him on the street, chances are you wouldn't even give him a second glance. He'd be just a nice-looking fellow whom you would be at a loss to describe—like the male lead in a Grade B movie, or the model for a necktie ad." Take that! Undated newspaper clipping in vol. 18 of the Arthur H. Vandenberg diaries, University of Michigan Bentley Library. Incidentally, Glad hated the picture on the cover of *Life*.

8. Gen Omar Bradley and Clay Blair, *A General's Life* (New York: Simon and Schuster, 1983), p. 478.

9. Vandenberg, Jr., interview. Apparently, columnist Drew Pearson got wind of the story and printed it, but Vandenberg ignored the flap, and Sandy continued to ride to school his last year.

10. Parrish interview. The project Glad envisioned probably concerned the Officers Wives Club. She was a founding member and thought all wives should play an active role.

11. Ltr., Hoyt to Collins, Jul 28, 1950, Vandenberg papers, LOC, box 77. Gladys remained lovely and was chosen as one of the ten best-dressed women in Washington. Undated news clipping, Vandenberg, Jr., collection.

12. Ltr., Vandenberg to Arnold, Oct 16, 1945, Arnold papers, LOC, box 72.

13. Burt correspondence.

14. Alan R. Gropman, *The Air Force Integrates, 1945–1964* (Washington: GPO, 1978), p. 85; Morris J. MacGregor, Jr., *Integration of the Armed Services* in *Defense Studies* series (Washington: GPO, 1981), pp. 21–23, 27, 82, 171–74, 271–74.

15. Ltr., Vandenberg to all commanding officers, Jan 12, 1949, Vandenberg papers, LOC, box 32; Lt Gen Idwal Edwards, interview with Maj Alan Gropman, Feb 10, 1973, USAFA, pp. 10–12, 26; MacGregor, p. 616.

16. Vandenberg, Jr., interview.

17. Vandenberg Jr., and Miller interviews; undated news clipping, Vandenberg, Jr., collection.

18. Vandenberg, Jr., interview; ltrs., Vandenberg to Sandy, Jun 11, 1943, and another, n.d., but probably during 1944, both in Vandenberg, Jr., collection.

19. Vandenberg, Jr., interview; ltr., Vandenberg to parents, Dec 8, 1949, Vandenberg, Jr., collection.

20. Vandenberg, Jr., interview.

21. Ibid.

22. *Aviation Week*, Apr 12, 1948, p. 7.

23. Norstad and Lee interviews; Puryear, pp. 116–17. Craigie and Vandenberg had been classmates at West Point; twenty-five years later their sons would share a cadet room.

24. Gen William F. McKee, interview with James C. Hasdorff, Mar 13–14, 1979, AFHO, p. 62.

25. Personal interview with Brig Gen Noel F. Parrish, July 11 and 13, 1984. Parrish is a particularly valuable source; not only was he one of Gen Vandenberg's aides, but he was also a trained historian, receiving his PhD from Rice University in 1975.

26. Ltr., Arthur Vandenberg to Lippmann, Jan 19, 1950, Lippmann papers, Yale University, file 2145, box 107.

27. Arthur Vandenberg, Jr., ed., *The Private Papers of Senator Vandenberg* (Boston: Houghton Mifflin, 1952), pp. xviii–ix.

28. Vandenberg, Jr., and Miller interviews. There were persistent rumors concerning the private life of Arthur Vandenberg, Jr. He never married, and the circumstances surrounding his death in 1968 are unclear.

29. Symington interview, pp. 17–18. For one of Vandenberg's detractors who held such beliefs, see Maj Gen Donald Wilson interview, p. 244. Even some friends thought the rumors were a possibility—Johnson and Joseph Smith interviews. Symington did not recall the date of the meeting with Spaatz and Eisenhower, but because he thought it necessary to consult the Army chief it implies that the discussion was before Air Force independence, perhaps even before Vandenberg's return from the CIG. If so, it would indicate that he was chosen deputy commander of the AAF with the clear intention that he would become the vice chief of staff after independence and then chief—a fairly long-range plan.

30. Robert L. Smith, "The Influence of USAF Chief of Staff Hoyt S. Vandenberg on United States National Security Policy," diss., American University, 1965, p. 18–19. Spaatz expressed this motive to Smith in a personal interview.

31. Arthur Vandenberg, Jr., chapter 22, passim.

32. Ltr., Gillespie to Wolfe, n.d., quoted in ltr., Whitehead to Kenney, Apr 29, 1947, Whitehead papers, AFSHRC, File 168.6008–3. Animosity apparently surfaced even before the war was over when Van received his third star in Mar 1945: "You may find some gratification in the knowledge that several of your friends here, including Monk Hunter who is visiting, have referred to you in sympathy in connection with Van's promotion." Ltr., Kuter to Hansell, Apr 6, 1945, Kuter papers, USAFA Archives, reel 4.

33. Ltr., Kenney to Vandenberg, Apr 2, 1948, Vandenberg papers, LOC, box 74. Fair-

child died of a heart attack in Mar 1950 and his place was taken by Nate Twining, commander of the Fifteenth Air Force during World War II. In 1950, he headed the Alaskan Command and was slated to retire. Vandenberg dissuaded him from that idea. Twining later succeeded Vandenberg as chief of staff and in 1957 became chairman of the JCS.

34. Robert L. Smith, p. 19.

35. "Warning Siren," *Time*, May 12, 1952, p. 23; *New York Times*, Apr 10, 1948, p. 13; Norstad interview.

36. "Exit Tooey," *Time*, Apr 12, 1948, p. 27; Beurket, ltr. to author.

37. Donald Wilson interview, pp. 245–46.

38. Norstad, Johnson, Lee, Pforzheimer, and Parrish interviews. Gen Albert C. Wedemeyer, ltr. to the author, Aug 8, 1983.

39. Ltr., Cronkite to Reynolds, Mar 7, 1980; undated news clipping, both in Vandenberg, Jr., collection.

40. *Time*, Mar 10, 1952, p. 28; *Time*, Apr 12, 1954, p. 29; Lee interview.

41. Giles, pp. 76–77; *U.S. News & World Report*, Aug 19, 1948, p. 37.

42. Ltr., Arnold to Vandenberg, Apr 27, 1948, Vandenberg papers, LOC, box 74. Note the imperial "we."

43. Jean E. Smith, ed., *The Papers of General Lucius D. Clay: Germany 1945–1949*, 2 volumes (Bloomington: Indiana University Press, 1974), II, p. 568. Smith says that the real reason for the cable was that Congress balked at the size of the military budget, and Clay was trying to prod them into granting more funds. A sensational charge, but Smith provides no source for his insight.

44. Leahy diary, Mar 6, 1948, LOC, box 6.

45. "CIA Review of World Situation," Apr 8, 1948 (S), NA, "Special File 4A: Berlin Crisis"; CIA Report: "Possible Program of Future Soviet Moves in Germany," Apr 28, 1948 (TS), from "CIA Reports" collection, UPA, reel 1; Millis and Duffield, p. 409.

46. Jean E. Smith, II, pp. 599–604.

47. Bradley and Blair, p. 478.

48. Lucius D. Clay, *Decision in Germany* (New York: Doubleday, 1950), p. 359.

49. Bradley and Blair, p. 481; Leahy diary, Jun 28, 1948; Millis and Duffield, p. 454; Truman, II, p. 123.

50. Jean E. Smith, II, pp. 709, 747; ltr., Vandenberg to LeMay, Jul 23, 1948 (TS), NA, RG 319, File 312TS.

51. Msgs., BJSM to Air Ministry, Jun 29 and Jul 20, 1948 (TS); memo by Secretary of State for Foreign Affairs, Sep 10, 1948 (TS), all in Air 20, File 8122, PRO. The fact that there were few stipulations attached to the use of British bases by American aircraft came as a shock to the British government when it was discovered in 1985. When I discussed this issue with the head of the RAF historical section, Air Commodore Henry A. Probert, he stated that there was widespread interest in the matter as a result of the American raid on Libya in 1985. Owing to the furor arising over the use of UK bases to launch the strike, a check of the archives was made; virtually nothing was uncovered. Vandenberg and Tedder were old friends; they did not need to commit things to paper. The issue of British control over the use of American bases is discussed at length in *The Long Wait: The Forging of the Anglo-American Nuclear Alliance, 1945–1958* by Timothy J. Botti (Westport: (Westport: Greenwood Press, 1987), chapter 9.

52. Carl M. Spaatz, "The Era of Air-Power Diplomacy," *Newsweek*, Sep 20, 1948, p. 26; Millis and Duffield, pp. 456–58.

53. LeMay interview, pp. 8–12. The original codename for atomic-capable aircraft was SILVERPLATE.

54. Teleconference between LeMay and Picher, Jun 29, 1948 (TS), NA, RG 319, File 312 TS; memo, Anderson to Maddocks, Jun 30, 1948 (TS), NA, RG 319, File 88, box 103; Col Theodore Severn, ltr. to the author, Aug 10, 1984. Severn was a B-29 aircraft commander deployed to England during the summer of 1948. The London *Times* stressed to its readers on several occasions that the B-29s were merely on routine training missions,

and the deployment was not connected with the Berlin crisis. Presumably their readers did not have a subscription to *Newsweek*. See especially the *Times* for Jul 17, 1948, p. 4, and Jul 19, 1948, p. 4. Actually, the B-29s did experiment with air dropping sacks of coal, but soon discovered that the impact reduced the coal to powder. Richard Collier, *Bridge Across the Sky* (New York: McGraw-Hill, 1978), p. 81.

55. The thesis that neither the planes nor the bombs were deployed to England is presented in Harry S. Borowski, *A Hollow Threat: Strategic Air Power and Containment Before the Korean War* (Westport, Conn.: Greenwood Press, 1982), chapter 7; "Strategic Air Command Official History for 1949," AFSHRC, File 416.01–49, pp. 91–94.

56. Memos, Vandenberg, no addressee, Jul 7, 1948 (TS), DDQI, 1978, p. 148B; Forrestal to Truman, Jul 21, 1949 (S), DDQI, Retrospective Collection (R), p. 67A; Lilienthal to Truman, Jul 21, 1948, DDQI, R, p. 9A; Webb to Truman, Jul 22, 1948 (S), DDQI, R, p. 921C; Truman to Forrestal, Aug 6, 1948 (S), DDQI, R, p. 912D; Lilienthal, II, pp. 338–92. One of Truman's aides wrote that the real reason the transfer was rejected dealt with political timing: elections were in the offing, and Truman did not want to arouse the public. Truman told his aide that the issue would be reconsidered after the election. MFR, by George Elsey, n.d., DDQI, R, p. 304A.

57. Little and Bowen, II, part 1, p. 234; Greenwood, p. 226; "Strategic Air Command Official History for 1948," AFSHRC, File 416.01–48, pp. 147–48; msg., BJSM to Landen, Jul 3, 1948 (TS), Air 20, File 8127, PRO; Millis and Duffield, p. 458.

58. Gen LeMay was an eminently quotable individual. Soon after taking over the command of SAC, he was asked if his outfit was combat ready. He responded that he had just gone into a hangar that was being guarded by an airman with a ham sandwich. Gen Kuter disputed the cold, gruff image the general presented, noting that LeMay had suffered from Bell's palsy as a child, a disease which severely affects the main facial nerve. As a result of its after-effects, LeMay found it difficult to keep his lower jaw up, so he usually chewed a cigar to help. In addition, the ailment made it very difficult for him to smile; the muscles simply would not permit it. Kuter interview, pp. 410–11.

59. Joseph Smith interview; LeMay interview, pp. 8–9.

60. Ltr., LeMay to Fairchild, Jun 22, 1948 (S), Fairchild papers, LOC, box 1.

61. Memo, Landry to Truman, Jul 16, 1948 (S); MFR, by Leahy, Jul 1, 1948 (TS), both in Leahy papers, NA, box 7; memo, Vandenberg to JCS, Jul 23, 1948 (TS); JCS 1907, "U.S. Military Courses of Action with Respect to the Situation in Berlin," Jul 19, 1948 (TS), both in "JCS: Strategic Issues, Part 1" collection, UPA, reel 5.

62. Jean E. Smith, II, pp. 614, 661, 674; Robert Murphy, *Diplomat Among Warriors* (Garden City, N.Y.: Doubleday, 1964), p. 315; WARINTELSUM, Mar 22, 1946 (TS), NA, RG 165, File OPD 355.05TS, box 75; memo, Vandenberg to Truman, Nov 26, 1946 (TS), "Vandenberg File," CIA Archives, Langley, Va. LeMay echoed this sentiment, commenting in his memoirs that "USAFE would be stupid to get mixed up in anything bigger than a cat-fight at a pet show." Gen Curtis E. LeMay and MacKinlay Kantor, *Mission with LeMay* (Garden City, N.Y.: Doubleday, 1965), p. 411.

63. Truman, II, pp. 124–26; Leahy diary, Jul 22, 1948; memo, Forrestal to NSC, Jul 22, 1948 (TS), NA, RG 319, File 312TS; Symington interview, p. 95; Robert Murphy, pp. 316–18; Clay, p. 368. Vandenberg already knew about the airfield at Tegel; his daily calendar indicates that on Jul 15 he discussed it with Admiral Whitney, remarking how it would allow MATS greatly to expand its operations. He was apparently stalling at the NSC meeting.

64. Kuter interview, pp. 479–80; William H. Tunner, *Over the Hump* (New York: Duell, Sloan and Pearce, 1964), p. 161; msg., Wedemeyer to Maddocks, Jun 29, 1948 (S), NA, RG 319, File 88, box 103. In a letter to the author, Gen Wedemeyer said that he was an old friend of Vandenberg and chided him when he later heard that Tunner had indeed been sent to Germany. Van admitted that Wedemeyer had been right and that Tunner was an excellent choice. It is possible that Vandenberg was reluctant to commit Tunner and a special airlift task force to Germany at an early stage because he was opposed to the whole idea of an airlift. Sending over this group would tend to become a self-fulfilling

prophecy; thus, he preferred to wait until the NSC made a definite commitment. Tunner was sent the week following the decisive Jul 22 meeting. Gen Smith emphasized that, although disappointed, he was not personally offended by the decision; Van was the chief and did what he thought best. When asked if he thought their friendship should have been taken into consideration, he replied, "Certainly not, Van was Chief of Staff; I was just a one-star." Joseph Smith interview. Although a man of great talent, Tunner had difficulty getting along with people. An efficiency report written by Gen Twining some years later noted his irascible personality and the detrimental effect it had on his leadership ability. In 1950, Vandenberg promoted Smith to major general and made him the MATS commander, bypassing Tunner, who remained vice commander.

65. Tunner, p. 161.

66. Ibid., pp. 162–66; Collier, pp. 111–23.

67. W. Phillips Davison, *The Berlin Blockade: A Study in Cold War Politics* (Santa Monica, Calif.: Rand Corp., 1957), p. 154.

68. Memo, Vandenberg to Symington, Dec 10, 1948, Vandenberg papers, LOC, box 32; Eugene M. Zuckert, interview with George M. Watson, Jr., Apr 27, 1982, AFHO, p. 44.

69. Collier, pp. 85–88, 105–109.

70. Memo, Symington to Vandenberg, Feb 4, 1949 (R), Vandenberg papers, LOC, box 40.

71. Ltr., Kuter to Vandenberg, Sep 22, 1948(S), NA, RG 319, File 88, Box 103; ltr., Vandenberg to Kenney, Dec 13, 1948, Vandenberg papers, LOC, box 46.

72. Memo, Vandenberg to Symington, Oct 11, 1948, Vandenberg papers, LOC, box 32. Each conversion would have cost $60,000 and taken four months to complete.

73. During the airlift there were 733 "harassment incidents" reported, most involving "buzzing and close flying." "Berlin Airlift Corridor Incidents by Soviets," Aug 10, 1948–Aug 5, 1949, AFSHRC, File 572.601A. In truth, the Soviets could have stopped the airlift at any time by merely jamming the radio marker beacons or the "ground controlled approach" radar that brought aircraft in to land during bad weather. Without such aids, it would have been virtually impossible for aircraft to land in Berlin during the winter months. Ltr., LeMay to Clay, Oct 14, 1948 (TS), Vandenberg papers, LOC, box 63; JCS 1907/15, "Possibility of Jamming Aircraft Landing Aids at Berlin Airfield," Oct 16, 1948 (TS), "Records of the JCS Part II: Strategic Issues, part 1" collection, UPA, reel 5. The Soviets showed restraint in this instance; they could easily have brought the airlift to a halt without firing a shot.

74. Memo, Landry to Leahy, Sep 28, 1948 (S), Vandenberg papers, LOC, box 9.

75. Robert H. Ferrell, ed., *Off the Record: The Private Papers of Harry S. Truman* (New York: Harper and Row, 1980), pp. 148–49.

76. "Plan HARROW," n.d. (TS), in Berlin File "Blitz Book," Vandenberg papers, LOC, box 38; ltr., Cannon to Vandenberg, Nov 16, 1948 (TS), Vandenberg papers, LOC, box 32.

77. Memo, Vandenberg to JCS, Oct 12, 1948 (TS), "Records of the JCS Part II: Strategic Issues, part 1" collection, UPA, reel 5; Kenneth W. Condit, *The Joint Chiefs of Staff and National Policy, Vol. II, 1947–1949*. JCS Historical Study (Washington: JCS, 1978), pp. 45–47.

78. Bradley and Blair, p. 481.

79. Winston Churchill, "United We Stand," *Vital Speeches of the Day*, Apr 1, 1949, p. 384.

80. Condit, p. 154; Bradley and Blair, p. 481; Avi Shlaim, *The United States and the Berlin Blockade, 1948–1949* (Berkeley: University of California Press, 1983), pp. 337–40.

81. Collier, pp. 161–66. Thirty-one were Americans; thirty-nine were British.

82. Quoted in Frank Johnson, "Airlift to Berlin," *Air Classics*, Sep, 1978, p. 30.

83. Arthur H. Vandenberg personal diaries, volume 15, p. 33, Arthur H. Vandenberg papers, Bentley Library, University of Michigan; ltrs., A. Vandenberg to MacArthur, Aug 17 and Sep 16, 1943, RG 10, Box 1, MacArthur Archives, Norfolk, Va.

84. Gen George C. Kenney, interview with Marvin M. Stanley, Jan 25, 1967, AFHO, p. 37; Cook interview, p. 329.

85. One of Kenney's wing commanders concluded that he simply did not care anymore once the war was over, and he was happy to let his deputy, Maj Gen Clements McMullen, run SAC. Lt Gen Clarence S. Irvine, interview with Robert M. Kipp, Dec 17, 1970, AFHO, p. 17.

86. Ltr., Hipps to Streett, May 10, 1946 (S), AFSHRC, File A4012.

87. Ltr., Bunker to Spaatz, Mar 28, 1948 (S), NA, RG 18, File AAJ, box 799; ltr., Brereton to Spaatz, Jul 7, 1947 (TS), NA, RG 341, File DCS/O, box 10.

88. Ltr., Vandenberg to Lilienthal, Jul 12, 1948 (S), Vandenberg papers, LOC, box 32. The problem was a classic "catch-22": the modifications were so secret no one could be found with a high enough security clearance to carry them out.

89. Little and Bowen, II, part 1, p. 154.

90. JCS 1745/5, "The Production of Fissionable Material," Jan 21, 1948 (TS), "Records of the JCS Part II: Strategic Issues, part 1" collection, UPA, reel 1.

91. Little and Bowen, II, part 1, pp. 223, 375; David Alan Rosenberg, "U.S. Nuclear Stockpile, 1945 to 1950," *Bulletin of the Atomic Scientists*, 30, No. 5 (May 1982), p. 29. Only one such exercise was conducted before July 1948; eight more were held the following year. Little and Bowen, II, part 1, pp. 102–109.

92. Memo, by Vandenberg, no addressee, Jul 7, 1948 (TS), DDQI, 1978, p. 149B. By June 1948, there were fifty bombs in the stockpile, but not enough ground crews to assemble them or flight crews to deliver them. Rosenberg, "Stockpile," pp. 26–28.

93. Rosenberg, "Stockpiling," pp. 27–28.

94. Ibid., p. 28.

95. 1947 SAC History, p. 98; Borowski gives an excellent outline of this program, pp. 57–60.

96. LeMay interview, pp. 37–39.

97. Stephen Leo, interview with George M. Watson, Jr., Aug 18, 1982, AFHO, p. 77.

98. Ltrs., Whitehead to Kenney, Jun 5 and Jul 4, 1948, Whitehead papers, AFSHRC, File 168.6008–3.

99. Ltr., Vandenberg to Kenney, May 10, 1948 (S), NA, RG 18, File AAJ, box 799; ltr., Vandenberg to Kenney, Jun 9, 1948 (R), Vandenberg papers, LOC, box 32; Borowski, pp. 46–47. Smith had been on Vandenberg's staff at the AEAF in 1944.

100. Ltr., Judge to commanders, Aug 4, 1948, AFSHRC, File 168.005–1; Vandenberg daily calendar, Aug 6, 1948, LOC, box 1.

101. "Lindbergh Report," Sep 14, 1948 (C), LeMay papers, LOC, box 61.

102. Brig Gen Paul W. Tibbetts, Jr., interview with James S. Howard, Lt Col Frederick Zoes, and Capt Barry J. Anderson, Feb 7, 1985, AFHO, pp. 43–45.

103. Norstad interview; Borowski, p. 149; 1948 SAC History, p. 265. Vandenberg also spoke several times to Gen Joe Cannon (LeMay's replacement in Europe) during this period. He, like Fairchild, Kenney, and McNarney, was of the Old Guard. Perhaps Vandenberg took special care to explain his reasons for Kenney's relief.

104. LeMay interview, pp. 13–14.

105. Ltr., Symington to Truman, Oct 5, 1948, Vandenberg papers, LOC, box 59. It was required by law that the SAC commander be a full general, so a waiver had to be obtained for LeMay's appointment.

106. Ltr., Whitehead to Kenney, Sep 24, 1948, Whitehead papers, AFSHRC, File 168.6008–3. Whitehead also saw Kenney's relief as a continuing attempt by the "European Generals" to displace those who had served in the Pacific. After the war the AAF was dominated by Spaatz, Eaker, Vandenberg, and Twining, not by Kenney, Whitehead, Millard Harmon, and Chennault.

107. LeMay interview, p. 37.

108. LeMay and Kantor, pp. 432–33.

109. LeMay interview, pp. 24–32.

110. When Sandy graduated from pilot training in 1952, his father advised him to choose a career in SAC: "I gave LeMay a blank check to rebuild that command. SAC is gonna

be in the driver's seat from now on." Sandy opted for fighters anyway. Vandenberg, Jr., interview.

V. WAR PLANS AND WAR PLANES

1. "Military Position of the United States in the Light of Russian Policy," Joint War Plans Committee (JWPC) 416/1, Jan 8, 1946 (TS), NA, RG 319, "ABC File" 384, box 469.

2. JCS 789/1, "Concept of Operation PINCHER," Mar 2, 1946 (TS), from "Records of JCS, Part II: The Soviet Union, part 1" collection, UPA, reel 2.

3. JPS 789/1, "Problems Deriving from PINCHER," Apr 13, 1946 (TS); JWPC 432/3, "Joint Basic Outline War Plan, Short Title: PINCHER," Apr 27, 1946 (TS), both from "Records of the JCS, Part II: The Soviet Union, part 1" collection, UPA, reel 2. The use of atomic bombs in the event of war was not yet official policy. In fact, in May 1948, Truman told Leahy that he wanted a war plan drawn up that did not contemplate the use of atomic weapons. The JCS attempted to write such a plan, but at the outset of the Berlin crisis, Forrestal authorized them to abandon these efforts. Leahy diary, May 5–6, 1948; Millis and Duffield, p. 466.

4. Greenwood, p. 228.

5. Memo, Vandenberg to Symington, Nov 5, 1947 (TS), DDQI, 1976, p. 241B.

6. Finletter related that in 1947 the JCS attempted to brief him on the emergency war plan while he chaired the president's Air Policy Commission, but after some lengthy and largely incoherent rambling by the chiefs, Eisenhower broke in to apologize and admit there really was no war plan. Thomas K. Finletter, interview with Marvin Stanley, Feb 1967, AFHO, pp. 36–37; "Lack of Strategic Plan Hampers Development of U.S. Air Power," *Aviation Week*, Mar 1, 1948, pp. 11–12.

7. "The Position of the United States with Respect to Soviet-Directed World Communism," NSC Study, Mar 30, 1948 (TS), "Documents of the National Security Council, 1947–1977" (Frederick, Md.: UPA, 1980), microfilm reel 1. It is neither surprising nor coincidental that this study strongly resembles the ideas propounded so often by Soviet expert George Kennan.

8. JCS 1844/0, "HALFMOON," Jun 18, 1948 (TS), NA, RG 319, File 312TS; Condit, pp. 275–83.

9. Elliott V. Converse, "United States Plans for a Postwar Overseas Military Base System, 1942–1948," diss., Princeton University, 1984, pp. 165–69, 217, 253; "Discussion following Air Force presentation to the Combat Aviation Subcommittee" (Hinshaw-Brewster board), Jan 21, 1948 (S), Vandenberg papers, LOC, box 47.

10. "Presentation to JCS Committee on the Development of the Air Force During Fiscal Year 1950," n.d. (TS), Fairchild papers, LOC, box 2.

11. Vandenberg quotations from speeches given on the date indicated, located in Vandenberg papers, LOC, box 89.

12. Memo, Maddocks to Wedemeyer, Aug 2, 1948 (TS), NA, RG 319, File 312TS. Sorting out war plan codenames is nearly as big a chore as keeping straight all the World War II codenames. For example: HALFMOON begat FLEETWOOD which became TROJAN, then DOUBLESTAR, father of OFFTACKLE, sire of SHAKEDOWN, whose son was CRASSPIECE, etc. Said a leading authority on the subject, David MacIsaac: "Both the air staff and joint planners continued work on a whole series of so-called war plans whose only long-range significance would be to provide historians the problem of trying to sort them out." David MacIsaac, "The Air Force and Strategic Thought, 1945–1951," Woodrow Wilson Fellow Working Paper, Jun 1979, p. 30.

13. "Requirements of the Stockpile of Atomic Weapons," Jan 12, 1949 (TS), from "Records of the JCS, Part II: Strategic Issues, part 1" collection, UPA, reel 1. Incidentally, the top five on the 1948 hit parade were Moscow, Leningrad, Gorky, Kuybyshev, and Baku; Stalingrad was nineteenth. JCS, "BUSHWACKER," May 8, 1948 (TS), NA, RG 319, File 312TS.

14. LeMay interview, p. 34. General LeMay goes on to say that the lack of a war plan did not particularly bother him because SAC had no capability at the time anyway.

15. JCS 1935, "U.S. Policy on Atomic Warfare," Sep 3, 1948 (TS), in "Records of the JCS, Part II: Strategic Issues, part 1" collection, UPA, reel 1; memo, Vandenberg to Symington, Sep 24, 1948 (TS), NA, RG 341, "General File," box 9.

16. David Alan Rosenberg, "The Origins of Overkill: Nuclear Weapons and American Strategy, 1945–1960," *International Security*, 7, No. 4 (Spring 1983), pp. 13–14; *Foreign Relations of the United States, 1948, Vol. I: The United Nations* (Washington: GPO, 1973), pp. 624–28.

17. Thomas L. Burns, manuscript of "History of the National Security Agency," NSA: Fort Meade, Md., 1987, chapter 4, passim; "Report to the Secretary of the State and the Secretary of Defense" (Brownell Committee Report), Jun 13, 1952 (TS), NA, RG 453, SRH-123.

18. JSPG 500/2, "BUSHWACKER," Mar 8, 1948 (TS), in "Records of the JCS, Part I: The Soviet Union, part 1" collection, UPA, reel 3; JCS 1844, "Emergency Plans," Mar 9, 1948 (TS), in "Records of the JCS, Part I: The Soviet Union, part 1" collection, UPA, reel 4.

19. Alfred Goldberg, ed., *A History of the United States Air Force, 1907–1957* (Princeton: D. Van Nostrand, 1957), p. 105.

20. "Air Board Meeting Notes," Apr 17, 1946 (S), AFHO, p. 36.

21. George C. Marshall, "Responsibility of Victory," *Vital Speeches of the Day*, Nov 15, 1945, p. 77.

22. Quoted in Noel F. Parrish, *Behind the Sheltering Bomb: Military Indecision from Alamagordo to Korea* (New York: Arno Press, 1979), p. 275.

23. Condit, pp. 163–73.

24. Press release by Defense Secretary James M. Forrestal, "Results of Key West Conference," Mar 27, 1948, Vandenberg papers, LOC, box 90.

25. Ibid., p. 8; "Air Board Meeting Notes," May 4–5, 1948 (S), AFHO, pp. 40–41.

26. Forrestal press release, pp. 12–21, in "Public Statements by the Secretaries of Defense, Part I: The Truman Administration, 1947–1953" (Frederick, Md.: UPA, 1980), microfilm reel 1.

27. Millis and Duffield, p. 392.

28. Memo, Gallery to Radford, Dec 17, 1947 (S), NA, RG 340, "Special File 4A."

29. "Chronology of Changes in Key West Agreements, April 1948–January 1958," JCS Historical Report, Feb 7, 1958 (TS), NA, RG 218, File CCS 337, box 96; "Air Board Meeting Notes," May 4–5, 1948 (S), AFHO. This interpretation is lent credence by a Navy commentary on a 1949 war plan. It states that the real objective of planning is to ensure effective application of forces in war. Ordinarily, this would entail accomplishing tasks in order of priority. However, sometimes "allocations to tasks of lesser priority are not contingent on adequate provision, even on a minimum basis, for tasks of higher priority." In other words, although antisubmarine warfare is a primary mission of the Navy, it may choose to ignore enemy subs if it would rather join the air offensive, which to the Navy was a secondary mission. JCS 1844/46, "Joint Outline of Emergency War Plan CRASSPIECE," Nov 8, 1949 (TS), from "Records of the JCS, Part I: The Soviet Union, part 1" collection, UPA, reel 6, pp. 355–56.

30. "Strategic Problems Discussed by Secretary Forrestal and Joint Chiefs," DOD Press Release, Aug 23, 1948, in "Public Statements by the Secretaries of Defense" collection, reel 1; Millis and Duffield, pp. 464–68.

31. Memo, Wilson to Vandenberg, Feb 2, 1948 (S), AFSHRC, File K143.519; Maj Gen K. D. Nichols, *The Road to Trinity* (New York: William Morrow, 1987), pp. 253–54. The Air Force candidate was Wilson; that of the Navy, Rear Admiral William Parsons.

32. Leahy diary, Mar 14, 1948.

33. James Forrestal, "First Annual Report of the Secretary of Defense," Washington, 1949, p. 9; *Newsweek*, Sep 20, 1948, pp. 26–27.

34. Memo, Vandenberg to Symington, Jul 9, 1947, Vandenberg papers, LOC, box 52.

35. Millis and Duffield, pp. 393, 466; "Press Release for Secretary Forrestal," Mar 26, 1948, in "Public Statements by the Secretaries of Defense" collection, reel 1.

36. Spaatz's letter quoted in memo, Vandenberg to Forrestal, Feb 8, 1949, Vandenberg papers, LOC, box 52.

37. Memo, Vandenberg to Forrestal, May 26, 1949, Vandenberg papers, LOC, box 52.

38. Ken Jones and Hubert Kelley, Jr., *Admiral Arleigh ("31–Knot") Burke* (Philadelphia: Chilton Books, 1962), p. 149; Vincent Davis, *The Admirals Lobby* (Chapel Hill: University of North Carolina Press, 1967), pp. 288–89. One of the best summaries of this controversy can be found in Ronald Schaffer's *Wings of Judgment: American Bombing in World War II* (New York: Oxford University Press, 1985), pp. 192–98.

39. Text of television address, Mar 2, 1949, Vandenberg papers, LOC, box 90. What Vandenberg did not mention was that another B-50 aircraft had made an attempt earlier that day and failed. Indeed, five different aircraft were standing by; it was hoped that at least one of them would make it all the way.

40. *Washington Post*, Apr 5, 1949, p. 1. What Denfeld failed to mention was that the Neptune was unable to land on the carrier and had to recover at an airfield on shore.

41. Robert S. Allen and William V. Shannon, *The Truman Merry-Go-Round* (New York: Vanguard Press, 1950), p. 446. It was also speculated that Johnson, a strong fund raiser for Truman in the 1948 election, was given the Defense job as a reward for his faithful political service.

42. *Newsweek*, Jul 25, 1949, p. 19.

43. Bradley and Blair, P. 503; Dean Acheson, *Present at the Creation* (New York: W. W. Norton, 1969), p. 374.

44. Memo, Denfeld to Johnson, Apr 22, 1949 (TS), Vandenberg papers, LOC, box 52. The flight deck of the *United States* was to be 158 feet longer and 77 feet wider than the largest existing carrier, the *Midway*. More importantly, the *United States* would have no large "island" above the flight deck, thus allowing aircraft with large wing spans to take off unimpeded. *Aviation Week*, Mar 24, 1948, p. 12.

45. "Supercarrier study," Mar 28, 1949 (TS), Vandenberg papers, LOC, box 97; "Air Force Knocks Out Navy's Super Carrier," *Life*, May 2, 1949, p. 47; Steven L. Reardon, *History of the Office of the Secretary of Defense, Vol. I: The Formative Years, 1947–1950* (Washington: GPO, 1984), p. 413.

46. Memo, Vandenberg to Johnson, Apr 23, 1949 (TS), Vandenberg papers, LOC, box 52.

47. Memo, Bradley to Johnson, Apr 22, 1949 (TS), Vandenberg papers, LOC, box 52.

48. Paul Y. Hammond, *Super Carriers and B-36 Bombers* (Indianapolis: Bobbs-Merrill, 1963), p. 28. Sullivan, out of town when Johnson announced his decision, had not been notified in advance of the project's cancellation.

49. Memo, Vandenberg to Johnson, n.d. (S), Vandenberg papers, LOC, box 52; ltr., Eisenhower to Forrestal, Dec 19, 1948 (S) and Eisenhower diary entry, Jan 27, 1949, both in Chandler and Galambos, X, pp. 380–81, 448–49.

50. Memos, Symington to Sullivan, Mar 15, 1948 (TS) and Royall to Symington, Mar 12, 1948 (TS), both in NA, RG 341, "General File," box 6; *Aviation Week*, Jan 26, 1948, p. 14 and Jul 11, 1949, p. 7.

51. Hammond, *Carriers*, p. 22.

52. Hanson W. Baldwin, "War Plane Orders Face Examination by Congressmen," *New York Times*, May 24, 1949, p. 1 and Jul 21, 1949, p. 3. John K. Northrop, president of Northrop Corporation that built the RB-49—competitor of the B-36—went to his death maintaining that corruption was involved in the cancellation of his "Flying Wing" contract. A recent PhD dissertation examined this matter closely and concluded that Northrop's allegations were false: the RB-49 was simply a substandard aircraft. Francis J. Baker, "The Death of the Flying Wing: The Real Reason Behind the 1949 Cancellation of Northrop Aircraft's RB-49," diss., Claremont Graduate School, 1984.

53. US Cong., House, hearings before the Armed Services Committee, *Investigation of the B-36 Bomber Program*, 81st Cong., 1st sess. (Washington: GPO, 1949), pp. 13–15. Forrestal noted in his diary that Johnson specifically asked him to conclude any decisions

on the B-36 before leaving office so that conflict of interest could not be charged. Millis and Duffield, p. 551; ltr., Vinson to Vandenberg, Jun 14, 1949, Vandenberg papers, LOC, box 42. The Odlums, Symingtons, and Vandenbergs were all friends; Mrs. Odlum was the famed aviatrix Jackie Cochran. There were some especially despicable rumors circulating regarding a *menage à trois* between Cochran, Symington, and Vandenberg.

54. *B-36* hearings, p. 242.

55. Ibid., pp. 172–79.

56. Stephen Jurika, ed., *From Pearl Harbor to Vietnam: The Memoirs of Admiral Arthur W. Radford* (Stanford, Calif.: Hoover Institution Press, 1980), p. 168.

57. *B-36* hearings, pp. 610–11. In a statement to the press afterwards, Worth described himself as a newsman, Hollywood scenario writer, naval reserve officer, and freelance writer. *New York Times*, Aug 25, 1949, p. 5.

58. *B-36* hearings, pp. 524–27, 599–600.

59. *Newsweek*, Aug 22, 1949, p. 16.

60. Hanson Baldwin, "The Unheard Opposition," *New York Times*, Aug 14, 1949, p. 30.

61. Murray Green, "Stuart Symington and the B-36," diss., American University, 1969, chapter 13, gives an excellent account of the court of inquiry. *Aviation Week*, Sep 8, 1949, p. 16.

62. *New York Times*, Sep 7, 1949, p. 1.

63. Baldwin, who had consistently opposed unification because it threatened civilian control of the military, nevertheless thought Crommelin was "courageous." *New York Times*, Sep 15, 1949, p. 13. Admirals Leahy and Halsey also hailed Crommelin for having the courage of his convictions. Leahy diary, Oct 6, 1949; *Aviation Week*, Sep 19, 1949, p. 16.

64. E. B. Potter, *Nimitz* (Annapolis: Naval Institute Press, 1976), p. 540.

65. MFR, by Fairchild, Feb 14, 1949 (C) and ltr., Vandenberg to LeMay, Feb 15, 1949 (C), both in Vandenberg papers, LOC, box 45.

66. "Evaluation of Effect on Soviet War Effort Resulting from the Strategic Air Offensive," (Harmon Report) May 11, 1949 (TS), located in Thomas H. Etzold and John Lewis Gaddis, eds., *Containment: Documents on American Policy and Strategy, 1945–1950* (New York: Columbia University Press, 1978), pp. 360–64.

67. Aaron L. Friedberg, "A History of the U.S. Strategic 'Doctrine'—1945 to 1980," *Journal of Strategic Studies*, 3, No. 3 (Dec 1980), pp. 46–47; Rosenberg, "Origins of Overkill," pp. 16–17; Borowski, pp. 182–83. At that time, the Weapons System Evaluation Group was also investigating the feasibility of carrying out the war plan. Its report was submitted in Feb 1950, after the B-36 hearings, and was somewhat less optimistic than the Harmon board. Because of the near total lack of sufficient target intelligence regarding the Soviet Union, the report thought it impossible to carry out the war plan. Nevertheless, it concluded that if such targeting information was available, SAC could expect to strike 70–85 percent of its intended targets, destroying two-thirds of them. The report suggested a greater emphasis be placed on intelligence matters, but also pushed for more and safer overseas bases, an operational air-refueling capability, and improved radar bombing for increased strike accuracy. "Report on Evaluation of Effectiveness of Strategic Air Operations," WSEG Study, Feb 8, 1950 (TS), DDQI, 1976, p. 159A.

68. US Cong., House, hearings before the Armed Services Committee, *The National Defense Program—Unification and Strategy* 81st Cong., 1st sess. (Washington: GPO, 1949), pp. 46–52.

69. Ibid., pp. 350–61.

70. "Shooting the Breeze," *Air Force*, Oct 1949, p. 4; Bradley and Blair, pp. 488, 507–10.

71. Quoted in ltr., Doolittle to Slessor, Dec 22, 1949, Vandenberg papers, LOC, box 12.

72. *Unification and Strategy* hearings, pp. 451–69.

73. Ibid., That same day, the president said in a press conference: "Nobody wants to take the air arm from the Navy. It is necessary that they have fighter protection all the

time. I don't think it is necessary for the Navy to go into the heavy bomber business." Harry S. Truman, *Public Papers of the Presidents, 1949* (Washington: GPO, 1964), p. 517.

74. Parrish interview by the author; Allen and Shannon, p. 476.

75. *New York Times*, Sep 16, 1949, p. 1. Crommelin eventually became involved in right-wing politics and was a supporter of Senator Joseph McCarthy.

76. Truman, *1949 Papers*, p. 536. Admiral Nimitz, Denfeld's predecessor, related that Matthews called him to ask for advice; Nimitz told him to relieve Denfeld; Matthews asked how; Nimitz wrote the letter for him. Potter, p. 541.

77. Capt Paul R. Schratz, "The Admirals' Revolt," *U.S. Naval War College Review*, Feb 1986, pp. 308–11.

78. Childs, p. 48; "State of the Unification," *Economist*, Oct 22, 1949, p. 893.

79. "Carrier Study File," Vandenberg papers, LOC, box 97. A memo from Gen Fairchild states that Maj Gen Hugh Knerr, who had just retired from duty on the Air Staff, had been retained by a shipping company as a "National Security Consultant on the matter of the 800 foot, 35–knot flush flying deck passenger liners they intend constructing within the next three years." He thought Van might want to know. Memo, Fairchild to Vandenberg, n.d. Fairchild papers, LOC, box 1.

80. Ltr., Johnson to Vandenberg, Apr 15, 1949, Vandenberg papers, LOC, box 3. It is also reported that when the USS *Missouri* ran aground in Chesapeake Bay in Jan 1950, Vandenberg offered to lend the Navy a B-36 to tow it off.

VI. ECONOMICS AND ATOMS

1. *Aviation Week*, Dec 8, 1947, pp. 7, 11–13.

2. Thomas K. Finletter (chairman), *Survival in the Air Age* (Washington: GPO, 1948), pp. 8–12, 25–28. Although Finletter succeeded Symington as Air Force secretary in 1950, it should not be interpreted that he was partial to air power at the time of this report. Finletter, as well as three of the other four members, had no professional experience with aviation before 1947. The exception was George Baker, a former vice-chairman of the Civil Aeronautics Board.

3. Hoyt S. Vandenberg, "Our 70–Group Air Force Emerges," *Popular Mechanics*, Dec 1948, p. 89.

4. "Report of the Congressional Aviation Policy Board," *Air Force*, Apr 1948, pp. 12–15, 38–39; *Aviation Week*, Mar 1, 1948, pp. 11–12; "Air Force of 35,000 Planes Is Urged," *U.S. Air Services*, Mar 1948, pp. 14–17.

5. Green, p. 74.

6. "Determination of Minimum Annual Airplane Weight," Jan 27, 1948 (TS), DDQI, 1976, p. 160A; memo, Forrestal to JCS, Mar 27, 1948 (S); "The Cost of a Balanced Armed Forces Program," JCS Report, Apr 11, 1948 (TS), both in "Records of the JCS, Part II: The United States" collection, reel 3; "Press Release by Secretary Forrestal," Apr 8, 1948, in "Public Statements by the Secretaries of Defense" collection, reel 1.

7. Memos, Truman to Forrestal, May 13, 1948; Truman to Vandenberg, May 13, 1948, both in Vandenberg papers, LOC, box 40.

8. Truman, *1949 Papers*, p. 58. Forrestal agreed with the president: "As long as we can outproduce the world, can control the sea and can strike inland with the atomic bomb, we can assume certain risks otherwise unacceptable." Millis and Duffield, p. 340.

9. Memo, Landry to Truman, Apr 16, 1949 (C), Vandenberg papers, LOC, box 13.

10. Memo, Symington to Truman, May 24, 1948, NA, RG 340, "Special File 4A"; memo, Symington to Forrestal, Jun 8, 1948 (S), Vandenberg papers, LOC, box 40. There is a copy of an interesting telegram in the Vandenberg papers from William Loeb, the noted conservative newspaper publisher, to Senator Joseph McCarthy. Loeb asks the senator: "Have you ever considered possibility that same type of people you have been uncovering in State Department are also scattered through budget bureau and White House Secretariat?" The Air Force was being crippled and it must stop. Loeb concluded that he hoped McCarthy could "find time to look into it." Vandenberg papers, LOC, box 83.

11. Millis and Duffield, pp. 502–5.

12. "Transcript of JCS Meeting," Oct 2, 1948 (TS) in "Records of the JCS, Part II, section 2, Strategic Issues" collection, reel 10.

13. Memo, Royall to Forrestal, Sep 7, 1948 (S), NA, RG 340, "Special File 4A."

14. Lilienthal, II, p. 351; Robert H. Ferrell, ed., *Off the Record: The Private Papers of Harry S. Truman* (New York: Harper and Row, 1980), pp. 134, 145.

15. Memo, Forrestal to JCS, Oct 6, 1948 (R), Vandenberg papers, LOC, box 40.

16. Memo, Vandenberg to Forrestal, Oct 7, 1948 (TS), Vandenberg papers, LOC, box 40.

17. Memos, Bradley to Forrestal, Oct 7, 1948 (TS), and Denfeld to Forrestal, Oct 7, 1948 (TS), both in Vandenberg papers, LOC, box 40.

18. Memo, JCS to Forrestal, Nov 8, 1948 (TS), Vandenberg papers, LOC, box 40.

19. Millis and Duffield, pp. 508–11, 536; memo, Forrestal to Truman, Dec 1, 1948, Vandenberg papers, LOC, box 40; Reardon, p. 351.

20. Memo, Forrestal to secretaries, Nov 8, 1948, Fairchild papers, LOC, box 3; memo, Forrestal to JCS, Nov 9, 1948 (TS), Vandenberg papers, LOC, box 40. Forrestal merely told his subordinates not to criticize each other in public; if they did, they were to advise him in advance. Millis and Duffield, pp. 516–17.

21. Zuckert interview, p. 34; Symington interview, p. 36.

22. Memo, Vandenberg to Forrestal, Nov 9, 1948, NA, RG 340, "Special File 4A." In a memo to Symington, Vandenberg stressed the need for a JCS chairman, suggesting Eisenhower for the position. Memo, Vandenberg to Symington, Jan 17, 1949, Vandenberg papers, LOC, box 32.

23. Memo, Vandenberg to Johnson, Jan 18, 1950, Vandenberg papers, LOC, box 40. Vandenberg wrote an even stronger indictment of the JCS system to Symington on Mar 21, 1949, Vandenberg papers, LOC, box 32.

24. Testimony of Gen Vandenberg to Committee on National Security Organization (Hoover Commission), Jun 29, 1948, Vandenberg papers, LOC, box 49.

25. For the full text of the 1949 NSA amendments, as well as the recommendations of Forrestal, the Hoover Commission, and President Truman, see Alice Cole et al., eds., *The Department of Defense: Documents of Establishment and Organization, 1944–1978* (Washington: GPO, 1978), pp. 63–107; Millis and Duffield, pp. 497–98.

26. Charlotte Knight, "Mystery Man of the Pentagon," *Colliers*, Jan 22, 1954, pp. 34–36; Reardon, p. 362; Condit, p. 271.

27. Ltr., Vandenberg to Symington, Jan 12, 1949, Victor Emmanuel File, Herbert Hoover Presidential Library, West Branch, Iowa; ltr., Vandenberg to Symington, Mar 5, 1949, Vandenberg papers, LOC, box 49; Daily Staff Digest, Jan 24, 1950 (S), NA, RG 341, DSD File, box 10; "Management Control Through Cost Control," Jul 8, 1948, Vandenberg papers, LOC, box 58; Gen Edwin Rawlings, *Born to Fly* (Minneapolis: Great Way Publishing, 1987), pp. 46, 56–57.

28. Hoyt S. Vandenberg, speech to Associated Industries of Massachusetts, Oct 27, 1949, copy in Vandenberg papers, LOC, box 90; Zuckert interview, pp. 24–26.

29. Memo, Vandenberg to Forrestal, Aug 10, 1949 (TS); Edwards to Vandenberg, Mar 28, 1950 (S), both in Vandenberg papers, LOC, box 41.

30. US Cong., Senate, hearings before the Appropriations Committee, *National Military Establishment Appropriations Bill for 1950*, 81st Cong., 1st sess. (Washington: GPO, 1949), pp. 80–90.

31. Arnold A. Rogow, *James Forrestal* (New York: Macmillan, 1963), p. 295. *Aviation Week*, Jun 14, 1948, p. 7. Truman was asked about this alleged conflict, but denied it. Truman, *1949 Papers*, p. 473; Zuckert interview, p. 35. Although both Symington and the president were Missouri Democrats, by the time Symington left office their relationship was strained, and Symington received no support from the president when running for the Senate.

32. *Second Report of the Secretary of the Air Force for the Fiscal Year 1949.* (Washington: GPO, 1950), p. 241. The "equivalent" statement refers to Vandenberg's decision

to include more aircraft in each group rather than form new groups. Thus, combat capability increased although the actual number of groups remained constant.

33. Eisenhower diary entry, Feb 2, 1949, in Chandler and Galambos, X, pp. 461–62.

34. Eisenhower diary entry, Feb 19, 1949; memo, Eisenhower to Chiefs, Feb 28, 1949 (S), both in Chandler and Galambos, X, pp. 497–98, 515.

35. Smith to Vandenberg, Apr 5, 1950 (S), Vandenberg papers, LOC, box 41. US Cong., House, hearings before the Appropriations Committee, *National Military Establishment Appropriations for 1950*, 81st Cong., 1st sess. (Washington: GPO, 1949), pp. 228, 240.

36. Eisenhower diary entry, Feb 9, 1949, in Chandler and Galambos, X, pp. 482–83; Condit, pp. 246–54.

37. Memo, Vandenberg to Johnson, Aug 10, 1949 (TS), Vandenberg papers, LOC, box 41.

38. Memo, Vandenberg to Eisenhower, May 23, 1949 (TS), Vandenberg papers, LOC, box 32.

39. Eisenhower diary entry, Feb 9, 1949; memo, Eisenhower to Johnson, Jul 14, 1949; ltr., Eisenhower to Hazlett, Nov 17, 1949, all in Chandler and Galambos, X, pp. 482–83, 699–703, 831–35.

40. MFR, by Eisenhower, Mar 28, 1950, in Chandler and Galambos, XI, pp. 1041–43; Condit, pp. 263–65.

41. Omar Bradley, address to Command and General Staff College, Jul 1, 1949, Vandenberg papers, LOC, box 42; memo, Vandenberg to Johnson, Aug 10, 1949 (TS), Vandenberg papers, LOC, box 41; Condit, pp. 265–66.

42. Condit, pp. 270–71.

43. *Report of the Secretary of Defense for the Fiscal Year 1950* (Washington: GPO, 1951), pp. 11–14.

44. Ltr., Vandenberg to Senator Wherry, Sep 20, 1949, Vandenberg papers, LOC, box 40.

45. Edward A. Kolodziej, *The Uncommon Defense and Congress, 1945–1963* (Columbus: Ohio State University Press, 1966), p. 79.

46. Quoted in Warner R. Schilling, Paul Y. Hammond, and Glenn H. Snyder, *Strategy, Politics and Defense Budgets* (New York: Columbia University Press, 1962), p. 79.

47. Ltr., Truman to Johnson, Nov 8, 1949, Vandenberg papers, LOC, box 40; Truman, *1949 Papers*, pp. 538–39.

48. Lewis L. Strauss, *Men and Decisions* (Garden City, N.Y.: Doubleday, 1962), pp. 201–204; memoes, Norstad to Royall, Sep 3, 1947, DDQI, 1978, p. 356A and Royall to Eisenhower, Sep 5, 1947 (TS), DDQI, 1978, p. 356B; memo, Eisenhower to Spaatz, Sep 16, 1947 (TS), in Chandler and Galambos, IX, p. 1918.

49. MFR, by AEC, Jul 21, 1948 (TS), DDQI, R, p. 8G; memo, Barrons to Hillenkoetter, Feb 9, 1948 (TS), NA, RG 341, "General File," box 10; ltr., Kepner to Vandenberg, May 20, 1948, Vandenberg papers, LOC, box 56; Lilienthal, II, p. 384.

50. Memos by DCI (Hillenkoetter), no addressee, Sep 9 and 27, 1949 (TS), both in "CIA Research Reports: The Soviet Union, 1946–1976" collection, 1980, reel 1; Hewlett and Duncan, II, pp. 362–66.

51. Hewlett and Duncan, II, pp. 367–68; Lilienthal, II, pp. 569–72; Truman, *Memoirs*, II, p. 307. Several have stated that Johnson and Truman never really believed the Soviets had exploded a bomb in 1949. Gregg Herken, *Winning Weapon*, pp. 302–3; Noel Parrish, *Behind the Sheltering Bomb*, p. 324; Truman, *1949 Papers*, p. 485. Note the generic term "explosion" rather than "bomb," "device," or "weapon." Maj Gen K. D. Nichols, head of the Special Weapons Group, referred to the "Russian device" in a conversation with Truman. In military jargon, atomic weapons are usually referred to as devices; it sounds less aggressive. Truman apparently interpreted Nichol's use of the word "device" to mean some type of experimental gadget mounted on a platform, and thus not a true weapon. Nichols, p. 272.

52. Lilienthal, II, p. 580.

53. Memo, Hillenkoetter to Truman, Jul 1, 1949 (TS), DDQI, 1979, p. 18B; Norstad briefing to Truman, Oct 26, 1946 (TS), Vandenberg papers, LOC, box 63. In late July 1949, Gen Bradley testified that the Soviets could have the bomb by 1950, but more likely not before 1952. US Cong., Senate, hearings in executive session before the Armed Services Committee, *Military Assistance Program*, 81st Cong., 1st sess. (Washington: GPO, 1973), p. 93; "Did the Soviet Bomb Come Sooner Than Expected?" *Bulletin of the Atomic Scientists*, 5, No. 10 (Oct 1949), pp. 261–64, gives a series of quotations by various scientists all fairly accurately predicting the date for Joe I. However, all of the statements had been made in 1945–46, and at that time it was standard to use a figure of five years for Soviet development (the length of time it had taken the US), but as the five years drew to a close, many extended their estimates. The CIA estimate of July 1949—in which the Air Force concurred—predicted mid-1950 as the earliest date, with mid-1953 as "most probable." Memo, DCI to Truman, Jul 1, 1949 (TS), "CIA Reports, 1946–1976" collection, reel 1; Gen Charles P. Cabell, unpublished memoir, "Memoirs of an Unidentified Aide," n.d., AFSHRC, File 1025181, p. 262.

54. Ltr., Vandenberg to LeMay, Apr 1, 1950 (TS), LeMay papers, LOC, box 198.

55. MFR, by Fairchild, Sep 30, 1949 (S), Fairchild papers, LOC, box 1; Gen Hoyt Vandenberg, interview with James Strebig, May 9, 1950, Vandenberg papers, LOC, box 90; Richard F. McMullen, *Air Defense and National Policy, 1946–1950*, 2 volumes, Air Defense Command Historical Study No. 22 (Peterson Field AFB, Colo: Air Defense Command, 1964), p. 53.

56. Memo, Vandenberg to JCS, Nov 16, 1949 (TS), Fairchild papers, LOC, box 1.

57. "The Proposed Acceleration of the Atomic Energy Program," NSC Report, Oct 10, 1949 (TS), DDQI, R, p. 303G; Truman, *1949 Papers*, p. 523.

58. Gregg Herken, *Counsels of War* (New York: Alfred A. Knopf, 1985), pp. 26–29; Fred Kaplan, *The Wizards of Armageddon* (New York: Simon and Schuster, 1983), pp. 38–40. Both of these books rely heavily on the Brodie papers concerning the targeting issue. The subject is not mentioned in either the Vandenberg or the LeMay papers.

59. Barry H. Steiner, "Using the Absolute Weapon: Early Ideas of Bernard Brodie on Atomic Strategy," *Journal of Strategic Studies*, 7, No. 4 (Dec 1984), pp. 381–83; Herken, *Counsels of War*, pp. 28–32; Kaplan, pp. 41–49; ltrs., Brodie to Vandenberg, Nov 28, 1950, and Vandenberg to Griswold, Nov 30, 1950, both in Vandenberg papers, LOC, box 21.

60. J. Robert Oppenheimer, "Physics in the Contemporary World," *Bulletin of the Atomic Scientists*, 4, No. 3 (Mar 1948), p. 66.

61. Stanley A. Blumberg and Givinci Owens, *Energy and Conflict: The Life and Times of Edward Teller* (New York: Putnam's, 1976), p. 240.

62. General Advisory Commission Report, Oct 30, 1949 (TS) in *Foreign Relations of the United States, 1949, Vol. I: National Security Affairs; Foreign and Economic Policy* (Washington: GPO, 1976), pp. 569–73. Of significance, Maj Gen James McCormack was the highest ranking member of the Military Liaison Committee to the AEC and its chief weapons expert. He was deliberately excluded from the October meeting, and he believed it was because of his previously expressed strong support for the super. The GAC simply did not want to hear from proponents. Philip M. Stern, *The Oppenheimer Case: Security on Trial* (New York: Harper and Row, 1969), p. 150.

63. Nichols, p. 259.

64. U.S. Atomic Energy Commission, *In the Matter of J. Robert Oppenheimer: Transcript of Hearings before Personnel Security Board* (Cambridge, Mass.: MIT Press, 1971), p. 682; ltr., McMahon to Truman, Oct 7, 1949 (C), DDQI, R, p. 912F; memo, Lilienthal to Truman, Nov 9, 1949 (TS) located in *FRUS, 1949*, I, pp. 576–83.

65. *Oppenheimer* hearings, p. 778; David Alan Rosenberg, "American Atomic Strategy and the Hydrogen Bomb Decision," *Journal of American History*, 66, No. 1 (Jun 1979), pp. 80–83.

66. Ltr., Dean to Truman, Nov 9, 1949 (TS) located in *FRUS, 1949*, I, pp. 583–84.

67. Ltr., Strauss to Truman, Nov 25, 1949 (TS) located in *FRUS, 1949*, I, pp. 596–99.

68. *Oppenheimer* hearings, pp. 127, 682–83; ltr., McMahon to Truman, Nov 21, 1949 (TS) in *FRUS, 1949*, I, pp. 588–92.

69. Maj Gen Roscoe C. Wilson, interview with Lt Col Dennis A. Smith, Dec 1–2, 1983, AFHO, pp. 107, 113. When the first tactical atomic weapon was exploded in Jan 1951, Gen Collins is reported to have exclaimed: "Now we've got it!" Stewart Alsop and Dr Ralph E. Lapp, "Can the New A-Bomb Stop Troops in the Field?" *Saturday Evening Post*, Sep 29, 1951, p. 20.

70. Memo, Vandenberg to JCS, Mar 11, 1951 (TS), DDQI, 1976, p. 240C.

71. Memo, JCS to Johnson, Nov 23, 1949 (TS) in *FRUS, 1949*, I, pp. 595–96.

72. Memo, JCS to Johnson, Jan 13, 1950 (TS) located in *FRUS, 1950, Vol. I: National Security Affairs; Foreign and Economic Policy* (Washington: GPO, 1977), pp. 503–11.

73. Robert J. Lamphere and Tom Shachtman, *The FBI-KGB Wars: A Special Agent's Story* (New York: Random House, 1986), pp. 185–88. According to Agent Lamphere, the information supplied by Fuchs led directly to the arrest of Julius and Ethel Rosenberg, who controlled an extensive Soviet spy network throughout the US. Ibid., pp. 214–16. See also Edward Teller with Allen Brown, *The Legacy of Hiroshima* (Garden City, N.Y.: Doubleday, 1962), p. 46; "Dr. Klaus Fuchs to Stand Trial for Espionage," *Bulletin of the Atomic Scientists*, 6, No. 3 (Mar 1950), p. 68. There are two recent biographies of Klaus Fuchs; for an excellent review of these works, see Stephen Toulmin, "The Conscientious Spy," *New York Review of Books*, Nov 19, 1987, pp. 54–60.

74. Herbert F. York, *The Advisers: Oppenheimer, Teller and the Superbomb* (San Francisco: W. H. Freeman, 1976), p. 66.

75. Isaacson and Thomas, p. 487.

76. David Lilienthal, "Special Report to the President," Jan 31, 1950 (TS) in *FRUS, 1950*, I, 513–23.

77. Lilienthal, II, pp. 632–33.

78. Hewlett and Duncan, II, pp. 369–409. A Gallup poll taken in Feb 1950 revealed that 73 percent of those surveyed advocated development of the hydrogen bomb. George H. Gallup, *The Gallup Poll: Public Opinion, 1935–1971*, 3 volumes (New York: Random House, 1972), II, p. 888.

79. Memo, Loper to LeBaron, Feb 16, 1950 (TS), DDQI, R, p. 67C. Rosenberg gives his opinion regarding the impact of the Loper memo in his *JAH* article on the hydrogen bomb decision, p. 84.

80. Ltr., Johnson to Truman, Feb 24, 1950 (TS), DDQI, 1977, p. 304A.

81. *Oppenheimer* hearings, pp. 85, 313–15, 723, 746, 755; Teller and Brown, pp. 53–62.

82. For one of the more detailed and biased studies, see memo, Brooks to McNarney, Sep 27, 1948 (TS), Vandenberg papers, LOC, box 40.

83. Truman, *1950 Papers*, pp. 46–53.

84. Ibid.

85. Omar Bradley, "A Soldier's Farewell," *Saturday Evening Post*, Aug 22, 1953, p. 63; J. Lawton Collins, "*Lightning Joe*," p. 440.

86. Symington interview, p. 55.

87. US Cong., Senate, hearings before the Appropriations Committee, *Department of Defense Appropriations for 1951*, 81st Cong., 2nd sess. (Washington: GPO, 1950), pp. 8–20.

88. Ibid., p. 73. It should be remembered that the AEC budget was separate from the DOD budget.

89. Ibid., pp. 223–27.

90. Noel Parrish, *Behind the Sheltering Bomb*, p. 324; Truman, *1950 Papers*, p. 285.

91. Parrish interview.

VII. THE WAR FOR ASIA

1. For the events in Korea before 1950, see Leon Gordenker, *The United Nations and the Peaceful Unification of Korea* (The Hague: Martinus, 1959), Akira Iriye, *The Cold War in Asia* (Englewood Cliffs: Prentice-Hall, 1974), and Russell D. Buhite, *Soviet-American Relations in Asia, 1945–1954* (Norman: University of Oklahoma Press, 1981).

2. CIA Study, "Estimates of the Effects of the Soviet Possession of the Atomic Bomb upon the Security of the United States," Apr 6, 1950 (TS), in "CIA Reports, 1946–1976" collection, UPA, reel 3. MacArthur's staff also admitted among themselves that they had been caught by surprise. Gen Earle E. Partridge diary, Jun 26, 1950, AFSHRC, File 168.7014.1.

3. "Minutes of meeting between Acheson, Johnson and JCS," Apr 24, 1950 (TS), in "Official Conversations and Meetings of Dean Acheson, 1949–1953" (Frederick, Md.: UPA, 1980), reel 2.

4. This account of the Blair House meeting is taken from a lengthy memorandum written by Ambassador at Large Philip Jessup that is published in *Foreign Relations of the United States, 1950, Vol. VII: Korea* (Washington: GPO, 1976), pp. 156–61. Jessup's is one of the few contemporary accounts of this crucial meeting as well as of those that followed in the weeks ahead. Although the memoirs of participants are also available—Truman, Acheson, Bradley, and Collins—they were not published until several years later and were based, therefore, either on memory or personal notes that are not available. All substantially agree with Jessup's more detailed account.

5. *FRUS, 1950, Korea*, pp. 156–61.

6. Ibid. According to Jessup, the emphasis was placed on the Soviet Union, with China scarcely mentioned; it was assumed that the Kremlin had instigated the invasion. Finletter interview, p. 17.

7. Gen Omar Bradley, "U.S. Military Policy: 1950," *Reader's Digest*, Oct 1950, pp. 143–54.

8. Lt Gen Edward Almond, "United Nations Operations in Korea," speech to the Air University, Oct 8, 1951 (S), AFSHRC, File K239.716250–67(S); ltr., Weyland to Vandenberg, Oct 10, 1950 (S), Twining papers, USAFA, box 2; Lt Gen Edward Timberlake, interview with Burt Case, May 1965, AFHO, pp. 17–18. Timberlake, one of Vandenberg's classmates from A Company at West Point, was vice commander of the Fifth Air Force in Jun 1950.

9. Partridge diary, Jun 26, 1950. After World War II, the Air Force changed the "P" designation (pursuit), to "F" (fighter); hence, the F-51s were merely WWII-vintage Mustangs. The F-80 was the first operational jet in the American inventory, and the F-82 was an unusual and not altogether successful design—a twin-boomed Mustang that was flown by two pilots. Actually, the Fifth Air Force had just completed its annual Operational Readiness Inspection and was "flat on its back" when the invasion occurred. That Partridge was able to respond at all is remarkable. Ltr., O'Donnell to LeMay, Jul 10, 1950 (S), LeMay papers, LOC, box 65.

10. *FRUS, 1950, Korea*, p. 179.

11. Ibid.; James F. Schnabel and Robert J. Watson, *The Joint Chiefs of Staff and National Policy, Vol. III: The Korean War*, JCS Historical Study (Washington: JCS, 1979), p. 92.

12. Partridge USAFA interview, p. 39; Almond speech. When Johnson and Bradley visited Tokyo the week before the invasion, they had reiterated to MacArthur and his staff that US control of Formosa was "mandatory." No mention was made of Korea. Partridge diary, Jun 20, 1950.

13. *FRUS, 1950, Korea*, p. 217.

14. Ibid., pp. 240–41. It was also on the twenty-ninth that President Truman first referred to the Korean situation as a "police action." Truman, *1950 Papers*, pp. 502–506.

15. Msgs., Johnson to Vandenberg, Jul 9, 1950, Johnson to Norstad, Jul 10, 1950,

LeMay to Norstad, Jul 10, 1950, all TS and all in Vandenberg papers, LOC, box 56; msgs., BJSM to AMC, Jul 9, 1950 and MOD to BJSM, Jul 10, 1950 both TS and both in PRO, Air 20, File 8122. Maj Gen Leon Johnson was commander of the 3rd Air Division in England at the time. He had gained fame during World War II in leading the bombing raid against Ploesti in August 1943, for which he was awarded the Medal of Honor. A few months before the Korean crisis when Vandenberg and his son visited Europe, they were entertained by the Johnsons. Sandy was attracted to his hosts' daughter, Sue, and the two eventually married.

16. Msg., Vandenberg to Stratemeyer, Jul 3, 1950 (TS), Vandenberg papers, LOC, box 86; Lt Gen George E. Stratemeyer, personal diary, Jul 4, 1950, AFSHRC, File 168.7018–16.

17. Ltr., O'Donnell to LeMay, Jul 11, 1950 (S), LeMay papers, LOC, box 65; Stratemeyer diary, Jul 11, 1950.

18. Ltrs., Stratemeyer to Vandenberg, Jul 10 and Aug 7, 1950 (TS), Vandenberg papers, LOC, box 86.

19. Robert F. Futrell, *The United States Air Force in Korea, 1950–1953*, revised edition (Washington: GPO, 1984), p. 92.

20. Memo to Gen Bolte, including transcript of conversation between Gens MacArthur, Vandenberg, and Collins, Jul 17, 1950 (TS), DDQI, 1976, p. 243A; Stratemeyer diary, Jul 14, 1950; J. Lawton Collins, *War in Peacetime* (Boston: Houghton Mifflin, 1969), pp. 81–83. To repel the invaders was the stated US and UN objective at the time—not to unify Korea.

21. Stratemeyer diary, Jul 12, 1950; Partridge diary, Jul 13, 1950.

22. Bradley and Blair, pp. 654–55.

23. Msg., JCS to MacArthur, Aug 29, 1950 (TS), MacArthur Archives, RG 9, box 43; Schnabel and Watson, p. 215.

24. David Rees, *Korea: The Limited War* (New York: St. Martin's Press, 1964), p. 96.

25. RB-29 reconnaissance flights probed the borders of both China and the Soviet Union on a periodic and frequent basis, but did not usually penetrate their airspace. An exception was made on August 25, 1951, when an RB-29 overflew Shanghai on a photo reconnaissance mission. John T. Farquhar, "A Cold War in Flames: The Impact of Aerial Reconnaissance on US-Soviet Relations, 1948–1960," thesis, Creighton University, 1986, chapters 1 and 2, passim.

26. Msgs., Vandenberg to Stratemeyer, Sep 1, 1950 (TS), Stratemeyer to Vandenberg, Oct 10, 1950 (TS), both in Vandenberg papers, LOC, box 86; msgs., JCS to MacArthur, Aug 6, 29 and Oct 11, 1950, all TS and all in MacArthur Archives, RG 9, box 43. Partridge noted dryly in his diary that prosecuting the two "youngsters" would be difficult: the only witnesses were in Russia and were unavailable to testify! Partridge diary, Oct 31, 1950.

27. Memo, Eisenhower to Forrestal, Nov 14, 1947 (S), Vandenberg papers, LOC, box 97. Emphasis in original.

28. Ibid.

29. J. J. Lichman, *History of Continental Air Command, 1 Dec 1948 to 31 Dec 1949*, USAF Historical Study, (Maxwell AFB, Ala.: Air University, n.d.), pp. 7–9. Momyer referred to the escort mission as "an obsolete concept from the last war." Momyer later rose to the rank of general and commanded the Seventh Air Force and then TAC during the Vietnam War.

30. Ibid., p. 28; Lee interview. The perceived necessity for forming CONAC is well documented by Thomas A. Sturm, "Organizational Evolution," *Air Force*, Sep 1970, pp. 68–84. Gen Lee succeeded Quesada as TAC commander in 1948. Ralph D. Bald, *Air Force Participation in Joint Army-Air Force Training Exercises, 1947–1950*, USAF Historical Study No. 80 (Maxwell AFB, Ala.: Air University, 1955), p. 71. For an excellent discussion of TAC doctrine from 1945 to 1950 see Joseph W. Caddell, "Orphan of Unification: The Development of United States Air Force Tactical Air Power Doctrine, 1945–1950," diss. Duke University, 1984.

31. Quesada interview, p. 22.

32. Ltr., Quesada to Vandenberg, Feb 23, 1951, Vandenberg papers, LOC, box 22. The letter was addressed, "To the Chief of Staff," and signed, "E. R. Quesada." It was the only letter I have come across from a senior commander that was not addressed "Dear Van" and signed with only a first name.

33. Ltr., Alexander, Voorhees et al., to Royall, Apr 19, 1950 (TS), MacArthur Archives, RG 6, box 1.

34. MFR, "Tactical Support of the Ground Forces," by Larsen, May 5, 1949 (C), Twining papers, USAFA, box 2; ltr., Whitehead to Vandenberg, May 11, 1949 (S), Vandenberg papers, LOC, box 43; "USAF Forms Tactical Air Force," *Aviation Week*, Jul 25, 1949, p. 16.

35. Ltr., Lee to Vandenberg, Aug 17, 1949, Vandenberg papers, LOC, box 45; Bald, pp. 68–71. Lee later maintained that the Army was getting "plenty of joint training, but they always wanted more. They were never satisfied." Lee interview. "Final Report of PORTREX Exercise," Apr 10, 1950 (R), Lee papers, USAFA.

36. "Report of the USAF Board of Review for Tactical Operations, 10 June 1949—Oct 1949," n.d. (S), Quesada papers, LOC, box 6.

37. Memo, White to Vandenberg, May 4, 1950 (C), Vandenberg papers, LOC, box 47.

38. Ltrs., Doolittle to Vandenberg, Jul 26, 1950 (S), and Stratemeyer to Vandenberg, Jul 28, 1950 (S), both in Twining papers, USAFA, box 2.

39. Maj Gen Samuel Anderson, interview with Hugh N. Ahmann, Jun 28–Jul 1, 1976, AFHO, pp. 350–53; Weyland interview, pp. 189–91.

40. Ltr., Weyland to Vandenberg, Oct 10, 1950 (S), Twining papers, USAFA, box 12; Stratemeyer diary, Jul 14, 18, and Aug 1, 1950.

41. Memo, Ford to Vandenberg, Jul 9, 1951, Vandenberg papers, LOC, box 50; Almond speech; ltr., Almond to Sauce, Jan 25, 1951 (S), Almond papers, MacArthur Archives, RG 38, box 3.

42. Weyland to Vandenberg, Oct 12, 1950 (S), Twining papers, USAFA, box 2; Weyland interview, pp. 191–200.

43. Ltr., Weyland to Ridgway, Jul 9, 1950 (S), Ridgway papers, AHI, box 19; Stratemeyer diary, Jul 7, 10, and Aug 1, 1950.

44. Operations order, by MacArthur, Jul 15, 1950 (S), MacArthur Archives, RG 6, box 2; Stratemeyer diary, Oct 17, 1950; Partridge USAFA interview, p. 37.

45. Futrell, pp. 122–23, 128–29. James A. Field, Jr., *History of United States Naval Operations: Korea* (Washington: GPO, 1962), pp. 141–44. It was fortunate that the Navy's operational area kept them clear of Mig Alley; carrier fighters were no match for the Soviet-built MIG-15. Navy pilots shot down only sixteen enemy aircraft during the war, and their one ace was a "Corsair" pilot who claimed five "bedcheck Charlie" open-cockpit biplanes in mid-1953.

46. Ltrs., Doolittle to Vandenberg, Jul 26, 1950 (S), and Weyland to Vandenberg, Oct 10, 1950 (S), both in Twining papers, USAFA, box 2; Stratemeyer diary, Oct 2, 1950.

47. Msgs., Norstad to Stratemeyer, Aug 14 and 21, 1950 (C), Vandenberg papers, LOC, box 86.

48. Msg., Stratemeyer to Norstad, Aug 16, 1950 (TS), Vandenberg papers, LOC, box 86.

49. Memo of interview between MacArthur and Stearns, Nov 22, 1950 (S), Twining papers, USAFA, box 12. General Almond concurred in these views. Almond speech. Of interest, MacArthur had expressed much the same sentiments to his Army colleagues. Memos of conferences between MacArthur, Harriman, Norstad, Ridgway, and Almond, Aug 8, 1950, and between MacArthur, Collins, Sherman, and Almond, Aug 24, 1950, both TS and both in MacArthur Archives, RG 6, box 1.

50. Memo, Stearns to Finletter, Jan 16, 1951, Twining papers, USAFA, box 2.

51. Collins, p. 113; ltr., Doolittle to Vandenberg, Jul 26, 1950 (S), Twining papers, USAFA, box 2. Maj Gen William B. Kean of the 25th Division said in Sep 1950 that the Fifth Air Force had "saved his division many times." Futrell, p. 143. Lt Gen James Van Fleet said as late as Apr 1953 that his command had only 25 percent of the heavy artillery it had been authorized. Ibid., p. 537.

52. Ltr., Stratemeyer to Vandenberg, Jul 25, 1950 (S), Twining papers, USAFA, box 2; Futrell, p. 123. Walker used the term "astounding" to describe the cost of Marine air support.

53. GHQ UN Report, "Military Intelligence Summary," Nov 14, 1950, and memo, Rawlings to Twining, Nov 18, 1950, both TS and both in Twining papers, USAFA, box 2; "Has the Air Force Done Its Job in Korea?" *Air Force*, Mar 1951, pp. 41–43.

54. Stratemeyer diary, Aug 9, 1950; US Cong., House, hearings before the Appropriations Committee, *The Supplemental Appropriations Bill for 1951*, 81st Cong., 2nd sess. (Washington: GPO, 1950), p. 235.

55. Futrell, pp. 112, 133–34; ltr., Twining to LeMay, Jan 24, 1951 (TS), LeMay papers, LOC, box 197. Vandenberg said much the same thing during the MacArthur hearings of May 1951.

56. Memo, unsigned to Vandenberg, Apr 17, 1950 (S), Vandenberg papers, LOC, box 97. Emphasis in original.

57. Walter S. Poole, *The Joint Chiefs of Staff and National Policy, Vol. IV: 1950–1952*, JCS Historical Study (Washington: JCS, 1979), pp. 60–63.

58. Ferrell, *Off the Record*, pp. 189–93. The quotes were from Truman's diary entries on Sept 7 and 14, 1950.

59. Truman, *1950 Papers*, pp. 622–23.

60. Bradley and Blair, p. 552; Acheson, p. 441; Noel Parrish, *Behind the Sheltering Bomb*, p. 365. Harriman explained to Stewart Alsop—Parrish's source for the story—"after all, we Groton boys have to stick together." A similar explanation is given in Tyler Abell, *The Drew Pearson Diaries, 1949–1959* (New York: Holt, Rinehart and Winston, 1974), pp. 131–32, 350. Because Truman had written in his diary the week before that he intended to replace Johnson, it is unlikely that the political back-stabbing was the main reason for relief, but perhaps a last straw.

61. Stratemeyer diary, Nov 2, 1950; Partridge diary, Nov 2, 1950; memo, Stratemeyer to MacArthur, Nov 1950 (TS), MacArthur Archives, RG 9, box 1; *FRUS, 1950, Korea*, pp. 1076–77.

62. Msg., MacArthur to JCS, Nov 7, 1950 (TS), MacArthur Archives, RG 9, box 43; Stratemeyer diary, Nov 7, 1950. Stratemeyer had sent much the same message of impending doom to Vandenberg. Memo of conference between Acheson, Lovett, and Rusk Nov 6, 1950 (TS), in "Official Conversations of Dean Acheson" collection, reel 3; Schnabel and Watson, pp. 290–94. Vandenberg had directed Stratemeyer on Nov 6 not to attack targets within five miles of the Manchurian or Soviet borders. Msg., Vandenberg to Stratemeyer, Nov 6, 1950 (TS), Vandenberg papers, LOC, box 86.

63. Memo, Collins to JCS, Nov 20, 1950 (TS), in "Records of the JCS, Part II: The Far East" collection, reel 9; msgs., Stratemeyer to Vandenberg, Nov 7, 1950 (TS), and Vandenberg to Stratemeyer, Nov 30, 1950 (TS), both in Vandenberg papers, LOC, box 86; Stratemeyer diary, Nov 29, 1950.

64. Msgs., Stratemeyer to Vandenberg, Nov 30, 1950 (TS), and Vandenberg to Stratemeyer, Dec 15, 1950 (TS), Vandenberg papers, LOC, box 86; Stratemeyer diary, Dec 1, 1950.

65. *FRUS, 1950, Korea*, p. 1330. Actually, Vandenberg had advocated such punitive strikes as early as Nov 21. "NSC Meeting Notes," Nov 21, 1950 (TS), in "Official Conversations of Dean Acheson" collection, reel 3.

66. Msg., LeMay to Vandenberg, Dec 2, 1950 (TS), LeMay papers, LOC, box 196. In Mar 1951, Stratemeyer suggested to LeMay that he launch a B-36 strike against North Korea from American bases; *that* would send the Chinese a signal! LeMay declined; the logistical problems were too great. Ltrs., Stratemeyer to LeMay, Feb 6, 1951 (S) and LeMay to Stratemeyer, Mar 6, 1951 (S), both in Twining papers, LOC, box 54.

67. Msg., JCS to LeMay, Dec 6, 1950 (TS), LeMay papers, LOC, box 197.

68. Memo, Stratemeyer to MacArthur, Jan 9, 1951 (TS), MacArthur Archives, RG 9, box 1.

69. Bradley and Blair, p. 582; *New York Times*, Jun 1, 1951, p. 1. Since the first week

of the war, American leaders had pondered the question of what to do should the Soviet Union enter the war. Their conclusion: "the US should prepare to minimize its commitment in Korea and prepare to execute warplans." Memo, JCS to Johnson, Jul 10, 1950 (TS), DDQI, 1975, p. 272D.

70. Truman, *1950 Papers*, p. 727. Later in the day, Charles G. Ross, the presidential press secretary, clarified Truman's statement: "Any nation possessing atomic weapons would have to consider their use under certain circumstances, but only the president would authorize American employment of them. This the President has not done." Hewlett and Duncan, II, p. 533.

71. Roger M. Andrus, ed., *Forging the Atomic Shield: Excerpts from the Office Diary of Gordon E. Dean* (Chapel Hill: University of North Carolina Press, 1987), pp. 137–38; Hewlett and Duncan, II, p. 539.

72. Daily Staff Digest, Jul 20, 1950 (TS), NA, RG 341, LDS File, box 24; London *Times*, Sep 2, 1950, p. 5; John H. Scrivner, Jr., "Pioneer into Space: A Biography of Major General Orvil A. Anderson," diss., University of Oklahoma, 1971, chap. 11. Since early June, both private observers and public officials had discussed the efficacy of using atomic weapons in Korea; virtually all agreed that they would be neither necessary nor desirable. See especially "Atomic Weapons and the Korean War," *Bulletin of the Atomic Scientists*, 6, No. 7 (Jul 1950), pp. 194, 217; White House memo, Jul 6, 1950 (TS), DDQI, 1979, p. 471C. Vandenberg was opposed to the use of atomic bombs at this stage of the war. He feared that the mountainous terrain and primitive industrial base of North Korea would mitigate the effectiveness of the bomb. Atomic weapons were nearly as important for psychological reasons as for military ones. Vandenberg did not wish to squander his psychological chips. Nichols, p. 280. In April 1950, Kenney had written Vandenberg urging a preemptive strike on the Soviet Union: "It would not be preventive war, because we are already at war." But Kenney's remarks were made in private, through channels; Anderson's were not. Ltr., Kenney to Vandenberg, Apr 29, 1950 (TS), AFSHRC, File 168.15–10.

73. Memo, Collins to Vandenberg, Nov 21, 1950 (S), Vandenberg papers, LOC, box 83.

74. Msg., Collins to MacArthur, Nov 16, 1950 (TS), Twining papers, LOC, box 12.

75. Ltr., Vandenberg to Collins, n.d., but probably around Nov 25, 1950, Vandenberg papers, LOC, box 83.

76. Ltr., Vandenberg to Cannon, Sep 28, 1950 (TS), Vandenberg papers, LOC, box 86; ltr., Leach to Vandenberg, Nov 22, 1950 (S), Twining papers, USAFA, box 12; "Semiannual Report of the Secretary of Defense, Jan 1 to Jun 30, 1951," p. 200.

77. Schnabel and Watson, pp. 345–46; *FRUS, 1950, Korea*, pp. 1259–60.

78. Matthew B. Ridgway, *The Korean War* (Garden City: Doubleday, 1964), p. 62. Ridgway had been the director of athletics when Vandenberg was a cadet.

79. Schnabel and Watson, pp. 366, 377–80; *FRUS, 1950, Korea*, pp. 1439–40; MFR, by unsigned JCS representative, Dec 1, 1950 (TS), DDQI, 1975, p. 73B.

80. *FRUS, 1950, Korea*, pp. 1570–73

81. *FRUS, 1951, Vol. VII: Korea* (Washington: GPO, 1983), pp. 67–68; MFR, by Acheson, Jan 12, 1951 (TS), in "Official Conversations of Dean Acheson" collection, reel 5.

82. Noel Parrish, *Behind the Sheltering Bomb*, p. 366. The official report of this visit, signed by Collins and Vandenberg, states that MacArthur spoke "with some emotion" about his predicament and the possibility of evacuation. Memo, Collins and Vandenberg to JCS, Jan 19, 1951 (TS), in "Records of the JCS: The Far East" collection, reel 2.

83. Stratemeyer and Partridge diaries, Jan 16, 1951; Maj Gen Edward Timberlake diary, Jan 16, 1950, AFSHRC, File 168.7077; undated news clipping, Vandenberg, Jr., collection; US Cong., Senate, hearings before the Armed Services and Foreign Relations Committees, *The Military Situation in the Far East*, 82nd Cong., 1st sess. (Washington: GPO, 1950), p. 329. Gen Marshall later referred to Vandenberg's exploit as a "remarkable reconnaissance." The Army official historian was less gracious, saying that Vandenberg showed great courage but poor judgment. James F. Schnable, *Policy and Direction: The First Year* in *United States Army in the Korean War* series (Washington: GPO, 1972), p. 327.

84. Memo, Collins to Marshall, Jan 19, 1951 (TS), Vandenberg papers, LOC, box 83; Acheson, p. 516.

85. *FRUS, 1951, Korea*, p. 104.

86. This account appears to be from the diary kept by Gen Bradley at the time that he referred to during the MacArthur hearings in May 1951. It was originally classified top secret and is located in the Vandenberg papers, LOC, box 83. Bradley's aide later said that after the JCS meeting of Sunday, Bradley told him they were all fed up with MacArthur's "petulance and ill-tempered complaints." MacArthur also seemed to be losing confidence in himself and was growing jealous of Ridgway's success in stopping the Communist advance. Schnabel and Watson, p. 542.

87. Bradley and Blair, pp. 632–33; MFR, by Acheson re: phone conversation with Marshall, Mar 24, 1951 (TS), in "Official Conversations of Dean Acheson" collection, reel 5.

88. Brig Gen Noel F. Parrish, interview with James Hasdorff, June 10–14, 1974, AFHO, p. 213. All of the chiefs were careful to point out later that they did not *recommend* removal, but rather *concurred* in the recommendation made by their superior, Secretary Marshall.

89. Ibid. Actually, President Truman had directed the JCS to meet with Harriman, Acheson, and Marshall to "discuss and agree on objectives and procedures to follow in preparation for the MacArthur hearings." The president wanted no loose cannons before the Senate committee. Memo, Carter to Bradley, Apr 23, 1951 (S), Bradley papers, NA, box 3. Once the hearings began, they were carefully orchestrated by the Democratic senators. After they testified, a Senate aide would debrief the individuals on their performance and what steps should be taken to clear up any "fly specks" in the administration's case. Memos, Matthews to Bradley, May 15, 1951, and Matthews to JCS, May 23, 1951 (C), both in Bradley papers, NA, box 3.

90. *Far East* hearings, Vandenberg: pp. 1391, 1419, 1441–43; Marshall: pp. 325, 416–17; Bradley: pp. 878–81; Collins: p. 1187; Sherman: p. 1537. It would seem that Vandenberg was also the main proponent of this view at the Apr 8 meeting; at least none of the others used this as a justification for MacArthur's dismissal before the Senate.

91. Ibid., pp. 1404, 1461. MacArthur planned to widen the war by using atomic bombs to destroy Manchurian airfields, sow radioactive waste across the northern portion of Korea, and employ Chinese Nationalist troops. For an interesting examination of this strategy, see Edgar O'Ballance, "The MacArthur Plan," *Royal United Services Institute Journal*, 110, No. 639 (1965), pp. 248–53.

92. *Far East* hearings, pp. 1378–80, 1393–94, 1399–1400, 1447, 1502. This line of thought was not simply for public consumption. At the same time, Vandenberg presented a classified lecture to the National War College that used the same arguments against an expansion of the war. May 25, 1951 (S), Twining papers, USAFA, box 19.

93. *Far East* hearings, uncensored transcript, pp. 3690–94, 3705, 3945–52. Official administration policy was also opposed to hot pursuit. Ltr., Acheson to Marshall, Nov 21, 1950 (TS), DDQI, 1975, p. 73A.

94. Stratemeyer diary, Dec 23, 1950. Emphasis in original.

95. Ibid., Oct 21, 1950, for the DFC incident; Nov 13, 1950, for the Medal of Honor; on Apr 3, 1951, MacArthur told Stratemeyer that George Marshall "has gone nuts"; on Apr 4, 1951, Stratemeyer informed newsmen that he agreed with MacArthur: "We can't win the war with our hands tied behind our backs"; Apr 6, 1951, was the meeting with Congressmen William J. Bryan and O. K. Armstrong; on Apr 25, 1951, Vandenberg directed Stratemeyer to refrain from commenting on the war, and on May 20, 1951, Stratemeyer suffered a heart attack.

96. *Far East* hearings, pp. 1399, 1426, 1430–35, 1494–96.

97. Ibid., pp. 1434–35.

98. Ibid., p. 1427. MacArthur had told the senators earlier that month that the quality of the air support given to his troops "has perhaps never been equaled in the history of modern war," p. 309. Unwittingly, the senior North Korean delegate at the truce talks, Maj Gen Nam Il, gave this unsolicited endorsement for American air power: "Without the

support of the indiscriminate bombing and bombardment by your air and naval forces, your ground forces would have long ago been driven out of the Korean peninsula by our powerful and battle-skilled ground forces." Futrell, p. 372.

99. *Far East* hearings, pp. 1398–99, 1430–32, 1495–96.

100. Ibid., p. 1384.

101. Ibid., p. 1385.

102. Ibid., p. 1417.

103. Ibid., pp. 1470–71.

104. Behind the scenes, the JCS often debated an expansion of the war, but always resolved in the end to keep the war limited. Memo, Finletter to Truman, Jun 26, 1951 (TS), DDQI, 1979, p. 372D; memo, JCS to Marshall, Jul 13, 1951 (TS), DDQI, 1975, p. 18A; memo, JCS to Lovett, Nov 3, 1951 (TS), DDQI, 1975, p. 18C.

105. Ltr., Weyland to Vandenberg, Oct 10, 1950 (S), Twining papers, USAFA, box 2.

106. "The U.S. Air Force and Its Boss Are Ready," *Newsweek*, Feb 19, 1951, p. 24. Another of Vandenberg's favorite analogies was to compare interdiction to trying to stop a water sprinkler by putting your fingers over all the holes; it may succeed, but you'll get awfully wet. It's better just to turn off the spigot. Interview with Vandenberg by Martin Hayden, Sep 20, 1950, Twining papers, USAFA, box 12.

107. "An interview with General Vandenberg," *Aviation Age*, Feb 1952, p. 32. One study maintains that STRANGLE cut the total truck production of China and the Soviet Union by at least 15 percent. FEAF Operations Analysis, "An Evaluation of the Interdiction Program in Korea," Nov 19, 1951 (S), AFSHRC, File K720.3104–49; Futrell, p. 407. Actually, enemy inactivity made STRANGLE appear ineffective because the Communists were slowly able to stockpile supplies for the few occasions when they took the offensive. For an excellent though critical review of the Korean interdiction campaign, see Edmund Dews and Felix Kozaczka, "Air Interdiction Lessons from Past Campaigns," RAND Note No. N-1743 PA&E, 1981.

108. Stratemeyer diary, Aug 14, 1950; msgs., Vandenberg to Stratemeyer, Aug 20, 1950, and Nov 15, 1950, both TS and both in Vandenberg papers, LOC, box 86.

109. Ltr., Twining to LeMay, Jan 24, 1951 (TS), LeMay papers, LOC, box 197; Futrell, pp. 325–31, 453–61; Joe G. Taylor, *Development of Night Air Operations, 1941–1952*. USAF Historical Study No. 92 (Maxwell AFB, Ala.: Air Force Archives, 1953), passim; Gen James Van Fleet, *Rail Transport and the Winning of Wars* (Washington: Association of American Railroads, 1956), passim.

110. Memo of mtg., Secretary of State [Acheson], June 27, 1951 (TS), Acheson papers, Truman Library; Vandenberg interview in *Aviation Age*, p. 31; Hoyt S. Vandenberg, "Air Force Hasn't Been Doing the Job It Can Do in Korea," *U.S. News & World Report*, Nov 30, 1951, pp. 16–19.

111. Futrell, p. 404; ltr., Kelly to LeMay, Oct 29, 1951 (S), LeMay papers, LOC, box 65.

112. Futrell, pp. 692–95.

113. *FRUS, 1952–54, Vol. XV: Korea* (Washington: GPO, 1984), p. 121; *Far East* hearings, uncensored transcript, p. 3625; SITTREP No. 6, Jul 4, 1950 (S), DDQI, 1979, p. 31D; Schnabel and Watson, p. 253.

114. Vandenberg, "Air Force in Korea," pp. 16–19.

115. Memo, Grussendorf to Vandenberg, Nov 16, 1951 (S), Vandenberg papers, LOC, box 83; ltr., Kelly to LeMay, Nov 7, 1951 (S), LeMay papers, LOC, box 65; London *Times*, Nov 22, 1951, p. 4.

116. Futrell, pp. 477–80.

117. Msg., MacArthur to JCS, Feb 26, 1951 (TS), MacArthur Archives, RG 9, box 43; JIC Report 557/1, Feb 15, 1951, and memo, Vandenberg to JCS, May 1, 1952, both TS and both in "Records of the JCS: The Far East" collection, reel 10; *FRUS, Korea, 1952–54*, pp. 52–54, 130.

118. *FRUS, 1952–54, Korea*, pp. 356–57.

119. Futrell, pp. 483–89.

120. Ibid.; *FRUS, 1952–54, Korea*, pp. 352–54.

121. Vandenberg and other military leaders had been urging such attacks almost since the beginning of the war. Ltr., O'Donnell to LeMay, Aug 20, 1950 (S), LeMay papers, LOC, box 65; memo, Edwards to Twining, Jan 31, 1951 (S), Twining papers, LOC, box 54; "US Objectives and Courses of Action in Korea," Dec 7, 1951 (TS), in "Documents of the National Security Council: First Supplement" (Frederick, Md.: UPA, 1981), reel 1; MFR, conversation between Acheson and Lovett, Feb 19, 1951 (TS), in "Official Conversations of Dean Acheson" collection, reel 5; memo, Vandenberg to JCS, Aug 10, 1951 (TS), in "Records of the JCS: The Far East" collection, reel 10.

122. *FRUS, Korea, 1952–54*, gives an exhaustive account of these discussions. Vandenberg was adamantly opposed to forced repatriation, pp. 41–42, 68–69.

123. Msgs., Vandenberg to JCS, Mar 14, 1952 and Jun 12, 1952, both TS and both in "Records of the JCS: The Far East" collection, reel 10.

124. Daily Staff Digests, Jan 16, 25, and Dec 4, 1950 (TS), all in NA, RG 341, LDS File, boxes 10 and 24; memo, Twining to Air Materiel Command, Jan 15, 1952 (TS), Twining papers, LOC, box 56.

125. *FRUS, 1952–54, Korea*, pp. 527–32. The argument that such weapons were used in Korea on an experimental basis is made by Stephen L. Endicott, "Germ Warfare and Plausible Denial," *Modern China*, 5, No. 1, Jan 1979, pp. 79–104.

126. *FRUS, 1952–54, Korea*, p. 1062. The JCS had discussed the issue among themselves in March of that year. "Future Courses of Action in Connection with the Situation in Korea," JCS memo, Mar 28, 1953 (TS), DDQI, 1981, p. 165A. The contrast between this proposed strategy with that of gradual response later employed in the Vietnam War "Rolling Thunder" campaign is striking.

127. *FRUS, 1952–54, Korea*, p. 1069. The issue of whether Eisenhower made such threats to China has been debated for years. The most recent, authoritative, and plausible treatment of the subject is by Edward C. Keefer, "President Eisenhower and the End of the Korean War," *Diplomatic History*, 10, No. 3 (Summer 1986), pp. 267–89. Keefer's conclusion: "Ultimately, Eisenhower ended the war by accepting the possibility of atomic warfare and even global conflict."

128. *FRUS, 1951, Korea*, pp. 51, 367–68.

129. *FRUS, 1952–54, Korea*, pp. 33, 52–54.

130. Ibid., pp. 480–81.

131. Hoyt S. Vandenberg, speech to the Air War College, May 6, 1953 (TS), AFHO File K239.716253–126. It is also significant that at this same time the administration was considering aid to the French in Indochina. Vandenberg was adamantly opposed to such schemes; he wished to end one war, not begin another. *Foreign Relations of the United States, 1952–1954, Vol. XIII: Indochina* (Washington: GPO, 1982), pp. 496–502, 518.

VIII. TWILIGHT

1. Norstad and Parrish interviews; Finletter interview, p. 19; *Newsweek*, May 10, 1952, p. 30. One of Finletter's books, *Power and Policy* (New York: Harcourt, Brace, 1954) posited that only American strategic air power could protect the West from Soviet aggression.

2. Parrish interview with author; McKee interview, p. 32.

3. Norstad, Smith, Parrish, and McHugh interviews.

4. Kuter interview, pp. 532–33. Gen Norstad stated that thereafter when a deputy was called into Finletter's office, several would always go along as well; this effectively defeated the secretary's "divide and conquer" attempts. Norstad interview.

5. *Aviation Week*, Jun 18, 1951, p. 13; *Washington Daily News*, Apr 21, 1950, p. 1; msg., Vandenberg to all commanders, Jun 19, 1951, Vandenberg papers, LOC, box 72; *New York Times*, Jun 23, 1951, p. 7. Vandenberg was aware of his potential predicament soon after taking over as chief, asking an aide what his options would be at the end of his statutory four-year tour. Memo, Boatner to Vandenberg, Dec 1, 1948, Vandenberg papers, LOC,

box 79. An undated news clipping in the Vandenberg, Jr., collection even suggested that Vandenberg would be selected as ambassador to Moscow.

6. *New York Times*, Mar 1, 1952, p. 6; "Vandenberg-LeMay-Twining Team Puts Air Force Back on Top," *U.S. News & World Report*, Mar 14, 1952, pp. 62–64; *Aviation Week*, Mar 10, 1952, p. 15; *Washington Post*, Feb 21, 1952, p. 1.

7. *Army, Navy, Air Force Journal*, Mar 8, 1952, p. 828; *New York Times*, Mar 1, 1952, p. 6; James Haggerty, "Will Vandenberg be Reappointed?" *American Aviation*, Mar 3, 1952, p. 15. The London *Times* scoffed that the president's decision was merely a refusal to make a decision. The contenders for Vandenberg's position were too powerful to risk slighting one of them, and so Truman compromised and stuck with the one man respected and acceptable to all parties. London *Times*, Mar 3, 1952, p. 3.

8. *Aviation Week*, Mar 17, 1952, p. 12; *Washington Daily News*, Mar 4, 1952; *Washington Post*, Mar 4, 1952.

9. *Army, Navy, Air Force Journal*, May 3, 1952, p. 1077.

10. Vandenberg daily calendar, May 6 and 7, 1952, Vandenberg papers, LOC, box 5; memo, Armstrong to Twining, Jul 18, 1952 (C), Twining papers, LOC, box 122; msg., Twining to all commanders, May 7, 1952, Vandenberg papers, LOC, box 87; record of telephone conversation between Twining and Symington, May 8, 1952, Twining papers, LOC, box 1. In a telephone conversation with Gen Joseph Cannon on May 8, Twining said: "He [Van] has had an inkling for some time, but you know him, you can't get him to go to a doctor. Said he hasn't had a physical for so long he was afraid to take one." Record of telephone conversation between Twining and Cannon, May 8, 1952, Twining papers, LOC, box 1.

11. "Generals Shift. . . Big Bombers Lose Favor," *Business Week*, Aug 16, 1952, p. 35; memo, Craig to Twining, Nov 15, 1951, Twining papers, LOC, box 55; msg., HQUSAF to All Major Commands (ALMAJCOM), May 15, 1952, LeMay papers, LOC, box 60. Brig Gen Godfrey McHugh, Vandenberg's aide, recalled that Mrs. LeMay was at the Twining quarters measuring windows for drapes when word was announced that there would be no transfer after all. McHugh interview. Kuter was deputy chief of staff for personnel at the time.

12. Ltr., Vandenberg to Truman, Jun 25, 1952, Vandenberg papers, LOC, box 77; ltr., Norstad to Vandenberg, Sep 8, 1952, Vandenberg papers, LOC, box 87; *New York Times*, Aug 26, 1952, p. 10; *Air Force Times*, Dec 13, 1952, p. 31.

13. NSC-68, Apr 14, 1950 (TS), copy in *FRUS, 1950, Foreign and Economic Policy*, pp. 236–292.

14. Poole, pp. 6–7.

15. Poole, p. 8; Paul Y. Hammond, "NSC-68: Prologue to Rearmament," in *Strategy, Politics and Defense Budgets* (New York: Columbia University Press, 1962), pp. 287–89.

16. "NSC-68," p. 4.

17. Ibid., p. 44.

18. Ibid., pp. 57–59. Poole states that NSC-68 called for nearly tripling the annual defense budget to $30 billion, but that figure is nowhere mentioned in the original document.

19. *FRUS, 1950, Foreign and Economic Policy*, pp. 298–306.

20. Hammond, "NSC-68," p. 331. Much of this debate is recounted in *FRUS, 1950, Foreign and Economic Policy*, pp. 307–24.

21. Acheson, p. 374.

22. Poole, pp. 37–42; memo, Finletter to Vandenberg, Mar 6, 1951 (TS-Cosmic), Vandenberg papers, LOC, box 88.

23. Poole, pp. 44–46; US Cong., House, hearings before the Appropriations Committee, *Second Supplemental Appropriations Bill for 1951*, 81st Cong., 2nd sess. (Washington: GPO, 1950), p. 10.

24. Poole, p. 59.

25. Ibid., p. 63.

26. Ibid., pp. 67–70; "Short Summary of the Development of US Air Power Since the End of World War II," Jan 11, 1953 (S), DDQI, 1976, p. 239E.

27. Memos, Fetcheler to JCS, Sep 12, 1951 (TS), and Collins to JCS, Sep 13, 1951 (TS), both in Vandenberg papers, LOC, box 88.

28. Poole, pp. 95–99; memo, Finletter to Marshall, Jul 16, 1951 (TS), Twining papers, LOC, box 122; memo, Finletter to Vandenberg, Jul 11, 1951 (TS), Vandenberg papers, LOC, box 83.

29. Glenn Snyder, "The 'New Look' of 1953," in *Strategy, Politics and Defense Budgets* (New York: Columbia University Press, 1962), p. 384; memo, JCS to Lovett, Oct 3, 1951 (TS), DDQI, 1976, p. 160B.

30. Snyder, p. 386.

31. Nathan F. Twining, *Neither Liberty nor Safety* (New York: Holt, Rinehart, and Winston, 1966), p. 39.

32. This view is argued by Donald J. Mrozek in "A New Look at 'Balanced Forces': Defense Continuities from Truman to Eisenhower," *Military Affairs*, 38, No. 4 (Dec 1974), pp. 145–51.

33. Poole, p. 109.

34. Ibid., p. 112; Kolodziej, pp. 153-56.

35. Kolodziej, p. 157.

36. Memo, JSPG to JCS, Jan 4, 1952 (TS), DDQI, 1976, p. 157A.

37. Poole, p. 113; "Summary of Air Power."

38. Memo, Finletter to Vandenberg, Jul 16, 1952 (C), Vandenberg papers, LOC, box 84; memo, JCS to Lovett, Mar 11, 1952 (TS), DDQI, 1977, p. 291A.

39. Gen Hoyt S. Vandenberg, "Air Power Build-Up Only Half Completed," *Planes*, Dec 1952, pp. 1–3.

40. Memo, Vandenberg to JCS, Oct 15, 1952 (TS), Twining papers, USAFA Archives, box 5. In August 1951, Vandenberg had pointedly requested from the CNO a detailed report of the Navy's atomic capability. The Navy had consistently claimed they could deliver atomic weapons more effectively and cheaply than the Air Force, but had supplied little proof of that assertion. Admiral Fetcheler's response was interesting in that he proposed a "retardation" mission for atomic capable Navy aircraft, to slow down a Soviet advance through Europe by employing tactical atomic weapons. Memo, Vandenberg to JCS, Aug 22, 1951 (TS), DDQI, 1976, p. 248B; memo, Fetcheler to JCS, Sep 7, 1951 (TS), DDQI, 1977, p. 292D.

41. Daily Staff Digest, Sep 12, 1950 (TS), NA, RG 341, LDS File, box 24; "History of Project Lincoln," Dec 10, 1952 (S), AFSHRC, File K243.04-2.

42. MFR, by Fairchild, Sep 30, 1949 (S), Fairchild papers, LOC, box 1; "History of Project Lincoln."

43. "Final Report of Project Charles," Aug 1, 1951 (S), AFSHRC, File 146.02-4.

44. Memo, Zacharias to Hill, Jun 13, 1952, and "Agenda for Project," Aug 26, 1952 (R), both in Oppenheimer papers, LOC, box 187.

45. *Oppenheimer* hearings, pp. 597–600.

46. "Project Vista Interim Report No. 1," Mar 7, 1952 (S), AFSHRC, File K146.003-137.

47. "Sworn affadavit by J. R. Oppenheimer," May 12, 1954, Oppenheimer papers, LOC, box 218; *Oppenheimer* hearings, pp. 496– 98. Norstad had advised Vandenberg of the implications of tactical nuclear weapons in Aug 1951, saying that the Air Force should initiate a study "before someone else does and produces results we don't like." Msg., Norstad to Vandenberg, Aug 25, 1951 (TS), Vandenberg papers, LOC, box 86. Norstad apparently was given the idea of an Air Force study by Brig Gen Roscoe Wilson, the atomic energy expert on the Air Staff. Memo, Wilson to Norstad, May 31, 1950 (TS), DDQI, 1978, p. 361C.

48. *Oppenheimer* hearings, p. 754; York, p. 139. Vista was funded largely by the Air Force, but its findings were surreptitiously briefed to Gen Eisenhower, the NATO commander. Vandenberg and Finletter were outraged by this, the secretary exclaiming that he had been "knifed in the back." To counter this ploy, Vandenberg had Norstad thoroughly brief both the Vista scientists and Eisenhower on official Air Force doc-

trine regarding strategic air power. *Oppenheimer* hearings, pp. 749–50, 892; Stern, pp. 182–83.

49. For the semiofficial Air Force reaction to Lincoln and Vista, see "The Truth About Our Air Defense," *Air Force*, May 1953. For the opposing view see, Stewart Alsop and Ralph E. Lapp, "We Can Smash the Red A-Bombers," *Saturday Evening Post*, Mar 21, 1953.

50. Gen Hoyt S. Vandenberg, "Address to the Field Officers Course," May 6, 1953, AFSHRC, File K239.716253–126, pp. 13–15.

51. Ambrose, pp. 86–91; Robert H. Ferrell, ed., *The Eisenhower Diaries* (New York: W. W. Norton, 1981), pp. 235–36; "Summary of Air Power." Defense Secretary Charles E. Wilson was the former president of General Motors and was referred to as "Engine Charlie," to distinguish him from Charles E. Wilson, head of the Defense Production Authority, who was the former president of General Electric and thus called "Electric Charlie."

52. "Actions Limiting Air Force Programs," Mar 29, 1953 (TS); memo, Paul to Vandenberg, Jun 2, 1953 (TS), both in Vandenberg papers, LOC, box 48; memo, JCS to Wilson, Mar 19, 1953 (TS), DDQI, 1977, p. 291C; US Cong., Senate, hearings before the Armed Services Committee, *Joint Chiefs of Staff Nominations*, 83rd Cong., 1st sess. (Washington: GPO, 1953), pp. 32–34.

53. Kolodziej, pp. 169–70. An excellent discussion of the entire budget battle of 1953 can be found in Robert J. Watson, *The Joint Chiefs of Staff and National Policy, Vol. V, 1953–1954*, JCS Historical Study (Washington: JCS, 1986), chapter 3.

54. There are several letters between Eisenhower and Vandenberg located in the Eisenhower papers concerning invitations to football games, parties, and other social events. Although clearly a superior-subordinate relationship, it seemed to be a warm one nevertheless. Eisenhower papers, Eisenhower Library, Abilene, Kansas.

55. Parrish interview with author. Parrish was Vandenberg's speech writer.

56. US Cong., Senate, hearings before the Appropriations Committee, *Department of Defense Appropriations for 1954*, 83rd Cong., 1st sess. (Washington: GPO, 1953), pp. 218–21. Vandenberg also testified before the House in March on the budget and again in June, the week following the controversial Senate hearings. His basic thrust was much the same on all three occasions, but he was most vocal before the Senate. US Cong., House, hearings before the Appropriations Committee, *Department of the Air Force Appropriations Bill for 1954*, 83rd Cong., 1st sess. (Washington: GPO, 1953), pp. 3–37, 957–89.

57. Senate hearings, *Department of Defense Appropriations for 1954*, pp. 230–31.

58. Ibid., p. 232.

59. Ibid., pp. 232–36.

60. Ibid., pp. 265, 368–70.

61. *Newsweek*, Jun 15, 1953, p. 26. When completing testimony before the House the following week, Democratic Congressman George H. Mahon paid him an even more glowing tribute: "No military officer who has appeared before us has been more unbending and devout and conscientious and courageous in expressing his view, regardless of where the chips might fall, than you have. I am glad we can live in a country where we can do things like that and have officers who perform like that." House hearings, *Department of the Air Force Appropriations Bill for 1954*, p. 989. Vandenberg admitted, however, that the hearings were difficult, writing Shedd: "Brother, was it rough!" Ltr., Hoyt to Shedd, Jun 18, 1953, Vandenberg papers, LOC, box 77.

62. *Air Force Times*, Jun 13, 1953, p. 4.

63. *Washington Star*, Apr 2, 1954, p. 1; E. Bruce Geelhold, *Charles E. Wilson and Controversy at the Pentagon, 1953–1957* (Detroit: Wayne State University Press, 1979), pp. 74–76.

64. Hoyt S. Vandenberg, speech to National Press Club, Jun 22, 1953, copy in Vandenberg papers, LOC, box 91. After his retirement, Vandenberg apologized for his strident remarks, but commented: "The moral thing in our democracy, I hope, will always be for a responsible military man to respond candidly when Congress asks his opinion, even though his opinions may not be comforting." *Air Force*, May 1954, p. 32.

65. *Army, Navy, Air Force Journal*, Jul 4, 1953, p. 1342.

66. Col Ernest E. Gossett, ltr. to the author, Dec 18, 1984.

67. Msg., Vandenberg to all commanders, Jun 30, 1953, Kuter papers, USAFA Archives, reel 8.

68. Vandenberg, Jr., interview; Burt correspondence; ltr., Vandenberg to Shedd, May 28, 1953, Vandenberg papers, LOC, box 77.

69. Vandenberg, Jr., interview. Collins VandenBerg died in Dec 1953 at age eighty-four, but Hoyt was never told.

70. "Information on funeral for Gen Vandenberg," Apr 2, 1954, Vandenberg papers, LOC, box 75. *New York Times*, Apr 6, 1954, p. 29. Twenty years later Brig Gen Hoyt Vandenberg, Jr., was selected as commandant of cadets at the Air Force Academy.

71. Futrell, *Ideas, Concepts, Doctrine*, p. 332. Maj Gen Hugh Knerr was a protégé of Gen Frank Andrews and was the first chief of staff of the GHQ Air Force in 1935. A zealous strategic bombing advocate, in 1942 he wrote a strong plea for an independent air force, *The Fight for Air Power*. Because such thinking was contrary to official Army policy at the time, he could not take credit for his work; instead, popular journalist William Bradford Huie appeared as the author.

72. Tris Coffin, "Vandenberg Runs Our Air Force Team," *Colliers*, Jul 1951, p. 99.

73. Ltr., Eisenhower to Butcher, Dec 10, 1942 (S) located in Chandler and Galambos, II, pp. 822–25. Also quoted in James, *A Time for Giants*, p. 273.

74. Futrell, *Ideas, Concepts, Doctrine*, p. 277; Lt Gen Laurence Kuter, "Air Force Headquarters," lecture at Air War College, Feb 23, 1949, Kuter papers, USAFA Archives, reel 12; msgs., Vandenberg to Norstad, Feb 2, 1952 (TS), and Norstad to Vandenberg, Feb 4, 1952 (TS), both in Vandenberg papers, LOC, box 87. The incident concerned a member of Norstad's staff who had ignored a directive from then Maj Gen Kuter, the deputy chief of staff for personnel.

75. Coffin, p. 99.

76. LeMay interview, p. 32; Johnson interview.

77. Rawlings, p. 67.

78. Kuter, "Air Force Headquarters."

79. Coffin, p. 99.

80. McKee interview, p. 79.

81. Ltr., Vandenberg to Chidlaw, n.d., but probably late 1950, Twining papers, LOC, box 121. This was not a subtle attempt to put Chidlaw out to pasture; in mid-1951 Vandenberg promoted him to full general while giving him the Air Defense Command.

82. Vandenberg, Jr., interview; Clay Blair, *Beyond Courage* (New York: Ballantine Books, 1955), pp. 75–77.

83. Ltr., Kuter to Vandenberg, Sep 17, 1953, Kuter papers, USAFA Archives, reel 4. Note that this letter was written before Vandenberg entered the hospital.

84. Gen Nathan Twining, speech to Mid Pines Club, May 8, 1954, copy in Twining papers, USAFA Archives, box 15; Wedemeyer, ltr. to the author, Aug 8, 1983.

85. London *Times*, Apr 11, 1954, p. 11.

86. James C. Derieux, "What Shifts Will Eisenhower Make in Our Military Setup?" *Colliers*, Dec 27, 1952, p. 32. Arthur Vandenberg, Jr., President-elect Eisenhower's appointments secretary, confided to his cousin, Hoyt, Jr., that Eisenhower had intended to appoint Gen Vandenberg as next JCS chairman. Hoyt Vandenberg, Jr., interview. Brig Gen Noel Parrish recalled Vandenberg's political ambitions, remarking that when the chief was to give a speech in Milwaukee he specifically asked for the text to be typed in extra large print so he would not have to wear his glasses. He expected Vandenberg to run for the Senate in his home state of Wisconsin. Parrish interview. Ltr., Kress to Vandenberg, Aug 23, 1952, Vandenberg papers, LOC, box 27, for talk of a fifth star. This proposal was not far-fetched; the three former chairmen—Leahy, Eisenhower, and Bradley—had all held that rank, and Vandenberg was also a recognized war hero.

87. Vandenberg, "Address to Field Officers Course." Emphasis in original.

BIBLIOGRAPHY

MANUSCRIPT COLLECTIONS

The Library of Congress contains the papers of several noted airmen; the most important for this study are those of Hoyt Vandenberg. This collection contains ninety-seven document boxes, of which approximately half are listed as classified and kept in the vault. Very little of the material is actually still sensitive, however, and the library has been supportive in getting relevant documents downgraded. There are, unfortunately, large gaps in the Vandenberg papers; virtually nothing before 1944 and very little before 1947. There is no reference to his tenure as Army G-2 or director of the Central Intelligence Group. There is also very little information dealing with atomic energy, special weapons development, or technology. These topics have been researched with material from other archives, interviews, correspondence, and secondary sources.

Other collections examined at the LOC:

Stewart and Joseph Alsop
Gen Henry H. Arnold
Gen James H. Doolittle
Gen Ira C. Eaker
Gen Muir Fairchild
Adm William D. Leahy
Gen Curtis E. LeMay
J. Robert Oppenheimer
Lt Gen Elwood R. Quesada
Gen Carl M. Spaatz
Gen Nathan F. Twining
Gen Thomas D. White

The Air Force Historical Office in Washington, D.C., contains microfilm copies of most documents in the official Air Force Archives located at Maxwell AFB, Alabama, including the annual command histories. AFHO also has copies of the papers of Gens George C. Kenney and Lauris Norstad.

The Air Force Academy Archives contain the voluminous papers of Gen Laurence Kuter and a partial, but very important, collection of Twining papers. In addition, the following collections also proved useful:

Maj Gen Jarred V. Crabb
Maj Gen Haywood S. Hansell
Maj Gen Hugh J. Knerr
Gen Robert M. Lee
Maj Gen George McDonald
James Parton

The Academy also has many of the hundreds of oral history interviews conducted by the USAF and the Columbia University Project over the past twenty-five years.

The National Archives contain a wealth of information, but it is difficult to filter out the important data. Fortunately, certain files have been separated from the mass and are very useful: the JCS files and the Admiral Leahy and General Bradley papers pertaining to their years as JCS chairmen.

The official US Air Force Archives are located at the Simpson Historical Research Cen-

259

ter at Maxwell AFB, Alabama, and are absolutely essential for any topic dealing with Air Force history.

The US Army Military History Institute at Carlisle Barracks, Pennsylvania, contains the records of the Army War College. It also holds the very valuable papers of Gen Matthew Ridgway, Lt Gen Edward Almond and Chester B. Hansen, Omar Bradley's aide during World War II.

The Gen Douglas MacArthur Archives in Norfolk, Virginia, are invaluable for studying the Korean War.

The CIA archives at Langley, Virginia, and the NSA archives at Fort Meade, Maryland, provided extremely important information on Vandenberg's tenure at G-2 and the CIG.

In England there are two repositories of importance for this work. First is the Public Records Office in Kew Gardens, London, which contains the official records of the RAF. Also located there are the papers of ACM Sir Trafford Leigh-Mallory, including his World War II diary when Commander of the AEAF. At the Imperial War Museum in London are the papers of AVM E. J. Kingston-McCloughry. Of lesser value to this study are the Royal Air Force Archives in the RAF Museum at Hendon. They contain a small collection of Leigh-Mallory's personal papers.

The Bentley Library at the University of Michigan has the Arthur H. Vandenberg collection, but there is almost nothing pertinent to the senator's nephew.

Contact was made with the Hoover, Truman, and Eisenhower presidential libraries, and copies of some valuable documents were thus obtained.

INTERVIEWS

Anderson, Maj Gen Frederick L., by W. J. Paul, Albert Simpson, and Arthur Goldberg, AFHO, May 28, 1947.

Anderson, Maj Gen Samuel, by Hugh N. Ahmann, AFHO, Jun 28–Jul 1, 1976.

Cook, Gen Orval R., by Hugh N. Ahmann and Richard Emmons, AFHO, Jun 4–5 and Aug 6–7, 1974.

Doolittle, Lt Gen James H., by Lt Col Robert M. Burch, Maj Ronald R. Fogelman, and Capt. James P. Tate, USAFA, Sep 26, 1971.

Eaker, Lt Gen Ira C., by Donald Shaughnessy, Columbia University, 1960.

——, by the author, Mar 30, 1978.

Edwards, Lt Gen Idwal D., by Maj Alan Gropman, USAFA, Feb 10, 1973.

Finletter, Thomas K., by Marvin Stanley, AFHO, Feb 1967.

Hitchcock, Col Edward C., telephone interview by the author, Jan 30, 1987.

Irvine, Lt Gen Clarence S., by Robert Kipp, AFHO, Dec 17, 1970.

Johnson, Gen Leon, by the author, Feb 21–23, 1984.

Kenney, Gen George C., by Marvin Stanley, AFHO, Jan 25, 1967.

Kuter, Gen Laurence S., by Hugh N. Ahmann and Thomas A. Sturm, AFHO, Sep 30 and Oct 3, 1974.

Lee, Gen Robert M., by the author, Aug 29, 1986.

LeMay, Gen Curtis E., by John T. Bohn, AFHO, Mar 9, 1971.

Leo, Steven, by George Watson, Jr., AFHO, Aug 18, 1982.

McHugh, Brig Gen Godfrey, by the author, Jul 13, 1984.

McKee, Gen William F., by James C. Hasdorff, AFHO, Mar 13–14, 1979.

Miller, Gloria, telephone interview by the author, Jun 24, 1984.

Norstad, Gen Lauris, by the author, Feb 22, 1984.

Parrish, Brig Gen Noel F., by the author, Jul 11 and 13, 1984.

——, by James C. Hasdorff, AFHO, Jun 10–14, 1974.

Partridge, Gen Earle E., by Thomas A. Sturm and Hugh N. Ahmann, AFHO, Apr 24–25, 1974.

——, by Lt Col Jon Reynolds, Maj Robert Bartanowicz, and the author, USAFA, Feb 16, 1978.

Pforzheimer, Walter, by the author, Jan 30, 1987.

Quesada, Lt Gen Elwood R., by Lt Cols Steven Long and Ralph Stephenson, AFHO, May 12–22, 1975.

Smith, Gen Frederick H., by James C. Hasdorff, AFHO, Jan 7–8, 1976.

Smith, Lt Gen Joseph, by the author, Jul 11, 1984.

Spaatz, Gen Carl M., by Arthur Goldberg, AFHO, May 19, 1965.

Spaatz, Ruth, by James C. Hasdorff, AFHO, Mar 3, 1981.

Symington, W. Stuart, by Hugh N. Ahmann and Herman S. Wolk, AFHO, May 2 and Dec 12, 1978.

Tibbetts, Brig Gen Paul W., by James S. Howard, Lt Col Frederick Zoes, and Capt Barry J. Anderson, AFHO, Feb 7, 1985.

Timberlake, Lt Gen Edward, by Burt Case, AFHO, May 1965.

Tunner, Lt Gen William H., by James C. Hasdorff, AFHO, Oct 5–6, 1976.

Vandenberg, Maj Gen Hoyt S., Jr., by the author, Feb 21–23, 1984, Jan 10–11, 1987.

Weyland, Gen Otto P., by Brig Gen Noel Parrish and James C. Hasdorff, AFHO, Nov 19, 1974.

Wilson, Maj Gen Donald, by Hugh N. Ahmann, AFHO, Dec 10–11, 1975.

Wilson, Maj Gen Roscoe, by Lt Col Dennis A. Smith, AFHO, Dec 1–2, 1983.

Zuckert, Eugene M., by George M. Watson, Jr., AFHO, Apr 27, 1982.

CORRESPONDENCE

Beadle, Col Frank L., Sep 8, 1984.

Bennett, Col W. G., Aug 13, 1984.

Best, CMSgt Vince, Dec 22, 1984.

Beurket, Col Raymond T., Jun 24, 1984.

Booth, Lt Gen Donald P., Jun 13, 1984.

Bowen, Col C. H., Feb 25, 1985.

Burt, Col William R., Oct 20, Nov. 12, 1984; Feb 7 and 20, 1985; Oct 25, 1986.

Cary, Col Milo G., Sep 20, 1984.

Clarke, Gen Bruce C., Jun 27, 1984.

Cothran, Frank E., Sep 30, 1984.

Evans, Col R. B., Jul 8, 1984.

Felt, Adm Harry D., Aug 11, 1984.

Gettys, Col Charles W., Jun 2, 1984.

Goddard, Col N. B., Sep 15, 1984.

Gossett, Col Ernest E, Dec 18, 1984.

Hansell, Maj Gen Haywood S., Jr., May 13, 1974.

Hitchcock, Col Edward C., Mar 3, 1987.

Holmes, Brig Gen Ernest V., Jun 14, 1984.

des Islets, Col R. E. M., Jun 20, 1984.

Johnson, Lt Gen Alfred L., Jun 17, 1984.

Johnson, Col Wendell, May 30, 1984.

Kindleberger, Charles P., Jan 19, 1985.

Kuter, Ethel, Aug 11, 1984.

LeMay, Gen Curtis E., Nov 19, 1986.

Lynch, Maj Gen Edmund C., Aug 20 and 26, and Oct 2, 1984.

MacArthur, Jeanne, Nov 6, 1986.

McCarley, J. Britt, May 28 and Jun 10, 1987.

McDaniel, Maj Gen Edward H., Jun 13, 1984.

Marcus, Col Morris H., Sep 12, 1984.

Mesick, Col B. S., Jun 29, 1984.

Neal, Col Ralph M., Jun 23, 1984.

Nichols. Maj Gen Kenneth D., Dec. 7, 1987.

Nutter, Maj Gen William H., Jun 18, 1984.
Parrish, Brig Gen Noel F., Nov 23, 1983.
Plummer, Thomas F., Jun 13, 1984.
Rostow, Walter W., Nov 30, 1984.
Samuel, Maj Gen John S., Jan 27, 1985.
Scudder, Nathan F., Mar 28, 1984.
Severn, Col Theodore, Aug 10 and 21, 1984.
Shelley, Col James M., Feb 2, 1985.
Spalding, Maj Gen Sidney P., Jul 28 and Aug 26, 1984.
Sullivan, Col Carroll F., Sep 13 and 24, 1984; Feb 27 and Apr 9, 1985.
Sweany, Brig Gen Kenneth S., Jun 17, 1984.
Tolley, RAdm Kemp, Jul 21, 1984.
Thompkins, C. David, Dec 13, 1983, Oct 4, 1984; Aug 21, 1986.
Triplet, Col William S., Jun 9, 1984.
Vandenberg, Maj Gen Hoyt S., Jr., numerous letters and telephone conversations from
    1983 to 1987.
Vandenberg, Shedd, May 15 and Jun 3, 1984.
Wedemeyer, Gen Albert C., Aug 8 and Sep 24, 1983.
Weikert, Maj Gen John M., Jun 9, 1984.
Wilson, Col Harry E., Aug 2, 1984.
Zuckerman, Lord Solly, Sep 24, 1984.

MICROFILM COLLECTIONS

The following microfilm collections of primary documents, published by the University
Publications of America, were also extremely useful:
"CIA Research Reports: The Soviet Union, 1946–1976," 1980.
"Documents of the National Security Council, 1947–1977," 1980.
"————: First Supplement," 1981.
"————: Second Supplement," 1983.
"The Military Situation in the Far East and the Relief of General MacArthur," 1977.
"Minutes of Meetings of the National Security Council, With Special Advisory Reports,"
    1982.
"Official Conversations and Meetings of Dean Acheson, 1949–1953," 1980.
"Public Statements by the Secretaries of Defense, Part I: The Truman Administration,
    1947–1953," 1982.
"Records of the Joint Chiefs of Staff, Part 1: 1942–45: Meetings," 1981.
"————: The European Theater," 1981.
"————: The Pacific Theater," 1981.
"————: The Soviet Union," 1981.
"————: Strategic Issues," 1983.
"Records of the Joint Chiefs of Staff, Part 2: 1946–53: The Soviet Union," 1979.
"————: The Far East," 1979.
"————: Europe and NATO," 1980.
"————: The United States," 1980.
"————: Strategic Issues, Section 2," 1981.

GOVERNMENT PUBLICATIONS

Finletter, Thomas K. (chairman), *Survival in the Air Age.* Washington: GPO, 1948.
Foreign Relations of the United States: 1943, The Conferences at Cairo and Teheran. Wash-
    ington: GPO, 1961.
————: *1947, Vol. I: The United Nations.* Washington: GPO, 1973.
————: *1948, Vol. I: The United Nations.* Washington: GPO, 1973.

————: *1949, Vol. I: National Security Affairs; Foreign and Economic Policy*. Washington: GPO, 1976.

————: *1950, Vol. I: National Security Affairs; Foreign and Economic Policy*. Washington: GPO, 1977.

————: *1950, Vol. VII: Korea*. Washington: GPO, 1976.

————: *1951, Vol VII: Korea*. Washington: GPO, 1983.

————: *1952–1954, Vol. XIII: Indochina*. Washington: GPO, 1982.

————: *1952–1954, Vol. XV: Korea*. Washington: GPO, 1984.

Report of the Secretary of Defense for the Fiscal Year 1950. Washington: GPO, 1951.

Rockefeller, Nelson R. (chairman), *Commission on CIA Activities within the United States*. Washington: GPO, 1975.

Second Report of the Secretary of the Air Force for the Fiscal Year 1949. Washington: GPO, 1950.

US Cong., hearings before the Select Committee on Post-War Military Policy, *Proposal to Establish a Single Department of Armed Forces*. 78th Cong., 2nd sess., Washington: GPO, 1944.

US Cong., House, hearings before the Appropriations Committee, *Department of the Air Force Appropriations Bill for 1954*. 83rd Cong., 1st sess., Washington: GPO, 1953.

US Cong., House, hearings before the Appropriations Committee, *National Military Establishment Appropriations Bill for 1950*. 81st Cong., 1st sess. Washington: GPO, 1949.

US Cong., House, hearings before the Appropriations Committee, *The Second Supplemental Appropriations Bill for 1951*. 81st Cong., 2nd sess. Washington: GPO, 1950.

US Cong., House, hearings before the Appropriations Committee, *The Supplemental Appropriations Bill for 1951*. 81st Cong., 2nd sess. Washington: GPO, 1950.

US Cong., House, hearings before the Committee on Expenditures, *The National Security Act of 1947*. 80th Cong., 1st sess. Washington: GPO, 1982.

US Cong., Senate, *Final Report of Select Committee to Study Governmental Operations with Respect to Intelligence Activities*, IX Books. 94th Cong., 2nd sess., Washington: GPO, 1976.

US Cong., Senate, hearings before the Appropriations Committee, *Department of Defense Appropriations for 1951*. 81st Cong., 2nd sess. Washington: GPO, 1950.

US Cong., Senate, hearings before the Appropriations Committee, *Department of Defense Appropriations for 1954*. 83rd Cong., 1st sess. Washington: GPO, 1953.

US Cong., Senate, hearings before the Appropriations Committee, *National Military Establishment Appropriations Bill for 1950*. 81st Cong., 1st sess. Washington: GPO, 1949.

US Cong., Senate, hearings before the Armed Services and Foreign Relations Committees, *The Military Situation in the Far East*. 82nd Cong., 1st sess. Washington: GPO, 1950.

US Cong., Senate, hearings before the Armed Services Committee, *Investigation of the B-36 Bomber Program*. 81st Cong., 1st sess. Washington: GPO, 1949.

US Cong., Senate, hearings before the Armed Services Committee, *Joint Chiefs of Staff Nominations*. 83rd Cong., 1st sess., Washington: GPO, 1953.

US Cong., Senate, hearings before the Armed Services Committee, *The National Defense Establishment*. 80th Cong., 1st sess. Washington: GPO, 1947.

US Cong., Senate, hearings before the Armed Services Committee, *The National Defense Program—Unification and Strategy*. 81st Cong., 1st sess. Washington: GPO, 1949.

US Cong., Senate, hearings in executive session before the Armed Services Committee, *Military Assistance Program*. 81st Cong., 1st sess. Washington: GPO, 1973.

UNPUBLISHED STUDIES

Baker, Francis J. "The Death of the Flying Wing: The Real Reasons Behind the 1949 Cancellation of Northrop Aircraft's RB-49." Diss., Claremont Graduate School, 1984.

Caddell, Joseph W. "Orphan of Unification: The Development of United States Air Force Tactical Air Power Doctrine, 1945–1950." Diss., Duke University, 1984.

Converse, Elliott V. "United States Plans for a Postwar Overseas Military Base System, 1942–1948." Diss., Princeton University, 1984.

Davis, Vincent. "Admirals, Politics and Postwar Defense Policy: The Origins of the Postwar U.S. Navy, 1943–1946." Diss., Princeton University, 1961.

Farquhar, John T. "A Cold War in Flames: The Impact of Aerial Reconnaissance on US–Soviet Relations, 1948–1960." Thesis, Creighton University, 1986.

Goldstein, Donald. "Ennis Whitehead, Aerospace Commander and Pioneer." Diss., Denver University, 1971.

Green, Murray. "Stuart Symington and the B-36." Diss., American University, 1969.

Julian, Thomas A. "Operation FRANTIC and the Search for American- Soviet Military Co-operation, 1941–1944." Diss., Syracuse University, 1968.

Legere, Laurence J. "Unification of the Armed Forces." Diss., Harvard University, 1950.

MacIsaac, David. "The Air Force and Strategic Thought." Woodrow Wilson Fellow Working Paper, June 1979.

Moll, Kenneth S. "Nuclear Strategy, 1945–1949: America's First Four Years." Thesis, University of Omaha, 1965.

Nye, Roger H. "The United States Military Academy in an Era of Educational Reform, 1900–1925." Diss., Columbia University, 1968.

Reynolds, Jon A. "Education and Training for High Command: Hoyt S. Vandenberg's Early Career." Diss., Duke University, 1980.

Scrivner, John H., Jr. "Pioneer into Space: A Biography of Major General Orvil A. Anderson." Diss., University of Oklahoma, 1971.

Smith, Robert L. "The Influence of USAF Chief of Staff Hoyt S. Vandenberg on United States National Security Policy." Diss., American University, 1965.

HISTORICAL STUDIES

Air Phase of the North African Invasion. USAF Historical Study No. 105. Maxwell AFB, Ala.: Air University, n.d.

Bald, Ralph D. Air Force Participation in Joint Army–Air Force Training Exercises, 1947–1950. USAF Historical Study No. 80. Maxwell AFB, Ala.: Air University, 1955.

Bidwell, Col Bruce W. History of the Military Intelligence Division. 8 volumes. Department of the Army Historical Study. Washington: US Army Historical Office, 1959–61.

Chronology, Functions and Composition of the Joint Chiefs of Staff, 1942–1978. JCS Special Historical Study. Washington: JCS, 1979.

A Concise History of the Organization of the Joint Chiefs of Staff, 1942–1978. JCS Special Historical Study. Washington: JCS, 1979.

Condit, Kenneth W. The Joint Chiefs of Staff and National Policy, Vol. II, 1947–1949. JCS Historical Study. Washington: JCS, 1978.

Dews, Edmund, and Felix Kozaczka. Air Interdiction Lessons from Past Campaigns. RAND Note No. N-1743 P&AE. Santa Monica, Calif.: RAND Corporation, 1981.

Finney, Robert T. History of the Air Corps Tactical School, 1920–1940. USAF Historical Study No. 100. Maxwell AFB, Ala: Air University, 1955.

Futrell, Robert F. Ideas, Concepts, Doctrine: A History of Basic Thinking in the United States Air Force, 1917–1964. 2 volumes. USAF Historical Study No. 139. Maxwell AFB, Ala: Air University, 1971.

Greer, Thomas H. The Development of Air Doctrine in the Army Air Arm, 1917–1941. USAF Historical Study. Maxwell AFB, Ala: Air University, 1955.

Kaysen, Carl. Notes on Strategic Air Intelligence in World War II (ETO). RAND Study No. R-165. Santa Monica, Calif.: RAND Corporation, 1953.

Lichman, J. J. History of Continental Air Command, 1 Dec 1948 to 31 Dec 1949. USAF Historical Study. Maxwell AFB, Ala: Air University, n.d.

Little, R. D., and Lee Bowen. The History of Air Force Participation in the Atomic Energy Program, 1943–1953. 5 volumes. USAF Historical Study. Maxwell AFB, Ala.: Air Force Archives, n.d.

McMullen, Richard F. *Air Defense and National Policy, 1946–1957.* 2 volumes, Air Defense Command Historical Study No. 22. Peterson AFB, Colo.: Air Defense Command, 1964.

Poole, Walter S. *The Joint Chiefs of Staff and National Policy, Vol. IV, 1950–1952.* JCS Historical Study. Washington: JCS, 1980.

Russel, Robert R. *Expansion of Industrial Facilities under Army Air Force Auspices, 1940–1945.* USAF Historical Study. Maxwell AFB, Ala.: Air University, 1946.

Schnabel, James F. *The Joint Chiefs of Staff and National Policy, Vol. I, 1945–1947.* JCS Historical Study. Washington: JCS, 1979.

————, and Robert J. Watson. *The Joint Chiefs of Staff and National Policy, Vol. III, The Korean War.* JCS Historical Study. Washington: JCS, 1978.

Sunderland, Riley. *Evolution of Command and Control Doctrine for Close Air Support.* USAF Historical Study. Washington: Air Force Historical Office, 1973.

Taylor, Joe G. *Development of Night Air Operations, 1941–1952.* USAF Historical Study No. 92. Maxwell AFB, Ala.: Air Force Archives, 1953.

The Liberation of North West Europe. 6 volumes. RAF Historical Study. London, Air Ministry, n.d.

Watson, Robert J. *The Joint Chiefs of Staff and National Policy, Vol. V, 1953–1954.* JCS Historical Study. Washington: JCS, 1986.

Williams, Edwin L., Jr. *Legislative History of the AAF and USAF, 1941–1951.* USAF Historical Study No. 84. Maxwell AFB, Ala.: Air University, 1955.

BOOKS

Abell, Tyler. *The Drew Pearson Diaries, 1949–1959.* New York: Holt, Rinehart, and Winston, 1974.

Acheson, Dean. *Present at the Creation.* New York: W. W. Norton, 1969.

Albion, Robert G., and Robert H. Connery. *Forrestal and the Navy.* New York: Columbia University Press, 1962.

Allen, Robert S., and William V. Shannon. *The Truman Merry-Go-Round.* New York: Vanguard Press, 1950.

Ambrose, Stephen. *Duty, Honor, Country: A History of West Point.* Baltimore: Johns Hopkins University Press, 1966.

————. *Eisenhower, Vol. 2: The President.* New York: Simon and Schuster, 1984.

Andrus, Roger M., ed. *Forging the Atomic Shield: Excerpts from the Office Diary of Gordon E. Dean.* Chapel Hill: University of North Carolina Press, 1987.

Arnold, Henry H. *Global Mission.* New York: Harper and Bros., 1949.

Atomic Energy Commission. *In the Matter of J. Robert Oppenheimer: Transcript of Hearings before the Personnel Security Board.* Cambridge, Mass.: MIT Press, 1971.

Ball, Harry P. *Of Responsible Command: A History of the US Army War College.* Carlisle Barracks, Pa.: Alumni Association of the Army War College, 1983.

Bamford, James. *The Puzzle Palace: A Report on America's Most Secret Agency.* Boston: Houghton Mifflin, 1982.

Bar-Zohar, Michel. *The Hunt for German Scientists.* New York: Hawthorn Books, 1967.

Beverley, George H. *Pioneer in the U.S. Air Corps.* Manhattan, Kans.: Sunflower University Press, 1982.

Blair, Clay. *Beyond Courage.* New York: Ballantine Books, 1955.

Bland, Larry I., Sharon R. Ritenour, and Clarence E. Wunderlin, Jr., eds. *The Papers of George Catlett Marshall, Vol 2: "We Cannot Delay" July 1, 1939–December 6, 1941.* Baltimore: Johns Hopkins University Press, 1986.

Blumberg, Stanley A., and Givinci Owens. *Energy and Conflict: The Life and Times of Edward Teller.* New York: Putnam's, 1976.

Bohlen, Charles E. *Witness to History, 1929–1969.* New York: W. W. Norton, 1973.

Borden, Norman E., Jr. *Air Mail Emergency: 1934.* Freeport, Maine: Bond Wheelwright Co., 1968.

Borowski, Harry S. *A Hollow Threat: Strategic Air Power and Containment Before the Korean War*. Westport, Conn.: Greenwood Press, 1982.

Botti, Timothy J. *The Long Wait: The Forging of the Anglo-American Nuclear Alliance, 1945–1958*. Westport: Greenwood Press, 1987.

Bradley, Gen Omar, and Clay Blair. *A General's Life*. New York: Simon and Schuster, 1983.

Brereton, Lewis. *The Brereton Diaries*. New York: William Morrow, 1945.

Brodie, Bernard. *Strategy in the Missile Age*. Princeton: Princeton University Press, 1959.

Buell, Thomas B. *Master of Sea Power: A Biography of Fleet Admiral Ernest J. King*. Boston: Little, Brown, 1980.

——. *The Quiet Warrior*. Boston: Little, Brown, 1974.

Buhite, Russell D. *Soviet-American Relations in Asia, 1945–1954*. Norman: University of Oklahoma Press, 1981.

Butcher, Capt Harry C. *My Three Years with Eisenhower*. New York: Simon and Schuster, 1946.

Calvocoressi, Peter. *Top Secret Ultra*. New York: Ballantine Books, 1980.

Caraley, Demetrios. *The Politics of Military Unification*. New York: Columbia University Press, 1966.

Chandler, Alfred D., and Louis Galambos, eds. *The Papers of Dwight David Eisenhower*. 11 volumes. Baltimore: Johns Hopkins University Press, 1970–86.

Chennault, Claire. *Way of a Fighter*. New York: Putnam's, 1949.

Churchill, Winston. *The Second World War*. 5 volumes. Boston: Houghton Mifflin, 1950.

Clay, Lucius. *Decision in Germany*. New York: Doubleday, 1950.

Clayton, Aileen. *The Enemy Is Listening*. New York: Ballantine Books, 1980.

Clifford, John G. *The Citizen Soldiers: The Plattsburg Training Camp Movement*. Lexington: The University Press of Kentucky, 1972.

Cline, Ray S. *Secrets, Spies and Scholars: Blueprint of the Essential CIA*. Washington: Acropolis Books, 1976.

——. *Washington Command Post: The Operations Division* in United States Army in World War II series. Washington: GPO, 1961.

Coffey, Thomas M. *Iron Eagle: The Turbulent Life of General Curtis E. LeMay*. New York: Crown Publishers, 1986.

Cole, Alice et al. *The Department of Defense: Documents of Establishment and Organization, 1944–1978*. Washington: GPO, 1978.

Cole, H. M. *The Lorraine Campaign* in United States Army in World War II series. Washington: GPO, 1950.

——. *The Ardennes: The Battle of the Bulge* in United States Army in World War II series. Washington: GPO, 1965.

Collier, Richard. *Bridge Across the Sky*. New York: McGraw-Hill, 1978.

Collins, J. Lawton. *War in Peacetime*. Boston: Houghton Mifflin, 1969.

——. *"Lightning Joe": An Autobiography*. Baton Rouge: Louisiana State University Press, 1979.

Conn, Stetson, and Byron Fairchild. *The Framework of Hemisphere Defense* in United States Army in World War II series. Washington: GPO, 1960.

Cozzens, James Gould. *A Time of War: Air Force Diaries and Pentagon Memos, 1943–1945*. Columbia, S.C.: Buccoli Clark, 1984.

——. *Guard of Honor*. New York: Harcourt, Brace, 1948.

Craven, Wesley F., and James L. Cate. eds. *The Army Air Forces in World War II*. 7 volumes. Chicago: University of Chicago Press, 1948–51.

Cullum, George W. Biographical Register of the Officers and Graduates of the U.S. Military Academy at West Point, New York, Supplement Vol. VII, 1920–30. *Chicago: Lakeside Press, 1930*.

Dastrup, Boyd L. *The U.S. Army Command and General Staff College: A Centennial History*. Manhattan, Kans.: Sunflower University Press, 1982.

Davis, Vincent. *The Admirals Lobby*. Chapel Hill: University of North Carolina Press, 1982.

Davison, W. Phillips. *The Berlin Blockade: A Study in Cold War Politics*. Santa Monica, Calif.: RAND Corp., 1957.

Deane, John R. *The Strange Alliance: The Story of our Efforts at Wartime Co-operation with Russia*. New York: Viking, 1946.

Demaris, Ovid. *The Director: An Oral Biography of J. Edgar Hoover*. New York: Harper's Magazine Press, 1975.

Dennett, Raymond, and Joseph E. Johnson, eds. *Negotiating with the Russians*. Boston: World Peace Foundation, 1951.

Donovan, Robert J. *Conflict and Crisis: The Presidency of Harry S. Truman, 1945–1948*. New York: W. W. Norton, 1977.

Douglas, Sholto. *Years of Command*. London: Collins, 1966.

Dupuy, R. Ernest. *Men of West Point: The First 150 Years of the United States Military Academy*. New York: William Sloane, 1951.

Etzold, Thomas H., and John Lewis Gaddis, eds. *Containment: Documents on American Policy and Strategy, 1945–1950*. New York: Columbia University Press, 1978.

Feis, Herbert. *Churchill—Roosevelt—Stalin*. Princeton: Princeton University Press, 1967.

Ferrell, Robert H., ed. *The Eisenhower Diaries*. New York: W. W. Norton, 1981.

———. *Off the Record: The Private Papers of Harry S. Truman*. New York: Harper and Row, 1980.

Field, James A., Jr. *History of United States Naval Operations: Korea*. Washington: GPO, 1962.

Finletter, Thomas K. *Power and Policy*. New York: Harcourt, Brace, 1954.

Futrell, Robert F. *The United States Air Force in Korea, 1950–1953*. Revised edition. Washington: GPO, 1984.

Gallup, George H. *The Gallup Poll: Public Opinion, 1935–1971*. 3 volumes. New York: Random House, 1972.

Ganoe, William A. *MacArthur Close-Up*. New York: Vantage Press, 1962.

Geelhold, E. Bruce. *Charles E. Wilson and Controversy at the Pentagon, 1953 to 1957*. Detroit: Wayne State University Press, 1979.

Goldberg, Alfred, ed. *A History of the United States Air Force, 1907–1957*. Princeton: D. Van Nostrand, 1957.

Gordenker, Leon. *The United Nations and the Peaceful Unification of Korea*. The Hague: Martinus., 1959.

Greenwood, Jim, and Maxine Greenwood. *Stunt Flying in the Movies*. Blue Ridge Summit, Pa.: Tab Books, 1982.

Gropman, Alan R. *The Air Force Integrates, 1945–1964*. Washington: GPO, 1978.

Hammond, Paul Y. *Organizing for Defense*. Princeton: Princeton University Press, 1961.

———. *Super Carriers and B-36 Bombers*. Indianapolis: Bobbs-Merrill, 1963.

———, Warner R. Schilling, and Glenn H. Snyder. *Strategy, Politics and Defense Budgets*. New York: Columbia University Press, 1962.

Hansen, Laurence J. *What It Was Like Flying for "Ike."* Largo, Fla.: Aero Medical Consultants, 1983.

Harriman, W. Averell, and Elie Abel. *Special Envoy to Churchill and Stalin, 1941–1946*. New York: Random House, 1975.

Hastings, Max. *OVERLORD: D-Day and the Battle for Normandy*. New York: Simon and Schuster, 1984.

Herken, Gregg. *Counsels of War*. New York: Alfred A. Knopf, 1985.

———. *The Winning Weapon: The Atomic Bomb in the Cold War, 1945–1950*. New York: Alfred A. Knopf, 1980.

Hewlett, Richard G., and Francis Duncan. *A History of the Atomic Energy Commission*. 2 volumes. University Park: Penn State University Press, 1969.

Hinsley, F. H., E. E. Thomas, C. F. G. Ransom, and R. C. Knight. British Intelligence in the Second World War. 4 volumes. London: Her Majesty's Stationery Office, 1979–88.

Holley, Irving B, Jr. Buying Aircraft: Materiel Procurement for the Army Air Forces in United States Army in World War II series. Washington: GPO, 1964.

Howe, George. Northwest Africa: Seizing the Initiative in the West in United States Army in World War II series. Washington: GPO, 1957.

Howitzer: The Yearbook of the United States Corps of Cadets. West Point, N.Y.: USMA Printing Office, 1919–23.

Hunt, Frazier, The Untold Story of Douglas MacArthur. New York: Devin-Adair Co., 1954.

Hurley, Alfred F. Billy Mitchell: Crusader for Air Power. New York: Franklin Watts, 1964.

Infield, Glenn B. The Poltava Affair: A Russian Warning: An American Tragedy. New York: Macmillan, 1973.

Iriye, Akira. The Cold War in Asia. Englewood Cliffs: Prentice-Hall, 1974.

Irving, David. War Between the Generals. London: Allen Lowe, 1981.

Isaacson, Walter, and Evan Thomas. The Wise Men: Six Friends and the World They Made. New York: Simon and Schuster, 1986.

James, D. Clayton. The Years of MacArthur. 3 volumes. Boston: Houghton Mifflin, 1970–1985.

———. A Time for Giants: The Politics of the American High Command in World War II. New York: Franklin Watts, 1987.

Johnson, Brig Gen Bruce. The Man with Two Hats. New York: Carlton Press, 1968.

Jones, Ken, and Hubert Kelley, Jr. Admiral Arleigh ("31-Knot") Burke. Philadelphia: Chilton Books, 1962.

Jones, Vincent C. Manhattan: The Army and the Atomic Bomb in United States Army in World War II series. Washington: GPO, 1985.

Jurika, Stephen, ed. From Pearl Harbor to Vietnam: The Memoirs of Admiral Arthur W. Radford. Stanford, Calif.: Hoover Institution Press, 1980.

Kaplan, Fred. The Wizards of Armageddon. New York: Simon and Schuster, 1983.

Keiser, Gordon W. The US Marine Corps and Unification, 1944–1947: The Politics of Survival. Washington: National Defense University Press, 1982.

Kesaris, Paul L., ed. Ultra and the History of the United States Strategic Air Force in Europe vs. the German Air Force. Frederick, Md.: University Publications of America, 1980.

King, Ernest J., and Walter M. Whitehill. Fleet Admiral Ernest J. King: A Naval Record. London: Eyre and Spottiswoode, 1953.

Kingston-McCloughry, E. J. The Direction of War. New York: Praeger, 1958.

Kinnard, Douglas. The Secretary of Defense. Lexington: The University Press of Kentucky, 1980.

Kintner, William R. Forging a New Sword: A Study of the Department of Defense. New York: Harper Bros., 1958.

Kirkpatrick, Lyman B. The Real CIA. New York: Macmillan, 1968.

Knightley, Philip. The Second Oldest Profession: Spies and Spying in the Twentieth Century. New York: W. W. Norton, 1986.

Kohn, Richard H., and Joseph P. Harahan, eds. Air Superiority in World War II and Korea. Washington: Air Force Historical Office, 1983.

Kolodziej, Edward A. The Uncommon Defense and Congress, 1945–1963. Columbus: Ohio State University Press, 1966.

Korb, Lawrence J. The Joint Chiefs of Staff. Bloomington: Indiana University Press, 1976.

Lamphere, Robert J., and Tom Shachtman. The FBI-KGB Wars: A Special Agent's Story. New York: Random House, 1986.

Lasby, Clarence G. Project Paperclip: German Scientists and the Cold War. New York: Atheneum, 1971.

Leahy, William D. I Was There. New York: McGraw-Hill, 1950.

Leary, William M., ed. *The Central Intelligence Agency: A History and Documents*. University: University of Alabama Press, 1984.

LeMay, Gen Curtis E., and MacKinlay Kantor. *Mission with LeMay*. Garden City, N.Y.: Doubleday, 1965.

Lilienthal, David. *The Journals of David Lilienthal, Vol. 2: The Atomic Energy Years, 1945–1950*. New York: Harper and Row, 1964.

Loftus, John. *The Belarus Secret*. New York: Alfred A. Knopf, 1982.

MacArthur, Douglas. *Reminiscences*. New York: McGraw-Hill, 1964.

MacCloskey, Monro. *TORCH and the Twelfth Air Force*. New York: Richards Rosen Press, 1971.

MacDonald, Charles B. *The Siegfried Line Campaign* in United States Army in World War II series. Washington: GPO, 1963.

MacGregor, Morris J., Jr. *Integration of the Armed Services* in Defense Studies series. Washington: GPO, 1981.

Matloff, Maurice. *Strategic Planning for Coalition Warfare, 1943–1944* in United States Army in World War II series. Washington: GPO, 1959.

———, and Edwin M. Snell. *Strategic Planning for Coalition Warfare, 1941–44*. 2 volumes, in *United States Army in World War II* series. Washington: GPO, 1953.

Messenger, Charles. *"Bomber" Harris and the Strategic Bombing Offensive, 1939–1945*. London: Arms and Armour Press, 1984.

Millis, Walter, and E. S. Duffield, eds. *The Forrestal Diaries*. New York: Viking, 1951.

Mitchell, William. *Skyways: A Book on Modern Aeronautics*. Philadelphia: J. B. Lippincott, 1930.

Morgan, Lt Gen Sir Frederick. *Overture to Overload*. London: Hodder and Stoughton, 1950.

Morton, Louis B. *The Fall of the Philippines* in United States Army in World War II series. Washington: GPO, 1953.

Murphy, Robert. *Diplomat Among Warriors*. Garden City, N.Y.: Doubleday, 1964.

Mylander, Maureen. *The Generals*. New York: Dial Press, 1974.

Nichols, Maj Gen K. D. *The Road to Trinity*. New York: William Morrow, 1987.

Overy, R. J. *The Air War, 1939–1945*. New York: Stein and Day, 1981.

Pappas, George S. *Prudens Futuri: The U.S. Army War College, 1901–1967*. Carlisle Barracks, Pa.: Alumni Association of the Army War College, 1967.

Parrish, Noel F. *Behind the Sheltering Bomb: Military Indecision from Alamogordo to Korea*. New York: Arno Press, 1979.

Parrish, Thomas. *The Ultra Americans: The U.S. Role in Breaking the Nazi Codes*. New York: Stein and Day, 1986.

Patton, George S., Jr. *War As I Knew It*. Boston: Houghton Mifflin, 1947.

Pogue, Forrest C. *George C. Marshall: Ordeal and Hope, 1939–1942*. New York: Viking, 1966.

———. *George C. Marshall: Statesman*. New York: Viking, 1987.

Potter, E. B. *Nimitz*. Annapolis, Md.: Naval Institute Press, 1976.

Powers, Richard G. *Secrecy and Power: The Life of J. Edgar Hoover*. New York: Free Press, 1987.

Powers, Thomas. *The Man Who Kept the Secrets: Richard Helms and the CIA*. New York: Alfred A. Knopf, 1979.

Puryear, Edgar F., Jr. *Stars in Flight: A Study in Air Force Character and Leadership*. Novato, Calif.: Presidio Press, 1981.

Rawlings, Gen Edwin. *Born to Fly*. Minneapolis: Great Way Publishing, 1987.

Reardon, Steven L. *History of the Office of the Secretary of Defense, Vol. I: The Formative Years, 1947–1950*. Washington: GPO, 1984.

Rees, David. *Korea: The Limited War*. New York: St. Martin's Press, 1964.

Reynolds, Quentin. *The Amazing Mr. Doolittle*. New York: Appleton-Century-Crofts, 1953.

Ridgway, Matthew. *The Korean War*. Garden City, N.Y.: Doubleday, 1964.

Rogow, Arnold A. *James Forrestal*. New York: Macmillan, 1963.

Rositzko, Harry. *The CIA's Secret Operations*. New York: Reader's Digest Press, 1977.

Rostow, Walter W. *Pre-Invasion Bombing Strategy: General Eisenhower's Decision of March 25, 1944*. Austin: University of Texas Press, 1981.

Salisbury, Harrison E. *Without Fear or Favor: An Uncompromising Look at the "New York Times."* New York: Times Books, 1980.

Schaffer, Ronald. *Wings of Judgment: American Bombing in World War II*. New York: Oxford University Press, 1985.

Schilling, Warner R., Paul Y. Hammond, and Glenn H. Snyder. *Strategy, Politcs, and Defense Budgets*. New York: Columbia University Press, 1962.

Schnabel, James F. *Policy and Direction: The First Year* in *United States Army in the Korean War* series. Washington: GPO, 1972.

Shepley, James, and Clay Blair. *The Hydrogen Bomb: The Men, the Menace, the Mechanism*. New York: David McKay, 1954.

Sherry, Michael S. *The Rise of American Air Power: The Creation of Armageddon*. New Haven: Yale University Press, 1987.

Shiner, John F. *Foulois and the U.S. Army Air Corps, 1931–1935*. Washington: GPO, 1984.

Shlaim, Avi. *The United States and the Berlin Blockade, 1948–1949*. Berkeley: University of California Press, 1983.

Smith, Jean E., ed. *The Papers of General Lucius D. Clay: Germany, 1945–1949*. 2 volumes. Bloomington: Indiana University Press, 1974.

Smith, Perry McCoy. *The Air Force Plans for Peace, 1943–1945*. Baltimore: Johns Hopkins University Press, 1970.

Stern, Phillip M. *The Oppenheimer Case: Security on Trial*. New York: Harper and Row, 1969.

Stimson, Henry L., and McGeorge Bundy. *On Active Service in Peace and War*. New York: Harper and Bros., 1948.

Strauss, Lewis L. *Men and Decisions*. Garden City, N.Y.: Doubleday, 1962.

Strong, Maj Gen Sir Kenneth. *Intelligence at the Top: The Recollections of an Intelligence Officer*. Garden City, N.Y.: Doubleday, 1969.

Tedder, [Arthur] Lord. *With Prejudice*. Boston: Little, Brown, 1966.

Teller, Edward, with Allen Brown. *The Legacy of Hiroshima*. Garden City, N.Y.: Doubleday, 1962.

Terraine, John. *A Time for Courage: The Royal Air Force in the European War, 1939–1945*. New York: Macmillan, 1985.

Thomas, Lowell, and Edward Jablonski. *Doolittle: A Biography*. Garden City, N.Y.: Doubleday, 1976.

Thompkins, C. David. *Senator Arthur H. Vandenberg: The Evolution of a Modern Republican, 1884–1945*. Lansing: Michigan State University Press, 1970.

Thompson, Wayne, ed. *Air Leadership*. Washington: Air Force Historical Office, 1986.

Toledano, Ralph de. *J. Edgar Hoover: The Man in His Time*. New Rochelle, N.Y.: Arlington House, 1973.

Troy, Thomas F. *Donovan and the CIA*. Frederick, Md.: University Publications of America, 1981.

Truman, Harry S. *The Memoirs of Harry S. Truman*. 2 volumes. Garden City, N.Y.: Doubleday, 1956.

———. *Public Papers of the Presidents, 1948–1952*. Washington: GPO, 1964.

Tunner, William H. *Over the Hump*. New York: Duell, Sloan and Pearce, 1964.

Twining, Nathan F. *Neither Liberty nor Safety*. New York: Holt, Rinehart, and Winston, 1966.

Ungar, Sanford. *FBI*. Boston: Little, Brown, 1975.

US Atomic Energy Commission. *In the Matter of J. Robert Oppenheimer: Transcript of Hearings before Personal Security Board*. Cambridge, Mass.: MIT Press, 1971.

Vandenberg, Arthur, Jr., ed. *The Private Papers of Senator Vandenberg*. Boston: Houghton Mifflin, 1952.

Van Fleet, Gen James. *Rail Transport and the Winning of Wars*. Washington: Association of American Railroads, 1956.

Watts, Barry D. *The Foundations of US Air Power Doctrine: The Problem of Friction in War*. Maxwell AFB, Ala.: Air University Press, 1984.

Webster, Charles, and Noble Frankland. *The Strategic Air Offensive Against Germany, 1939–1945*. 4 volumes. London: Her Majesty's Stationery Office, 1961.

Weigley, Russell F. *Eisenhower's Lieutenants*. Bloomington: Indiana University Press, 1981.

Wolk, Herman S. *Planning and Organizing the Postwar Air Force, 1943–1947*. Washington: GPO, 1984.

Wyson, Humphrey, and Susan Young. *Prelude to Overlord*. Novato, Calif.: Presidio Press, 1983.

York, Herbert F. *The Advisers: Oppenheimer, Teller and the Superbomb*. San Francisco: W. H. Freeman and Co., 1976.

Young, Kenneth, ed. *The Diaries of Robert Bruce Lockhart, Vol. 2: 1939–1965*. London: Macmillan, 1980.

Zuckerman, Solly. *From Apes to Warlords*. New York: Harper and Row, 1978.

ARTICLES

Abbot, Ernest H. "The Boys of Plum Island." *The Outlook*, Aug 23, 1916, pp. 950–58.

———. "The Plum Island Idea." *National Service*, Aug 1917, pp. 349–56.

Air Corps Newsletter. Mar 1927; Jul 1930; Jan, Apr 1936; Jul 1937.

"Air Force Knocks Out Navy's Super Carrier." *Life*, May 2, 1949, p. 47.

Air Force Times, Dec 13, 1952, p. 31; Jun 13, 1953, p. 4.

"Air Force of 35,000 Planes Is Urged." *U.S. Air Services*, Mar 1948, pp. 14–17.

Alsop, Joseph, and Stewart Alsop. "We Accuse!" *Harper's Magazine*, Oct 1954, pp. 25–45.

Alsop, Stewart. "U.S. Quietly Laying Foundation for Competent Secret Service." *New York Herald Tribune*, Jun 30, 1946.

———, and Ralph E. Lapp. "Can the New A-Bomb Stop Troops in the Field?" *Saturday Evening Post*, Sep 29, 1951, pp. 20–21, 89–92.

———. "We Can Smash the Red A-Bombers." *Saturday Evening Post*, Mar 21, 1953.

Army, Navy, Air Force Journal, Mar 8, 1952, p. 828; May 3, 1952, p. 1077; Jul 4, 1953, p. 1342.

"Atomic Weapons and the Korean War." *Bulletin of the Atomic Scientists*, 6, No. 7 (Jul 1950), pp. 194, 217.

Aviation Week, Dec 8, 1947, pp. 7, 11–13; Jan 26, 1948, p. 14; Mar 1, 1948, pp. 11–12; Mar 24, 1948, p. 12; Apr 12, 1948, p. 7; Jun 14, 1948, p. 7; Jul 11, 1949, p. 7; Jul 25, 1949, p. 16; Sep 8, 1949, p. 16; Sep 19, 1949, p. 16; Jun 8, 1951, p. 13; Jun 18, 1951, p. 13; Mar 10, 1952, p. 15; Mar 17, 1952, p. 12.

Baldwin, Hanson. "Intelligence—II." *New York Times*, Jul 22, 1948, p. 2.

———. "Set-up for Intelligence." *New York Times*, Apr 6, 1947, p. 38.

———. "The Unheard Opposition." *New York Times*, Aug 14, 1949, p. 30.

———. "War Plane Orders Face Examination by Congressmen." *New York Times*, May 24, 1949, p. 1.

Braden, Tom. "The Birth of the CIA." *American Heritage*, 27, No. 2 (Feb 1977), pp. 4–13.

Bradley, Omar N. "Security Is a Cooperative Venture." *Vital Speeches of the Day*, Mar 1, 1949, pp. 299–301.

———. "A Soldier's Farewell." *Saturday Evening Post*, Aug 22, 1953, pp. 20–21, 56–64.

———. "This Way Lies Peace." *Saturday Evening Post*, Oct 15, 1949, pp. 133, 168–70.

———. "U.S. Military Policy: 1950." *Reader's Digest*, Oct 1950, pp. 143–54.

Brown, Constance. "New Central Intelligence Badly in Need of Funds." *Washington Star*, Jun 16, 1946.

Childs, Marquis W. "The Battle of the Pentagon." *Harper's Magazine*, Aug 1949, pp. 47–53.

Churchill, Winston. "United We Stand." *Vital Speeches of the Day*, Apr 1, 1949, pp. 380–84.

Cline, Ray S., and Maurice Matloff. "Development of War Department Views on Unification." *Military Affairs*, XIII, No. 2 (Summer 1949), pp. 65–74.

Coffin, Tris. "Vandenberg Runs Our Air Force Team." *Coronet*, Jul 1951, pp. 96–101.

Coletta, Paolo E. "The Defense Unification Battle, 1947–1950: The Navy." *Prologue*, 7, No. 1 (Spring 1975), pp. 6–17.

Denfeld, Louis E. "The Only Carrier the Air Force Ever Sank." *Colliers*, Mar 25, 1950, pp. 32–33, 46–51.

"Did the Soviet Bomb Come Sooner Than Expected?" *Bulletin of the Atomic Scientists*, V, No. 10 (Oct 1949), pp. 261–75.

Derieux, James C. "What Shifts Will Eisenhower Make in Our Military Setup?" *Collier's*, Dec 27, 1952, p. 32.

Endicott, Stephen L. "Germ Warfare and Plausible Denial." *Modern China*, 5, No. 1 (Jan 1979), pp. 79–104.

"Exit Tooey." *Time*, Apr 12, 1948, p. 27.

Freund, James C. "The Revolt of the Admirals." *Aerospace Historian*, 4, No. 1 (Jan-Apr 1963), pp. 1–10.

Friedberg, Aaron L. "A History of U.S. Strategic 'Doctrine'—1945 to 1980." *Journal of Strategic Studies*, Vol. 3 No. 3 (Dec 1980), pp. 37–71.

"General Vandenberg Steps In." *Air Force*, May 1948, pp. 14, 45–46.

"Generals Shift . . . Big Bombers Lose Favor." *Business Week*, Aug 16, 1952, pp. 34–35.

Giles, John A. "General Van." *Flying*, Jul 1948, pp. 27, 76–77.

Graves, Harold. "Intelligence Untangled." *Providence Bulletin*, Jun 11, 1946.

Greenwood, John T. "The Emergence of the Postwar Strategic Air Force, 1945–1953." In *Proceedings of the Eighth Military History Symposium USAF Academy, 1978.* Washington: GPO, 1979, pp. 215–44.

Haggerty, James. "Will Vandenberg be Reappointed?" *American Aviation*, Mar 3, 1952, p. 15.

"Has the Air Force Done Its Job in Korea?" *Air Force*, Mar 1951, pp. 41–43.

Hicks, Lt Col F. H. "The Story of West Point." *The Mentor*, Sep 1924, pp. 3–17.

"Hidden Struggle for the H-Bomb." *Fortune*, May 1953, pp. 109–10, 230.

Holt, Lucius N. "An Educational Institution." *Infantry Journal*, 24, No. 5 (May 1924), pp. 553–62.

Huston, James A. "Tactical Use of Air Power in World War II: The Army Experience." *Military Affairs*, 14 (1950), pp. 166–85.

"An Interview with General Vandenberg." *Aviation Age*, Feb 1952, pp. 31–32.

Johnson, Frank. "Airlift to Berlin." *Air Classics*, Sep 1978, pp. 25–32.

Keefer, Edward C. "President Eisenhower and the End of the Korean War." *Diplomatic History*, 10, No. 3 (Summer 1986), pp. 267–89.

Kerns, Maj Harry N. "Cadet Problems." *Mental Hygiene*, Oct 1923, pp. 688–96.

Knight, Charlotte. "Mystery Man of the Pentagon." *Colliers*, Jan 22, 1954, pp. 30–36.

"Lack of Strategic Plan Hampers Development of U.S. Air Power." *Aviation Week*, Mar 1, 1948, pp. 11–12.

Lawrence, W. H. "Regrouping of Army Airmen in 3 Commands Set by Spaatz." *New York Times*, Mar 6, 1946, p. 1.

London Daily Express, Aug 10, 1948.

London Times, Jul 17, 1948, p. 4; Jul 19, 1948, p. 4; Sep 2, 1950, p. 5; Nov 22, 1951, p. 4; Mar 3, 1952, p. 3; Apr 11, 1954, p. 11.

Lukas, Richard. "Aircraft Commitments to Russia." *Air University Review*, 16, No. 5 (Jul-Aug 1965), pp. 44–53.

———. "The VELVET Project: Hope and Frustration." *Military Affairs*, 28, No. 4 (Winter 1964), pp. 145–62.

McFarland, Marvin W. "Air Power and the Warsaw Uprising," *Air Power Historian*, Oct 1956, pp. 185–95.

Marshall, George C. "Responsibility of Victory." *Vital Speeches of the Day*, Nov 15, 1945, pp. 76–78.

Maurer, Maurer. "A Delicate Mission: Aerial Reconnaissance of Japanese Islands before World War II." *Military Affairs*, 26, No. 2 (Summer 1962), pp. 66–75.

Maycock, Thomas J. "Notes on the Development of AAF Tactical Doctrine." *Military Affairs*, 14 (1950), pp. 80–91.

Miami Star Sun, Apr 8, 1948, p. 28.

Mitchell, Donald W. "Problems of Unification." *Current History*, 18, No. 105 (May 1950), pp. 263–66.

Mrozek, Donald J. "A New Look at 'Balanced Forces': Defense Continuities from Truman to Eisenhower." *Military Affairs*, 38, No. 4 (Dec 1974), pp. 145–50.

Murphy, Charles J. V. "The State of the Armed Forces." *Life*, Sep 2, 1946, pp. 96–108.

New York Times, Dec. 16, 1945; Apr 10, 1948, p. 13; Aug 14, 1949, p. 30; Sep 7, 1949, p. 1; Sep 15, 1949, p. 13; Sep 16, 1949, p. 1; Jun 1, 1951, p. 1; Jun 23, 1951, p. 7; Mar 1, 1952, p. 6; Aug 26, 1952, p. 10; Apr 6, 1954, p. 29.

Newsweek, Jun 2, 1947, p. 13; Sep 20, 1948, pp. 26–27; Jul 25, 1949, p. 19; Aug 22, 1949, p. 16; May 10, 1952, p. 30; Jun 15, 1953, p. 26.

O'Ballance, Edgar. "The MacArthur Plan." *Royal United Services Institute Journal*, 110, No. 639 (August 1965), pp. 248–53.

Oppenheimer, J. Robert. "Physics in the Contemporary World." *Bulletin of the Atomic Scientists*, 4, No. 3 (Mar 1948), pp. 65–68, 85–86.

Parrish, Noel F. "Vandenberg: Rebuilding the Shoestring Air Force." *Air Force Magazine*, Aug 1981, pp. 88–93.

Perkins, J. W. "Use of Heavy Bombers on Tactical Missions." *Military Review*, 26, No. 2 (May 1946), pp. 18–21.

"President Orders Exploration of Super Bomb." *Bulletin of the Atomic Scientists*, 6, No. 3 (Mar 1950), pp. 66–68.

"President's Secret Newspaper." *The Senior Scholastic*, Sep 23, 1946, p. 9.

"Report of the Congressional Aviation Policy Board." *Air Force*. Apr 1948, pp. 12–15, 38–39.

Rosenberg, David Alan. "American Atomic Strategy and Hydrogen Bomb Decision." *Journal of American History*, 66, No. 1 (Jun 1979), pp. 62–87.

———. "The Origins of Overkill: Nuclear Weapons and American Strategy, 1945–1960." *International Security*, Vol. 7 No. 4 (Spring 1983), pp. 3–37.

———. "U.S. Nuclear Stockpile, 1945 to 1950." *Bulletin of the Atomic Scientists*, 38, No. 5 (May 1982), pp. 25–30.

Sander, Alfred D. "Truman and the National Security Council." *Journal of American History*, 59, No. 2 (Sep 1972), pp. 369–88.

Schaffer, Ronald. "American Military Ethics in World War II: The Bombing of German Cities." *Journal of American History*, 67, No. 2 (Sep 1980), pp. 318–34.

Schratz, Capt Paul R. "The Admirals Revolt." *U.S. Naval War College Review*, Feb 1986, pp. 308–11.

Shalett, Sidney. "Army Intelligence Being Reorganized." *New York Times*, May 16, 1945, p. 14.

———. "General Vandenberg Set for New Post." *New York Times*, Feb 26, 1947, p. 18.

———. "Man on a Hot Seat." *Saturday Evening Post*, May 29, 1948, pp. 23, 136–38.

"Shooting the Breeze." *Air Force*, Oct 1949, p. 4.

Snyder, Glenn. "The 'New Look' of 1953," in *Strategy, Politics and Defense Budgets*. New York: Columbia University Press, 1962.

Spaatz, Carl M. "Concept for Peace." *Newsweek*, Apr 12, 1954, p. 36.

———. "The Era of Air–Power Diplomacy." *Newsweek*, Sep 20, 1948, pp. 25–28.

———. "If We Should Have to Fight Again." *Life*, Jul 5, 1948, pp. 34–36, 39–44.

"Spy Master." *Newsweek*, Jul 22, 1946, p. 34.

"State of the Unification." *Economist*, Oct 22, 1949, pp. 892–94.

Steiner, Barry H. "Using the Absolute Weapon: Early Ideas of Bernard Brodie on Atomic Strategy." *Journal of Strategic Studies*, 7, No. 4 (Dec 1984), pp. 365–93.

Sturm, Thomas A. "Organizational Evolution." *Air Force*, Sep 1970, pp. 68–84.

Time, Mar 10, 1952, p. 28; Apr 12, 1954, p. 29.

Toulmin, Stephen. "The Conscientious Spy." *New York Review of Books*, Nov 19, 1987, pp. 54–60.

Truman, Harry S. "Our Armed Forces Must Be Unified." *Colliers*, Aug 26, 1944, pp. 16, 63–64.

"The Truth About Our Air Defense." *Air Force*, May 1953, pp. 251–29, 34–36.

Tunner, William H. "Technology or Manpower." *Air University Review*, 5, No. 3 (Fall 1952), pp. 3–21.

"USAF Forms Tactical Air Force." *Aviation Week*, Jul 25, 1949, p. 16.

"U.S. Air Force and Its Boss Are Ready." *Newsweek*, Feb 19, 1951, pp. 22–24.

U.S. News and World Report, Aug 23, 1946, pp. 60–61; Aug 19, 1948, p. 37.

"US Tactical Air Power in Europe." *Impact*, May 1945.

Vandenberg, Hoyt S. "Air Force Hasn't Been Doing the Job It Can Do in Korea." *U.S. News & World Report*, Nov 30, 1951, pp. 16–19.

———. "Air Power Build-Up Only Half Completed." *Planes*, Dec 1952, p. 1.

———. "B-36: Superplane or 'Sitting Duck'?" *U.S. News and World Report*, Jul 1, 1949, pp. 41–43.

———. "The Middle Way." *Vital Speeches of the Day*, Dec 15, 1950, pp. 139–41.

———. "Our 70-Group Air Force Emerges." *Popular Mechanics*, Dec 1948, pp. 89–95, 250–54.

———. "Pursuit." *Flying and Popular Aviation*, 29, No. 3 (Sep 1941), pp. 54–62.

———. "The Truth About Our Air Power." *Saturday Evening Post*, Feb 17, 1951, pp. 20–21, 100–04.

"Vandenberg-LeMay-Twining Team Puts Air Force Back on Top." *U.S. News and World Report*, Mar 14, 1952. pp. 62–64.

"Warning Siren." *Time*, May 12, 1952.

Washington Daily News, Apr 21, 1950, p. 1; Mar 1, 1952.

Washington Evening Star, Jun 10, 1946.

Washington Post, Apr 5, 1949, p. 1; Feb 21, 1952, p. 1; Mar 4, 1952.

Washington Star, Apr 2, 1954, p. 1.

Wertenbaker, Charles H. "Back in Stride." *Time*, Jan 15, 1945, pp. 26–28.

Wilt, Alan F. "Coming of Age: XIX TAC's Roles During the 1944 Dash Across France." *Air University Review*, 36, No. 3 (Mar-Apr 1985), pp. 71–87.

Wolk, Herman. "The Defense Unification Battle, 1947–1950: The Air Force." *Prologue*, 7, No. 1 (Spring 1975), pp. 18–26.

INDEX